AF681518

Alcohol and Drug Abuse as Encountered in Office Practice

Editor

Frank Lynn Iber

Professor of Medicine
Stritch College of Medicine
Loyola University
Maywood, Illinois

Chief of Gastroenterology
Edward Hines Jr. Hospital
Hines, Illinois

CRC Press
Boca Raton Ann Arbor Boston

Library of Congress Cataloging-in-Publication Data

Alcohol and drug abuse as encountered in office practice/editor,
Frank Lynn Iber.
p. cm.
Includes bibliographical references.
Includes index.
ISBN 0-8493-0166-1
1. Alcoholism—Treatment. 2. Drug abuse—Treatment. 3. Family medicine. I. Iber, Frank L., 1928-
[DNLM: 1. Alcoholism—diagnosis. 2. Alcoholism—rehabilitation.
3. Substance Abuse—diagnosis. 4. Substance Abuse—rehabilitation.
WM 270 A35415]
RC564.73.A43 1990
616.86—dc20
DLC 90-2334

This book represents information obtained from authentic and highly regarded sources. Reprinted material is quoted with permission, and sources are indicated. A wide variety of references are listed. Every reasonable effort has been made to give reliable data and information, but the author and the publisher cannot assume responsibility for the validity of all materials or for the consequences of their use.

All rights reserved. This book, or any parts thereof, may not be reproduced in any form without written consent from the publisher.

Direct all inquiries to CRC Press, Inc., 2000 Corporate Blvd., N.W., Boca Raton, Florida 33431.

© 1991 by CRC Press, Inc.

International Standard Book Number 0-8493-0166-1

Library of Congress Card Number 90-2334
Printed in the United States

Dedication

In 1956 Tom Burnett and W. Dixon Gibbs of Baltimore convinced me that working with alcoholics was rewarding and showed me how to become effective; I have been involved in this labor ever since. This book is dedicated to the volunteers who help people with substance abuse.

ACKNOWLEDGMENT

This book required the participation of many workers. Our secretary Norma Jackson produced the manuscript. Gloria Kelly, R.N. assisted with editing. Billie Ladas produced all of the art work and Gerda Kirschner and Willie Marks made the photographs. John Cline of Hines, Pat Padgett of the NIH, and the many workers at Pracon Inc. Reston Va. provided many bibliographies and obtained many library references. A large number of colleagues critiqued one or more chapters, sharing their expertise and suggesting important information that might be included. I am grateful to these people for their excellent suggestions. Many of the best features of this book are because of their intervention, but I accept full responsibility for failure to fully carry out their ideas if errors appear. Richard Baum, M.D.; John Crayton, M.D.; Charles Davidson, M.D.; Carole Dorsch, M.D.; Walter Dorus, M.D.; Kathryn Eiler, M.D.; Barbara Ganem, M.D.; Richard Iber, B.S.; Robert Iber, J.D.; Gloria Kelly, R.N.; Harry Klinefelter, M.D.; U. Malkernecker, M.D.; Ron Medej, M.S.W.; Esteban Mezey, M.D.; Robert Miller, B.A.; Kevin O'Brien, M.D.; David Posner, M.D.; Jeanne Riley, M.B.A.; Herbert Trace, M.D.; and Janice Willms, M.D. responded to this need.

The ideas in this book came from a much wider group. I have shared responsibilities for the care of substance abuse patients at Johns Hopkins Hospital, Baltimore City Hospitals, Lemuel Shattuck Hospital, Boston Alcoholism Dependence Project, Baltimore Veterans Administration Hospital, Fort Howard VA Hospital, University Hospitals, and Edward Hines Jr. Hospital for more than 30 continuous years. These programs and the several hundred staff persons who worked with them through these years of may involvement were my teachers. To these who shared the work, the excitement of helping people, and the evolution of the ideas expressed here I direct my thanks and hope they share pride in what is put forth in this book.

PREFACE

I became active with substance abusing patients as a resident physician in internal medicine in the 1950s. At that time many physicians did not treat abuse and more than half the hospitals were reluctant to admit such patients. Volunteer and self-help groups filled the gap that hospitals and physicians left and I learned a great deal from them and helped with their half-way houses and homes for withdrawal. I began research on alcohol injury and recovery. The clear advantage of a physician cooperating with volunteer groups was apparent in the resources I could offer to my patients.

A few years later I was working in Boston and had an opportunity to establish large withdrawal facilities for derelict abusing patients and worked out programs that continue to this day. During these years I became active in teaching medical students and physicians about substance abuse. The need for a practical guide for office-based physicians seeing only the abuse problems in a standard private practice was then clearly apparent. Physicians were increasingly aware of abusing patients, but were not utilizing self-help groups and other trained persons in the recovery process. This book was delayed, for many books on the subject appeared but none quite hit the mark to which I was aiming.

This book is for the office-based physician doing a family or internal medicine practice. It is a guide to handle about 95% of the problems of abuse that come to attention in practice and to indicate clearly those which require other facilities. Its primary purpose is to point out that the skills that each of us physicians has learned can be used to great benefit for helping abusing patients. As with most chronic diseases, assistance at an early stage produces a much greater impact on future health and I hope with this guide such an improved outcome becomes more frequent.

Frank Iber, M.D.
Chicago, Illinois 1990

THE AUTHOR

Frank L. Iber, M.D., is Professor of Medicine at Loyola University in Chicago and Chief of Gastroenterology at Edward Hines Jr. Hospital. He received his A.B. and M.A. degrees from Miami University in Oxford, Ohio, his M.D. degree from Johns Hopkins University School of Medicine in Baltimore, and did postgraduate work at Hopkins and at the Postgraduate Medical School in London, England. He became an Assistant Professor at Hopkins in 1960, an Associate Professor in 1965, and Professor of Medicine at Tufts University in Boston in 1968. In 1973 he returned to Baltimore as Director of the Gastrointestinal Division at University of Maryland and the Baltimore VA Hospital. He is a founding member of the American Council on Alcoholism, director of programs for alcoholics and drug abuse at the Baltimore VA Hospital, the Lemuel Shattuck Hospital in Boston, and has established a model inner city program for derelict abusers in Boston. He has served on the board and as a backup physician for some 30 organizations providing services for abusing persons. The training divisions of these programs provided laboratory experience for more than 200 professionals in ministry, social work, psychology, nurse practioners, physicians, and physicians assistants, the majority of whom remain in addiction work.

Dr. Iber is a member of the American College of Physicians, the American Society of Addiction Physicians, Research Society in Alcoholism and some 15 other learned societies in medicine, liver disease, nutrition, and addictions. He has been the principal investigator on more than 50 grants from the National Institutes of Health, the Veterans Administration, and foundations and is an author of more than 200 publications, 25 book chapters, and 2 complete books. His research has been in the treatment of liver disease and its complications, nutritional problems of the addictions, medical problems associated with addictions, and evaluations of treatment. His current research interests are in the formation of gallstones in cirrhosis of the liver, evaluation of treatment, and training.

TABLE OF CONTENTS

Chapter 1

Introduction to Abused Substances

I. INTRODUCTION

Addictive substances that are important to primary-care physicians in several different ways are presented briefly in this chapter and covered in much more specific detail later. Table 1 indicates ways in which addictions affect a doctor's patients.

Clearly the physician, by training and disposition, will undertake the management of some of these problems (such as the chronic obstructive lung disease of cigarette smoking), but may not choose to treat some of the psychiatric emergencies (such as panic or hallucinosis) and will appropriately refer such patients. The American Medical Association (AMA) has developed guidelines as to the responsibilities of the physician in such situations, and these guidelines are discussed in a later section of this chapter.

No physician can avoid patients who use addictive substances. Caffeine addiction will not be discussed in this book because it is so ubiquitous and creates very few health problems. Assisting patients with cessation of smoking is a common practice of physicians, and the health problems resulting from smoking and from alcohol abuse exceed by far the problems produced by all other addictions combined. Some 90% of American adults use alcohol at least monthly, and at any time from 5 to 15% are abusers. At least 15% of Americans under age 40 use an illicit drug at least monthly, but only a small fraction of these are addicted. Modest use of tobacco, almost always in the form of cigarette smoking, exceeds abuse, but more than 20% of adults in all states except Utah use tobacco.[1]

TABLE 1
Impact of Addiction on Practice Decisions

1. Health-related toxicities of the addiction
2. Emergencies related to the addiction
3. Conditions often associated with addiction
4. Problems encountered during withdrawal
5. Aberrant responses to medication
6. Responsible requests to stop the addiction
7. Addictions in family members producing health problems in your patient

TABLE 2
Classification of Substances of Abuse

Class	Major members	Problems[a]
Sedatives	Alcohol, sedatives, hypnotics, anxiolytics	I, W, H
Caffeine	Caffeine, a few others, theophylline	I
Marijuana	Hashish	I, D
Amphetamines	Amphetamines, cocaine	I, W, D
Opiates		I, W, H
Nicotine	Tobacco	W
Hallucinogens	LSD, mescaline	I, P
Inhalants	Glue, ether, toluene	I, P
PCP		I, D, P

[a] I = intoxication, W = withdrawal, H = health problems, D = delirium, P = psychosis.

Throughout this book we will classify abused drugs into the broad groups outlined in Table 2.

II. HEALTH-RELATED TOXICITIES

Every physician is familiar with the coronary, vascular, and pulmonary problems associated with chronic cigarette smoking and with the cirrhosis of the liver associated with alcohol, which facts emphasize that different drugs have different health effects. Nearly all physicians are familiar with the endocarditis and abscesses in strange locations associated with use of nonsterile intravenous drugs and with the human immunovirus (HIV) and hepatitis B infections associated with shared intravenous needles.

The panic reactions associated with use of marijuana, hallucinogens, PCP, and solvents are less familiar. Although alcohol and opiate withdrawal are well publicized, many physicians have no clear plan for management of these difficulties in their own offices and have not thought about specific criteria for recommending hospitalization. Chronic organic brain syndrome is known to most physicians as a consequence of alcohol abuse, but it is also a consequence of every group of drugs except perhaps marijuana.

III. EMERGENCIES

Schuckit delineates a priority system using initial physical examination to guide physicians in addressing the most urgent problem first. In his scheme,[2] severely compromised vital signs are *most* important; only when these are stable at acceptable levels can one address signs or symptoms of withdrawal. If the vital signs are in an acceptable range for safety and there is no withdrawal, then confusion can be addressed. If none of these problems are present but there are hallucinations and/or delusions without insight, this represents a psy-

TABLE 3
Medical Conditions Associated with Drug Addiction

Common to all	Depressants
Increased trauma	Overdose, psychosis
Increased suicide	Organic brain syndrome
Malnutrition	Withdrawal
Common to all i.v. use	Stimulants
Hepatitis, AIDS	Overdose, psychosis
Endocarditis, abscesses	Hallucinogens
Common to all smoking	Panic reactions
Allergic bronchitis	Opiates
Emphysema	Overdose, withdrawal
Alcohol	Phencyclidine (PCP)
Cirrhosis, pancreatitis	Overdose
Brain injury, withdrawal	Neuritis

chosis. Schuckit's scheme thus offers a straightforward method for prioritizing emergencies and deciding where and how to care for them.

Other urgent patients have panic reactions, ''dry drunks,'' or flashbacks, which are discussed in Chapters 10, 17, 18, and 20.

IV. CONDITIONS FREQUENTLY ASSOCIATED WITH ADDICTIONS

Table 3 lists some of the common medical problems associated with specific substances of abuse; a great deal more detail is presented in the subsequent chapters of this book.

V. PROBLEMS DURING WITHDRAWAL

Alcohol and opiates produce the most marked withdrawal reactions, with reactions to other sedatives being infrequently encountered but of similar severity. Withdrawal reactions occur only after tolerance has developed. There is biochemical adaptation to the chronic presence of the drug, as a part of tolerance development associated with increase in the rate and intensity of use. As the drug is removed, the unopposed addicted person has manifestations in all systems of the body. The autonomic nervous system, muscles, and central nervous system participate in these reactions. Multiple receptor systems are overactive during withdrawal, but particularly prominent features of hyperactivity of the norepinephrine, dopaminergic, and gababenzodiazepine receptors occur.

The setting for withdrawal to occur starts with sufficient regular use of the agent to produce biochemical adaptation or tolerance. In a tolerant person the same amount of drug produces less effect. For some agents this involves increased numbers of receptors, for others altered rates of production of neurotransmitters. To attain identical effects the user must increase the dose, frequency of use, or both, and this constitutes tolerance and is the setting for withdrawal.

For withdrawal to occur in such a susceptible person, the level of the drug must fall to less than half its usual level. In drugs with very short half-lives (such as alcohol, with a half-life of about 90 min in an addicted person), this occurs overnight during sleep, and some withdrawal signs occur very soon. Many alcoholics awaken to take an additional drink. For long-acting drugs such as phenobarbital, withdrawal may occur only a week or more after stopping the drug. Thus, withdrawal is a complex reaction related to the intensity and

TABLE 4
Means by Which Addicting Drugs Alter the Effects of Medicinal Agents

1. Tolerance blunts the effects of similar drugs e.g., pain medications are ineffective in heroin addicts
2. Potentiation through different systems occurs e.g., Nonfatal doses of ethanol + barbiturate may be fatal in combination
3. Addiction may induce hepatic P-450 enzymes e.g., Alcoholism lowers prothrombin levels in patients on coumadin
4. Unrecognized withdrawal produces a temporary erratic drug response which becomes toxic when withdrawal is complete e.g., Aggressive hypertension treatment in alcoholics may lead to hypotension a few days later

duration of the addiction, the abruptness of the withdrawal, and other factors such as emotional state, malnutrition, and the calmness or threatening nature of the environment.

VI. ABERRANT RESPONSE TO MEDICATION

Most addicting substances act directly or as a side effect on receptors that are used as regular regulatory pathways and by therapeutic agents. Thus alcoholics are notoriously resistant to anesthesia induction with benzodiazepine drugs, often requiring five- to tenfold the usual dose. Opiate addicts are nearly insensitive to ordinary doses of opiates as pain medications when they develop pancreatitis. Many other examples are obvious. Table 4 lists mechanisms by which an addictive drug might influence subsequently used medicinal agents.

Most addicting substances have side effects associated with both the class of agents (such as constipation for opiates) and the specific molecules. Although these may be acceptable at normal doses of use, often as tolerance develops, the side effects may be exaggerated. Sophisticated addicts often utilize a second drug to partly allay the side effects. Thus, most alcoholics use great quantities of caffeine to remain a little more alert. Many opiate users employ amphetamines to combat the effects on alertness and intensify the "high" that they obtain.

The concept that addicted persons may handle drugs in an erratic fashion is important. Physicians can best handle this problem in practice by using a limited number of drugs and knowing their utility well. Chapter 5 covers the pharmacology needed by therapists, and Chapter 13 includes this author's choices of useful drugs. A limited formulary of drugs will increase one's ability to manage abusing patients. Nearly all abused drugs will have disappeared from the body in a few days to a few weeks after use ceases.

VII. RESPONSIBLE REQUESTS TO ASSIST IN CESSATION OF THE ADDICTION

Primary-care doctors in any one year provide care and consultation to some 50% of active alcoholics and about 25% of those suffering other addictions. As part of a health evaluation, a diagnosis of substance abuse is made and communicated to the patient. This may prove to be contributory to or the major condition for which the person is seeking medical help. A sincere desire to give up the addiction is expressed and an appeal for assistance is made. Since substance abuse is widely presented as a health problem, every practitioner needs some sort of appropriate response. Table 5 lists levels of care that physicians may choose to provide, but the problem cannot be ignored. The physician's minimal responsibility is to assess immediate health needs and advise care appropriate to the person's needs and economic position.

The level at which an individual physician participates and the abused substances for which the physician is willing and prepared to treat are his or her choice after the urgent aspects are attended to. To undertake any of this treatment requires some specific knowledge, and it is the purpose of this book to provide that for all physicians.

TABLE 5
Levels of Care a Physician May Provide in the Treatment of an Addicted Subject

1. Minimal
   a. Evaluate for urgent needs and make referral appropriate to these needs
   b. Assist with detoxification
   c. Treat health problems in the patient
2. Intermediate
   a. Supervise inpatient or outpatient withdrawal
   b. Complete medical assessment and treat
   c. Evolve treatment plan with patient, continue to see patient for support
   d. Provide some of the treatment
   e. Make and follow up on referrals
3. Marked
   a. Provide all professional aspects of treatment, including medical and behavioral modification and/or psychiatric therapy

The AMA Council on Scientific Affairs in 1979 adopted guidelines for physician involvement in the care of substance-abusing patients, and these have been widely distributed to professional and lay organizations.[3] In these guidelines they distinguish three levels of care, as listed in Table 6.

When an ongoing doctor-patient, or more commonly doctor-family relationship exists, it is sometimes easier for the doctor to provide information on the type of drug- or alcohol-related treatment needed. In this situation the physician may provide valuable aid to the family in suggesting types of therapy that are appropriate (Table 6, I.E). At a time of crisis, often engendered by drugs or alcohol, a decision is sometimes made to enter a very costly short-term treatment facility to provide a feeling that something is being done. Often the same funds invested in longer-term treatment will accomplish much more toward changing the habit. To accomplish these various goals the physician must equip himself and his office appropriately; ways to do this are discussed in Chapters 26 and 31.

It should be emphasized with regard to Tables 5 and 6 that, apart from diagnosis and referral, and a few genuine emergencies that may occur in the office, the physician can select a level of involvement in the treatment of substance abuse. Almost no physician, however, can completely eliminate involvement with abusing patients, for they are ubiquitous. There is in fact evidence that the abusing patient is more demanding of physicians' time and more likely to bring a legal action of malpractice than the nonabusing subject.

TABLE 6
Levels of Care as Defined by AMA[3]

I. Level I: All physicians with clinical responsibility for diagnosis and treatment
   A. Recognize dysfunction caused by abuse
   B. Be aware of medical complications
   C. Include detailed history of drug and alcohol use in any complete evaluation
   D. Evaluate patient needs and community resources to assure adequate care
   E. Refer to appropriate resource

II. Level II: Physicians accepting limited treatment responsibility
   A. Assist in becoming substance free, treat withdrawal
   B. Recognize and treat or refer complicating illness
   C. Apprise patient of the addiction and requirements for recovery
   D. Evaluate health, social, economic, and interpersonal resources to formulate a recovery plan
   E. Determine the need for involving significant others in a short-term and later in a longer-term recovery plan
   F. Develop a long-term recovery plan with the patient's participation

III. Level III: Physicians accepting responsibility for long-term treatment
   A. Acquire specific necessary knowledge
   B. Provide and supervise:
      1. A supportive, therapeutic, nonjudgmental relationship
      2. Define the conditions and limits of the therapy
      3. Periodically review and update the recovery plan with the patient
      4. Involve the patient with an abstinent peer group
      5. Know about — and be able to use — social, vocational, and spiritual support systems
      6. Evaluate significant others, and involve them in treatment
   C. Continually monitor the patient's medication needs
   D. Be knowledgeable about the proper use of pharmacotherapy
   E. Throughout treatment, look for and treat or refer complicating illness or relapse
   F. Be available to the patient as needed for an indefinite period of recovery

REFERENCES

1. Behavioral risk factor surveillence — selected states, 1987, *JAMA*, 262, 753, 1989.
2. **Schuckit, M. A.,** *Drug and Alcohol Abuse, A Clinical Guide to Diagnosis and Treatment,* 3rd ed., Plenum Press, New York, 1989.
3. **Bowen, O. T. and Sammons, J. H.,** AMA guidelines for physician involvement in the care of substance-abusing patients, in pamphlet distributed by American Medical Association, Chicago.

Chapter 2

Terminology, Definitions, Classification of Abused Substances, and Diagnostic Criteria

I. INTRODUCTION

This chapter discusses the terminology that will be used throughout this book. Some commonly used classifications and diagnostic criteria are also outlined. Ambiguity and confusion abound in the field of substance abuse because of the widespread use of the same term to mean many things. A person who abuses a drug means different things to a law enforcement officer, a physician, and a court trying the person for a crime allegedly committed under the influence of that drug. A glossary is provided as an appendix to this book for easy reference.

A. TERMS USED INTERCHANGEABLY

Throughout this book we will use some terms interchangeably without regard for the subtle differences. Thus, alcohol as a specific noun and ethanol will mean the same thing. Table 7 lists several pairs of words that will be so employed.

TABLE 7
Words Used Interchangeably in This Book

alcohol ↔ ethanol	opiate ↔ opioid
abuser ↔ addict	tolerant ↔ addicted ↔ dependent
drug free ↔ abstinent	

TABLE 8
Terms Used in a Restrictive Sense in This Book

Treatment	Substance abuse therapist
Social drug use	Self-help groups
Inpatient treatment	Outpatient treatment
Treatment program	

B. TERMS USED IN A RESTRICTIVE SENSE

A few terms are deliberately used in a sense appropriate to a physician and health team audience, and different from the broader use of the term in substance abuse literature. Table 8 lists these terms, which will be discussed further in this section.

Treatment in this text is restricted to therapy administered or directed by a person with specific training, usually an M.D., Ph.D., M.S.W., or training in clinical psychiatry, for which a fee is charged or the therapist receives a salary for administering the treatment. Assistance limited to family or self-help groups is not included under the term treatment. Though these may be a part of a treatment program, the key feature is direction by a specifically trained person. A *substance abuse therapist* is a person with specific training in the treatment of substance abuse or an advanced degree in assisting patients. A few largely self-taught men and women provide help with substance abuse exceeding that of many therapists with many degrees, but this type person is disappearing from the field and many unqualified persons offer ineffective therapy.

Inpatient treatment refers to a residential program directed by a therapist. Residential programs directed and operated solely by self-trained or self-help groups are not included in inpatient treatment in this text.

Outpatient treatment refers only to patients who come to a treatment facility run by a trained person as noted in the previous paragraph, but who do not reside there. *Self-help groups* consist of persons with substance abuse problems who are in various stages of recovery and who join together in some sort of formal organization. In some communities informal groups, often church-affiliated, provide services or shelter to homeless addicted persons. These are not considered self-help groups because they include many persons who are not recovering from the problem.

Social use of a drug or alcohol refers to use on more than one occasion, usually at least monthly, as part of a group activity with other persons. The drug may be legal or illegal, the use may be as frequent as daily, but there is no evidence of tolerance, harm to health, or harm to job or interpersonal relationships. Thus, a weekly user of "crack" cocaine who gets a toxic reaction has transcended "social use" and has become an abuser. A person who uses cocaine weekly in total secrecy is not considered a social user in this book: he is an abuser.

II. FOOD AND DRUG ADMINISTRATION CLASSIFICATION

Drugs with a potential for addiction are regulated by the Food and Drug Administration (FDA) and are assigned to specific "schedules" that are related to both their medical utility

TABLE 9
FDA Schedules for Drugs with Abuse Potential

Not assigned, permits limited to experimental work
 "High abuse, no medical use"
 Synthetic opiates with high addiction potential
 Synthetic amphetamines with no unique properties
Schedule I, "high abuse, very low usefulness"
 Heroin
 Hallucinogens
 Marijuana
Schedule II, "high abuse, major medical use"
 Opiates (most potent)
 Cocaine
 Barbiturates (most)
 Methaqualone
 Ketamine (PCP)
 Amphetamines
Schedule III, "moderate abuse, moderate usefulness"
 Codeine in combinations with NSAIDs
 Paregoric
 Glutethimide
Schedule IV, "moderate abuse, high usefulness"
 Phenobarbital
 Chloral hydrate
 Benzodiazepines
 Propoxyphene
Schedule V, "low abuse, high usefulness"
 Narcotic-atropine mixtures
 Codeine mixtures (up to 200 mg)

and their potential for abuse. Alcohol is regulated separately. Most substances of low potential for addiction or in use for a long time, such as caffeine, tobacco, and most inhaled vapors, are not regulated. Some new molecules — "designer drugs" — often escape regulation for a time until there is insufficient published experience with their addiction potential.

Pharmacists, physicians, dentists, veterinarians, and manufacturers as well as some others with need for use are licensed to use drugs within specific schedules. Record-keeping responsibilities vary within the schedule and the volume of activity. Table 9 lists the schedules that are now used and some examples.

The FDA schedules have a valuable regulatory influence, decreasing the entry of drugs into the hands of abusers via physicians and pharmacies, but have had a very limited influence on the diversion of large quantities of drugs into illicit channels at the manufacturing level. Illicit laboratories manufacturing amphetamines, PCP, and designer drugs, and the illicit importation of purified drugs from outside America, are more important sources of abused substances. From my reading and experience I would estimate that most cases of abused prescription medication arise from inappropriate prescribing habits; most amphetamine, PCP, and barbiturate abuse arises from American-manufactured drugs illegally reaching the street trade, and cocaine, opiate, and marijuana abuse relies largely on imported supplies.

III. FDA CLASSIFICATION OF EXPERIMENTAL DRUGS FOR HUMAN USE

An additional FDA classification often seen in the literature is "investigational drugs" for which an IND (Investigational New Drug) permit has been issued. This classification applies to all new agents undergoing clinical trials. No drug can be studied in the U.S.

TABLE 10
Investigational Drug Classification

Phase I: initial trial in man, applied to first 10 to 200 normal persons, seeking dose, pharmacology dose, tolerance, and preliminary side-effect profile. Usually limited to male adults under age 55.
Phase II: trial of a limited population of 50 to 200 patients presenting the disease to be treated. Dose changes are permitted but a control group must be presented, with random assignment to the new treatment.
Phase III: expanded controlled and open clinical trials under the same conditions or new conditions. The drug cannot be sold. At conclusion, an NDA (New Drug Application) is filed.
Phase IV: after marketing is permitted, continued surveillance for rare complications. A larger sample of a certain type of treatment population may be required.

across state lines without prior approval by the regulatory agency. Table 10 indicates the major features of this classification. More details are given by Iber et al.[1]

IV. DSM III-R DEFINITIONS AND CLASSIFICATIONS

The American Psychiatric Association (APA) has undertaken the task of codifying specific criteria for diagnosis or exclusion of psychiatric disorders to help physicians toward uniformity of diagnosis. Their work with the various addictive disorders can be very useful to all workers in the field, for they define quite precisely the criteria necessary to make diagnoses. A few minutes of browsing in the *Diagnostic and Statistical Manual of Mental Disorders* (DSM III-R)[2]) will convince any physician of the precision of diagnosis, and a look from time to time will allow him to sharpen his criteria for making a specific diagnosis, particularly if he does not frequently deal with these problems. In my own work I have found that DSM III-R provides simple guidelines for me to follow to avoid embarrassment in diagnosis and documentation.

Figure 1A reproduces the chart in DSM III-R on diagnostic criteria for psychoactive substance dependence. Figure 1B reproduces the criteria for severity. These figures illustrate the utility of this source in giving the physician a clear basis for making a diagnosis and supporting that diagnosis to the patient and his family. Subsequent parts of this text elaborate on the application of the criteria.

A further example in Figure 2 reproduces the DSM III-R table for diagnosing uncomplicated alcohol withdrawal.

DSM III-R is the best available reference for precise diagnosis, and is increasingly being used by agencies dealing with psychiatric diseases and their costs. Internists and family medicine specialists are often a bit less familiar with this source and the diagnostic criteria. The examples in Figures 1 and 2 illustrate that this guide is very practical and easy to apply.

A. At least three of the following:

(1) substance often taken in larger amounts or over a a longer period than the person intended.

(2) persistent desire or one or more unsuccessful efforts to cut down on control substance use.

(3) a great deal of time spent in activities necessary to get the substance (e.g., chain smoking), or recovering from its effects

(4) frequent intoxication or withdrawal symptoms when expected to fulfill major role obligations at work, school, or home (e.g., does not go to work because hung over, goes to school or work "high", intoxicated while taking care of his or her children), or when substance use is physically hazardous (e.g., drives when intoxicated)

(5) important social, occupational, or recreational activities given up or reduced because of substance use.

(6) continued substance use despite knowledge of having persistent or recurrent social, psychological, or physical problem that is caused or exacerbated by the use of the substance (e.g., keeps using heroin despite family arguments about it, cocaine-induced depression, or having an ulcer made worse by drinking)

(7) marked tolerance : need for markedly increased amounts of the substance (i.e., at least a 50% increase) in order to achieve intoxication or desired effect, or markedly diminished effect with continued use of the same amount

Note: The following items may not apply to cannabis, hallucinogens, or phencyclidine (PCP):

(8) characteristic withdrawal symptoms (see specific withdrawal syndromes under Psychoactive Substance - induced Organic Mental Disorders)

(9) substance often taken to relieve or avoid withdrawal symptoms

B. Some symptoms of the disturbance have persisted for at least one month, or have occurred repeatedly over a longer period of time.

FIGURE 1A. Diagnostic criteria for psychoactive substance dependence. (From American Psychiatric Association, *Diagnostic and Statistical Manual of Mental Disorders,* 3rd ed., rev., American Psychiatric Association, Washington, D.C., 1987 — permission granted for reproduction.)

Mild: Few, if any, symptoms in excess of those required to make the diagnosis, and the symptoms result in no more than mild impairment in occupational functioning or in usual social activities or relationships with others.

Moderate: Symptoms functional impairment between "mild" and "severe"

Severe: Many symptoms in excess of those required to make the diagnosis, and the symptoms markedly interfere with occupational functioning or with usual social activities or relationships with others

In Partial Remission: During the past six months , some use of the substance and some symptoms of dependence.

In Full Remission: During the past six months, either no use of the substance, or use of the substance and no symptoms of dependence.

FIGURE 1B. Criteria for severity of psychoactive substance dependence. (From American Psychiatric Association, *Diagnostic and Statistical Manual of Mental Disorders,* 3rd ed., rev., American Psychiatric Association, Washington, D.C., 1987 — permission granted for reproduction.)

A. Cessation of prolonged (several days or longer) heavy ingestion of alcohol or reduction in the amount of alcohol ingested, followed within several hours by coarse tremor of hands, tongue, or eyelids, and at least one of the following:

(1) nausea or vomiting
(2) malaise or weakness
(3) autonomic hyperactivity, e.g., tachycardia, sweating, elevated blood pressure
(4) anxiety
(5) depressed mood or irritability
(6) transient hallucinations or illusions
(7) headache
(8) insomnia

B. Not due to any physicial or other mental disorder, such as Alcohol Withdrawal Delirium.

FIGURE 2. Diagnostic criteria for uncomplicated alcohol withdrawal. (From American Psychiatric Association, *Diagnostic and Statistical Manual of Mental Disorders,* 3rd ed., rev., American Psychiatric Association, Washington, D.C., 1987 — permission granted for reproduction.)

REFERENCES

1. **Iber, F. L., Riley, W. A., and Murray, P. J.,** *Conducting Clinical Trials,* Plenum Press, New York, 1987.
2. American Psychiatric Association, *Diagnostic and Statistical Manual of Mental Disorders,* 3rd ed., rev., American Psychiatric Association, Washington, D.C., 1987.

Chapter 3

The Molecular Basis of Action of Abused Substances

I. INTRODUCTION

Advances in neurochemistry, including an understanding of the nature of neurotransmitter substances and their membrane receptors and the manner in which these receptors alter either ion channels or second messengers inside the cell, have provided the molecular basis for the action of many substances of abuse; yet there is no single molecular hypothesis that covers all addictions in a common understanding. In this chapter we will first provide some very simple definitions and then apply these definitions to describe the available information on the molecular basis of activity of abused substances. In the next chapter we will contrast the behavioral differences of alcohol and other abused substances.

A. CELL WALL RECEPTORS

The membrane of every cell (called the plasma membrane) has specialized sites called receptor sites. These sites, which serve urgent regulatory functions of the interior of the cell and usually have an external process, extend through the two layers of lipid that make up the plasma membrane and often have an internal process. The external process by its spatial arrangement is quite specific for molecules that can interact with the receptor. These include simply highly charged molecules (e.g., acetylcholine), simple hormone molecules (e.g., thyroid), peptide hormones (insulin), and a few other substances.

When the sterically specific molecule combines with a specific receptor, a number of things may occur. In some cases the receptor internalizes the molecule and transports it within the cell to the site where it is active. Androgenic steroids act on the nucleus and reach it by this means. Other materials are internalized and released into the cell cytoplasm. A common effect produced by most hormones is to activate synthesis inside the cell of a potent cell regulator or second messenger. Second messengers include cyclic adenosine monophosphate (AMP), guanosine monophosphate (GMP), and (inositol triphosphate (IP3) that broadly change the activity of a cell. In this manner minute amounts of a hormone (present in concentrations of 10^{-7} mole) can effect a great deal of change.

Another common effect of receptors in combination with their specific hormone is to change ion entry channels into the cell. Thus, the inhibitory neurotransmitter substance gamma-aminobutyric acid (GABA) blocks an important channel that allows chloride to enter cells and in doing so changes many functions of that cell. Other receptors affect ionic calcium or potassium.

Cells adjust to need by increasing or decreasing the numbers of receptors in the surface. If there are more receptors (up regulation), the cell becomes more sensitive to the hormone; the opposite is true for down regulation (fewer receptors).

Many substances act locally on the cells immediately surrounding their production and release site, and reach the receptors through the extracellular fluid. Release often occurs near receptors (synapse is the name of the releasing site and the receptor when closely approximated), and enzymes such as cholinesterase destroy excess hormone to prevent it from acting at a distance.

Abused substances greatly affect regulatory processes; some of the known methods by which they act will be discussed in later sections.

B. NEUROTRANSMITTER SUBSTANCES

Certain simple molecules are used as regulators throughout the animal kingdom. Acetylcholine and epinephrine were among the earliest of these that were discovered, but we now know of many more. Common ones include serotonin, dopamine, GABA, and glutamic acid. In addition, many peptides also serve as regulators. These include the encephalins, cholecystokinin, gastrin, and at least 30 others. Each of these combines with receptors on a variety of different cells, causing a chain of reactions specific to each cell type.

C. PLASMA MEMBRANE PROPERTIES

Each cell of the body is surrounded by a two-layered membrane that is freely permeable to water but impermeable to charged particles. This cell wall or plasma membrane protects the inside of the cell from the outside. A large number of lipoproteins are positioned across the membrane, with processes on both the outside and inside. Many of these are receptors, as noted above; others serve for transport by attaching to ions or other molecules outside, then flip-flopping in such a way as to transport something into the cell or out of it. Still others form a channel that permits a specific ion to pass freely along a concentration gradient, moving by diffusion from areas of high concentration to areas of low concentration.

II. ALCOHOL AND VOLATILE ANESTHETICS AND INHALED AGENTS

A. ANESTHETICS AND INHALED AGENTS

Anesthetics and other inhaled agents are highly lipid-soluble, usually water-insoluble materials that dissolve specifically in the lipid plasma membranes of every cell in the body. Alcohol is both water- and lipid-soluble, and shares this property with anesthetic agents. When sufficient anesthetic agent has entered the plasma membrane to make up 1 or 2% of the volume, the properties of the membrane change such that the lipoproteins that must flip-flop through the membrane are retarded, so that function slows or even stops if enough more material is added. Volatile abused solvents, including toluene, benzene, ether, and nitrous oxide, share this property. During anesthesia, lighter doses affect the higher centers and produce a "high," which for ether, toluene, and aerosols is prolonged. Larger doses produce progressive lethargy, interference with motor function, and unconsciousness; extreme doses produce brainstem depression and death.

This is the mode of action of the volatile anesthetic agents and of ethanol at concentrations greater than 400 mg/dl. Of great interest is animal experimentation showing that prolonged and chronic exposure to ethanol results in host adaptation to these plasma membrane changes such that the impairment is less in the chronically exposed animal; this host adaptation is associated with specific changes in the composition of the cellular membranes. Such changes appear after 2 to 3 weeks of chronic ethanol exposure and disappear about 1 week after cessation of such treatment. During withdrawal this compensation is unbalanced, producing symptoms. These results, however, do not explain the clear fact that alcohol produces effects on behavior at a level well below that needed to alter plasma membrane function.

B. ALCOHOL

Although alcohol may be unique among the addicting substances in having no receptor, Tabakoff and Hoffman note that alcohol produces changes in a variety of receptors analogous to those caused by other abused substances.[1] Thus, the effect of alcohol seems most marked on membranes near binding sites. Tabakoff and Hoffman found that an amino acid receptor in the brain that controls the entrance of calcium, called the N-methyl-D-aspartate receptor, is inhibited by ethanol in concentrations of 40 to 50 mg/dl (a level found in the blood after the ingestion of two drinks in a normal-sized person). The effect was seen predominantly in areas that process memory, including the hippocampus and the cerebellum. Blockage of this system effectively slowed the generation of the second messenger cGMP. This system is the first that is appreciably changed by levels of alcohol at which normal persons are aware of altered function.[2] Effects on the GABA-benzodiazepine receptor chloride ionophore have also been found effective at levels of 100 mg/dl. The effect of ethanol is to potentiate chloride flux in the same manner that GABA and benzodiazepines act. This mechanism is of interest because it requires a PCP-like material as part of the complete chloride flux channel. Ethanol preferentially inhibits opiate binding to the delta receptor. This has been recently reviewed.[3] Many other neurosubstances are altered in alcoholism, including catecholamines.[4] Thyrotropin-releasing hormone has recently been shown to antagonize ethanol inebriation.[5]

III. SUBSTANCES OF ABUSE FOR WHICH THE MECHANISM OF ACTION SEEMS TO BE UNDERSTOOD

It is now believed that all substances that are effective in milligram quantities act through entry into the central nervous system by binding to specific receptors and in this manner increase or decrease a regulatory process through interference with the usual action of an already existing internal structure. Many but not all of these regulatory systems have been discovered.

A. COCAINE AND AMPHETAMINES

Cocaine and amphetamines are sympathomimetic drugs and increase dopaminergic and noradrenergic transmitters at the neuronal synapses. Cocaine blocks reuptake of norepinephrine, and amphetamines both augment release and block reuptake, in effect accounting for prolonged and exaggerated adrenergic response,[6] with both drugs increasing the amount of DOPA and noradrenaline at the receptor site and in circulation. Addicts cannot distinguish between these amphetamines and cocaine when given intravenously, and a recent analysis of the composition of street drugs suggested that about 20% of the cocaine supplied on the street is actually a less expensive amphetamine. Dopaminergic blockade extinguishes self-administration behavior in rats for both classes of agents.[7] This is in contrast to the failure of either alpha- or beta-adrenergic blockade to extinguish self-administration in similar rats.

B. OPIOIDS

Addicting opiates, both natural and synthetic, share binding with a group of normal peptides called encephalins, of which some 20 are now known. Native morphine has at least four distinct receptors. The mu receptor, located mostly in the central nervous system, has the behavior-altering characteristics which we associate with addiction; it is far more sensitive to chemicals such as morphine and less sensitive to peptides. Other receptors in the brain and in the intestine have activity with most opiates, but show a different spectrum of responses. More detail is presented in Chapter 19. The delta receptor is predominantly for encephalins, and there is a binding site almost specific for dynorphin called the K site.[8] It is known that only mu agonist supports self-administration and addiction-producing behavior in rats.

C. PHENCYCLIDINE

Phencyclidine has effects similar to those of amphetamines and barbiturates. This agent enhances the sedative effects of both ethanol and barbiturates. Binding occurs at two disparate central nervous system sites. The omega opiate binding is highly specific, but the functional alteration is unknown. It also binds to the GABA-benzodiazepine ionophore chloride channel. This component is required to complete that regulatory system.

D. BENZODIAZEPINES

The benzodiazepines open up an important chloride channel in central nervous system tissues. There is cross reaction with alcohol and GABA, but a benzodiazepine-like agent is critical to the function of this system. The natural substance controlling this reaction has now been identified as a metabolite of diazepam, and the distribution of these receptors can be defined by PET scanning using labeled analogs of benzodiazepines.

E. BARBITURATES

Barbiturates act on the same synaptic systems as GABA and depress the sensory cortex, decrease motor activity, and produce sedations. They act primarily at the level of the thalamus, inhibiting ascending conduction in the reticular formation and in this manner interfering with the transmission of impulses to the cortex.

F. ATROPINE AND OTHER ANTICHOLINERGIC DRUGS

Atropine and other anticholinergic drugs are behavior-altering agents that interfere with acetylcholine transmission in the central nervous system. Different drugs have different profiles in the nicotinic and muscarinic synapses.

G. CAFFEINE AND OTHER THEOPHYLLINES

Caffeine and other theophyllines act on specific smooth muscle receptors and cause the immediate increase of cAMP inside the cell. Other neuroreceptors are stimulated by these agents.

H. NICOTINE

Nicotine is an agonist to nicotinic receptors in the peripheral and central nervous systems, producing both stimulant and depressant phases of action on all autonomic ganglia. The result is a release of catecholamines.

I. AGENTS FOR WHICH THE MOLECULAR BASIS OF ACTION IS UNKNOWN

Marijuana blocks bicarbonate ion transport, which makes it useful in the treatment of glaucoma, but the molecular basis for its behavioral changes is unknown. Hallucinogens bind to central nervous system centers, suggesting specific binding sites, but only the regions of the brain involved are known.

IV. ANIMAL MODELS OF ADDICTION

Olds and Milner[9] described a model of intracranial electrical stimulation in adult rats which will reward animals sufficiently with this ''pleasurable'' system that animals will work to exhaustion or undertake unpleasant stimuli. All addicting substances lowered the threshold of this phenomenon, usually with a U-shaped curve with much higher levels raising the threshold. These results led these workers and Kornetsky and Bain[10] to postulate that addicting drugs have in common a hedonistic center or reward center present in all people that the drug awards, and that this sets up its own behavior. This theory has strong support in several different animal models.

A variety of self-administration paradigms of addiction are employed. A widely used model implants catheters into the cerebral ventricles of a rat and pumps drug into the animal in accord with its behavior or problem solving. Such models are often used to demonstrate that a substance has addicting potential by its ability to replace an addicting opiate or its ability to cause drug-seeking behavior. Although these models reproduce the addiction, including withdrawal, they have not contributed in a major way to an understanding of just what factors are essential to initiation.

REFERENCES

1. **Tabakoff, B. and Hoffman, P. L.,** Biochemical pharmacology of alcohol, in *Psychopharmacology, The Third Generation of Progress,* Meltzer, H. Y., Ed., Raven Press, New York, 1987, 1521.
2. **Hoffman, P. and Weight, F.,** Only two drinks may affect memory, *JAMA,* 261, 2604, 1989.
3. **Charness, M. E., Simon, R. P., and Greenberg, D. A.,** Ethanol and the nervous system, *N. Engl. J. Med.,* 321, 442, 1989.
4. **Hunt, W. A. and Majcrowicz, E.,** Alterations in the turnover of brain norepinephrine and dopamine in alcohol-dependent rats, *J. Neurochem.,* 23, 549, 1974.
5. **Knutsen, H., Dolva, L. A., Skrede, S., Bjorklund, R., and Morland, J.,** Thyrotropin-releasing hormone antagonism of ethanol inebriation, *Alcoholism: Clin. Exp. Res.,* 13, 365, 1989.
6. **Woolverton, W. L.,** *Pharmacologist,* 26, 1621, 1984.
7. **Risner, M. C. and Jones, B. E.,** Dopaminergic blockade but not adrenergic blockade extinguishing self administration of cocaine, *Biol. Psychiatr.,* 11, 625, 1976.
8. **Chavkin, C., James, I. F., and Goldstein, A.,** Morphine receptors in the central nervous system, the kappa binding system, *Science,* 215, 413, 1984.
9. **Olds, J. and Milner, P.,** Positive reinforcement produced by electrical stimulation of setal area and other regions of rat brain, *J. Comp. Physiol. Psychol.,* 47, 419, 1954.
10. **Kornetsky, C. and Bain, G.,** Neuronal bases for hedonic effects of cocaine and opiates, in *Cocaine: Clinical and Biobehavioral Aspects,* Fisher, S., Raskin, A., and Uhlenhuth, E. H., Eds., Oxford University Press, New York, 1987, 66.

Chapter 4

Etiology of Substance Abuse and Similarities in Alcoholism and Drug Abuse

I. ETIOLOGY

A. INTRODUCTION

Most addicts and their families, in reflective moments, want to identify the small flaw in the addict's earlier life that will provide understanding of the destructive addiction. The simplistic search for ''an etiology'' of harmful substance abuse likens the problem to a sore finger caused by a splinter. If only the splinter could be plucked out, the problem would disappear. This form of thinking creates an urgency to find the cause of addiction, for its removal represents the ''cure.''

The same person energized to identify the cause clearly understands and appreciates the pervasive changes produced by substance abuse yet does not extend this comprehension to doubt the ''splinter'' theory. Thus, the search for a cause, though highly illogical, occupies an inordinate amount of time of professionals, abusers, and their families. Physicians and the many health-oriented advocacy groups among the population share some of the responsibility for the notion that there is a singular cause for each disease and that its removal, like an operation for an abscess or benign tumor, will result in a cure.

It is my view that programs aimed primarily at altering the pathological behavior produced by the addiction and eliminating drug use are far more effective than programs aimed at removing "the cause."

Each person who studies one or more of the addictions discovers that there is obfuscation and confusion about exactly what is required in order to declare a given person addicted, and just what behavior should be targeted as the criterion for success beyond limitation of substance use. This is in part brought about because of the many different perspectives that are brought to bear on addictions. The physician treating cirrhosis in an alcoholic, the judge weighing repeated driving offenses while under the influence of alcohol, the school counselor helping an underachieving child, and the psychologist aiding the wife of a drinking man all have different definitions, concerns, and goals for treatment of the problem of addiction. The doctor considers himself successful if the liver disease compensates and the patient regains health, His Honor pleases his constituency by imposing a long prison sentence, the counselor is delighted with good grades, and the psychologist may be pleased with a separation from an abusive marriage for his client. These diverse objectives are occasionally pooled to indicate treatment outcomes, yet none has addressed the primary problem of alcoholism.

Many different disciplines have contributed to the etiology of alcoholism and drug abuse, yet there is no satisfying identification of just why a small fraction of users become abusers. Genetic studies, longitudinal studies of specific populations, and epidemiological studies have provided data of value, and to some degree the discoveries of one field can be generalized to populations well outside the one investigated. Alcohol has been much more completely studied as an abused substance than have others, and there is a greater amount and diversity of material on its abuse than for any other single substance.

B. THOUGHTS ON DRUG ABUSE

Alcoholism research supports a genetic cause for alcoholism, with possibly as much as 20% of alcoholism being due to inheritance, though most studies put the figure lower. No other single factor has emerged as being more important. For all addictive behavior there must be an available supply and an acceptance of its use. Settings that are quite intolerant of use seem less associated with the behavior than tolerant ones. It is usually held that there are some hedonistic, anxiolytic, or antidepressive effects on behavior that play a role in getting a person into use initially, but this formulation fails to explain why some people become addicted and others do not. In any population of recreational users of a mind-altering drug, only a minority become addicted though tolerance will develop in nearly all. This is well understood among alcohol users (no more than 6% become alcoholics), patients requiring long-term use of opiates for cancer pain, and heroin users. Probably the incidence of addiction is among the highest with cocaine, and even here it represents only 15% of users. Once addiction occurs, it is clear to all that it has a "life of its own," meaning that science cannot explain which people get better and which ones go on to die from advanced complications of their problem.

C. CONCLUSIONS ON THE ETIOLOGY OF ALCOHOLISM BY VAILLANT

A remarkable book by Vaillant,[1] taking advantage of two good longitudinal studies extending over more than 45 years and many related studies but limited to alcoholism, addresses etiological issues in men in Boston. The study uses information on an inner-city group of adolescents, many from broken homes, and a group of college sophomores.

The Vaillant book confirms a few previously held conclusions about alcoholism but questions many firm convictions that were simply generalizations from acecdotal experience or limited studies. The conclusions in this thoughtful book probably apply to drug abuse also.

The prospective studies found independent contributions of heredity, ethnicity, and premorbid antisocial behavior to subsequent alcoholism. Both alcoholic fathers and mothers influence subsequent alcoholism. Ethnic groups that tolerated drunkenness and that did not teach responsible drinking in the home had a higher incidence of alcoholism. Parental conflict, poor maternal supervision, and many moves of the household during adolescence contributed to future alcoholism. Those individuals who had a good home environment and successes in life before age 12 had no problems with abuse of alcohol in later life, but among those coming from broken or irregular families or those who had behavior problems through the teens, about half did not become alcoholic and about half did. A major difference between the conclusions of Vaillant's prospective studies and the many retrospective studies is that underlying psychopathology is rare in the premorbid alcoholic. The characteristic personality of the alcoholic is a consequence of the drinking behavior and not its cause. Alcoholism is *not* a symptom of underlying distress; the abuse of alcohol produces much of the distress that is seen. Socializing healthy drinking practices to permit life-long conscious choice is one of the better suggestions that emerges.

II. SIMILARITIES BETWEEN ALCOHOL AND DRUG ABUSE

A. INTRODUCTION

Everyone who works with addictions has noticed many common features that addicted persons have. If one observes addicts of a similar age and social-economic background, the similarities are even more prominent. Those conducting treatment commonly experience patients addicted to one substance acquiring an addiction to another substance during the course of treatment. The choice of a substance of abuse, though probably never made from a vast and fully complete menu, seems to be dependent upon one's family and peers. The family values of one's upbringing and the peers in one's social and work environments heavily influence to which substance one will be exposed and will utilize if abuse occurs. At early ages, 6 to 12 years, influences of the home, including older siblings and parental substance use, are predominant. Multiple studies show that the school exercises a substantial influence in modulating family and peer input.

Two widely distributed transport systems in the central nervous system, the GABA-benzodiazepine chloride ionophore and a glutamate-sensitive one, are altered by many different addicting substances, as described in Chapter 3. Ethanol, opiates, PCP, and sedatives alter the GABA-benzodiazepine chloride transport system (ionophore). The glutamate calcium transport system is exquisitely sensitive to alcohol and PCP, but is also modulated by opiates, cocaine, and amphetamines. Thus, through the mediation of these two fundamental systems there may be widespread changes that have more in common than differences.

Alcohol is the most commonly used substance subject to abuse. It is heavily ingrained in our culture, with more than 90% of adults living in metropolitan areas using alcohol at least yearly. The movement from use to abuse is a widely experienced transition. Alcohol is the major drug of abuse in persons over age 40 and in middle-class, home-owning groups. Despite ready availability, however, even the most generous estimates find that less than 10% and possibly as few as 5% of users become abusers.

Prescription-requiring items such as sedatives and amphetamines are abused by those who regularly see doctors. Some 80% of prescriptions for benzodiazepine drugs are given legally to abusers by physicians. Changes in FDA regulations and assignment of more restrictive schedules for amphetamines have diminished the numbers of doctor-supplied abusers and made these drugs much more common in street trade.

Marijuana and cocaine have been the drugs of the "smart set" of employed middle-class men and women. Use started with peer participation and continued because of ensnarement by the highs produced. The attractiveness of a group activity using an illicit drug and sharing in a "high" is widespread — a similar disregard of the law during Prohibition was so pervasive that an estimated 70% of the U.S. metropolitan population used illicit alcoholic beverages weekly.

Other illicit drugs used by underprivileged youth in large metropolitan areas seem to be an expression of rebellion and a means to escape boredom. This accounts for the disproportionate numbers of poor, underprivileged, and large-city minority groups among those with unmet needs for treatment.

B. SOCIAL ASPECTS

Drug use as a ritualistic feature of some major cultural groups is prominent in history. It has been independently discovered with various drugs in all parts of the world for seven millennia of recorded history. Alcohol, coffee, tea, tobacco, coca leaves, cannabis, opiates, mescaline, and many other psychoactive substances were used in rituals preceding the recorded histories of the cultures in which they were first discovered. In most cultures a complex and well-organized ritual has evolved for use of the drug. A clear leader, use of the drug by many in the group, and interdiction to nongroup use are prominent features. In this early cultural use of drugs there is a complex ceremony involving large segments of the population (sometimes limited to men) gathered together under leadership who conduct the ceremony. As a part of the ritual some or all of the individuals ingest the drug. A burst of unusual behavior brought about by the action of the drug is followed by an ordered response from the group, always under leadership and evolving from long experience.[2,3] The use of beer in ancient Inca culture and mescaline in western Native American ceremonies are excellent examples. Such use of drugs in primitive societies may be important in keeping younger men an active part of the tribe, gaining support for current leaders, and diminishing contention for leadership. In these societies individual repetitive abuse is rarely found because of the societal sanctions against nongroup experimentation with the agents. Thus, a monopoly restricts availability of the substance. There are many clear analogies between these societies and our own. Cultural groups that use agents with abuse potential in group enterprises with clear acceptance of the limitations have fewer problems than those who do not. Thus, use of alcohol in Italian, Jewish, and traditional Chinese families is associated with almost no abuse.

In contrast, startling epidemics of substance abuse have broken out in more recent history, associated with mass inexpensive availability of the agent, sometimes legal, sometimes illegal, as reviewed by Kissin.[4] Examples include the use of gin in England in the eighteenth century, the use of alcohol by Native Americans, the use of amphetamines in Japan, as well as current use of cocaine.

As societies become more developed, the use of various substances is integrated by social codes and customs, but ritual aspects are preserved. Thus, the use of tea in the Orient and Russia preserves many rites that have survived their utility in an earlier time. For some substances, the ceremonial and symbolic importance has created a social imperative that individuals cannot resist. Thus, the nuptial glass of wine in Jewish marriage ceremonies transcends the desire of the individual to avoid alcohol. Westermeyer, through anthropological studies of substance use, has observed that the alcoholic is more socially deviant in Asia than the opium users; Moslems are unconcerned about cannabis use; members of the Native American Church are encouraged to use peyote in certain ceremonies.[5] Yet in America and Europe alcohol is accepted and these other substances are deemed deviant.

Students of outbreaks of substance abuse[6] find that trends toward secularism and away from traditional religious influences are essential but usually not sufficient. Rapid social changes such as those brought about by extensive migrations, unusual infusions of prosperity, great new unemployment, or war are usually required in the correct setting. Examples are the gin epidemics in England, the high use of marijuana in the U.S. in the depression of the 1929—1933 era, amphetamine epidemics in Sweden and Japan during the turbulent

1950s, the heroin epidemic of the 1960s in the U.S., and the more recent crack cocaine epidemic in the U.S. in the late 1980s. The epidemics have always been with a substance new to the population. Coffee and tobacco, when introduced to Europe, went through much of the furor that amphetamines and other street drugs have gone through in our time.

At the height of certain epidemics peak substance abuse of 10% of the population was described although 50% was reported for selected segments. The use of daily alcoholic portions of wine by Portuguese peasants and French farm workers or the use of cocoa leaf on a daily basis by Peruvian laborers in rural areas suggests that at least 1 in 3 are tolerant, with the prevalence of use approaching 95%. This shows that some popularly accepted habits can be fully as destructive as epidemics, and that control is much more difficult because it requires altering a society's fabric of tradition, mores, and acceptance.

Societies control new and old substances by prohibition, taxation, and regulation of availability and public use. This control has varying degrees of efficiency. When there are large numbers of users, immense profits from illicit supply lines to be made, and wide public tolerance, these modalities are of limited use. It is remarkable that alcohol, opiates, cocaine, and amphetamines are similar in their regulatory problems and in the ambiguity of the laws governing their availability.

C. PSYCHOLOGY OF ADDICTION

Predicting drug or alcohol use based on characteristics determined before age 12 or before exposure to addicting agents suggests only that maladjusted children have more of a chance of becoming abnormal users than well-adjusted children. Genetic or home factors appear to be at least as strong as factors, and we must conclude that there is no typical personality that leads to alcoholism or addiction; in fact, the better prospective studies support the idea that addiction produces abnormal personality.

In contrast to the predictive value of personality factors, the development of an addiction produces certain stereotyped personality and behavioral patterns, which are remarkable similar for different types of addictions. The age profile of abusers of alcohol is older than that for abusers of amphetamine or heroin, in part because of the much longer use-before-addicted time for alcohol. Developing drug abuse and tolerance requires the potential addict to obtain the drug, and as part of the process to maintain secrecy, protect supplies, and sequester the time and money to support the habit. This leads to a pattern of secretiveness, aloofness, apartness, substantial sequestration of time and resources from the attention of those close to the person. These features are widespread among addicts and usually appear in personality studies. Otherwise there is great diversity. Most studies show low self-esteem and sensitivity to disapproval (see Carroll[7]). As problematic use occurs, most addicts use the drug to build confidence or relieve symptoms. They exhibit wide mood swings, with anger, anxiety, and remorse usually prominent. Poor judgment, dominated by their next usage, and reduced interest in nondrinking or nondrug projects is common. Cocaine and amphetamine users have prominent hedonistic natures,[8] which may be less marked in heroin users.[9]

Using the testing protocols of the Minnesota Multiphasic Personality Inventory (MMPI), alcohol or heroin abusers were distinguished from normal control subjects but not one from another.[10] Keeley and Solomon, in both their book[11] and a subsequent review,[12] cover many differences between nonabusers and abusers and similarities between alcoholics and other abusers. However, the study groups are often small, and it is difficult to extrapolate from one study to another.

D. TREATMENT

There are significant differences in the medical illnesses that accompany addictions. Alcoholism produces more nutritional problems, with cirrhosis, chronic brain injury, and pancreatitis prominent. Intravenous addicts have more infectious complications, including hepatitis B, AIDS, endocarditis, and abscesses in remote portions of the body. Withdrawal states and their treatments are different and are discussed in Chapter 27.

Once withdrawal is completed, there is much more common ground in treatment, and most programs treat addicts with various addictions in the same facilities. Schuckit outlines such programs and the rationale in his book,[13] and this is discussed further in Chapters 26 and 28. It is apparent that the elements of drug and alcohol rehabilitation programs can be run together and that a single program can even be operated effectively for both.

The problems of mixing adolescents with the elderly pose greater challenges than mixing various addictions. It is estimated that 60% of cocaine abusers become alcohol abusers during recovery; our own studies suggest that at least 10% of veterans initiating treatment for alcoholism use another illicit drug at least weekly.

Prevention programs are usually quite different when directed toward alcoholism or toward other agents. This is in part because prevention of alcoholism in the workplace was actively organized as early as the 1940s and has continued with independent funding and goals. In the schools there has been concern that a drug prevention program directed to children under age 10, when such information is essential, may actually present them with new information. Often, therefore, such programs are cleansed of specifics and become vague guidelines for better mental hygiene as sloganized by Nancy Reagan's "Just Say No!" program. Nonetheless, excellent units of information are available for use in school systems.[9]

Industry, particularly with programs addressed toward decreasing overall health costs, has recognized the value of health maintenance including self-recognition of smoking, drinking, and drug use problems. These programs, aimed widely at the addictive disorders, usually provide screening questionnaires for recognition of severity of a problem, counseling to verify desires and needs for treatment, and entry into cessation programs as part of workplace health benefits. Success rates of 80% for smoking, drinking, and illicit drug use are commonly experienced in short-term evaluations, and up to 40% in much longer ones.

REFERENCES

1. **Vallaint, G.,** *The Natural History of Alcoholism,* Harvard University Press, Cambridge, MA, 1972.
2. **Lewis, I. M.,** *Ecstatic Religion,* Penguin Books, Baltimore, MD, 1971.
3. **La Barre, W.,** *Flesh of the Gods,* Furst, P. T., Ed., Praeger Publ., New York, 1972, 261.
4. **Kissin, B.,** An historical review of alcohol and drug use, in *Alcohol and Drugs: Similarities and Differences,* Solomon, J. and Keeley, K., Eds., PSG Publ., Littleton, MA, 1981.
5. **Westermeyer, J.,** Sociocultural aspects of alcohol and drug use and abuse, in *Alcohol and Drugs: Similarities and Differences,* Solomon, J. and Keeley, K., Eds., PSG Publ., Littleton, MA, 1981.
6. **Leighton, A. L.,** *My name is Legion,* Basic Books, New York, 1959.
7. **Carroll, J. F. X.,** Personality and psychopathology, comparison of alcoholic and drug dependent persons, in *Alcohol and Drugs: Similarities and Differences,* Solomon, J. and Keeley, K., Eds., PSG Publ., Littleton, MA, 1981.
8. **McGrath, J. H.,** Adolescent pill users, *Int. J. Addictions,* 5, 173, 1970.
9. **Milkman, H. and Frosch, W. A.,** On the preferential abuse of heroin and amphetamine, *J. Nerv. Ment. Disorders,* 156, 242, 1973.
10. **Apfeldorf, J.,** Alcoholism scales of the MMPI, contributions and future directions, *Int. J. Addictions,* 13, 17, 1978.
11. **Solomon, J. and Keeley, K. A., Eds.,** *Alcohol and Drugs: Similarities and Differences,* PSG Publ., Littleton, MA, 1981.
12. **Keeley, K. A. and Solomon, J.,** New perspectives on the similarities and differences of alcoholism and drug abuse, *Curr. Alcoholism,* 8, 99, 1981.
13. **Schuckit, M. A.,** *Drug and Alcohol Abuse, A Clinical Guide to Diagnosis and Treatment,* 2nd ed., Plenum Press, New York, 1984.

Chapter 5

Essential Pharmacology of Abused Drugs

I. INTRODUCTION

Most primary-care physicians understand the use of medicinal drugs from both their training and daily care of patients. In this chapter we review absorption, metabolism, some factors influencing entry into the central nervous system (CNS), and tolerance of addicting drugs. Details about each drug are provided in later chapters describing each class of agents. For most classes of abused drugs there are several similar chemical forms that may be abused. Opiates, amphetamines, barbiturates, and benzodiazepine drugs are families with many representatives. Within each family there is a similarity of mode of principal action, cross tolerance is exhibited, but the methods of removal and the side effects are often quite different. New substances in each class are discovered each year, both by the legitimate pharmaceutical industry and by hidden chemists making "designer drugs" with potential for illicit use and profits.

Most agents are taken in quantities of micromoles to millimoles and provide blood and tissue concentrations in the range of 10^{-7} to 10^{-5}, which is usually 10 to 1000 times the concentration of the natural substance that they are replacing at a receptor site. An exception is ethanol, which is ingested in molar quantities and reaches concentrations of 20 to 30 m*M*/l during mild intoxication.

II. ABSORPTION OF DRUGS

A. ROUTES OF ABSORPTION

Abused drugs are taken by mouth, smoked, inhaled directly onto the mucous membranes, or injected intravenously. The method of taking the drug is determined by the chemical form of the drug and some of its basic properties. All drugs taken by mouth have a relatively slow absorption, with peak after one hour. There is substantial metabolism by the liver as they are absorbed, which removes a great deal of the drug *before* the desired effect is obtained. This "first-pass effect" and the long wait for the "high" make oral ingestion a less preferred route of administration. The first-pass effect varies from very low for hallucinogens and atropine to intermediate (10 to 20%) for alcohol and some amphetamines, to high (up to 85%) for opiates.

"Snorting" pure drug into the nasal mucosa leads to absorption that is more rapid than ingestion, but slower than intravenous or inhalation routes. There is no first-pass effect, but only fairly pure drugs are absorbed through these membranes. Betel nut is absorbed through the buccal mucosa by chewing the nut and leaf with alkali in the form of lime to enhance absorption. Snorting, widely employed for cocaine and other pure drugs, is accomplished by inhaling a linearly arranged row of powder from a glass surface. A straw or rolled paper inserted into the nostril facilitates the process. With insufflation the high lasts longer than that following intravenous administration, but absorption is less than 100% complete.

Drugs that can be inhaled directly, such as ether or toluene, or drugs that can be vaporized by heating (smoking), such as "crack" cocaine, opiates, or nicotine, and inhaled into the lungs are absorbed rapidly, with a peak effect almost the same as intravenous injection. "Crack" is the free base of cocaine, which vaporizes at lower temperature to permit smoking; salts of cocaine vaporize at much higher temperatures and therefore do not deliver comparable doses. Figure 3 illustrates the differences in rates of absorption and the effective blood or CNS levels for the identical dose of cocaine taken by various methods. The total absorbed dose is the same for intravenous (i.v.) and intramuscular (i.m.) use (not illustrated), but is less complete for nasal insufflation or smoking, for these processes are typically 80% complete for highly pure material and as low as 25% complete for impure material. None of these routes has a first-pass effect. Oral ingestion has a large first-pass effect, usually 30 to 70%.

B. IMPORTANCE OF pH

Many drugs are bases that ionize under acidic conditions and cannot be absorbed by diffusion. Betel nut is such a drug, so it is chewed with alkaline lime to enhance its absorption. Basic drugs ionize in the stomach and will not be absorbed until they reach the alkaline milieu of the small intestine. These drugs include opiates, amphetamines, barbiturates, and some individual members of other drug classes. The pH of the gastrointestinal tract influences the amount and rate of drug absorption.

III. TRANSPORT, METABOLISM, AND REMOVAL OF DRUGS

A. TRANSPORT

Protein binding holds drug in the serum and retards its movement into the central nervous system and into the liver for metabolic alteration or into the liver and kidney for excretion. All water-soluble agents exhibit some protein binding, but it varies from little (<15%) to marked (>60%). Protein binding diminishes the concentration of drug available for diffusion into the brain and liver, and of course, decreases glomerular filtration at the kidney. Occasionally, albumin binding of a drug is altered by another drug that binds even more tightly, displacing the initial drug. Protein binding is also influenced by conditions that alter blood

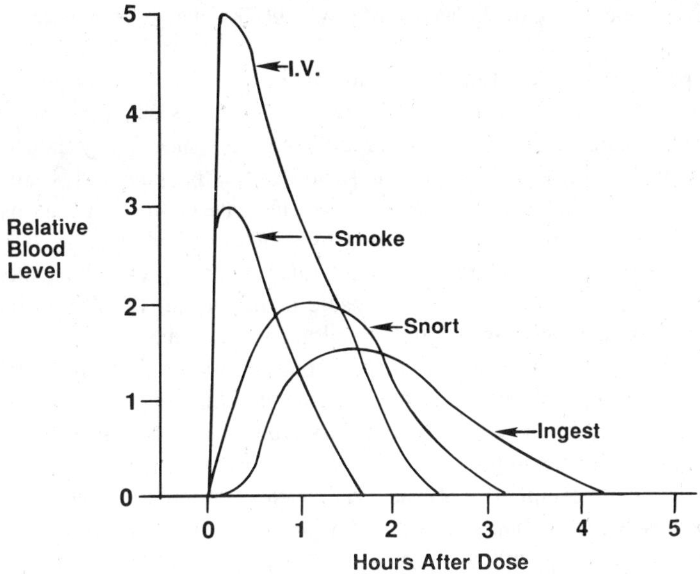

FIGURE 3. Absorption and duration of action after identical doses of cocaine taken by various routes. Note that the intravenous route delivers the highest dose. Smoking and snorting do not deliver all of the active material, and ingestion has a substantial first-pass effect. Snorting and ingestion have the most prolonged effects. The high occurs almost immediately after smoking or intravenous injection, but is delayed after ingestion. It is intermediate following snorting.

pH. A highly bound agent requires as much as 20 min for the high to be perceived, even after intravenous administration.

Ethyl alcohol is fully soluble in water, and its volume of distribution is relatively low. Ether is highly lipid-soluble and has a very high volume of distribution because it dissolves in lipid stores. Some amphetamines are tightly bound to albumin in the plasma and have a volume of distribution that is about the same as the albumin space. Drugs with a high volume of distribution take longer to be removed from the body than those with a low volume. Excretion, liver biotransformation, and renal excretion can take place only on that portion of drug in the circulation. Drug in other sites must diffuse into the circulation before these modes of removal can occur. When biotransformation occurs, the lipid solubility is diminished and the water solubility is increased, a fact which nearly always decreases the volume of distribution and accelerates the removal of the biotransformed product.

Lipid-soluble and water-insoluble agents (inhalants) are rapidly transported from the lungs after inhalation via the blood to the central nervous system, moving primarily along a concentration gradient. Ethanol is lipid- and water-soluble, so that it distributes into the body water of the subject. None of these agents is appreciably protein bound.

B. BIOTRANSFORMATION

Nearly all drugs are biotransformed, usually in the liver, to a different chemical form. In this process most drugs are rendered biologically inactive, and the new, more polar products are more readily excreted by either the kidney or liver or both. A few drugs are converted into active products by this process. Thus, codeine and heroin are both biotransformed to morphine, but at different rates; the morphine is the active form. Diazepam is metabolized to many different products, nearly half of which are biologically active. Biotransformation always converts drugs to a form that is more readily excretable by the liver or kidney. Highly lipid-soluble drugs are converted to water-soluble ones, making biliary or renal excretion much more likely; as part of this solubility change the volume of distribution is diminished.

The endoplastic reticulum of the liver is the major site of biotransformation where lipid-soluble drugs are acted upon by oxidative or conjugative steps using the enzymes P-450 to produce the new chemical species. These processes are nonspecifically induced to increase their metabolism with increased use of drugs, and as this happens drugs are converted to inactive products more rapidly. This nonspecific increase in drug metabolism is one of several factors that account for the increased tolerance of alcoholics for barbiturates and other drugs. Increase in the metabolic disposition rate is generally called metabolic tolerance. The drug-metabolizing enzymes are also capable of inhibition. Disulfiram inhibits one of the major enzymes metabolizing alcohol, resulting in the accumulation of acetaldehyde. Cimetidine inhibits many P-450 enzymes, producing a modest slowing down of drug metabolism. P-450 enzymes are present in the intestine and the kidney, but the most important collection is in the liver. Biotransformation occurs even in advanced liver disease, with these other sites assuming greater importance.

Alcohol, unlike almost all other substances, is nearly completely metabolized to energy, with the products being carbon dioxide and water. The initial steps of oxidation occur predominantly in the liver with the formation of acetaldehyde followed by acetate. The acetate is then metabolized throughout the body.

C. EXCRETION

The inhaled volatile drugs, such as ether, toluene, amyl acetate, acetone, and nitrous oxide, are excreted largely through the lungs. The urine is the most important route of excretion for most agents, with biliary excretion sharing excretion of many agents. In general, these drugs are biotransformed by the liver into more water-soluble and less lipid-soluble forms that can be excreted by the kidney; the bile is the second most important route of excretion, but because of the difficulty of collecting samples, the least well studied. Glutethimide is extensively excreted into the bile.

Products of biotransformation that are not ionized are excreted largely by glomerular filtration, but those with a charge at body pH are often actively secreted by the renal tubules. Urinary excretion often is in the form of conjugates, such as glucuronides or sulfates; many of these are weak acids or bases. Alkalinization of the urine increases the excretion of weak acids such as most barbiturates. Acidification of the urine increases the excretion of basic metabolic products such as those from amphetamines, methadone, nicotine, and PCP. As a person ages, there is a systematic and predictable decline in renal function, thus most drugs persist longer in older people than in young ones.

IV. PHARMACOKINETICS

The rate of alteration of the plasma level is described by pharmacokinetics. The usual measure is the blood or plasma half-persistence time (also called half-clearance time or half-time) and is that amount of time in which the plasma level falls by 50%. For nearly all drugs, the total metabolism and excretion is faster at high levels than at low levels, because some major drug removal processes are linearly related to concentration. Thus, glomerular filtration and diffusion are faster at high concentrations than at low concentrations. Processes controlled by such forces have a similar half-clearance time at both low and high levels. This most common type of plasma disappearance is called first-order kinetics; when the logarithm of the blood concentration is plotted against time, the graph forms a straight line. This defines removal processes that are related to blood levels.

When the amount of drug disappearing from the blood is the same at both high and low levels (the concentration is linear with time), a process that is saturated is indicated. This is the case with alcohol removal at levels above 200 mg/dl and with high doses of methadone. This is called zero-order kinetics and indicates a carrier or enzyme-mediated system that is constantly saturated, analogous to a fully loaded train of 100 cars moving a massive coal pile from city A to city B. An equal amount is moved in each unit of time, regardless of the size of the coal pile in city A.

The half-life is important in determining the effect of multiple doses. If a second, similar dose is given at a time interval of less than the half-life, cumulation will occur; if it is given at longer than the half-life interval, the blood level will decline. Since excretory processes most frequently increase with blood levels, a maximal level will be attained at any dosing level. Usually the dosing level reaches a plateau at five half-lives.

V. RECEPTORS, TOLERANCE, AND ANTAGONISTS

A. RECEPTORS

With the exception of inhalants, anesthetics, and alcohol, all drugs bind to specific receptors as part of their action. Drugs are often present in a concentration 10 to 100 times that of the natural agonist for which the receptor was designed, indicating less efficient binding. Only that portion of the drug in the receptor is effective. Drug at other sites does not exert its action. The substance for which the receptor was designed (e.g., norepinephrine) binds much more tightly to the receptor than the unnatural one (e.g., amphetamines), thus higher concentrations are required for an effect. If the natural substrate is increased (such as with extreme fear or excitement), the effect of the drug may be totally ameliorated because the system is flooded with the more efficient natural binding material.

Receptors are known to increase in density on a cell, or to diminish in density. Both changes are common means of adjusting systems to increase sensitivity to a material by increasing the numbers of receptors per cell (up regulation) or diminish sensitivity (down regulation).

B. TOLERANCE

As any drug is used repeatedly, higher and higher doses are required to obtain the same effect physiologically or psychologically. There are two distinct components of tolerance. Metabolic tolerance refers to an increased rate of metabolism of a drug through repeated exposure, usually through increases in the amounts of P-450 enzymes in the liver brought about by induction. This is manifest by a shortened half-time and lower blood levels for a fixed dose and has been demonstrated to be widely present in alcoholics and opiate addicts. A second form of tolerance is psychological or neurological. In this tolerance the attainment of the same degree of sedation or psychic high requires a much higher blood level than in the drug-naive person. This tolerance usually comes about through alterations of receptor density producing fewer receptors per cell. This mechanism is well established in animal models of addiction, but has not been widely measured in humans, though it is reliably predicted to exist. To attain the measured end point let us assume that a minimum of ten receptors must combine with the neurotransmitter each minute. If there are fewer receptors by a factor of 50%, then the opportunity of a given concentration of neurotransmitter is reduced by 50% and in this fashion diminishes the sensitivity. Put another way, the stimulus must be twice as strong to attain the same effect. Such adjustment of the receptor levels to produce tolerance is a necessary prerequisite before withdrawal can occur.

The setting for tolerance to occur seems to be use of sufficient dose to more than saturate available binding sites. When narcotics are used for pain control in cancer, tolerance does not develop very frequently. This is probably because saturation of binding sites does not occur. As the pain worsens and higher doses are required, the worsening pain is associated with more binding sites.

C. ANTAGONISTS

Antagonists occupy binding sites without an effect similar to the agonist, but prevent the agonist activity or even reverse that activity. Although experimental antagonists are known for most drugs, only nalorphine as a pure antagonist to opiates is in common use. An antagonist to the benzodiazepine drugs is available and will be released for use largely as an anecdote for these agents when used for anesthesia in ambulatory units, such as for dentistry, endoscopy, and cystoscopy.

Chapter 6

Issues of Law and Custom

I. INTRODUCTION

The law in the U.S. regarding behavior-modifying substances is a complex mixture of concern for the welfare of citizens, protection of one citizen from the behavior of others, and protection of citizens from themselves. The Food and Drug Administration, initially responsible for the purity of food, gradually became involved on the national level with the safety of medicines. This function has slowly expanded to include efficacy of medicines, including over-the-counter agents, and the regulation of addicting substances through the Bureau of Narcotics. Alcohol regulation, on the other hand, except under national prohibition, has been regulated largely at the local level, with federal intervention only with regard to taxation and assuring that very limited amounts of beverage alcohol are produced without taxation.

The rules controlling the manufacture and availability of drugs and alcohol are continually changing, reflecting changing customs in America. Frequently a single dramatic event captures the attention of lawmakers or regulators, resulting in many new and occasionally inappropriately restrictive actions, but sometimes correcting regulation long neglected. The occurrence of major limb defects at birth among children born of mothers taking thalidomide changed early drug evaluation regulations. The pointed protests of MADD (Mothers Against Drunken Driving) has impressively changed federal and local regulation of driving while intoxicated, and the entry of Betty Ford into abuse treatment changed federal funding for such programs.

Custom — what social leaders are doing or what young people have set as trends —

often influences new behaviors and leads to public acceptance even though the behavior may be in conflict with the law. Clearly the use of amphetamines in the 1940s, marijuana in the 1960s, and cocaine in the 1980s are examples of custom that have set major trends, even though all are illegal. The healthy trend in shifting from concentrated distilled liquor to wines and beers as the alcohol use pattern in young people is noteworthy.

A. PROHIBITION

In the decade prior to and in the period of recovery and prosperity following World War I, a trend toward urbanization and industrialization from a farm-based population, and mobilization and then release of many people as part of the war effort, started new social trends including alcohol use in many. Use of beer and distilled liquors spread rapidly in the urban areas. Drunkenness, family disruption, alcohol-related crime, motor accidents, and impairment of work increased. Temperance movements that had been present in America before the turn of the century grew, and more and more citizens accepted the simplistic view that the availability of alcohol was the cause of many twentieth-century urban-associated social problems. The Volstead Act (the Eighteenth Amendment to the Constitution) prohibiting the manufacture, importation, or distribution of fermented or distilled beverages with an alcohol content greater than 3% (all beers and wines have more alcohol than this), was approved in 1919 and phased into effect in the next few years. It was not repealed until 1933. This period of prohibition was a failure. Somewhat analogous to our current epidemic use of cocaine, the laws did not adequately reflect public practice and custom. There was not widespread support for prohibition among the populace. The substantial profits made in the illicit supply of distilled alcohol beverages encouraged organized crime to meet the demand. Bribery, corruption of police, judges, and others in the public trust, and flaunting of the laws were common during this period.

In the 3 years after passage of the Eighteenth Amendment, the distilling industry of America was converted to other uses and the stocks of alcoholic beverages were destroyed. However, the inhabitants of metropolitan America were unwilling to give up the consumption of alcohol. Quantities of alcoholic beverages were concealed from destruction, smuggling occurred at most American borders, and a major industry of illegal importation, production, and distribution was established. The potential for large profits was a major attraction to criminal organizations with their accompanying violence.

This steady supply and availability of alcoholic beverages spawned a popular culture among the young in metropolitan areas of the country. The illegal nightclub (speakeasy) became widely available, and most of America turned a deaf ear to the prohibition laws. At one time it was believed that more than 70% of adult Americans were using illegal beverages.

We learned some things from our experience with prohibition. The customs and widespread popular habits of the people are not always adequately protected by new or old laws. Prohibition did not control the social ills it set out to correct. It produced many new and somewhat unanticipated ones in bringing fortunes to organized crime, encouraging many toward illegal behavior, and making drinking the "sophisticated" thing to do. New laws that are in conflict with the customs of many people are usually flaunted. It is clear, however, that the cirrhosis rate declined during the prohibition years, indicating that the high levels of alcohol use required for this complication to occur were less available.

Our legal efforts at the control of marijuana and even to some degree the use of cocaine among the well-to-do has similarly met with widespread flaunting of the law. Our culture has available many mind-altering and addicting substances, yet only a few of these are intensely regulated or completely interdicted. Older drugs, such as caffeine in tea and coffee and tobacco, were treated as transient fads at the time of their introduction to Americans. Religious groups were against their use, and there were wide differences between those who tolerated their use and those who felt that they should not be used.

The use of marijuana, stimulants and amphetamines to stay awake, concentrated alcohol, smoking or drinking by women in public, and certainly "street drugs" have produced a variety of divergent but initially negative views and opinions within the many sides of public opinion. Each substance and its mode of use has had a substantial following, often among the rebellious or the adventuresome. The perception that the use of a particular drug can provide a lot of good or pleasure and very little harm has been widely promulgated for each of these substances.

Because there are so many different views on the proper place of these substances, we do not have very clear policies for their use. When there is a consistent and uniformly negative view of a substance or a behavior within a tightly knit social group, most often a religious or ethnic group, there results complete interdiction of that substance or behavior. When, however, the influence of that group is weakened or there are mixed views, individual choice is tolerated. This is seen in members of the Church of Latter Day Saints (commonly called Mormons), who as a group interdict alcohol, tobacco, coffee, tea, and use of street drugs. In Salt Lake City and that state of Utah the use rate of these substances is the lowest in the nation, but among Mormons living in other portions of the world the use rate is substantially higher.

To a major degree, ambivalence about the role of alcohol, over-the-counter drugs, and marijuana leads to tolerance among most American adults of the use of these materials. Public nudity and certain sexual practice variations are less tolerated than is substance utilization, including use of illicit substances. The American ethos allowing individual differences to exist side by side permits a great deal of acceptance of many varieties of substance use as long as it is not clearly harming others. Friends and neighbors are indignant about reporting illicit drug use to authorities and occasionally ostracize those who take such actions, but there seems a shift toward recognizing the tremendous harm that widespread abuse is causing. Our laws often ignore a major area (such as prosecution of the user of an illicit substance) and are overly stringent in others. Most of us also become a little cynical about respect for the law when many instances of irregular enforcement, corrupt judges and police, and ambivalent laws are often in the news. To a large degree we are quite tolerant of use and even abuse of alcohol, some over-the-counter drugs, and the minor street drugs such as marijuana. America is a melting pot of many cultures and customs, and our neighbors and neighborhoods respect the right to be different. Currently, we become much more agitated over issues of abortion on demand, nudity, and tolerance of certain sexual aberrations than we do over working people's use of illicit substances or alcoholism in our neighbors. This tolerance, bordering on indifference, is one of the reasons that widespread use of illicit substances continues.

The current increasing endemic use of cocaine in America has many features of the experience of prohibition. The wide use of the agent by employed people creates a high demand. This in turn provides immense profits for the illicit drug trade. The power of these profits clearly has overcome the policies of police and courts in some isolated instances. These include the more often than occasional appearance of confiscated cocaine back in street trade through its disappearance from custody, the intimidation of witnesses in court cases, and the negligible prosecution of prominent personalities who are identified as drug users. It may well be that legalization of certain abused substances may be the only way to attain control. The "war against drugs" under the Reagan and Bush administrations has been most characterized by increasing expenditures on control, increasing arrests, but also increasing availability and use.

II. THE LAW

The law is clear on which substances are legal (alcohol, caffeine, tobacco) and which are clearly illegal to use and possess. Clear exceptions are made for the manufacture, possession, and medical use of otherwise illegal substances. The Food and Drug Administration (FDA) is charged by the federal government with the definition and regulation of such substances. Newer addicting molecules for which there is limited animal or human experience, molecules designed by chemists that are analogs of existing narcotics, and unusual drugs of plant origin used in other parts of the world but rarely imported into the U.S. are not regulated by the FDA.

Ambivalence about drug law arises from the widespread criminal prosecution of manufacturers and suppliers of illicit drugs, while millions of individual users of illegal substances continue their usage with relative impunity. Further, in a few states, illegally obtained prescription agents and marijuana under a specific limit, defined for personal use, are legal to possess; only amounts in excess of these defined amounts are illegal. Interviews indicate that approximately half of Americans have used an illegal substance at least once, suggesting that existing laws have not heavily influenced them in this choice.

In the remainder of this chapter I pose a number of substantive questions important to the physician treating substance abuse. The answers are generalized to consider all regions of the U.S.; should they appear to be in conflict with local regulation, the advice of an attorney should be sought.[1-4]

1. *Does the physician identifying use of an illicit substance have any legal responsibility for reporting?*

There is currently no legal duty on any citizen in any state to report criminality. *When called upon,* however, every citizen has the duty to give information in his or her possession to proper authorities. The key here is "when called upon". This is duty under common law. In many states there is a legislated duty upon physicians to report contagious diseases to health authorities, but many physicians do not fully comply with this when it involves a substantial embarrassment to them or their patients. An example is the reporting of venereal disease encountered in the course of private practice. In many states physicians are required to report incidents of convulsions to the bureau of motor vehicles, but this is very infrequently complied with, because the resultant loss of drivers' licenses leads to repercussions on the physician. Although the law is clear, enforcement is very lax.

The Hippocratic oath, widely supported and promulgated by physicians and their professional and regulatory societies, provides guidance that has standing in society even though it does not take precedence over established law. The oath states that "whatever in connection with my professional practice, or not in connection with it, I see or hear in the life of men which might not be spoken of abroad, I will not divulge as reckoning that all such should be kept secret;" the American Medical Association has concluded that "A physician may not reveal the confidences entrusted to him in the course of medical attendance, or the deficiencies he may observe in the character of patients, unless he is required to do so by the law or unless it becomes necessary in order to protect the welfare of the individual or of the community".[5]

2. *Are the records of such a physician open to subpoena?*

There are areas of confidentiality protected by the law, such as attorney/client, accountant/client, clergy/parishioner, and physician/patient. The physician/patient privilege is statutory and is so recognized in most but not all states. This means that a physician may not be compelled to reveal his or her records *or* any information divulged by a patient in the course of medical treatment. Many states, however, have abrogated this statutory privilege in criminal cases, sometimes in differing ways. Louisiana, for instance, has provided an exception to the privilege to make hospital records (not office records) available in criminal trials. In other states the privilege is limited to civil actions. Laws in various states are slowly evolving to increasingly diminish the protection of physician/patient privilege.

3. *Is an addicted person who commits a criminal act under the influence of the drug to which he is addicted liable for the consequences of his act?*

Voluntary intoxication with a legal or illegal substance does not excuse a criminal act. In some instances, when the intoxication was of sufficient degree that the person could not form the intent required in the definition of the crime, courts have found the person innocent. Thus, on occasion, proof of intoxication has been held to negate the specific-intent requirement for robbery, larceny, burglary, attempted rape, and assault with intent to murder. Similarly, first-degree murder has been reduced to second-degree murder, with voluntary intoxication negating the element of premeditation. In these rare cases, it was held that due to intoxication the defendent could not form the intent of malice necessary in the greater crime of first-degree murder. In contrast, general-intent crimes such as rape cannot use voluntary intoxication to prove lack of intent. The intent is implied from the act itself. Thus, the general rule is that voluntary intoxication is never allowed as an absolute defense; however, some jurisdictions allow the intoxication to negate an element of the crime, in effect creating a defense.

Involuntary intoxication is treated differently. A defendant who can prove involuntarily induced intoxication may be excused from criminal responsibility, i.e., it may be a defense in and of itself. There have been five different types of involuntary induced intoxications recognized. These are (1) coercive intoxication (fault of another), (2) inadvertent intoxication (innocent mistake), (3) accidental intoxication (medical prescription), (4) temporary insanity, and (5) compulsion. The first three defenses are not widely held by the legal system. For a temporary insanity plea, "a person is not responsible for criminal conduct if at the time of such conduct as a result of mental disease or defect he lacks the substantial capacity either to appreciate the criminality (wrongfulness) or his conduct or to conform his conduct to the requirements of the law." This is the language that determines insanity in the majority of U.S. courts. A limited number of jurisdictions have accepted the theory that a drug addict when out of drugs is incapable of refraining from acts to replenish his or her supply; i.e., there is compulsion. The insanity defense has been used successfully in this instance, but has only infrequently been accepted. Another infrequently accepted defense is the "psychotic hangover". In this the defendant addict argues that through years of drug abuse he or she has become insane.

Although intoxication with drugs or with alcohol is treated the same under the law, there is a general prejudice about the use of illegal drugs. Since such use constitutes an illegal act, there is the unstated argument that subsequent actions were a foreseeable effect of illegal drug use. Courts do not frequently reward a defendant on trial for committing any illegal act by allowing his or her illegal intoxication to serve as a mitigator or defense.

4. *Do laws regarding driving while intoxicated apply to all substances?*

Specific language of "driving while under the influence of intoxicants" is ordinarily used, and intoxicants are separately defined. Since there is variation from state to state in the language used, it is well to have the specific laws reviewed in the state in which such a case arises.

5. *What is a physician's liability when an abusing patient leaves his or her care or refuses to carry out medical advice?*

The liability is the same as in other malpractice cases. The recommendations must be clearly documented in the patient's record. If the patient leaves the physician's care or does not follow through with appointments, this too should be documented. When such patients fail to keep appointments, the process of notification and rescheduling used by the physician's office should be noted. As with any other patient, when a reasonable number of failures to follow through have occurred, it is of value to send the patient a letter terminating his or her care.

Only when the physician feels that a person is suicidal, homicidal, or in no condition to drive does he or she have extra responsibility. With suicide or homicide, consultation with a psychiatrist or even involvement of security people or the police is possible, but a highly sedated patient or one who somehow became intoxicated while under medical care and now plans to drive to another location poses a problem that can only be handled by reasoning with the patient.

A patient who rejects therapy for substance abuse to the point where the physician does not feel they are accepting advice for their care should be discharged from care by letter. In my experience these letters often gain cooperation that other means have failed to attain.

Since abusing patients are more likely to abuse medication, including overdose with the intent to commit suicide, it is important to provide written instructions and limit medication amounts to those the patient can handle. Outpatient detoxification and the dispensing of medications for this purpose is discussed in Chapter 27.

REFERENCES

1. **Iber, R. G.,** Personal communication in response to questions, Baltimore, 1989.
2. *Corpus Juris Secundum,* The American Law Book Co., Brooklyn, NY, 1964.
3. *American Law Reports,* The Lawyers Co-operative Publishing Co., Rochester, NY, 1989.
4. **Benton, E., Bor, A., Leech, W., Levy, J., Lipshie, S., Mitchell, T., and Brown, G.,** Special project on drugs and criminal responsibility, *Vanderbilt Law Rev.,* 33, 1145, 1980.
5. *Principles of Medical Ethics,* American Medical Association, Chicago, 1957.

Chapter 7

Attitudes Among Medical Staff That Influence Substance Abuse Care

I. INTRODUCTION

Substance abuse victims have chronic disease that requires long-term support and intervention if the outcome is to be influenced. Early interactions between abusing clients and medical staffs involved in their diagnosis and subsequent care profoundly influence whether or not the client will remain in some sort of relationship with treatment facilities or will eschew such contacts. It is the purpose of this chapter to discuss some of the adverse attitudes that doctors and their staffs may have, and to provide some suggestions for change if these are identified.

We must all recognize that it is not possible to avoid contact with substance-abusing subjects and at least part of their treatment except by denying the existence of substance abuse in our practices. Chapter 1 presented some of the many ways in which physicians are called upon to assist abusing subjects and their families, and Chapter 6 presented some of the responsibilities that the law, society, and medical organizations impose upon each of us. The importance of substance abuse is increasingly recognized as the basis of mild hypertension, hyperlipidemia, and problems of obesity. It plays a substantial role in traumatic accidents, abuse of children and the elderly, suicide attempts, and marital separations occurring after 10 or more years of marriage. These issues in our patients bring abusing patients to almost all doctors, and recognition of abuse is important if our interventions are to be successful.

Three substantial problems will be discussed in subsequent sections. First, there is often a perception that intervention and treatment of substance abuse is of little or no value. If it is undertaken, it requires a great deal of time and resources. This attitude derives from generally accurate information and experience concerning *derelict* or street-dwelling chronic addicts and is erroneously extended to the entire population of abusers. A second problem is economic. All health facilities are caught in a financial vise brought about by forces demanding more services but diminishing reimbursement. Abusers are widely perceived to require more services and to provide on the average less likelihood of reimbursement. The third problem is concern for the health and safety of medical staff and other patients. The image of a smelly, dirty, unkempt, noisily offensive patient is known to everyone. Occasional violent acts carried out under the influence of drugs or alcohol are publicized in the media out of proportion to their frequency. Finally, it is common knowledge that AIDS, hepatitis B and C, and venereal disease are more widespread among street addicts than in the population at large. Exaggeration of the magnitude of these three problems is widespread in medical facilities and among their staffs and often influences treatment.[1]

II. THE "TYPICAL SUBSTANCE ABUSER" AND THE INFLUENCE OF TREATMENT

The "typical" abuser coming to the attention of a medical practice has the same features as the average patient in that practice over age 13 years. More than 90% are employed and reasonably healthy. The derelict alcoholic or drug addict makes up less than 3% of all alcoholics and 5% of all other drug abusers and is found largely in inner-city metropolitan areas because they are tolerated there. Much teaching of doctors and other health professionals is carried out in large university and Veterans Administration hospitals located in major cities, where substantial numbers of such derelict patients are treated and subsequently observed. It is experience with this group of patients that is largely responsible for establishing the attitude that abusing persons are often dirty and unkempt, riddled with communicable diseases, and infrequently rehabilitated. The chronic derelict addict or alcoholic clearly has the poorest prognosis for recovery of all abusing people.

In contrast, the abuser who is employed and has a family often shows excellent response to even a small amount of treatment; this area is explored more thoroughly in Chapter 27. Those who treat substance abuse among employed patients find the work rewarding in the many patients who are restored to their former potential through modest interventions.

III. ECONOMICS, HAZARDS TO STAFF

A. ECONOMICS

Physicians' offices are placed in a financial stricture resulting from increased expenses and decreased revenues. Documentation, adequate doctor-patient relationships, and extensive forms for third-party reimbursement consume time without contributing to reimbursement. Abusing patients encountered during the course of evaluation for disease require extensive counseling to overcome denial of abuse, and family members often require extended and repeated explanations. Substance-abusing patients often have financial problems, become unemployed, and exhaust the willingness of close family members to handle their obligations. Expired insurance, inability to pay reasonable fees, and failure to follow through with applications for assistance for treatment are frequent among abusing patients. However, treating abusing patients just like other patients avoids most of these problems. Each office has an entry process that rapidly identifies the means of payment. Prolonged and costly treatments are discussed with the patient, and when an inability to afford them is identified, alternative cares may be suggested and the patient assisted in attaining them.

The care of abusing adolescents and employed adults is one of the major growth industries in America, largely because such treatment is identified as useful, is paid for by third-party providers, and provides excellent reimbursement for the time spent. Physicians are appropriately reimbursed for initial screening, planning and discussing proposed therapy, supervising such therapy, and specific treatment of particular problems. Much of the actual program of treatment is administered by other professionals in the form of counseling, group therapy, work and discussion activities, and family therapy. An appropriate charge is rendered for each of these services by the professional who administers the activity. Doctors usually do not seek reimbursement for extended interviews that constitute family counseling or prolonged telephone interviews that provide assistance. Assessing an appropriate charge for all services administered to abusing patients makes such work as financially rewarding as other forms of treatment.

Each physician's office should determine how much care they wish to provide to abusing patients who neither appear for emergency assistance nor are associated with the office for another major and appropriate reason. This decision should be based at least partly on the physician's skills and available time. Should there be occasional patients who cannot afford appropriate care through the physician's office, referral to a volunteer or publicly funded program is preferable to an inadequate program or one that will add a major debt to the addict's existing problems.

B. HAZARDS

The risk to staff and other patients with regard to violence, acquiring disease, or even frightening away "paying" patients is extremely low and diminishes even further in a well-run office. Staff training to anticipate potential problems will almost always avoid them. Should an intoxicated or acutely psychotic patient appear, the staff should intercede immediately to assist with appropriate care and remove the patient from the common waiting area. Nearly all abuse programs promptly dismiss patients who are clearly intoxicated. A new appointment is scheduled for a time when the patient will be more able to participate, and transportation is arranged. If there is an emergency, the physician can be interrupted to deal with it, most often by directing the patient to an appropriate facility or calling an ambulance or cab if needed. Abusing patients avoid unpleasantness; intoxicated patients simply do not present themselves at facilities that have a firm policy of not permitting them to remain. In most offices a very unkempt person can be taken to an examining room and the problem dealt with in a professional manner out of sight of the waiting-room group.

Violence is rare indeed; it is discussed in Chapters 10 and 33. Although communicable diseases such as AIDS, hepatitis B and C, and many venereal diseases are more prevalent in abusing subjects, office techniques of handwashing, cleanliness, and sterilization of penetrating instruments totally prevents spread of these conditions from one patient to another or to staff. Body lice and scabies are very rare problems, and are more common in a pediatrics practice than in one devoted to substance abuse; even in these practices they are largely limited to those who are obviously filthy.

The standard training of office staff in preventing the spread of disease and continual review of cleanliness techniques, disposal of blood-contaminated sharps, and other hygienic discipline is sufficient for care of abusers and will protect all. A special plan to deal with intoxicated patients should be discussed and even rehearsed so that it will function smoothly should it every be required.

TABLE 11
Origin of Negative Attitudes Toward Substance Abusers

1. Large experience with derelict addicts
2. Perception that treatment is hopeless
3. Fear of violence, contagion
4. Utilization of M.D. and staff time with low reimbursement
5. The abuse personality — inflicts pain on all who touch and creates anger
6. Relapse in addicts well treated with great skill, compassion, and time

IV. ORIGINS OF POOR ATTITUDES TOWARD ADDICTS

Table 11 shows some of the common causes of negative attitudes toward addicts. Although not all of these factors can be altered, through education and improvement in skills of the physician and staff the influence that they have on the medical staff can be changed. The prevalence of training experience with derelict addicts and the negative image that this creates regarding disease, unpleasant associations, and the hopelessness of treatment has been discussed. This can be countered by examples of actual patients in your practice who are different. It is usually easy to identify instances of success with addiction without breaching confidentiality. This is the most powerful method of letting the entire medical staff see addicts in a different light.

Your actual experience will best reinforce the knowledge that addicts emerge from all levels of the socioeconomic scale, all races, and all neighborhoods.

Problems of reimbursement have been discussed in the previous section. The solution is to subject the abusing patient to the same evaluation and interview process as other patients in the practice. All services should be appropriately billed, so it will soon be found that utilized time generates income.

A. THE ABUSE PERSONALITY

Many personality traits of chronic addicts often alienate them from other people. Abusers develop extensive skills and habits of lying to protect time, substance use, and resources, and this is often detected in interview. Denial of abuse usually leads to alternative explanations of difficulties with work, family, or other persons. The misery of abusers is great and quickly extends to include you, the therapist, as in, "if you can only help me with my health I will be alright," implying that their problems are related to your poor skills or obstinacy in assisting them. Medical suggestions are often not accepted, or not complied with. The net effect is that the therapist is made to feel inadequate in skill and creates a genuine motivation in the doctor to avoid such encounters in the future.

Through understanding, the addictologist gently but firmly confronts the denial. Lying or blaming others may be confronted when effecting therapy, but in planning treatment the nature of the problem must be made extremely clear — e.g., the addiction, not the ulcer, is the basis of the problem. The exact responsibilities of the patient and of the doctor are defined, and are reinforced on subsequent visits.

B. RELAPSE AFTER PROLONGED THERAPY

When any of us has worked for a long time with a patient and feel that we have given the patient our best in compassion, skill, and time, we are disappointed by relapse and often interpret it as a personal rejection or a failure of our skills. Vaillant[2] repeatedly emphasizes that addictions "have a life of their own", with many relapses occurring during the course of a person's lifetime. These relapses are not deliberate and are almost never a rejection of the therapist but a clear part of the destructive behavior that is the addiction. Understanding this is sometimes difficult, but it should never result in dismissing the patient from treatment.

Addicts will often relapse, usually at a time that is inconvenient to all concerned. This is one of the major challenges in the treatment and management of addiction.

C. FURTHER SOLUTIONS

Recognition of the barriers to doctor-patient and staff-patient communications is important in treating abusers and keeping them in treatment.[3] Allowing the abusing person to have dignity, privacy, and self-respect is a very important part of office practice that is sometimes neglected. Attitudes are not fixed; they change with even modest education of both doctors and staff.[4]

REFERENCES

1. **Olbrisch, M. E. and Levenson, J. L.,** Liver transplantation for alcoholic cirrhosis, *JAMA,* 261, 2958, 1989.
2. **Vaillant, G.,** *The Natural History of Alcoholism,* Harvard University Press, Cambridge, MA, 1972.
3. **Quill, T. E.,** Recognizing and adjusting to barriers in doctor-patient communication, *Ann. Intern. Med.,* 111, 51, 1989.
4. **Chappel, J. N., Jordan, R. D., Treadway, B. J., and Miller, P. R.,** Substance abuse attitudes, changes in medical students, *Am. J. Psychol.,* 134, 379, 1977.

Chapter 8

Obtaining an Accurate Drug and Alcohol History

I. INTRODUCTION

Alcohol use is a part of the lifestyle of 95% of adult Americans and is the most frequently abused substance. Approximately 30% of Americans have been given a prescription containing a sedative, tranquilizer, or sleeping preparation.Some 15% of persons under 35 years have tried cocaine, PCP, or opiates. An additional 15% have used marijuana. Although the personal sampling of legal and illegal substances is commonplace, only a small fraction of those who sample become regular users or abusers.

The uncertain legal status of users of illicit substances encourages them to be silent and secretive about use unless a clear need to disclose is demonstrated. Sometimes the trust in the physician-patient relationship is insufficiently established to allow the patient to provide this information. Alcohol and doctor-provided agents, when used in large amounts, require constant attention to maintaining supplies. This usually leads to secretiveness, use of multiple sources (such as several doctors prescribing the same drug), and diverting money for payment from other needs. Thus accurate information is not readily revealed.

Most persons who use a substance, legal or illegal, do not either become abusers or develop tolerance. Among patients with chronic pain treated with high doses of opiates, tolerance is occasionally induced, but interference with aspects of living and work is infrequent and serious addiction is rare. Similar experience is found with street drugs. Approximately 80 to 90% of the people who undertake recreational use of a drug at one time or another do not become addicts and should not be so labeled on the basis of admission of use. Cocaine in the form of "crack" may be the most addicting of the commonly abused substances. The highest estimate of users becoming abusers that I have identified is 20%.

A. PURPOSE

The purpose of a substance use history is threefold. First, the relationship of the current consultation to substance use can be established. Second, the pattern of use and how this interdigitates with lifestyle largely determines the strategy that will successfully modify the use. Third, planning for future good health may indicate a need to modify substance use, both licit and illicit. Together with the physical examination, data from the laboratory, and possibly information from collateral sources, a diagnosis and a treatment plan can be made.

B. SOURCES OF INFORMATION

There are several different ways to obtain a history of substance abuse. The most common is directly from the patient, but this may create concern when confidence in the doctor-patient relationship has not yet been established. A self-administered questionnaire used by all new patients is an excellent alternative, providing similar information without creating alarm that the abusing patient is being treated differently.

Obtaining a history from household contacts or other collateral sources creates special problems of its own. Testing blood or urine for drugs raises legal issues of invasion of privacy that are not always addressed satisfactorily.

Each of these methods has its limitations. The direct history is sometimes inaccurate and almost always fails to indicate casual or very infrequent drug use. Self-administered questionnaires are excellent screening vehicles and provide more information than all but the most skillfully taken abuse history. Talking with relatives or household contacts if the patient is unable to provide a history creates tension between the physician and the patient because of the implication that the patient cannot be trusted. Obtaining information about drug and alcohol levels in the urine without specific prior approval from the patient creates no problem when the information is required for emergency decisions in a subject unable to provide such consent. Obtaining such information during an office visit carries the risk of legal action, but this risk is usually slight. Many obstetric clinics obtain urines for drugs on all patients to protect the unborn child, and this practice has been upheld by the courts at least in Illinois and California.

Chapter 7 addressed issues of attitude in the physician or staff that may interfere with relating to the abusing patient and obtaining an accurate history of substance use. It is generally believed that even under optimum circumstances some proportion of use will not be openly acknowledged. Of subjects tested and found positive for PCP, fully one third repeatedly deny exposure.

II. SUGGESTED APPROACH FOR OBTAINING AN ALCOHOL OR DRUG USE HISTORY

Screening for substance abuse is part of the evaluation of all patients. To avoid building a wall to communication, the person identified as a likely user must not in any way perceive this identification at the initial contact. Physicians with an aversion to the extreme alcohol or drug abuser must identify and eliminate this aversion before they can successfully work with abusers. As in all patient encounters, there should be an introductory period of friendliness and warmth to establish the basis of mutual respect, trust, and communication. Privacy is essential, comfortable seating valuable, and eye contact a necessity. Touching the hand or shoulder of the client as part of the introduction is valuable. Avoid being interrupted by phone calls or other staff. Abusers are often embarrassed or even demoralized by the seeking of treatment, and the therapist must reverse this feeling by showing very clearly that the problem is important. Abusers are often hypersensitive and interpret interruptions as rejection. Accept the humanity and worth of each individual and seek islands of value that you can clearly identify and point out to the patient. Do not be judgmental. Keep the questions and words few and get to the point as part of your usual evaluation.

A smile as you come to the patient, eye contact, and a statement, "I am Dr. Rodriguez, your new doctor," is a good beginning. This should be followed by a handshake, and if appropriate, assisting the person to the proper comfortable chair from which eye contact is easily possible. A few words about the person before talking about the consultation are very valuable. "I understand you are a student in the art institute" can initiate conversation before asking about the health problem. Unless the chief complaint involves substance abuse — "I'm here for my drinking," or "I'm losing my memory from drugs" — the substance use should be put into its appropriate place. Early in the interview, explicitly settle the issue of confidentiality of both your comments and written records about illness and drug use. "The information you provide during this evaluation is confidential. It will not be released to anyone without your permission." Having made this statement, it is mandatory that this guides your disclosures. When a parent or employer has engaged your services, it is important to clarify this relationship at the beginning of the interview. If precise copies of your reports are to go to them, you must so indicate. "An exact copy of my report will be sent to your insurance company" is a sufficient statement. Should a portion of the history be highly sensitive and not the basis of the consultation, it is sometimes appropriate to omit it from the report in order to preserve patient cooperation. Consider a patient who uses alcohol daily and develops cirrhosis with ascites. As part of his history, he also indicates that he is a homosexual. The patient's blood is negative for hepatitis B and C. There is no need to include his homosexuality in the history that is returned to his company, for it is not pertinent to his primary illness.

Sometimes a patient may ask you to suppress addiction in your report when it is a substantial portion of their problem and essential to the resolution of their illness. On the infrequent occasions that I have done this, it has invariably been a mistake. Patients can always refuse permission for you to send a report to their company, and everyone who is of legal age can refuse to have reports sent to family members. When a person suppresses key addiction information from insurers, it is part of denial and retards recovery.

The physician should assume the attitude that some medicine, alcohol, and illicit drug use is so common as to be normal. With this attitude, as the interviewer asks about medications or habits, he may say, "How do you use alcohol?" Later he may ask, "What medicines and drugs do you take?" and, during the answers, clarify "prescription, drug store, or street drugs?" and when and where the use occurs. Any positive answers offer an opportunity to learn about use in the most recent period. Empathy with the pressures of life that expose one to substances and the clearly projected attitude that it could happen to anyone are valuable. Indicate confidence in working with people on drugs. If you are comfortable with street terminology, it may facilitate communication to use that language with many clients rather than the more formal medical terminology.

Some clear "do's" include:

1. *Do* hear the person out completely before deciding on a diagnosis.
2. *Do* try to understand the precise reason for the patient's visit and acquire information to meet that need.
3. *Do* avoid moral judgments on substance use and lifestyle.
4. *Do* define just what your skills may accomplish toward a solution to the patients problem, what the patient must accomplish, and the limitations of both.

TABLE 12
Major Components of an Alcohol and Substance Abuse History Useful for Diagnosis and Treatment

1. Substances used and amount in past 3 months
2. Has tolerance or dependence developed now or in the past?
3. Does the patient believe he or she is now abusing the agent?
4. Age of first use/abuse, periods of abstinence
5. Time and drug of heaviest lifetime use
6. Use of other substances, which ones and when
7. Experiences with withdrawal, unusual features such as convulsions, violence
8. History of hallucinations, psychosis, or hospitalization for toxic reaction
9. Patient's perception of what he or she derives from the drug
10. Treatments undertaken for abused substances, particularly in the most recent year

III. DETERMINATION OF THE CIRCUMSTANCE OF THE CONSULTATION

The precise reason for the patient's visit needs to be determined. Often in substance abuse cases the patient has one perception and the physician has a different one, neither clearly articulated.

Determining who initiated the consultation is a useful starting point. Consultations may be initiated by patients, their families, their employers, or even their lawyers. Identification of the route to consultation leads logically to a discussion of the patient's expectation from the consultation. Is he seeking relief from some symptomatic problem? Is he seeking support that his current lifestyle is not destructive? Is he corroborating a diagnosis made elsewhere? Often the motive remains obscure in the early portion of the interview, but it needs to be clarified in order to be met.

Often the entry interview by clerical staff identifies the source of referral, e.g., self-referred, and to whom reports should be sent, and may be a clear basis for discussion of the motive and expectations. I usually ask at the time of summing up the health findings what the patient hopes to accomplish. An answer such as "I wanted an opinion on how bad my liver is" or "I want to know if I am a junky like my wife tells me" is a clear entry to further discussion.

IV. USEFUL COMPONENTS OF A DRUG HISTORY

Table 12 lists the necessary information for a complete drug history. This is needed for all patients in whom abuse is suspected in order to assist with treatment of the addiction. For assistance, with the present illness or for preventive medicine the substances used and the amounts employed in recent months are of the greatest importance.

A. SUBSTANCES USED

A majority of patients will freely discuss substance use in the recent period of their life, particularly with a health worker. They are almost always inaccurate in their estimation of the amount used. Use of multiple agents is common, with approx. 20% of alcoholics and 33% of emergency room visits by street drug users showing the presence of another substance upon toxicological screen. In identifying the pattern of use in recent months, patients often provide useful medical information from previous contacts with doctors and hospitals. Curiosity about drug sources or how they were paid for often causes the patient to withdraw and stop communicating. Current withdrawal and diseases that need attention are almost exclusively a function of drugs used in the most recent 3 to 6 months.

B. TOLERANCE

"Does the same amount of drug produce the same feeling as it did 3 months ago or when you started use?" usually identifies increasing tolerance, for the answer reveals escalating doses over time. Tolerance indicates less physiological effect from the same dose — thus an increased dose requirement for the same physiological effect. Tolerance occurs with all substances of abuse. Its presence indicates a regular user of that class of substances, and if the patient is using depressants or opiates a significant withdrawal syndrome may be anticipated. Sometimes the patient will identify tolerance by his answer to the question, "What happens when you don't get a fix?"

C. ABUSE

Abuse, as distinguished from use, indicates that some harmful effect has occurred in relation to finances, job or family performance, or health. A surprising number of patients have clear insight into these effects and are concerned; others ignore flagrant signs and signals or have denial highly developed. Abuse often occurs without recognizable tolerance, but most frequently both are present.

D. AGE OF FIRST USE OF THE ABUSED SUBSTANCE

Determining at what age the abused substance was first used will help establish the difficulty one will have with rehabilitation. Early onset of use often indicates a more established and difficult-to-reverse pattern than short-term use. Teen users often delay the development of adult personality features and may never develop them. Essentially all users have periods of abstinence, some spontaneous, some enforced. The genesis and duration of abstinence periods indicates something of the pattern of success/failure in this patient. Treatments that seemed to be of value are identified, and insight on the part of the patient and his or her family and friends is revealed.

Rehabilitation from a lifestyle centered on abuse must build a new life and self-esteem away from the abuse culture. Subjects who have had a substantial adult life before abuse became a major portion of their daily existence have more experiences upon which to build this program.

E. EXPERIENCES WITH WITHDRAWAL

Previous experience often predicts unique management problems that the patient may encounter with the current withdrawal. Severity is often predicted by the intensity and duration of drug use. However, patients with histories of convulsions, full psychosis, violence, and other exaggerated patterns typically have stereotyped withdrawals. Choice of site of treatment of the withdrawal and medications to be used may be more appropriate when based on prior experience history. Thus a patient who usually has a grand mal seizure during withdrawal is appropriately treated with potent anticonvulsives to prevent this event (see Chapter 27).

F. MEANING OF THE SUBSTANCE USE TO THE PATIENT

Many patients cannot articulate the all-consuming importance of the substance use to them, but some can provide clear statements. "It takes away the pain of my failures", "it relaxes me", "I can live with myself", "I can undertake sexual relations" are examples of statements that can be utilized in treatment. Sometimes early counseling can be directed to alternative, less destructive ways to relax, be at ease with the opposite sex, or enjoy an interpersonal activity. Some patients continue substance use to avoid a frightening withdrawal; assistance with a safe, anxiety-free detoxification may provide a major bond for future treatment. Occasionally a person wants only oblivion from the drug, to escape all earthly concerns. Often such persons have severe depression or other psychoses that will be assisted by specific diagnosis and treatment. Although the majority cannot tell you what their substance means to them early in treatment, it is a valuable insight when it occurs and many can describe this clearly after many months of sobriety.

G. PREVIOUS EXPERIENCES WITH TREATMENT

There are many different treatments for substance abuse to match the many different needs, and each is effective in selected subjects. Treatments that were effective in the past should be noted for possible repetition; treatments that clearly did not succeed should be avoided in your recommendations.

Primary-care physicians have a substantial advantage in planning a treatment in having available a wide menu of treatments to which they can refer and may well have one that matches a good outcome from the patient's past. Specialists often become so involved with a small number of programs that this wide menu is no longer available. Such elements of treatment as age and training of the therapist, duration of the program, primary modalities used, prominence of recovering addicts among the counselors, and relations with the patient's family, employer, and friends can be determined and matched with what is now feasible for the patient.

V. SPECIFIC THINGS TO AVOID IN TAKING A HISTORY OF SUBSTANCE ABUSE

1. Passing judgments, particularly negative ones about the drug abuse, the associated lifestyle, or the consequences. If you possess factual medical information, provide it to the patient but remain silent on other areas.
2. Being manipulated to reject the patient or his behavior. Many addicted persons understand the requirement for abstinence as a part of treatment. However, if they successfully manipulate the therapist into rejecting them because of the outrageousness of their action, they then justify continued abuse to themselves.
3. Interruptions of the interview process, which reinforce the concept that the patient is not important.
4. Allowing the patient to make unreasonable commitments — ''I'll never drink again in my life, and hope to be struck dead as God is my witness'', versus ''I'll stay off drugs today''.
5. Believing verbatim the subject's drug and alcohol history. Modest variation from facts is usually present, and nearly always the variation is in the direction that puts the patient in the better light.
6. Allowing major inconsistencies to remain unsettled, thus undermining the patient's credibility in your eyes. This can be handled nicely by ''I'm mixed up, you said in 1988 you were hospitalized three times for cocaine addiction, but later state you have never had drug treatment. Straighten me out on this please''.

This short list can be readily added to from your own experience. Addicts are sometimes so transparent and sensitive that they will share with you the many seemingly minor actions on your part that upset them greatly. With each such patient your ability to help other abusing patients increases. The issues are not unique to abusing patients but apply to all. Assisting each patient to feel better during the treatment process is part of feeling better from the treatment.

TABLE 13
Substance Abusers Who Present Unusual Difficulty in Obtaining Abuse History

1. Adolescents referred by parents
2. Paroled convicts
3. Physicians and other professionals
4. Mixed-drug users
5. Confused and psychotic patients

VI. SPECIAL PROBLEMS

Table 13 defines special groups of patients who present unusual difficulty in obtaining information regarding substance abuse. They are presented at this point in order to identify the specific problems and are discussed much more fully in later chapters of this book.

A. ADOLESCENTS

Adolescence is a particularly challenging age to treat, and drug abuse is no exception. Many teenagers experiment with drugs and alcohol as peer influence replaces home influences. They consider it their prerogative to experiment, use drugs, spend their money and conduct their lives as they see fit, and least of all the business of their parents. They sometimes provide an erroneous history or simply do not cooperate with any part of the evaluation or treatment process for they consider it Gestapo-like curtailment of their ''right'' to be a free spirit.

Programs that treat adolescents almost as adults, away from parental influence and without reporting details to parents, are often highly successful. Many young persons are labeled as drug and alcohol abusers without a clear confessed history from them. Though the process of evaluation and treatment is painful, the outcome is excellent — possibly because maturation recognizes the destructive force that abuse is.

B. PAROLED CONVICTS

Convicts on parole are usually required to be drug and alcohol free, but this requirement is overlooked by parole managers. Nonetheless, the risk of loss of freedom makes such persons extremely distrustful of questions regarding substance use, and the answers given are almost always what parole officers would prefer to hear. Clearly establishing that confidentiality will be respected and records will not be made available to authorities is only the first of many steps in gaining the confidence of such persons. Often essential judgments are made on probability or on the basis of urine testing.

C. PROFESSIONALS

Professionals are held to a higher standard of personal behavior than others, and use of legal substances in excess and any use of illicit substances may be the basis for loss of license to practice their profession. This reality leads to hostility and a noncooperative attitude on the part of the abusing professional, particularly the abusing physician. This attitude can be overcome by firm confrontation with facts or witnesses. Nearly all states have professional committees to facilitate recovery. Persons entering treatment have their anonymity preserved and continue their license to practice as long as they remain fully participatory in the recommended program. If the person fails to complete the evaluation or the treatment, the condition is publicly revealed and an open hearing reviews the appropriateness of continuing the license. This risk of public exposure with possible loss of the ability to practice the profession causes many doctors, lawyers, and dentists to submit to the full evaluation and treatment process. As many as 80% are fully rehabilitated to return to their practice.

Initially nearly all information comes from witnesses who have immunity under law to report to the evaluating committee, who keep the information confidential as long as the professional cooperates.

D. MIXED DRUG ABUSERS

The history is nearly always limited to the primary drug of abuse, such as heroin, cocaine, or amphetamines. The history of other drug use is seldom mentioned, for the abuser probably forgets the unpleasant times when a secondary drug was used regularly because the desired drug could not be obtained or could not be afforded.

Sometimes the minor drug is continued during treatment even though the patient abstains from using the major drug. The nature of mixed drug abuse is discovered most often by specific drug screens.

E. PSYCHOTIC PATIENTS

The mental pain and anguish of psychotic patients is relieved by the abused substance, and therefore preservation of the supply is utmost in the patient's conscious mind. Usually the abused substance is not mentioned. The symptoms of the abuse may not be clearly separable from the psychiatric symptoms. The diagnosis of which condition is of primary importance is often confusing, but there is agreement that treatment of either must start with becoming substance free.

VII. USE OF SELF-ADMINISTERED TESTS

Self-administered tests for alcoholism have been in use for several decades, and there are several excellent evaluations of their utility. They are particularly valuable in screening healthy patients for possible problems with substance abuse, as in employment physicals or entry examinations into a medical office.

Self-administered tests are useful for the individual in reviewing substance use as it becomes more and more frequent. Even among admitted abusers there is utility for planning therapy that focuses on the specific problems the test reveals.

The most widely used test is the Michigan Alcoholism Screening Test,[1] and the simplest is the CAGE questionnaire.[2] These tests are designed for use by alcoholics but can readily be modified for substance abuse. The CAGE questions can be incorporated into every history by asking verbally:

- Felt need to **C**ut down drinking?
- Ever felt **A**nnoyed by criticism of drinking?
- Ever had **G**uilt feelings about drinking?
- Ever taken a morning **E**ye opener?

By analogy, one could readily ask:

- Felt need to diminish your use of drugs?
- Ever felt annoyed by criticism of drug use?
- Ever had guilt feelings about drug use?
- Ever required a drug fix to get on with your day's activities?

The CAGE questionnaire addresses common reactions to abuse, including concern for harm, hypersensitivity to criticism, perception of guilt in the harm the abuse does to others, and the occurrence of habituation or tolerance requiring a repeated portion to stave off early withdrawal symptoms.

Vallaint, in his book on alcoholism,[3] listed 22 questions that he found useful in assessing the degree of addiction. I have reworded these and changed the order of presentation to illustrate how similar questions can be used in identification of abuse of all substances.

Circumstance of substance use — Do you use your substance (drink, shoot up, take a fix, etc.) after a disappointment or a quarrel or when the boss gives you a hard time? Do you use your substance more heavily than usual when you are having trouble or feel under pressure? Are there circumstances in which you feel quite uncomfortable if you cannot (drink, shoot up)? Do you usually have a reason for the occasions when you use heavily?

Concern about substance use and its effects on health — Do you ever wake up on the "morning after" and discover that you cannot remember part of the evening before, even though your friends tell you that you did not "pass out"? Have you often failed to keep promises you have made to yourself about controlling or cutting down on your (drinking, drug abuse)? Have you tried to control your (drinking, drug abuse) by making a change in jobs or moving to a new location? Are you having an increasing number of financial and work problems? Do you eat very little or irregularly when you are using your drug? Have you recently noticed that you cannot tolerate as much of your substance as you once did?

Guilt — Do you sometime feel guilty about your substance use? When you are substance free, do you often regret things you have said or done while drinking? Do you try to avoid family and close friends when you are drinking?

Tolerance — Have you noticed that you are able to handle more (drug, alcohol) than you did when you first started? When using drugs or alcohol with others, do you try to have a few extra portions when others will not know it? When you begin drinking or drug use, are you in more of a hurry to get the first portion into you than you used to be? Do you often find that you wish to continue drug use or drinking when your friends say they have had enough? Do you sometimes have the "shakes" or uneasiness in the morning and find that it helps to have a drink or a fix of your drug?

These questions are much more extensive than the simple CAGE ones, but illustrate ways in which the needed information may be developed.

VIII. MICHIGAN ALCOHOLISM SCREENING TEST

The Michigan Alcoholism Screening Test (MAST) is the best-validated self-administered screening test.[1] It evolved through study of groups of known alcoholics and working subjects thought not to be alcoholics. In this test a variety of simple direct questions are read and an answer of either yes or no is circled. Questions found to be of low discriminization value between alcoholics and nonalcoholics are given 1 point, those of high value are given 3 points, and those of intermediate value are given 2 points.

The high-value questions are

- Have you ever attended a meeting of Alcoholics Anonymous?
- Have you ever gone to anyone for help about your drinking?
- Have you ever been in a hospital because of your drinking?

Intermediate value questions are:

- Are you a normal drinker?
- Have you ever awakened the morning after some drinking the night before and found that you could not remember a part of the evening before?
- Can you stop drinking without a struggle after one or two drinks?
- Do friends or relatives think you are a normal drinker?
- Are you always able to stop drinking when you want to?

- Has drinking ever created problems with you and your wife?
- Has your wife ever gone to anyone for help about your drinking?
- Have you ever lost friends because of drinking?
- Have you ever gotten into trouble at work because of drinking?
- Have you ever lost a job because of drinking?
- Have you ever neglected your responsibilities because of drinking?
- Have you ever been told you have liver trouble or cirrhosis?
- Have you ever had delirium tremens or hallucinations?
- Have you ever been in a mental hospital or been seen in a mental health clinic and told that drinking was the problem?
- Have you ever been arrested because of drunk behavior?
- Have you ever been arrested for drunk driving?

For scoring, the total score on these and a few other questions is added up. Normals never score more than 4, alcoholics score more than 5. Although there are many questions regarding advanced abuse, it takes very few appropriate "alcoholic answers" to make the score 5 or more points.

REFERENCES

1. **Seltzer, M. L.,** The Michigan Alcoholism Screening Test, the quest for a new diagnostic instrument, *Am. J. Psychiatr.*, 127, 1653, 1974.
2. **Ewing, J. A.,** Detecting alcoholism, the CAGE questionnaire, *J. Am. Med. Assoc.*, 252, 1905, 1984.
3. **Vallaint, G.,** *The Natural History of Alcoholism,* Harvard University Press, Cambridge, MA, 1972.

Chapter 9

Recognizing the Alcoholic or Substance-Abusing Patient in Your Practice

I. INTRODUCTION

Some 6 to 9% of adult Americans are believed to be alcoholics, and at least 5% of adult Americans use some drug daily, with 30% using drugs occasionally. Thus every medical practice involved with persons over age 10 as patients or parents has these problems. It is estimated that only half the active alcoholics and one fifth of those using drugs are recognized in medical practice. A survey conducted in 1987 indicated that 51% of eighth-grade students and 63% of tenth-grade had tried smoking tobacco. Seventy-seven percent of eighth-grade and 89% of tenth-grade students had used alcohol, and 38% of the tenth graders had had five or more drinks on a single occasion in the most recent two weeks. Twenty-six percent of eighth-grade students and 38% of tenth-grade students had used marijuana; 4% of eighth-grade and 8% of the tenth-grade students had used cocaine.[1] Such data indicate that the problem is pervasive.

Recognition of users starts with knowledge of the substances used in the population from which your patients are drawn, and with knowledge of the acute and chronic manifestations of use of these agents. The substances used, the route of administration, and the patients likely to be abusers are different from one practice to another and in different

TABLE 14
Seminal Features of Substance Abuse Leading to Recognition

1. History clearly defines the problem (Chapter 8)
2. Physical examination strongly suggests abuse
3. History reveals problems that include addiction in the differential diagnosis
4. History and physical have a constellation of events suggesting chronic abuse
5. Diseases commonly associated with abuse are identified
6. Social and economic condition significantly less than predicted from early adulthood
7. Substantial record of underachieving in school
8. Extreme sensitivity, particularly about substance use
9. Episodic bizarre behavior, often denied by patient
10. Frequent job changes
11. History of suicide attempts
12. Multiple unexplained accidents or traumatic injury
13. Repeated failure in marriage or significant relationships

geographic regions. Substance abuse, however, spares no group. At its early stages it is quite responsive to treatment, which encourages early recognition.

Table 14 identifies some of the ways that alcohol or substance abuse is identified by the physician. Some of these will be discussed in subsequent sections.[2]

II. MEDICAL HISTORY

Chapter 8 discussed features in the medical history that may indicate substance abuse. Substance users and abusers are risk takers. The majority are also heavy users of caffeine and tobacco. As one takes the history, attitudes about risk become clearly apparent. The substance use history may precipitate extremely strong denial or unusual emotional display. If the protest and declaration of abstinence is excessive, the interviewer may correctly suspect abuse. Persons with a major habit must protect their time and resources. Job, interpersonal relationships, recreation all go by the wayside in pursuit of the addiction.

III. PHYSICAL EXAMINATION

A number of signs that appear upon physical examination may indicate drug use, possible abuse, and tolerance, and these may well be sufficient, alone or in combination with the history, to make a firm diagnosis of substance abuse. Only occasionally is it possible to identify the actual substance that is abused, but the route of abuse may leave a diagnostic trail.

A. FINDINGS RELATED TO THE ROUTE OF ADMINISTRATION

Drugs may be ingested or smoked with almost no tell-tale signs. Nasal insufflation (snorting) of drugs usually produces nasal congestion and erythema. There may be frequent blowing of the nose, with loss of nasal hair. Sinusitis may be present. Smoking of drugs, though usually no more than a few times daily, produces the same changes in the lungs as are produced by smoking cigarettes. Many abusers also use cigarettes. Intravenous drug use produces many physical findings (Table 15). The veins may be scarred, thrombosed, or pigmented from chronic injections.

B. NONSPECIFIC INDICATIONS OF SUBSTANCE ABUSE

Trauma and malnutrition are increased among the abusing population. Drug use is hazardous. Disordered consciousness and unsteady gait lead to falls and bumps. Motor accidents while driving or walking are frequent. Accidents at work or in the home are more

TABLE 15
Common and Occasional Findings in Chronic Users of Intravenous Drugs

I. Problems in veins
  A. Thromboses
  B. Many puncture marks
  C. Hematomas from unexplained venapunctures
  D. Absent veins in the usual sites due to overuse
  E. Thickened walls of veins
  F. Pigmented marks from destroyed or inflamed superficial veins
II. Problems in sterility
  A. Skin abscesses near venipuncture sites
  B. Fat pad abscesses, or atrophy from skin popping
III. Distant diseases
  A. Endocarditis, particularly staphylococcal
  B. Abscesses in unusual locations
  C. HIV infection
  D. Hepatitis B or C

common, including burns and lacerations. Addicts are easy victims for street criminals, and frequently by their own aggression become involved in physical altercations. Often the patient cannot explain adequately the events leading to the traumatic injury. It is not infrequent to see a patient with a broken wrist, or ribs, or a laceration that is unaccounted for in the history. Such a finding is highly suggestive of abuse.

When advanced and intensive drug use occurs, particularly with alcohol, opiates, and sedatives, malnutrition may become prominent. In economically deprived subjects there is usually marked weight loss and many associated deficiencies of vitamins and minerals. In persons with a regular income, the weight loss is often less marked, but there are specific deficiencies of nutrients such as folate, thiamin, zinc, vitamin A, and pyridoxine.

Advanced users often become unkempt, dirty, and odorous, and may be infested with body lice, crab lice, or even maggots. Such findings indicate continued drug stupor producing marked indifference to social values and the opinions of others. Alternatively, they may indicate major loss of mental faculties or psychosis.

C. CHANGES IN MENTAL STATUS

Depression is common in withdrawal from alcohol, sedatives, stimulants, and opiates. Panic disorders may occur with LSD, amphetamines, and glue sniffing.

Organic mental disorders, most commonly seen in alcoholics, can follow heavy use of almost any abused substance. It is quite common for a user to be mildly intoxicated when first seen and yet have no insight into the abnormality. Drunkenness is usually associated with unsteady gait, slurring of speech, and failure to adjust the timber of the voice appropriately. Sedatives and opioids produce a similar intoxication. Users are often dull in affect and in content of answers to questions. They are unable to remain attentive to the conversation. An evasive, suspicious person who avoids eye contact, or a sad, irritable person with rapid shifts in mood is highly suggestive of an abusing person.

D. CHANGES SEEN IN EXAMINATION OF THE HEAD

Table 16 lists common signs that suggest abuse.

E. CHANGES ENCOUNTERED IN THE CHEST AND HEART

The most frequent changes encountered in the chest and heart are those related to smoking, reflecting that more than 80% of all abusers are also users of cigarettes. Bronchitis, chronic obstructive lung disease, or more frequent asthmatic attacks are very common in

TABLE 16
Physical Findings of Abuse Observed During Examination of the Head

I. General
  A. Dirty, unkempt, lice
  B. Old or new trauma
II. Eyes
  A. Constricted pupils — opioids
     Dilated — amphetamines, opioid withdrawal
     Persistent light intolerance — cocaine
  B. Congested conjunctiva — cannabis, alcohol
  C. Persistent lacrimation — opiate withdrawal
     Irritation from insufflation
  D. Ophthalmoplegia — Wernicke's from alcoholism
  E. Nystagmus — alcohol withdrawal, PCP
  F. Loss of visual acuity — alcohol, methanol, tobacco
III. Nose
  A. Rhinitis or irritation — opiate withdrawal
     Drug insufflation, cocaine
  B. Acne rosacea — alcoholism
IV. Mouth
  A. Very poor teeth, neglect — alcoholism, opiates
  B. Perioral sores or rash — solvent use, avitaminosis
  C. Tongue — coated, heavy abuser; tremor, withdrawal
  D. Edema of uvula or soft palate — hashish use
V. Neck
  A. Skin wrinkled more than age suggests — alcohol, tobacco
  B. Nodding — opiates
  C. Rigidity, spasm — PCP, phenothiazine
  D. Spider angiomata — liver disease

TABLE 17
Abnormalities in the Physical Examination of the Heart Suggesting Drug Abuse

I. Arrhythmia: caffeine, alcohol, cocaine, stimulants, solvents
II. Cardiac murmurs
  A. High output: alcohol with disease or flushing malnutrition of alcoholism alcohol — disulfiram reaction sedative, opiate withdrawal
  B. Organic: endocarditis from i.v. abuse, acute cardiac dilatation — solvents

smokers and in those who do not use tobacco but who smoke street drugs frequently. Pulmonary edema is an occasional associated finding in cocaine and opiate toxic reaction and is a common consequent of adulterants used with these agents.

Table 17 outlines some occasional problems encountered in the examination of the heart.

F. CHANGES FOUND IN THE ABDOMEN

Signs of liver disease, intestinal dysfunction, stomach and pancreatic inflammation may be prominent in abusing persons. Table 18 lists some of the common findings.

G. FINDINGS IN THE GENITOURINARY SYSTEM

There are many findings in the genitourinary (GU) system that are suggestive of drug abuse. The bladder sometimes loses tone in chronic opiate users, with resultant distension and/or infection. In the male, testicular atrophy is prevalent in alcoholics and opiate users; if the testes are actually measured, this finding will be found to be present in the majority but sufficient to be striking only occasionally. All sexually transmitted diseases occur more commonly in abusing persons. In women a prominent cervicitis or vaginal discharge may

TABLE 18
Abnormalities in the Physical Examination of the Abdomen Suggesting Drug Abuse

I. Inspection
  A. Distension
    1. Tympanites, or air and fluid in bowel — opiates, solvents, use of high-dose antidepressants, sedatives
    2. Fluid — liver disease alcoholism
       Severe malnutrition — opiates, alcohol
  B. Multiple scars
    1. Unexplained trauma — alcoholism, opiates
    2. Surgical — alcoholism
  C. Other
    1. Xiphoid to umbilicus segment stretched, indicating hepatosplenomegaly — alcoholism
    2. Spiders, collateral veins — liver disease, alcoholism
    3. Severe pain, making person remain quiet — pancreatitis or perforated viscus, alcoholism
II. Palpation and auscultation
  A. Tenderness
    1. Liver — alcoholism, or hepatitis from i.v. abuse
    2. Stomach, ulcer gastritis — alcohol
    3. Diffuse with rebound, perferated viscus — alcoholism
       Pancreatitis — alcoholism
    4. Over cecum or sigmoid colon — opiate withdrawal
    5. Rectal — inflammation associated with infection — opiates
  B. Hyperactive bowel sounds
    1. Opiate withdrawal, sedative withdrawal
    2. Minimal ascites of liver disease — alcohol
    3. Malabsorption — alcohol, pancreatitis of alcohol abuse
  C. Hypoactive bowel sounds with distension
    1. Opiate use
    2. Stimulant use
    3. Intoxication
  D. Organomegaly
    1. Liver — alcohol abuse, hepatitis from i.v. drugs
       Severe malnutrition
    2. Splenomegaly — portal hypertension of liver disease; HIV, lymphoma of immunosuppression, heavy use habit
    3. Unclear mass — pancreatic pseudocyst of alcoholism
    4. Colon — obstipation due to high opiate use
  E. Ascites — liver disease, alcoholism, i.v. use
  F. Occult blood positive — alcoholism

be the clue that there is a problem. Chlamydia infections are much more common in abusing persons. Abusing females have many more gynecologial problems, including amenorrhea, meno-metrorrhagia, and apparent sterility, but these are not very specific.

H. MUSCULOSKELETAL AND NEUROLOGICAL PROBLEMS

A wide variety of addictions are associated with musculoskeletal wasting and weakness that is clearly toxic or disuse atrophy. The problem is symmetrical but may be striking. There is a form of acute rhabdomyolysis associated with intravenous cocaine and opioids, and infrequently with alcoholism that produces muscular tenderness that may be exquisite in the calf and upper arm areas. Muscle tenderness is common in alcoholics with weight loss, and may accompany almost any i.v. drug abuse, probably relating to embolization from the insoluble adulterant. Muscle tremors, fasciculation, are seen in withdrawal states from sedatives, opiates, and alcohol, and spasm is seen with PCP intoxication.

Asymmetrical palsies are common in abusers as a result of pressure exerted directly on the nerve, e.g., "Saturday night elbow", for the abuse voids the pain that would cause normal persons to move the limb before injury to the nerve occurred. Peripheral neuritis of a sensory form is common in malnourished persons, mostly alcoholics but also any abuser with a habit that places drug before food intake. Motor neuritis is infrequent and, when symmetrical, limited to alcoholics.

Tremors are common in heavy users during and for many weeks after withdrawal. These are symmetrical. Myasthenia gravis, Parkinson's, and essential tremor may be precipitated by a heavy bout of use, probably only in persons with the underlying condition. Liver encephalopathy may produce characteristic asterexis. Gait disorders are most common in alcoholics due to combinations of peripheral neuritis and cerebellar injury.

Loss of intelligence is common in all heavy-use syndromes but may be prominent in alcoholism, opiate, PCP, sedative, and hallucinogen use. Often specific psychological testing is required to be certain the person is abnormal and to chart improvement.

IV. CONSTELLATION OF FINDINGS

The concurrence of a setting of possible abuse and some historical and/or physical findings of possible abuse may lead the physician to pursue the possibility of abuse with specific questions or drug testing. Some examples are illustrative.

A housewife of 44 years, not working, has been overweight for years and complains of abdominal pain. Despite diets her weight is increasing and is now 164 lb on her 64-in. frame. She consults you for chronic fatigue, sleeping poorly, and nervousness. On physical she is normal except for a slight tremor. Among other things, amphetamine abuse was considered. Upon discussion, this possibility was verified. Her sources were discontinued and alternative weight reduction utilized.

A manufacturer's representative travels daily selling hardware. He is 51 and feels that he cannot keep up with the work. His specific complaints are fatigue and indigestion. The indigestion has the pattern of nausea in the morning, preventing him from eating breakfast but permitting him to eat a large evening meal. He does not take medicines or use drugs and has one beer daily. He is mildly obese, slightly tremulous, does not appear neat and clean, and has considerable unpleasant body odor and bad breath. Alcoholism was seriously considered despite the history; a blood test performed while in the office indicated a blood alcohol level of 180 mg/dl despite a statement that he had had no alcohol for two days. Upon confrontation the patient left the doctor's office, but entered an inpatient alcoholism program within the month under another doctor's care.

A university student has one C and four F's at the end of the first semester. He denies drug use, but drinks heavily at parties on the weekend although at no other time. He seems a little lethargic, responding quite slowly to simple questions, and is hyperactive in reflexes. You find yourself speaking very loudly to communicate with him. Regular drug use is suspected. He is unwilling to submit to a drug test, for he feels you are an agent of his parents, who arranged the consultation. After being dropped from school, this man was arrested for selling marijuana on campus and returned to you for treatment. History then revealed a pattern of heavy use of amphetamines and cocaine.

V. DISEASES COMMONLY ASSOCIATED WITH ABUSE

A variety of diseases have a close association with drug abuse, and whenever such a disease is encountered, consideration of abuse must be made in the differential diagnosis. Some of these diseases are listed in Table 19. The presence of one of these diseases is a strong signal to consider drug use or abuse as part of the differential diagnosis. Other corroborative evidence may appear. In Table 20 are listed some of the laboratory results that are often abnormal in abusing patients.

TABLE 19
Diseases Often Associated with Specific Addictions

Malnutrition — alcoholism, opiate addiction
Organic brain syndrome — alcoholism, opiates, PCP, solvents, hallucinogens
Cerebellar ataxia — alcoholism
Convulsions, new onset — alcoholism, stimulants, i.v. drugs
Peripheral neuritis — alcoholism
Nerve pressure palsies — any chronic addiction
Tuberculosis — alcoholism, i.v. drugs
Endocarditis, brain, liver abscess, osteomyelitis, i.v. drugs
Viral hepatitis — i.v. drugs
HIV infection — i.v. drugs
Sexually transmitted diseases — opiates, sedatives, PCP
Cirrhosis — alcoholism
Pancreatitis — alcoholism
Multiple trauma — sedatives, opiates, alcoholism
Cerebral vascular accident — i.v. drugs

TABLE 20
Aberrations in Common Laboratory Results Suggesting Addiction or Abuse

Elevated glucose — amphetamines, alcoholism
Low K, Zn PO_4, Mg — alcoholism
Elevated uric acid — alcoholism
Liver test abnormalities — alcoholism, i.v. drugs
Leukopenia — large spleen of alcoholism, i.v. drugs
Elevated amylase — alcoholism
Elevated cholesterol — alcoholism
Macrocytosis — alcoholism
Hyponatremia — opiates
Proteinuria — i.v. drugs, alcoholism
Hemoccult positive stools — alcoholism

VI. OTHER FEATURES

Drug addiction requires stealth and sequestration of resources to continue a habit if the person lives with family. Sometimes this strange behavior of secrecy about time or absences from home or penuriousness out of proportion to available resources is a tip-off. The person holding a job well beneath his abilities and training, or the feature of multiple changes in jobs, may suggest a problem of abuse. Many patients with a history of depression or suicide attempts are abusers.

REFERENCES

1. Results from the National Adolescent Student Health Survey of 1987, in *MMWR,* 38, 147, 1989; abstracted in *JAMA,* 261, 2025, 1989.
2. **Cotter, F. and Callahan, C.,** Training primary care physicians to identify and treat substance abuse, *Alcohol Health Res. World,* 11, 70, 1987.

Chapter 10

Emergencies in Drug and Alcohol Use and Their Management

I. INTRODUCTION

An emergency is any situation that the patient or his associates believe is life threatening, or that may result in the loss of sight, sanity, or property or loss of future health if not addressed promptly. Emergency rooms, walk-in centers, doctors on call, or previously consulted physicians often are contacted for assistance, and are expected to respond with an appropriate action. Using this definition, however, it is quite clear that many problems perceived as emergencies by the patient and his associates are less urgent in the eyes of the physician.

The emergency may be related directly to the drug or alcohol problem or only indirectly and a result of an automobile accident, fighting, related trauma, or attempted suicide. In this chapter we discuss only drug- and alcohol-related emergencies. Table 21 lists some of the emergencies encountered as well as the common classes of drugs that may cause them.

Medical complications of substance abuse are presented in Chapters 17 and 20, psychiatric complications in Chapter 18, and withdrawal recognition and treatment in Chapter 27.

TABLE 21
Types of Emergencies Encountered and Drugs to Which They Relate

Reaction	Classes of drugs responsible
1. Toxic/overdose	Commonly opiates, cocaine, occasionally depressants
2. Panic reaction	Hallucinogens, marijuana, stimulants, solvents
3. Psychosis	CNS stimulants, depressants
4. Withdrawal	Depressants, opiates, stimulants
5. Flashbacks, dry drunks	Hallucinogens, marijuana, alcohol
6. Violent behavior	All major classes

II. TOXIC REACTIONS

Toxic reaction is the preferred term for any reaction of sufficient severity to interfere with vital signs or consciousness. Some authors still use the term *overdose* for reactions that occur as a result of a dose vastly in excess of the intended one, and *toxic reaction* for those that occur when the intended dose is taken. Practically the differentiation is blurred, for these reactions are often the outcome of a confusional state in which the actual dose taken was unknown. Dose standardization is erratic, and adulterants common in illicit drugs further confuse the distinction.

The National Center for Health Statistics has listed unintentional poisonings since 1980, and in these reports there has been an increase from 1.9 to 2.3 deaths per 100,000 population. This increase is nearly all due to an increase in the death rate from drugs both prescription and illicit. Opiates and cocaine accounted for 75% of these deaths and, curiously, alcohol-ingestion deaths nearly equaled the total number of deaths from motor vehicle exhaust. The rate is higher for men than for women and higher for blacks than for whites, with the peak age at risk being young adult men 29 to 39 years of age. Thus, in 1986, 619 deaths nationwide resulted from opiates, 436 from cocaine, and 375 from alcohol, and the numbers are increasing. It is believed that this is misuse of drugs and alcohol,[1] and that these figures represent vast underreporting.

The recognition of cocaine (also i.v. amphetamines) and opiate toxic reaction is quite straightforward if the examining physician is suspicious of the possibility, even when there is no clear history of drug use. Figures 4 and 5 illustrate the major features of overdose of cocaine and of opiates (usually heroin).

A toxic reaction may occur from any route of administration, including smoking, but most commonly follows intravenous injection with tell-tale marks over the veins. Consciousness is almost always altered, but there are clear signs of CNS stimulation and hyperactivity with cocaine and depression with heroin. The pupils are pinpoint with heroin, enlarged with cocaine. Body temperature is increased with cocaine, normal or decreased with opiates, despite vasodilatation. Vital signs are alarming in both, but generally cocaine toxic reactions exhibit tachycardia and alarmingly elevated blood pressure, whereas blood pressure is usually low in opiate toxic reactions. Retching, vomiting, hallucinations, convulsions, and arrhythmia may occur in either.

In nearly all circumstances, naloxone (0.4 mg) should be given i.v. early in the treatment and repeated at least once after 2 to 5 min while looking for a response in the pupil or other abnormal CNS signs. This treatment produces no harm and will lighten the coma and alter the pupils in opiate toxic reaction. The airway should be maintained and the patient kept warm and in a position so that vomitus will not be aspirated. An i.v. route should be started and kept open with glucose solution. If there is not considerable reserve, or the response prompt, the patient should be maintained in the hospital. If there is a response to naloxone,

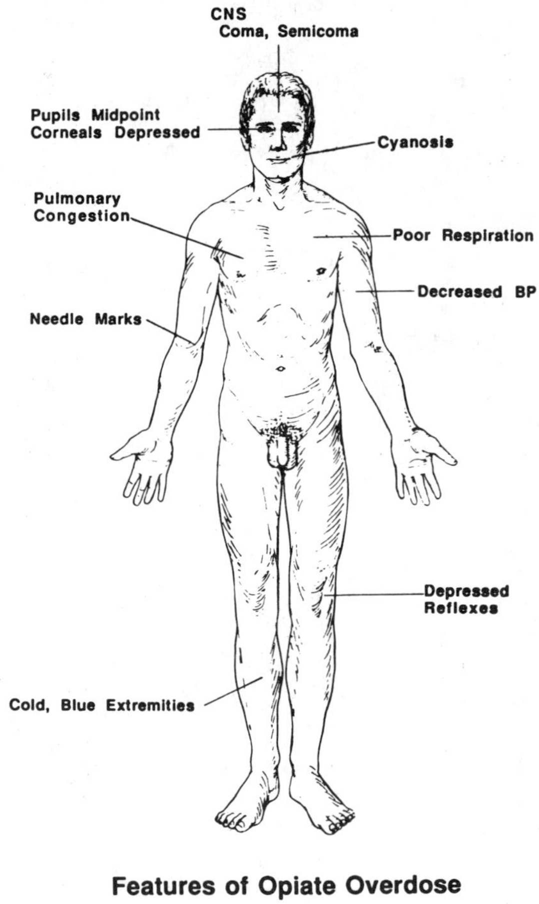

FIGURE 4. Features of opiate toxic reaction or overdose. The pupil size, unconsciousness, and lowered blood pressure are promptly reversed with naloxone. Contrast with Figure 5.

additional doses will be needed each 3 h. Alarming elevations of blood pressure will need to be lowered with i.v. drugs; hypotension may require support and hypoxemia may require oxygen.

Depressant overdose, usually as a suicide attempt, is illustrated in Figure 6. Although this reaction may mimic a heroin toxic reaction, the history is usually helpful. Naloxone administration will usually clarify the lack of response in depressant overdose. The most important part of the treatment is to maintain respiration and provide good nursing care to prevent aspiration. In the meantime the drug can be identified by checking with companions or by toxicological examination, but these drugs wear off in a few half-lives, usually within 48 h. The role of dialysis is discussed under the specific drugs.

III. PSYCHIATRIC EMERGENCIES

A. PSYCHOSIS

A diagnosis of psychosis is made when hallucinations and/or delusions are present in a patient who is *not* significantly disoriented or confused, *not* in withdrawal, and who has vital signs that are normal. Should any of these conditions not be met, then treatment of the withdrawal problem and/or support of the vital signs should be undertaken. A search

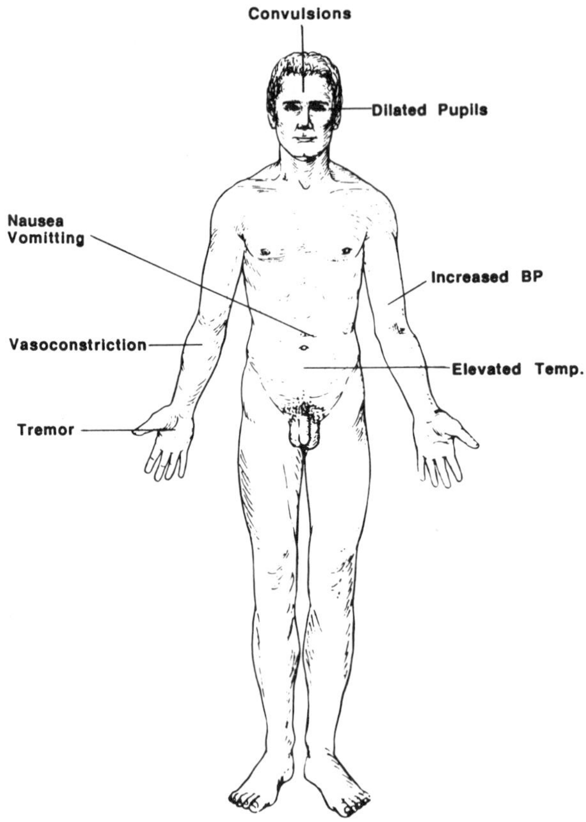

Features of Cocaine Overdose

FIGURE 5. Features of cocaine toxic reaction or overdose. The hyperactivity, manifested by elevated blood pressure, tremor, and dilated pupils with no response to naloxone, are quite specific for this condition or the identical-appearing toxic reaction to amphetamines. Contrast with Figure 4.

for alternative medical causes, including current intoxication, should be made in the patient who is disoriented or confused. Psychosis is most commonly encountered in the repeated user of stimulants or depressants, including the very popular cocaine and alcohol. The transition from normal to psychotic occurs within a few hours to a day and is a striking change, interfering almost totally with the patient's functioning. It is modestly alarming to the patient but strikingly so to his or her regular companions or associates, who are usually responsible for bringing the patient to you.

Such patients have no physical abnormalities, but with observation may demonstrate hallucinations or delusions. The process is self-limited, with reversal occurring in at the most 1 week. The laboratory is utilized to determine which drug or drugs were used by urine or blood screens. This sort of psychosis is always associated with positive tests for the agent. Some form of protected environment is usually required.

Treatment is based upon understanding, reassurance, and the provision of continuous companionship. Haloperidol may be used in milder cases (5 to 15 mg/day), but hospitalization may be necessary if the patient cannot be managed with these measures.

Persistence beyond a few days should lead to careful psychiatric evaluation for underlying disease or other diagnoses. Psychosis reactions do not seem to be recurrent.

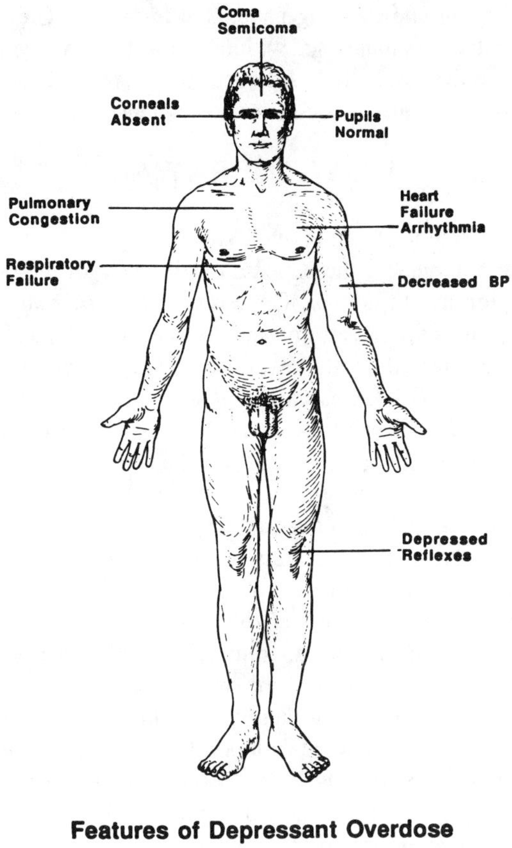

FIGURE 6. Features of depressant overdose. Very closely mimics toxic reaction to opiates as described in Figure 4 and the text, but there is no change with naloxone.

B. PANIC REACTIONS

The patient with a panic reaction is usually a new user of marijuana, a hallucinogen, or cocaine. Shortly after taking the drug the patient develops irrational fears of becoming insane, loses control, and becomes extremely anxious, agitated, and fearful. The agitation and fear are extreme and must be differentiated from withdrawal if the history is not clear. Often the fear of reprisals for use of an illicit drug leads to suppression of the history, and blood and urine testing must be performed.

The examination is usually thorough and appropriate to the age of the person to provide assurance that there is no serious problem. Sedation may be needed, but recovery is usually complete when the drug effects have left, most often in 6 to 12 h.

C. VIOLENCE

Although extremely rare, violent behavior is associated with drug or alcohol abuse in nearly three fourths of the cases in a recent report.[2] This study addressed the identification and prevention of violent episodes in a 700-bed Veterans Administration teaching hospital and over $2^1/_2$ years identified 46 such patients. Almost half had an underlying psychiatric disorder and substance abuse; an additional 25% had substance abuse alone. The study found that patients who displayed any sort of threatening or assaultive behavior against property, other patients, or employees were quite likely to repeat this behavior and thus had a means for early recognition. This group also defined an effective program to reduce violent behavior, based largely on identifying and flagging patients at high risk. They felt that patients with any form of psychiatric disorder diagnosed within the most recent 3 years, and clear evidence of substance abuse, were the single highest target group. Another recent study suggests that phencyclidine (PCP) simply is not associated with violence.[3]

IV. WITHDRAWAL

Recognition and treatment of withdrawal is discussed in more detail in Chapter 27. When presenting as an emergency, the patient is well aware of the problem, with agitation and hyperactivity the prominent findings. There is usually tremor and tachycardia, and there may be confusion, hallucinosis, and extreme anxiety. The neurological examination is normal unless old deficits are discovered. Withdrawal is a major problem with alcohol and opiates, a lesser problem with other CNS depressants, and almost no problem with stimulants. Onset occurs when the usual blood level of the abused substance is less than half the patient's customary value, and depends upon the agent. The behavioral and neurological aberrations progress rapidly over the day or two following initial symptoms and vary widely in both severity and precise symptoms, but mental and physical as well as autonomic hyperactivity are prominent. There may be psychosis, confusion, or even a state suggesting chronic organic brain syndrome, but recovery is complete.

In office or emergency-room contact, anxiety, confusion, autonomic hyperactivity with sweating, tearing, salivation, tachycardia, tremor, and hallucination are common. One or more grand mal seizures may precipitate the visit to the physician. At lesser stages the subject is extremely fearful of what is to happen. Treatment can be carried out with short-acting sedative (diazepam) for agitation, haloperidol for hallucination, and phenytoin for seizures, until the situation clarifies itself. A blood or urine drug screen will indicate the agents used to plan a more appropriate detoxification. Chapter 27 covers detoxification in more detail, including outpatient treatment.

V. OTHER INFREQUENT REACTIONS LEADING TO EMERGENCY VISITS

A. BLACKOUTS

Blackouts, most common in long-standing alcoholism, are periods of amnesia. A witness will be unaware that the patient is in any way unusual, but a short or substantial period of recent memory is erased. During this time the patient may have traveled some distance or transacted business, but may not know the outcome of an important issue occurring during that time. Physicians are often consulted urgently about these. Blackouts require no treatment, occur in half of all alcoholics, and disappear when the drinking ceases, but that may require several years. A close association of blackouts with loss of short-term memory has been noted.[4]

B. CONVULSIONS

Three types of convulsions are encountered in persons who abuse substances. These are idiopathic epilepsy, focal epilepsy associated with trauma, and withdrawal convulsions. If evaluated after the withdrawal period, the electroencephalogram and CT scan of the head can usually be used to reliably identify the first two of these. The occurrence of a convulsion is quite alarming and almost always leads such persons to the attention of the physician. The most common type is the onset of a generalized seizure occurring in an abusing person. The relation to withdrawal is unclear, for all abusers have fluctuations in their level of drug. It is infrequent for there to be multiple seizures, and status epilepticus is rare. Another form of convulsion is one that occurred or probably occurred during withdrawal. These are

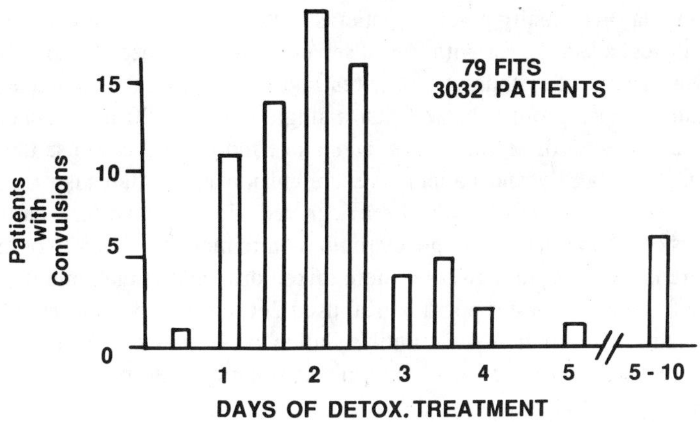

FIGURE 7. Occurrence of 79 generalized convulsions among patients admitted for detoxification treatment with alcoholism or mixed alcohol-drug abuse. The majority received a benzodiazepine drug, but none were given anticonvulsants. The convulsions occurred in the first 3 days after cessation of substance use in nearly all.

frequently not closely witnessed, and the history is unclear as to just what occurred, but the timing to cessation of drug 4 to 24 h previously is quite clear. These convulsions may recur with subsequent withdrawals but are infrequent.

Most seizures occur at home or at work and are promptly brought to emergency rooms. More than 90% of these are single, clearly a focal seizure at onset, and require little treatment to prevent those few that are recurrent in an actively abusing person.

The evaluation should include a neurological examination. Focal signs are meaningful for mass lesions or old trauma, and recent head trauma is common in addicts, often with no clear history of the event. Observation for an hour or two until the patient is mentally alert is much more valuable than acute skull films or CT scans. An EEG done after 1 week is helpful to identify epilepsy that requires long-term treatment.

Seizures in addicted persons have been best studied in alcoholics.[5] It is best to designate them withdrawal seizures until proven otherwise, for these are widely accepted as nonrecurrent and have none of the legal implications affecting occupation and driving of other forms of epilepsy.

Figure 7 illustrates seizures recorded from a large unit treating alcoholics and alcohol-drug addicts during withdrawal. The seizures occur shortly after admission, with 90% occurring in the first 72 h. Only 6% of these seizures were multiple, with no cases of status epilepticus observed. All except two of these patients had a history of seizures. In contrast, of a simultaneously observed group of alcoholics presenting at the emergency room with seizures, 17% were multiple and 2% were status. Evaluation of inpatient withdrawal seizures with CT scans and EEGs reveals that less than 10% have mass lesions or idiopathic epilepsy; a similar emergency-room series will identify 15 to 20%.

C. EPILEPSY

Treatment of epilepsy depends upon the etiology. Since fits do not tend to be recurrent in patients having their first convulsion after starting treatment for withdrawal, no further treatment is needed. If withdrawal treatment is carried out with benzodiazepine drugs with antiepilepsy potency (such as diazepam or lorazepam), no additional treatment is required, even in patients with a history of previous withdrawal convulsions. If treatment units utilize other benzodiazepines of low anticonvulsant potency or verbal control of agitation, a daily dose of phenytoin (300 mg/day), carbamezepine (200 mg/day), diazepam (10 mg/day), or lorazepam (2 mg/day) is usually given to patients with a history of convulsions upon withdrawal. These doses, adequate for withdrawal seizures, are also adequate to prevent seizures when there is a history of withdrawal seizures and are therefore recommended. A blind prospective study by our group[6] showed that a single dose of 300 mg of phenytoin given for 9 days prevented 90% of seizures. We have since modified this to use the drug only 5 days. The distress to family and patient of a convulsion more than justifies prophylactic treatment. Prevention of seizures has also been achieved with diazepam[7] and carbamezepine.[8]

Convulsions occurring in the emergency room require more medication for their effective treatment. There is more organic disease, more mixed drug addictions, and more likelihood of the epilepsy to recur. A recent positive trial used 260 mg i.v. phenobarbital as an initial dose and 130 mg i.v. each half hour until sedation was obtained. This both effectively managed the withdrawal and prevented subsequent seizures. The patients were sent home with companions when sedation was attained.[9]

Ng et al.[10] studied a large group of drinking men with new onset seizures. They concluded that the likelihood increased with intake of alcohol. This experience is also encountered in heavy users of cocaine and amphetamines. A similar study from France also examined first seizures. It found that patients under age 30 almost always used alcohol with or without other drugs as the basis of first seizures in patients without a history of trauma.[11]

D. DRY DRUNKENNESS OR FLASHBACKS

Both "dry drunk" and flashback refer to the recurrence of drug effects at a time the patient is not using an agent. Dry drunk indicates a reproduction of the patient's pattern of alcohol intoxication at a time remote from drinking. Flashback is most common with marijuana and hallucinogens. There is no satisfactory explanation for these infrequent occurrences, but they respond well to reassurance and continued companionship. They become less frequent as the interval of abstinence becomes longer.

VI. ASSESSMENT OF EMERGENCY

No matter how the patient presents, the evaluating physician needs to acquire as much pertinent history as possible, particularly gaining information from the patient or companions about substances possibly sampled, used, or abused and the temporal features of the presenting problem.

The mental state of the patient is well assessed during the interview, and the level of mental function, presence of hallucinations, reality orientation, and memory can be readily evaluated. The neurological examination must be meticulous, for head injuries are often encountered in this group and can mimic nearly all of the emergency problems with CNS manifestations. The vital signs should be taken early in the exam and repeated each 15 to 30 min in the severely ill person.

Often it is not possible to make a decision about what is happening in a patient with stable vital signs but some findings that are modestly alarming. A patient going into withdrawal may well be in an early stage of what will be alarmingly severe in a few more hours, and if that assessment is correct the patient will require treatment. A patient may seem to be obtunded from intoxication by drugs or alcohol, but the symptoms could also represent obtundity from a subdural hematoma. Under either circumstance it is sometimes possible to allow a few hours to pass and then reevaluate the patient. The family may take the patient home and then return with him or her for a reassessment. Intoxication will lessen in a few hours, but withdrawal will usually be clearly worse just a short time later. These issues are discussed further in Chapter 27 on evaluating and treating persons for withdrawal.

REFERENCES

1. **Litovitz, T. L., Schmitz, B. F., Matyunas, N., and Martin, T. G.,** 1987 annual report of the American Association of Poison Control Centers National Data Collection System, *Am. J. Emergency Med.*, 6, 479, 1988; cited in *MMWR*, 38, 153, 1989.
2. **Drummond, D. J., Sparr, L. F., and Gordon, G. H.,** Hospital violence reduction among high-risk patients, *JAMA*, 261, 2531, 1989.
3. **Brecher, M. and Morgan, J. P.,** Phencyclidine and violence: clinical and legal issues, *J. Clin. Psychopharmacol.*, 8, 397, 1988.
4. **Goodwin, D. W., Crane, J., and Guze, S. B.,** Loss of short term memory as a predictor of the alcoholic blackout, *Nature*, 227, 201, 1970.
5. **Victor, M. and Brausch, C.,** The role of abstinence in the genesis of alcoholic epilepsy, *Epilepsia*, 8, 1, 1967.
6. **Sampliner, R. E. and Iber, F. L.,** Diphenylhydantoin control of alcoholic withdrawal seizures, results of a controlled study, *JAMA*, 230, 1430, 1974.
7. **Devenyi, P. and Harrison, M. L.,** Prevention of alcohol withdrawal seizures with oral diazepam loading, *Can. Med. Assoc. J.*, 132, 788, 1985.
8. **Chu, N. S.,** Carbamazepine: prevention of alcohol withdrawal seizures, *Neurology*, 29, 1397, 1979.
9. **Young, G. P. and Dailey, R. H.,** Intravenous phenobarbital for the treatment of alcohol withdrawal seizures, *Epilepsia*, 29, 492, 1988.
10. **Ng, S. K. C., Hauser, W. A., Brust, J. C. M., and Susser, M.,** Alcohol consumption and withdrawal in new-onset seizures, *N. Engl. J. Med.*, 319, 666, 1988.
11. **Delangre, T., et al.,** Causes of first seizures in the adult according to age and sex, *Presse Med.*, 18, 1014, 1989.

Chapter 11

Laboratory Screening and Verification of Drug Use

I. INTRODUCTION

Modern laboratory testing of blood and urine, and occasionally other body fluids, breath, or body tissue has become so accurate and so sensitive that the use of addicting drugs of most major groups, even after 10 half lives, may be detected. In standard laboratory screening the emphasis is on certainty of significant levels rather than traces of drug. In this chapter we will discuss the use of the laboratory to confirm drug usage, and to establish which drugs have been used. A monograph is available.[1]

The quality of laboratory testing is of the utmost importance in using this means to establish drug use. In many instances, the information from the laboratory will appear in courts of law, occasionally to deprive a parolee of freedom, convict a recurrent DWI (driving while intoxicated) offender, or dismiss a person from a job or the military. For this reason, the laboratory industry in the United States in the late 1980s has been changing methods, quality control, and verification of positive tests to establish full specificity, reliability, and credibility. As of this writing, only the laboratories operated by the U.S. Navy and the commercial laboratories operated by Smith Kine & French and by American Medical Laboratory have been approved for this work, but many more are expected to follow in the next few years. Laboratories generally conduct screening by a thin-layer chromatographic method and confirm positive results by a more sensitive and specific method. These latter methods, often immunological, have been developed for the common drugs of abuse but are not available for the more exotic ones. This specificity of the confirmatory test is essential, if legal action is to be taken based upon the results. For medical purposes, however, usually only drug screens are used, in which high levels indicating current or very recent use are detected. Low cost of testing and rapid availability of results are more important than absolute certainty. Though the technology exists for forensic purposes there is no need for its use in ordinary clinical decisions.

Drugs have varied metabolism. Some such as nicotine have a short half life, but the major metabolite, cotinine, persists. Others such as caffeine have a slow half life and the parent drug is present in the blood and urine for many days. Metabolic products of marijuana persist for weeks and may be found by sensitive methods in the urine long after exposure. Other products, such as ethanol, leave the body in less than one day and leave behind no chemical footprints.

Selection of a laboratory is of course only part of the story. The collection, proper identification, and labeling of the specimen and at times proper preservation until analyzed are of equal importance. Addicts asked to provide a urine sample have been known to substitute someone else's specimen; these issues become critical as decisions of great future importance are sometimes based upon the results.

The assumption upon which all drug testing is tacitly based is that tolerant abusers cannot forgo use of their substance sufficiently long to allow it to clear their system completely. The validity of this assumption is examined in the section on breath tests.

II. LABORATORY TESTS COMMONLY ABNORMAL IN ADDICTIONS

During the 1970s and before, laboratory tests for street drugs were costly, not terribly sensitive, and gave results that varied markedly from laboratory to laboratory. Clinicians found that abuse led to certain associated diseases and metabolic abnormalities, particularly with alcohol, allowing one to suspect the addiction. The best known of these is the otherwise unexplained elevation of the mean corpuscular volume (MCV) of blood counts and the gamma-glutamyl transpeptidase (GGPT) enzyme, a liver measure of cholestasis and drug-metabolizing enzyme induction. Although both are elevated in other diseases, when they occur together or even alone, chronic alcoholism is one of the diagnoses that bears consideration. Other tests that provided value were minor changes in liver tests, particularly minimal elevation of the aminotransferase enzymes (ALT or AST), minor elevations of amylase, and decreases in phosphorous, magnesium, and zinc. The production of lactate in the metabolism of alcohol also raises the serum urate values.

Airline pilots were screened for alcoholism for two decades by use of standard electrolyte, liver test, amylase, and hematological examination. It was discovered that an elevated MCV of >102, abnormally low potassium, phosphate, or sodium, elevated GGTP (gamma-glutamyl transpeptidase), ALT (alanine aminotransferase) or amylase were sufficient markers to require review with an expert. In this way alcoholic pilots were detected, removed from flying status, treated, and restored with no clear accidents related to addiction. The short persistence of alcohol in the blood, saliva, or breath after drinking ceases, almost never as much as 12 h, makes these tests still of some clinical value. In general, the MCV and the GGTP are considered the best tests to screen for chronic alcoholism, and they are positive in about 90% of massive drinkers in Veterans Administration hospitals, but only about 50% of drinkers in private clinics.

No other markers among standard laboratory tests are as well established for other addictions. Among young persons anemia, hypoalbuminemia, mild liver test changes, and elevated serum muscle enzymes (such as CPK and aldolase) have been caused by heavy drug use, but on the whole the physical findings are much more suggestive.

TABLE 22
Hours After Most Recent Drug Use That a Urine May Be Collected and Be Positive

24 h or longer — thin-layer screen
- Amphetamines, all sorts
- Benzodiazepines
- Barbiturates
- Tricyclic antidepressants
- Methadone
- Propoxyphene
- Nicotine (and metabolite cotinine)
- Metabolites of marijuana
- Specific immunological tests
- Cocaine
- Methaqualone
- Morphine, heroin, codeine, hydrocodone
- Phencyclidine

3-12 h — thin-layer screen
- Opiates
- Pentazocine
- Cocaine
- Alcohol

Undetected in urine — thin-layer screen
- Marijuana
- Phencyclidine
- LSD and other hallucinogens

III. URINE TESTING

A properly collected urine, witnessed as coming from the patient and then sealed to prevent replacement and appropriately labeled, is essential if it is to be used for medical-legal purposes. Because urine substitution is common, there should in all cases be some consideration given to how one obtains urine form the patient under question. If analysis is not conducted promptly, the specimen should be stored at refrigeration temperature (4°C) until analysis is undertaken. Table 22 indicates the duration of positive urine findings to verify drug use *after* the last dose. It is apparent that urine obtained quite early during contact with the patient may be much more valuable than that obtained after a day or two.

Although the finding of drug or metabolic product of drug is highly sensitive and with verification quite specific, it depends upon several variables over which the testing group has no control. The exact time and size of the previous dose of drug relative to the urine sample, the volume of urine produced, and renal function determine the concentration of drug. The amount of urine actually used in the test and whether or not it was concentrated 10- or a 100-fold before being tested are variables within the laboratory. Although passive cigarette smoking (working in an area or living with smokers) may produce cotinine levels in nonsmokers of up to 10% of those of smokers, there are no examples of passive acquisition of positive tests for drugs. Newspapers avidly report the suspension of professional athletes from playing as a result of drug tests based upon these sensitive methods.

The excretion of many drugs is influenced by the pH of the urine. Conjugated drugs, or those with an active acidic or basic group and those tightly bound, are usually affected to some degree by changes in urine pH. The method of administration also substantially influences the dose absorbed and the amount excreted (see Figure 3 in Chapter 5).

TABLE 23
Duration of Positive Blood Tests for Drug After Use

Drug	Duration (h)
Cocaine	1/2—4
Tetrahydrocannabinol	6—10
Alcohol	6—16
Barbiturates	6—72

IV. BLOOD AND OTHER BODY FLUID TESTING

Highly water-soluble materials diffuse readily into all body fluids and reach equilibrium after 20 min. Thus ethanol levels in the blood, saliva, and urine are almost identical. Lipid-soluble materials such as toluene or ether are concentrated in lipids and appear in almost undetectable amounts in blood or urine. Still other agents are tightly bound to protein in the blood and remain there for a long time. Other drugs such as methaqualude may be concentrated in saliva.

Blood levels are a complex, changing process, reflecting absorption, entrance into the blood compartment, removal by diffusion into tissues, metabolism usually by the liver, and excretion by the liver and kidney. For many agents there is the release of a metabolic product (both codeine and heroin release morphine into the blood from the liver) into the blood, and its distribution and excretion are to be considered. Blood levels of alcohol and rates of metabolism have been sufficiently well established to allow one to predict accurately the blood level of alcohol at the time of a motor accident, a number of hours before, from the level now found in a sample of blood, breath or urine. These data do not exist for other agents. Agents that are protein bound, and agents that are water soluble, stay in the blood in sufficient concentrations to be measured. Since blood is usually collected from the patient by a technically trained person, there is less opportunity for fraudulently substituting another's body fluid. Table 23 lists agents that persist in the blood for a period of time, making testing of value. It is clear that blood levels are more limited in diagnostic value than urine.

Cocaine use has recently been detected by hair analysis, and the method has substantial use for forensic medicine. The subject has been reviewed.[2]

V. BREATH SAMPLES

Of all of the addicting substances, only alcohol appears in the breath in a precise relationship to the blood level. Breath alcohol (or blood if available) is used by law enforcement agencies to establish intoxication. A variety of accurate devices exist to measure breath alcohol. They usually report the concentration of blood alcohol. In most states a level of greater than 100 mg/dl blood level is considered driving under the influence of alcohol.

In emergency rooms dealing with large numbers of alcoholics, the availability of a device to measure breath alcohol is of great value. If a person is lethargic and confused, and unable to walk, the blood alcohol should be in excess of 200 mg/dl. If the measured level is substantially less than this value, one can conclude that there is another cause for the confusion, often another drug, but trauma may be present, thus directing the workup in another direction. The blood levels, as instantly available to emergency-room physicians, allow the detection of both alcohol poisoning and severe intoxication.

In office use, if one treats many abusing patients an inexpensive breath alcohol detection device (approximate cost, $300) will allow one to test patients for recent drinking. New

TABLE 24
Interview Data, Breath Testing in 1684 Clinic Visits by Patients with Alcoholic Liver Disease

Visit characteristic	N	Percent drinking in past week: Interview	Breath
1. All visits	1684	22	29
2. Admitted drinking	370	100	97
3. Drinking history negative	1314	0	8.3
4. History −, breath +	110	0	100

patients who deny drinking on the day of evaluation should read below the sensitivity of the instrument. A detectable alcohol level in a person who denies drinking, a common occurrence, establishes alcoholism. In a person who admits to drinking, if the level is 200 mg/dl or higher and the person appears normal with no signs of motor incoordination, one is dealing with advanced tolerance and, therefore, the person is a steady user. These breath-analyzing devices are of great utility in detecting mixed drug and alcohol use, for it is quite common for a former cocaine or opiate abuser to become an alcoholic during treatment.

The assumption that addicts cannot forgo the use of their drug for even as much as a day can be tested in alcoholism with the ready availability of the breath tests. A study of ours conducted over a period of 2 years measured breath alcohol at each clinic visit for patients with cirrhosis. Each patient was also interviewed independently by a counselor for alcoholism who did not have knowledge of the results of the breath testing. Table 24 records data abstracted from this study.[3]

Among patients who were negative for drinking on interview but who tested positive, there were 9 individuals who tested positive on every occasion (mean 4.3 visits). An additional 12 patients tested positive on breath test on every visit. Some of the patients admitted to drinking on some visits and denied drinking on other visits. Together these two groups accounted for 62% of the 110 patient visits in category 4. Of the other patients, only 41 of 1314 visits were history negative for drinking and test positive, and this represented 36 different patients. Of the 390 different patients in this study, 90 had alcohol present on almost every visit, and 90% of these admitted this history. Of the other 300 patients, 36 (12%) were documented as having used alcohol during the day of the visit. Since most of the patients were at the clinic site by noon, it is likely that only alcohol consumed on the day of the clinic visit was detected. Several conclusions emerge from this data: (1) most patients give reliable information on drinking (90%) when it is chronic; (2) most chronic drinkers show breath abnormality on each visit (94% of 90 patients with a mean of 4.7 visits); (3) occasional return to drinking (12%) occurs, and this is not admitted.

In this study all patients understood that testing would be done at each visit. Patients unwilling to be tested were referred to other care clinics. The fact of being tested, and being confronted by a physician with the test results, was not sufficient to prevent the patients from using alcohol.

VI. SCREENING TESTS

Screening tests are of great value in emergency rooms, as discussed previously. In office practice screening is highly useful to confirm suspected drug use that is denied, to detect poly-drug use when only one addiction is talked about, and to confirm that a person in a treatment program has remained free of drug. In my practice I inform patients that drug testing is used frequently and without warning, for it serves as an evaluation. Those with negative tests are informed of this finding and congratulated on staying drug free, and those with positive tests are involved in a discussion of this marker of a continuing problem.

The attitude of the physician must be one of understanding relapse. Testing is used to detect it before it is again destructive and is usually accepted in this way. Patients with positive tests are reassured that the laboratory is competent if they deny use and are encouraged with the other objective findings supporting success in treatment.

In our drug treatment clinics we collect a urine for screening on all patients just prior to seeing them or just after. We use a private toilet, check the temperature of each urine immediately after voiding, and place the samples in a controlled area. Only a small fraction are sent for analysis because of costs, but the principle of testing is clear. In alcoholism clinics we test each patient on each visit with a breath meter and share the readings with patient.

REFERENCES

1. **Hawks, R. L. and Chiang, C. N.,** Urine testing for drugs of abuse, *NIDA Res. Monogr. 73,* U.S. Department of Health and Human Services, National Institute on Drug Abuse, Rockville, MD, 1986.
2. **Bailey, D. N.,** Drug screening in an unconventional matrix; hair analysis, *JAMA,* 161, 3331, 1989.
3. **Iber, F. L., Wobbleton, J., Lavagnio, D., and Rubin, L.,** Abstinence in male veterans with cirrhosis treated in a liver clinic, unpublished.

Chapter 12

Cost-Effective Screening of Addicted Persons for Significant Illness

I. INTRODUCTION

This chapter is presented for the general physician called upon to evaluate a person who admits to substance abuse. The purpose may be required screening to enter a treatment program or consultation for overall health or a specific health problem. Alternatively, the patient may be seeking treatment of his or her abuse problem or consulting the physician to defuse a family crisis. The many medical and psychiatric crises that may be encountered are presented in detail in Chapters 17, 18, and 20. Here we review essential screening to identify important diseases that require early intervention, but we also wish to avoid unnecessary expense. Table 25 lists the major goals that are addressed in this form of screening.

These goals are best attained through the history and physical examination. Only when these give rise to a suspicion of specific problems should further consultation and more expensive procedures be undertaken. Screening procedures applied to all patients of a given age (such as hemoglobin, fecal occult blood measurement, urine analysis) should of course also be applied.

TABLE 25
Goals of Screening the Abusing Person

1. Confirm the diagnosis when possible
2. Identify major problems that might take life or result in disability if not found:
   a. Head trauma
   b. Internal bleeding
   c. Infection
   d. Major malnutrition
3. Identify major health problems unrelated to addiction
4. Identify major psychopathology affecting treatment and immediate future
5. Gain credibility by nonjudgmental thoroughness

II. CONFIRMATION OF DIAGNOSIS

Often the history, including confirmatory information provided by an employer, by a blood or breath test for alcohol, or by a family member, may be all that is needed. If the available history is not diagnostic, particularly at the time of urgency, such as during treatment of trauma, urine or blood chemical testing for specific substances is useful. Abusing persons are frequently unable to stop using substances long enough to pass screening tests. Many persons use multiple agents. These facts make screening tests of great value whenever the diagnosis is in doubt in providing firm confirmation of the diagnosis and information regarding multiple drug use. The urine or blood test, when positive, offers a basis for confronting denial; even the patient who consults you for assistance with drugs or alcohol may at a later time deny information given to you earlier, and the tests are useful in treatment. When positive tests are presented in an understanding manner, even though the patient has been confronted with a deliberate lie, it is effective in demonstrating thoroughness on your part and in providing some knowledge of the nature of the disease.

III. IDENTIFICATION OF MAJOR PROBLEMS

Head trauma, ruptured internal organ, hidden infection, and major interference with vital signs and consciousness must be identified early on. The taking of the history provides a great deal of information about the patient's mental function and his or her ability to cope with problems. If the person interacts normally and provides a reasonable amount of credible detail, then further testing is not needed. Measurements of vital signs, neurological testing, particularly of the cranial nerves, inspection of the mucous membranes for anemia, examination of the chest, abdomen, and limbs for pain, and careful auscultation of the chest for infection suffice for screening.

In a large personal experience screening street alcoholics for substantial illness, it was possible to train nurses, military corpsmen, or even highly interested college students to perform this assessment almost without error. The vital signs have particular importance and must be measured, including the temperature and respiratory rate. Fever and accelerated respiratory rate are rarely present unless associated with infection or other disease.

Sometimes the person screened is highly confused from the recent use of a substance. If it is short acting such as alcohol, heroin, or cocaine, screening the patient in a preliminary way, allowing him or her to remain nearby or to return in two or three hours, and repeating the observations is useful. Signs relating to intoxication should be strikingly less even after this short interval. On the other hand, if there is no change in the mental function of a patient on a short-acting drug, the likelihood of health injury is much greater.

IV. MAJOR HEALTH PROBLEMS UNRELATED TO THE ADDICTION

Each of us develops screening tests appropriate to the population with whom we work. All general physicians check blood pressure, most also check occult blood in those over age 50, blood glucose, and cholesterol, and comment on habits and nutrition. Similar checks are in order in the addicted person to preserve credibility. These screening tests help the patient understand that you expect him or her to recover and to use such tests to maintain future good health. All addicts exhibit anxiety from increased output of catecholamines after abstinence. This is nearly always associated with mild elevation of blood pressure, which will persist for up to 14 days. Treatment of this mild hypertension is not indicated, but all levels of elevation should be evaluated after this catecholamine effect has worn off. Many addicts fail to eat during periods of heavy use. As soon as they start to eat normally, blood sugar goes out of control and values in the diabetic range are common. Sugar in the urine is infrequent, but not unheard of. Again, such findings should be interpreted with caution, or the screening tests delayed for about a week in order to avoid labeling the person as diabetic.

Alcohol produces a rapidly reversible injury in many systems. Patients screened a day or two after intensive drinking will reveal stools positive for occult blood in 25%, abnormal liver tests in 25%, and elevated amylase in at least 25%. The majority of these are temporary alcohol injuries that reverse themselves by the fifth day for the hemoccult and amylase, and by one week for the liver tests. If the history and physical examinations do not identify reasons to test these levels, it is better to obtain screening tests in alcoholics after one week to avoid multiple retesting for the abnormality. Cholesterol levels, on the other hand, are often elevated in alcoholics, but this is sometimes an effective additional motivating factor for entering treatment.

Cigarettes are commonly used by addicts. There is disagreement among therapists as to whether to treat nicotine and other addictions simultaneously or to treat one form of substance abuse at a time. A recent conference on nicotine abuse advocated simultaneous treatment of all substance abuse.[1]

V. SCREENING FOR MAJOR PSYCHIATRIC ILLNESS

Features of depression are common in long-standing addiction ends, and are particularly prominent after depressant abuse (including alcohol) and use of stimulants, including cocaine. This diagnosis is often overlooked by screening doctors. Although modest depression associated with withdrawal reverses in about three weeks, severe depression, usually existing prior to the substance abuse, will be worsened during the withdrawal period and immediately afterward. Panic reactions, anxiety that is not believed to be a part of withdrawal, delusions, or hallucinations, or paranoia are features that are highly significant. These are usually uncovered during the interview and subsequent examination. Abusers often have suicidal thoughts and direct questioning about such ideas is essential to plan appropriate treatment.

A difficult problem is the person who is either too ill to provide an accurate history, or who is so quiet and withdrawn as to be bothered by talking, or who is hostile to the interview and examination process. However, by evaluating mental function as a regular part of taking history, one can often obtain the necessary information. If not, it is always possible to see the patient again at a later time or advise that the examination was incomplete. Another problem is the person who has been highly sedated for withdrawal treatment before your examination and is simply too drugged to cooperate. In such an instance certain key and essential portions of the examination, such as memory testing, must be deferred until the person is more alert. If the person is to enter a treatment facility and will not be seen again, one must clearly indicate the incompleteness of the examination for the benefit of subsequent observers.

VI. USE OF THE LABORATORY FOR SCREENING

The use of the laboratory for drug screening is presented in Chapter 11. As part of a general health screening, a few tests are obtained. In alcoholics, it is worthwhile to defer blood screening for liver, pancreatic disease, and diabetes for one week. Extensive blood tests are of limited value unless needed to answer a specific question arising from the physical or history. Hemoglobin and white blood counts are of the greatest value and should be obtained promptly. Measurements to detect modest abnormalities in liver function, nutrients, and electrolytes are usually of no therapeutic value, for they will repair themselves whether or not they are identified.

Certain patient groups have a higher than usual incidence of viral hepatitis, HIV infection, and venereal disease. I do not recommend screening unless the history is particularly suggestive or there is a specific purpose in mind for seeking the information. On the average I find that screening physicians often place false confidence on a great deal of laboratory work and too little on the history and physical.

VII. SCREENING IN RELATIONSHIP TO SUBSEQUENT CARE

Screening is extremely valid for the items in Table 22 at the time is is performed, but is probably least valuable in detecting all psychopathology and occasionally overlooks late head trauma or occult infection. All persons involved in the care of substance-abusing patients must be educated to the occasional need to refer a patient back to the screening physician or to another doctor, should new alarming findings occur. For this reason, some sort of sick call for complaints, a check of vital signs each day for the first week of abstinence, and a consideration of the mental outlook at each interview is useful in detecting conditions previously overlooked. As one becomes more experienced in treating addictions, a concept of normal recovery is evolved. At each stage or time period after abstinence begins, the usual amount of recovery of body and mind is known.When a person falls short of this, further evaluation is in order. For example, very heavy users of alcohol, opiates, or cocaine are often somewhat dull mentally for up to a month after cessation. Anything exceeding this needs further evaluation, and I usually obtain a CT scan in those few patients who persist in their lack of recovery. If there is no cortical atrophy, seek the consultation of a neurologist.

VIII. CURRENT SCREENING PRACTICES OF THE AUTHOR

A. MEN UNDER AGE 45

For men under 45, a standard history (using a checksheet) and careful physical examination is carried out. The neurological exam and auscultation of chest are very meticulous. A rectal is performed and a hemoccult done. Hemoglobin and white cell count are obtained. Only substantive findings suggesting head injury, psychosis, bleeding, infection, or acute abdomen are pursued at this time. Screening laboratory work is deferred for one week unless I have a high index of suspicion from the physical and history. A cholesterol, sugar, and liver tests are performed at that time. Elevated blood pressure is followed for at least 2 weeks without treatment unless it is alarming. Positive hemoccults on admission must be positive after 1 week, on at least one of three subsequent tests, to justify further evaluation. If there is a possible exposure to tuberculosis, skin testing is utilized.

B. MEN OVER AGE 45

Men over 45 are handled similarly to younger men, except a screening cardiogram is obtained if heart evaluation is not available from earlier records. Rectal examination and hemoccult testing is performed at the time of screening to counsel the patient on prostate problems if present. A blood screen after 1 week includes creatinine, sugar, liver tests, and cholesterol. A chest film is not routinely obtained, but a routine urine examination is included.

C. WOMEN OF ALL AGES

For women of all ages, breast and pelvic examination is undertaken as part of evaluation. If there is great agitation, the pelvic is deferred but not avoided. Appropriate PAP smears are made at that time. Other tests are the same as for older men.

REFERENCE

1. American Medical Association Workshop on Nicotine Abuse, Chicago, September 1989.

Chapter 13

Classes of Drugs Needed for the Successful Management of Addictions

I. INTRODUCTION

Pharmacotherapy of drug and alcohol dependence is a highly valuable portion of the physician's armamentarium, and all physicians need to be well acquainted with the range of agents used and their purpose. Even if doctors choose not to use drugs for specific purposes, they will often encounter new patients who are on these drugs. It is to be emphasized that pharmacotherapy should *never* be undertaken without establishing a physician-patient relationship including a clear articulation of the contract relating to drug use. Substance-abusing persons are at major risk to abuse therapeutic agents. Drug and alcohol addicts or abusers readily acquire abuse for other substances, almost always having a consumption of caffeine-containing beverages and cigarettes well above average. Any behavior-modifying drugs, particularly sedatives, soporifics, tranquilizers, and pain-controlling drugs, have a high potential for abuse so are used with care if at all. Table 26 lists the broad classes of drugs that will be discussed in this chapter.

II. BENZODIAZEPINE DRUGS

A. GENERAL

Though themselves addicting, the benzodiazepines are a highly useful class of agents, particularly in treatment of alcohol, sedative, and opiate withdrawal, and for crisis inter-

TABLE 26
Useful Drugs for Specific Problems in Addicted Persons

Drugs to treat withdrawal
- Benzodiazepines
- Phenobarbital

Drugs to treat or prevent convulsions
- Phenytoin
- Carbamezapine
- Diazepam, lorazepam
- Phenobarbital

Drugs to treat toxic and overdose reactions
- Opiate antagonists, naloxone
- Nalorphine, levallorphan
- Haloperidol

Drugs to Control Addiction
- Nicotine chewing gum
- Methadone
- Disulfiram

Ancillary drugs to control symptoms
- Clonidine
- Propranolol

TABLE 27
Useful Properties of Benzodiazepine Drugs

Property	Magnitude	Agent with property
	Oral Absorption	
Rapid	Complete in 30 min	Diazepam, chlordiazepoxide
Slow	Complete in 120 min	Oxazepam
	Intramuscular Use	
Erratic levels		Diazepam, chlordiazepoxide
Good absorption		Lorazepam
	No Active Metabolytes	
Long half life	10—20 h	Lorazepam
Short	5—15 h	Oxazepam
	Long-Acting Metabolytes	
Parent	10—24	Diazepam, chlordiazepoxide
Product	30—200	
	Anticonvulsant Activity	
Best		Diazepam
Some		Lorazepam
None		Chlordiazepoxide, oxazepam

vention in the ongoing care of abstinent addicts. These agents differ markedly one from another in several properties listed in Table 27 and are not interchangeable.

Table 27 contains information on the only four agents that are widely suggested for use in treatment of withdrawal from sedatives or opiates. The important differences among these drugs are in their anticonvulsant potency, their half lives, and the possible routes of administration. Diazepam is in my opinion the best drug for this purpose, for it has the greatest variety of effects for use in these patients and others. It cannot be used i.m. but has excellent, rapid absorption orally. All drugs require the liver for their metabolism and all are tightly bound to protein.

A suitable alternative with almost the same disadvantages is chlordiazepoxide. Lorazepam, which can be given intramuscularly, is included in our list of useful drugs. Though its half life is somewhat shorter, it is less potent as an anticonvulsant than diazepam but more potent that chlordiazepoxide. Its advantage is that it can be given intramuscularly. All benzodiazepine drugs are used to obtain a specific treatment goal determined by serial observation. Liver metabolism is utilized for all of these drugs, but diazepam and chlordiazepoxide are converted to active products with very long half lives.

B. DIAZEPAM

The half life of effective sedation with diazepam increases with age, for this agent has several metabolic products with similar activities. The sedation may have a half life as short as 12 h in young persons, rising to 70 h in 70-year-olds. It cannot be reliably given intramuscularly, but it is the best and most rapidly orally absorbed of this group of drugs. Excellent sedative, anticonvulsant, and skeletal muscle relaxation potency is present. Diazepam reaches steady state on the third to the fifth day. It may produce thrombophlebitis after i.v. injection. In addictions a safe unit dose is 10 mg, usually given orally. Repeated oral doses may be given after evaluation of effect each 1 to 2 h. Overdose is very infrequent and does not produce fatal disease unless there is major preexisting CNS suppression, liver encephalopathy, or marked anoxia. A rash occurs with sensitivity.

C. LORAZEPAM

Lorazepam (Ativan®) has a more fixed half life, shorter than diazepam. Its oral absorption is slower (2 to 3 h), but it may be used i.m. in all muscle groups with little pain and excellent absorption. It is metabolized by the liver but with no active metabolites, a fact that is often presented as an advantage but is not experienced in practice. It is less toxic intravenously and better absorbed intramuscularly. It is a little less potent as an anticonvulsant, and shorter acting than diazepam.

III. PHENOBARBITAL

Phenobarbital is a highly useful agent for withdrawal and treatment of convulsions. It is well absorbed orally, with some 15% removed in the first pass through the liver, and it may be given i.v. or i.m. It has a very long half life of about 80 h and as such is uniquely valuable in treating withdrawal from opiates, barbiturates, or benzodiazepines with longer half lives, and indeed any withdrawal. Its therapeutic/toxic ratio is about $^1/_4$, requiring more medical supervision of its use than the benzodiazepine groups of drugs. Phenobarbital is metabolized predominantly by the liver, with some 75% excreted in the bile and the remainder into the urine. It is about one-third bound to protein.

The dose used in adults is usually 260 mg as a loading dose i.v., with a repeated dose of 130 mg given each 30 to 60 min until drowsiness ensues. Because of the high protein binding, maximal effects after intravenous treatment may not be seen for 15 to 20 min. When the above regime is used, no further treatment is required. This dose has been highly effective in suppressing seizures in alcohol or alcohol-drug withdrawal and is superior to phenytoin. When the agents ingested are unknown, this is the agent of choice.

CNS toxicity may occur with respiratory depression, contraindicating the use of this drug when patients are not alert. Hypersensitivity is extremely rare. Acute dosing as drowsiness approaches is associated with many symptoms similar to drunkenness. In children, 8 mg/kg i.v. or i.m. is used.

IV. PHENYTOIN

Phenytoin is the most frequently used drug for control or prevention of convulsions, but its use is often inappropriate. It is slow and variable in its absorption, has a low first-pass effect, and requires about 3 h for absorption. It reaches a steady state in 7 to 10 days with daily oral dosing, and the therapeutic range is 15 to 20 μg/ml, with toxic levels noted above 25 to 30 μg/ml. It is metabolized by the liver and excreted by the kidney. It stabilizes neuronal membranes.

Withdrawal convulsions in alcoholics are prevented by daily oral dosing of 300 mg/day for 5 days when used with chlordiazepoxide or no medication. Phenytoin has failed to prevent recurrent convulsions in alcoholics presenting to emergency rooms and should not be used for this purpose.[1]

Phenytoin is the most commonly used treatment to control idiopathic epilepsy, common from trauma in alcoholics, but is used chronically, frequently in the continuous treatment of convulsions which occur during withdrawal. The toxicity of the drug and its slow onset of action make it an inferior choice to benzodiazepienes, phenobarbital, or carbamazepine in acute alcohol or opiate addiction.

V. CARBAMAZEPINE

Carbamazepine is a drug that is useful acutely to treat and prevent withdrawal convulsions and to provide sedation during withdrawal. It is erratically absorbed orally, with no first-pass effect and a long half life of about 35 h when initially used. It requires 4 to 6 h to reach a stable blood level of 8 to 15 μg/ml, which is the therapeutic level. It is metabolized by the liver and mostly secreted in the urine. It has been shown to prevent withdrawal seizures in doses of 400 mg/day. When first used it produces water retention with dilutional hyponatremia and may have sedative side effects when the plasma concentration is above 10 μg/ml. It has cross-sensitivity to the antidepressant tricyclics. In Scandinavia it is the most widely used anticonvulsant agent for preventing withdrawal seizures.[2]

VI. OPIATE ANTAGONISTS (NALOXONE, LEVALLORPHAN, NALORPHINE)

A. GENERAL

Used intravenously, the opiate antagonists promptly reverse respiratory depression caused by opioid drugs, even in neonates, and reverse many of the other effects of overdose of opiates and many related compounds. Although there are many subtypes of opiate receptors (see Chapter 2), naloxone interferes with the receptors in the respiratory center as well as all other types and in this fashion removes nearly all opioid effects and *may* precipitate withdrawal. Naloxone has no agonist activity, whereas levallorphan has some. The agonist effects of naloxone are much less than levallorphan, making the former the drug of choice.

B. NALOXONE

Naloxone (Narcan®) is given to adults in 0.4-mg increments; at other ages it is administered as 10 μg/kg body weight. It is always given i.v. when a vein can be found, but i.m. or s.c. administration is almost as effective. It may be repeated each 3 or 4 min after i.v. use, up to 2.0 mg in an adult. It may produce nausea and vomiting, restlessness and irritability. In high doses it may accelerate or even precipitate withdrawal. Its effect lasts only 2 to 3 h so repeated doses are needed after this interval if there is a response.

C. NALTREXONE

Naltrexone, an orally effective long-acting narcotic antagonist, is useful once a patient has been withdrawn from opiates for maintaining a drug-free state. Naltrexone blocks opiate effects, preventing the high.[3]

VII. HALOPERIDOL

Haloperidol is useful occasionally to treat hallucinations during withdrawal or in psychotic patients. Addicted patients who present with prominent visual and/or auditory hallucinations are readily controlled with this agent in doses of 2 to 10 mg. In patients who have hallucination from the time of initial contact with physicians, benzodiazepine agents are usually ineffective. Haloperidol can be given i.m., with peak concentration occurring in 10 to 20 min, or orally with only 70% absorbed and peak effect in 4 to 6 h. There is a substantial first-pass effect, so initial dosing is almost always intramuscular. The drug is metabolized by the liver and mostly excreted there. The half life is 24 h. Its major adverse side effect is hypotension, and it is contraindicated in patients with Parkinson's disease or with severe CNS depression.

The drug can produce extrapyramidal effects and, in the extreme, tardive dyskinesia. Muscular tremulousness and spasm may be observed. It is recommended that one use the drug initially as a 2-mg i.m. dose, repeating in 1 h. It is given for hallucination, almost always in conjunction with another drug, either phenobarbital or benzodiazepine. Up to 10 mg may be needed. Continued daily dosing after hallucination ceases should provide half the previous day's dose until 1 mg is reached. Abrupt discontinuation is not recommended. This drug is infrequently indicated.

VIII. METHADONE

The substitution of a legally available opiate upon request to addicts to replace street drugs has been used successfully in England and in many Eastern countries. When the synthetic drug methadone was discovered in 1964,[4] it was found that addicted persons exhibited a higher degree of physical and mental performance than did heroin addicts. It produces withdrawal prevention without the extreme high of other opiates and interferes less with mental and physiological function than others. In theory, the addict may be provided such an extreme habit with methadone that it is not possible to purchase street drugs to prevent withdrawal. It is useful in both detoxification and maintenance. It is well absorbed, with peak action in about 45 min, there is high protein binding and a first-pass effect. Its half life is about 24 h. It has all of the toxicity of other opiates. As a suppressant it is used at a level of 40 mg daily or twice daily.

Side effects almost always include sedation, sweating, some constipation, and decreased libido. These effects often disappear with chronic usage. The dosage is usually given as a liquid to prevent the addict saving up and selling the drug on the street. Because of the complex problems in opiate addicts, this drug may be given with disulfiram, neuroleptics, or antidepressants. The administration is nearly always supervised and associated with random testing for use of other illicit drugs. Naltrexone, a pure opioid antagonist without any agonist effects, is sometimes used to prevent opiate addicts from getting high, but naltrexone and methadone are not given together. Patients are placed on naltrexone only after they are clearly detoxified and often with a naloxone (Narcan®) challenge. Naltrexone is usually used for up to 2 years in a dose sufficiently high as to produce *no* effect from a regular heroin fix.[5]

IX. DISULFIRAM TREATMENT

Disulfiram blocks the conversion of acetaldehyde to acetate, leading to accumulations of acetaldehyde when alcohol is used in a person on disulfiram. The drug itself is taken daily in doses of 250 to 1000 mg. It is most often taken at bedtime, because it produces initial drowsiness. A few patients develop a metallic or garlic taste in the mouth, related to the secretion of CS2 in the breath, which is usually relieved by decreasing the dose. After a 3-day period of treatment and persisting for about 7 days after treatment ceases, the alcohol-disulfiram reaction occurs if alcohol is given.

The alcohol-disulfiram reaction begins within 30 min of the ingestion of alcohol; usually at least 10 g of alcohol (the amount in a usual portion of an alcoholic beverage) are required for the patient to perceive a reaction. The small amount of alcohol in medicines, cooking condiments, or absorbed from shaving lotions is too small to produce a reaction. Most reactions seen by physicians follow multiple drink ingestions. There is a marked vasodilatation, a feeling of warmth and excitement, usually occurring within 30 min of alcohol ingestion. The heart pounds, there is headache, increasing anxiety, and usually some element of nausea and vomiting. At a dose of 250 mg/day and a challenge of 10 to 15 g of ethanol (one drink), some 80% of people get a mildly unpleasant reaction. If a patient gets no reaction, it is appropriate to increase the dose of disulfiram.

Side effects of disulfiram that are serious and require discontinuation are allergy, mainly skin reactions usually observed in the initial 2 weeks of therapy, hepatitis observed in the first 6 weeks, optic neuritis (failing visual acuity) observed in the first 6 months, and acute psychosis also observed in the first 6 months. A peripheral neuritis may occur, usually detected after 1 or 2 years of treatment, thus emphasizing the need to know the condition of the patient when one initiates this drug.

Loss of potency or libido, often discussed as a side effect of disulfiram, is no more common in such patients than in those on placebo, but is frequently found in addicts and is readily attributed to the disulfiram. Compliance tests in both the breath and urine exist for this drug and have some utility.

The alcohol-disulfiram reaction is experienced by the majority of patients taking the drug for more than 3 months. It is never life threatening when the dose is 250 mg/day; a few deaths were reported with heavy drinking on doses of 1 g/day or higher. The reaction usually is controlled with sedatives and possibly a vasoconstricting drug to raise the blood pressure if it is alarmingly low. It is self-limited in 3 to 5 h, and patients who experience severe reactions maintain better sobriety than those who do not get such reactions. It has a long persistence of action, usually producing a reaction for 5 to 10 days after cessation of ingestion, and is often used under supervised conditions. As such it is taken 3 to 5 days a week under supervision, with the dose taken as a slurry of crushed tablets in about 2 ounces of water to prevent concealment. The other doses of the week are taken unsupervised.

The effectiveness of the drug seems to depend on a firm commitment to its use and the understanding that this is an enforced contract undertaken to prevent impulsive drinking. It is always used with other therapy.[6,7]

X. NICOTINE CHEWING GUM (NICORETTES®)

When nicotine bound to polacrilex resin is chewed, the nicotine is displaced by alkaline saliva and absorbed. It peaks if there is adequate saliva 15 to 30 min after chewing starts (much slower than the 30 s to peak after inhalation of tobacco). The average steady state of 11.8 ng/ml is from one fifth to one half that attained by a smoker. The gum is "exhausted" of nicotine in about 30 min of chewing and is ineffective in those without saliva. If beverages are used, sodium bicarbonate is needed to release the nicotine. Chewing tobacco produces about the same blood levels at substantially lower cost. There are many studies indicating that this is a positive aide to smoking cessation that is useful in highly motivated persons or when combined with other behavior modification.

XI. CLONIDINE (CATAPRES®)

Clonidine (Catapres®) is an alpha-adrenergic agonist-antagonist often used in the treatment of opiate withdrawal because it blocks areas in the locus ceruleus that are particularly activated. It has been used as an adjunct in alcohol withdrawal. The drug is well absorbed orally, metabolized by the liver, and excreted in the urine. It may lower the blood pressure as it reaches a peak concentration by 5 h; the effect may persist for 8 h.

One protocol for opioid withdrawal uses a test dose of 0.005 mg/kg to determine whether it relieves symptoms. Those with a positive response are given 0.017 mg/kg/day divided into two or three doses for 9 or 10 days, then are given half this dose on days 11 to 13 with cessation thereafter. This basic dose may be increased fourfold based on tolerance, with hypotension being of the greatest concern. Dopamine infusion to support blood pressure and atropine to reverse significant bradycardia may be needed if overdose is given. During this treatment patients should be cautioned about getting up promptly, for the blood pressure will usually respond in a slower-than-normal manner to changes in position. Clonidine has been used in alcohol withdrawal.[8]

An excellent review of its use in withdrawal exists.[9]

A recent summation suggests that clonidine is most effective during the final stages of withdrawal when doses of methadone or opiates are low.[10,11] It has also been reported to be of value in nicotine withdrawal.[12] It is insufficient as the only agent in treating major symptomatic withdrawal, but it leads to lower requirements for drugs with sedative side effects. Patients in protocols using clonidine are usually more mentally alert at all times after withdrawal treatment begins.

XII. PROPRANOLOL

A beta-adrenergic antagonist of great safety, propranolol is occasionally used for lysing anxiety symptoms in any form of withdrawal. When high doses of sedative drugs are needed because of unresponsive anxiety, propranolol is particularly beneficial.

Rapidly and completely absorbed, propranolol blocks beta-1 receptors in the heart and beta-2 receptors in other noncardiac sites. This agent and its many cousins are used in alcoholism and opiate addiction to treat the anxiety and the adrenergic hyperactivity of rapid heart rate, rapid breathing, fever, and extreme flushing that are often prominent during withdrawal. They are almost always adjunctive with benzodiazepines to lessen the amount of sedation.[13]

XIII. TRICYCLIC ANTIDEPRESSANTS

The wide variety of tricyclic antidepressants will not be discussed. Many therapists use these agents effectively to relieve dysphoric symptoms in alcohol- and opiate-dependent patients during the early months of recovery, but limited and poorly done controlled trials do not support such use in even a minority of patients. The treatment is not firmly established. On the other hand, when clear depression is established, these drugs are of marked benefit. The difficulty lies in diagnosing depression in the presence of active abuse. This difficulty is discussed more completely in Chapter 18.

XIV. INFREQUENTLY INDICATED BUT USEFUL AGENTS

A. ANTIHISTAMINES

Antihistamines are used as sedative hypnotics in both alcohol and opiate addiction during the early withdrawal period. Diphenydramine (Benadryl®), 50 or 100 mg at bedtime, is the most widely used. Although these agents are never used in my practice, they are used by many others.

B. PHENATHIAZINE ANTIEMETICS

The phenathiazine antiemetics are of very limited value, largely because they do not seem to be effective in abusing patients, particularly during withdrawal. Most often more complete treatment of withdrawal will allay nausea and vomiting.

C. ANALGESICS

Alcoholic or malnourished addicts are particularly sensitive to aspirin and nonsteroid analgesic drugs (NSAIDs), and these are usually avoided for a week or two until such damage is repaired. Codeine and meperidine can readily be habituating. Between these extremes, I recommend drugs starting with acetaminophen, moving to ibuprofen, and if necessary combination products with codeine. Analgesic abuse can readily occur and needs some caution.

D. INDIGESTION AIDS

Commercial antacids (Rolaids®, Alka Seltzer®, Pepto Bismol®, Sucralfate®) can be recommended as the patient desires for almost any symptoms. These are frequent in abusing persons, and treatment without diagnosis is recommended in the early weeks. Only if these symptoms persist is further diagnosis indicated. More potent agents such as H2-blocking drugs are to be avoided.

E. LAXATIVES

Laxatives are often needed in early recovery. Fiber, bulk laxatives, and lactulose are probably the best group from which to select treatment.

F. VITAMIN, MINERAL SUPPLEMENTS

Vitamin-mineral supplements are useful in all patients who have a history of malnutrition, but are needed for only a short period of time, rarely as long as 1 month. Very occasionally in specific disease states such as chronic pancreatitis, long-term use of supplements is required.

REFERENCES

1. **Young, G. P., Rores, C., Murphy, C., and Dailey, R. H.,** Intravenous phenobarbital for alcohol withdrawal convulsions, *Ann. Emergency Med.*, 16, 847, 1987.
2. **Sternebring, B., Holm, C. H., and Wadstein, A. M.,** Reduction in early alcohol abstinence fits by administration of carbamazepine syrup instead of tablets, *Eur. J. Clin. Pharmacol.*, 24, 611, 1983.
3. **Ginzburg, H. M.,** Naltrexone: its clinical utility, Alcohol, Drug Abuse and Mental Health Administration Publication ADM, Bethesda, MD, 84, 1358, 1984.
4. **Dole, V. P. and Nyswander, M. D.,** The use of methadone for narcotic blockade, *Br. J. Addict.*, 63, 55, 1968.
5. Report of the National Research Council on clinical evaluation of narcotic antagonists, Clinical evaluation of naltrexone treatment of opiate dependent individuals, *Arch. Gen. Psychiatr.*, 35, 335, 1978.
6. **Brewer, C.,** Patterns of compliance and evasion in treatment programmes which include supervised disulfiram, *Alcohol and Alcoholism,* 4, 385, 1986.
7. **Brewer, C.,** Disulfiram treatment of alcoholism, *JAMA,* 257, 926, 1987.
8. **Manheim, P.,** Alcohol withdrawal: effects of clonidine, *Alcoholism: Clin. Exp. Res.*, 9, 238, 1985.
9. **Walinder, J. and Svensson, T. L., Eds.,** Pharmacological treatment of abstinence reactions, clonidine: a new treatment mode, *Acta Psych. Scand.*, Supplement, 327, 73, 1, 1986.

10. **Gold, M. S., Pottash, A. C., Sweeney, D. R., and Kleber, H. D.,** Opiate withdrawal using clinidine: a safe, effective and rapid non-opiate treatment, *JAMA,* 293, 343, 1980.
11. **Schnoll, S. H. and Karan, L. D.,** Substance abuse, *JAMA,* 261, 2890, 1989.
12. **Glassman, A. H., Stetner, F., Walsh, B. T., et al.,** Heavy smokers, smoking cessation and clonidine: results of a double blind randomized trial, *JAMA,* 259, 2863, 1988.
13. **Kraus, M. L., Gottleib, L. D., et al.,** Randomized clinical trial of atenolol in patients with alcohol withdrawal, *New Engl. J. Med.,* 313, 905, 1985.

Chapter 14

Informing the Patient of the Diagnosis of Abuse and Motivating Him or Her to Treatment

I. INTRODUCTION

This chapter discusses a very difficult process in the management of substance abuse. Physicians must guide presentation so that it is clearly perceived even in the face of militant patient denial while at the same time avoid so alienating or discouraging the patient that he or she abandons all treatment on the basis of perceived insult. Our training as physicians does not give us the extraordinary sensitivity required in this endeavor, and our early experiences are often ineffective and bad ones. We can all recall instances when we were successfully intimidated in one way or another so that we avoided the issue of abuse, only later to acknowledge that we had missed a splendid opportunity for intervention.

There is no single circumstance that brings abusing individuals to a physician's attention, so generalizations as covered in this chapter must be tempered by the actual situation. Some users accept the existence of a problem and really want assistance in getting and staying off the drug. Others want relief from temporary pressure of job, marriage, or the law but have almost no desire *or intention* of abandoning the habit. Still others have such well-developed denial that they firmly believe the problems lie with others' inaccurate perceptions.

TABLE 28
Factors That Should Be Present When The Diagnosis of Abuse Is Discussed with Patient

1. Patient knowledge of the physician's thoroughness in forming the diagnosis
2. Clear acceptance by the physician of the patient as an individual
3. A nonjudgmental approach to the fact of abuse
4. Perception that there is hope for improvement
5. A clear plan for continuity of care; nonabandonment
6. Objective evidence of abuse that clearly outweighs the patient's reasons for doubt
7. Timing for presentation of the diagnosis similar to that for other diseases

Throughout this book we will emphasize honesty, thoroughness in diagnosis, and nonjudgmental acceptance of the addict. These characteristics are essential to this initial discussion of the fact of abuse. This chapter will present problems that often arise during the first serious discussion of the diagnosis of abuse and consider strategies that may be successful in avoiding or coping with them. The attitudes of physicians and other professionals and their staffs that may lead to failure, discussed more fully in Chapter 7, will also be discussed here.

II. TIMING PRESENTATION OF THE DIAGNOSIS OF ABUSE

Table 28 lists important considerations that usually must be present in order for the "fact of abuse" to have an excellent chance of acceptance. It is clear from Table 28 that the majority of these factors are under the physician's control and also depend upon some feedback from the patient as to whether each of the goals has been accomplished.

Major impairments in establishing a basis for treatment or acceptance of treatment arise from ignorance about the nature of substance abuse (on the part of either party), concern with the futility and hopelessness of the current endeavor (on the part of either party), and fear of abandonment as soon as this transaction is completed (on the part of the patient). The physician needs knowledge of the methods of intervention and the probability of success at various stages in order to share this information with the patient. The physician needs to examine his or her attitudes to determine which clients can in fact be assisted (see Chapter 7), and a contractual arrangement to "see this through" needs to be spoken early in the transaction to avoid an attitude of "why bother" on the part of the patient. None of these items, though readily enumerated, comes easily, for they may enter into and alter the very fabric of the therapist. But if one is to be effective, these issues must be confronted and worked with internally. Often the genesis of fear in the management of the substance-dependent person is the fear of failure. A knowledge of average outcomes with treatment is beneficial in helping the patient to know something of his or her chances of attaining and maintaining abstinence.

During the taking of the history and completing the physical examination, each of the issues in Table 28 can be assessed and the perception of the patient at least partially evaluated. Your acceptance of the individual in a nonjudgmental manner and your willingness to "see this illness through" can be communicated. It cannot be sufficiently emphasized that the thoroughness of your evaluation of the patient's general condition in both history and physical is substantially the grounds upon which the patient will accept or reject you as a therapist. The manner in which you take and discuss the drug-alcohol history (see Chapter 8) can go a long way toward establishing your own manifested attitudes.

The impartial weighing of the medical certainty of the diagnosis versus the reasonable doubts that denial in the patient will raise must be particularly addressed. When the person presents with the statement, "I'm hooked on cocaine and I need help", the situation is totally different than when a hostile teenager is forced to come by his parents because of a possible cocaine problem that is nearly totally denied. As the history unfolds along with the ancillary evidence, it will become fairly clear how much acceptance there is. It follows that the physician may need less evidence of the fact of addiction when there is acceptance than when there is major resistance and doubt on the part of the client.

Presentation of the fact of addiction should always follow the initial evaluation and, if pertinent, receipt of the necessary laboratory values. Using this time and more than one visit will increase the confidence the patient has in your thorough evaluation and in your diagnosis. The outside limit for the confrontation is tempered by your usual habits in discussing the diagnosis with the patient. If you commonly await laboratory and consultant confirmation, then this is completely appropriate in drug abuse; but if you commonly discuss diagnosis at the end of the first or second visit, then it should be undertaken at that time. The patient will usually be sensitive to your ambivalence about the discussion, and if this diagnosis is delayed or is substantial and deferred, may even intimidate you into retracting your diagnosis.

Vaillant[1] addresses this brilliantly: "Once the clinician has made the diagnosis of alcoholism, the diagnosis must be communicated to the patient. The patients need to be shown, not told." In the early stage, when the clinician and the patient doubt the diagnosis, Vaillant suggests instructing the patient to drink freely but never to exceed three drinks in a given day. A patient who is unable to follow this simple restriction for a month may become convinced that he or she is an alcoholic. Vaillant identifies the challenge as the need to convince the addict that he or she is a decent person who has an insidious disease, and that the disease is the primary cause of distress. This straightforward approach developed for alcoholism can be modified for other addictions.

The mild dementia present, at least temporarily, in all addicts requires that the instructions be kept simple, unambiguous, and focus on the addiction as the primary problem. The simple maxims of Alcoholics Anonymous and Al-Anon, which have carried over into all the self-help groups, are useful in the presentation of all addictions. At all times the element of treatability and hope should be emphasized. Presentation of the pain and misery of the addiction in the person's life need to be repeated over and over on subsequent visits and interviews.

III. MOTIVATING THE PATIENT TO TREATMENT

As part of the discussion of the diagnosis of addiction, the treatment and recovery process must be discussed to assure that treatment will in fact proceed. This should be done with the patient's willing acquiescence if not enthusiastic endorsement. Once the "fact of addition" has been presented, nearly all of the skills of the mature physician may be called upon to keep the patient moving toward effective therapy. The wide spectrum of necessary skills is required because of the wide spectrum of acceptances of the presentation of the "fact of addiction". The response of the patient to the presentment of the "fact of addiction" dictates the physician's actions. This next action by the physician substantially determines what the patient will undertake in the way of therapy. The physician must maintain hope and optimism about the patient's future, continue an attitude of compassion and acceptance, and avoid either rejecting or abandoning the patient. Statements said with sincerity, such as "Your situation is not that unusual in my practice," or "This problem can happen to anyone with your stresses/ambition/responsibilities," help the patient understand these things. Table 29 lists features of a physician therapist that keep the majority of clients in a therapeutic relationship.

Many abusers feel hopeless about their problem. Some knowledge of the most common addictions and treatment outcomes is often of great relief to them. An enthusiastic view of the future, as emphasized in any Alcoholics Anonymous or other self-help meeting, is an important viewpoint to utilize in motivating people to treatment, even to the point of underemphasizing the effort required.

TABLE 29
Physician Characteristics That Preserve Patients' Intent to Enter and Complete Therapy

1. Flexibility — never run out of treatment alternatives and options
2. Perceptive charity — accept hostility as anxiety, caution as the norm, negativity as a form of uncertainty
3. Evangelical optimism about eventual outcome
4. Helpfulness with all possible problems, at least to the degree of identifying resources
5. Firmness about the problem
6. Understanding:
   - Of the client as an individual
   - Of your responsibilities
   - Of your attitudinal problems

The credibility of motivation is based upon the treatment plan that is devised for *this particular patient*. Your role may be limited to counseling and supervising recovery from medical or psychiatric problems, supervising a portion of the treatment, or undertaking a large portion of the treatment, but you must be prepared to discuss just what you will be offering. Fear of rejection from a new contact and fear of abandonment from you who have been judged OK is an important part of cessation of therapy and can be overcome by forthrightness in defining just what you will do and who you will depend upon, and by assuring the client that the transition from one therapeutic modality or site to another includes no possibility of rejection.

More than three decades ago, Morris Chafitz confirmed the obvious at the Massachusetts General Hospital.[2] When alcoholics were accompanied from one referral to another by staff whom they had met, some 90% were kept; when they were referred into the unknown, only 30% of such appointments were met. This is an important lesson for all of us who choose to refer our patients: Make certain that the referral is smoothed by some participation through staff, a phone call, or a bit of personal involvement.

IV. STRATEGIES TO OVERCOME FREQUENT IMPEDIMENTS TO ENTRY INTO THERAPY

A. RELUCTANCE TO ACCEPT THE DIAGNOSIS

Sometimes reluctance to accept the diagnosis is a form of denial and no certitude of diagnosis will be sufficient, but often a cautious and reserved approach by the physician may play a motivating role. In the initial presentment, offer little doubt. "You have an alcohol problem that we must address together" is much more often accepted than "You may have a little drinking problem." Be firm in your assessment, be willing to discuss the basis of your diagnosis, but do not back down from your facts unless there has clearly been an error. If necessary, do not hesitate to use hard facts known to you, such as "You have cirrhosis" or "IBM did not promote you because of your fights with your wife." The denial process overlooks many obvious events, and at the same time as the misery of the current existence is discussed, the hope that things can be better is held out for the person to see. Now and then a discussion with a person who has been through a similar addiction and has recovered is highly valuable. All self-help groups will gladly work with doctors to assist patients in accepting treatment.

B. SETTING IMPOSSIBLE CONDITIONS TO ENTER THERAPY

Occasionally an addict will state "I'll undertake treatment if you can get my wife and kids back with me," or "I'll undertake treatment if it is only between you and me, but I don't want to get involved with others''. Helping the abuser appreciate that he or she is the one with the problem goes part way in overcoming the difficulty. There is little advantage in a blatant confrontation about the condition. Thus, it is appropriate to say that you will talk with the wife and to define that part of the treatment that you are trained to give, but not to make commitments on the full transaction. Sometimes there is great fear of new experiences, often anticipated to be demeaning, and staying with a pleasing helper is desired. This can be overcome by emphasizing that you will continue with the therapy but that others are needed to address specific parts of the treatment. Convincing the patient that you are in this together is usually all that is required. Do not reluctantly commit yourself to services that you cannot provide, for the breach of trust will be even more serious than accurately defining your role now.

C. OUTLANDISH, BOORISH, OR INAPPROPRIATE BEHAVIOR

Using outlandish, booring, or unappropriate behavior is an attempt to attain rejection and dismissal is an occasional experience. Abusers sometimes orchestrate rejection by the helpers and subsequently declare that the failure of therapy was a function of this rejection. Do not condone inappropriate behavior (missed appointments, intoxication, or highly abusive behavior to yourself or your staff), but do not allow it to be a basis for rejection. At the time of confrontation, the destructive nature of the behavior should be presented with its possible consequences. The presentation is best accepted and most instructive when the way that you the physician feel is the basis of the reprimand rather than the deficiency of the patient. Thus, for the late patient or one who skips appointments, it is appropriate to say that you like to keep on time for all of your patients and you become anxious and upset when someone is late because you cannot provide them appropriate care. For someone using abusive language, ''I get so upset over something like this that I (or my secretary) cannot help you appropriately for the next 30 minutes or so, so please help me serve you better by not doing this. By offering referral, longer waits since you cannot rely on their being present for an appointment, less time available for therapy since sorting out the consequences of bad behavior takes some of the time you have budgeted for the patient, but not rejection, you can usually communicate effectively without losing the patient to treatment.

D. LETTING THE PATIENT MAKE CHOICES

At each stage in the planned treatment, offer the patient opportunities to select the modalities of treatment. This participation improves motivation and if skillfully presented the patient will nearly always make the choice you wish. Abusing patients usually have cynical outlook toward therapists. By including self-help groups, religion, extensive physical conditioning, and some other alternative lifestyle-altering programs in the menu submitted for choice, patients gain an opportunity to examine what they really desire from professionally directed treatment.

REFERENCES

1. **Vaillant, G.,** *The Natural History of Alcoholism,* Harvard University Press, Cambridge, MA, 1981.
2. **Chafetz, M. E.,** *The Alcoholic Patient, Diagnosis and Management,* Medical Economics Books, Oradell, NJ, 1983.

Chapter 15

What Can be Learned from Smoking and Nicotine Addiction

I. INTRODUCTION

Tobacco, a New World plant, spread to Europe and Asia only after the discovery of the Americas. Its addicting ingredient, nicotine, was isolated in 1828. Although nicotine is quite poisonous to insects in the larval and pupal stages, it currently has no medicinal use. Tobacco may be chewed or insufflated into the nose as snuff, with absorption by both routes, but the most popular method of use by far is combustion just outside the lips with subsequent inhalation of the nicotine-laden smoke. Nicotine is absorbed through the mouth, nasopharynx, gastrointestinal, and pulmonary mucosa essentially completely because of its high water solubility and pK_a of 8.5. At acid pH it is largely ionized and not absorbed, but in the small intestine, where more alkaline conditions occur, it is readily taken into the body. It is known that pulmonary absorption from inhalation of nicotine-laden smoke is as rapid as i.v. injection with substantial blood levels reached 10-15 s after the first inhalation. A single cigarette contains about 20 mg of nicotine, of which less than 1 mg is delivered in smoke but all of which may be absorbed should the cigarette be ingested.

II. EFFECTS

Nicotine affects CNS and peripheral receptors and mimics acetylcholine at ganglionic sites and to a lesser degree on both striated and certain smooth muscle functions. Small doses are stimulatory, particularly on the autonomic nervous system, larger doses produce an autonomic blockade. Peak concentrations in those who smoke and inhale by taking the smoke into the lungs are 25 to 50 μg/ml. The half life is 1 to 2 h.

Most commonly the drug produces tachycardia by the excitement of sympathetic cardiac nerves while inhibiting the vagus, but in addicted persons, little effect or even bradycardia is observed. Heavy users of the order of 20 cigarettes daily have mild muscle tremors. Respiration is stimulated even when the drug is taken orally. The EEG shows stimulation with behavioral arousal, improved cognition and memory, and usually decreased appetite.[1,2] There is inhibition of gastric contractions, slowing of gastrointestinal emptying, and mild constipation in nearly all. The initial use of the drug after days of abstinence, or in the naive user, always stimulates salivation and heart rate, and there are usually other effects of norepinephrine release.

The addicting property seems to have its onset within seconds of inhalation of the smoke and is a perception of psychic arousal and alertness and a feeling of being more alive. Smokers given centrally active ganglionic blockers such as mecamylamine immediately increase their consumption of cigarettes, while smokers given nicotine intravenously decrease cigarette consumption. Heavy smokers keep a constant blood level by consuming and inhaling each puff, taking almost the same number of puffs per cigarette, and using a new cigarette each 20 to 40 min. If cigarettes varying in nicotine content are used, the smoker adjusts by more frequent smoking and deeper inhalation.

Once addicted, which can occur in 3 to 7 days of continuous use, absence of tobacco produces intense craving associated with restlessness, headache, impairment of concentration, and other symptoms.

Toxic doses, such as follows the eating of cigarettes by children (one or two may prove fatal), or the taking of nicotine-containing tablets or insecticides, can produce convulsions, nausea, and vomiting.

III. HEALTH EFFECTS OF SMOKING

Smoking of tobacco is probably associated with more ill health than any other addiction in the world and accounts for at least one third of the avoidable premature deaths in the United States. The addiction is due to nicotine, but the ill-health effects are mostly related to carcinogenic, cardiovascular, and pulmonary destructive components of combustion. Thus chronic bronchitis, emphysema and nasopharyngeal allergic complications are increased in smokers, as are carcinoma of the lung, esophagus, stomach, pancreas, colon, breast, and female organs. In addition there is a marked increase in coronary artery events and death, as well as increased peripheral and central nervous system vascular disease in smokers. A recent review of the mortality and morbidity of smoking in California indicated that $7.1 billion was the yearly cost in this one large state and accounted for one sixth of the deaths in smokers.[3] The health effects of nicotine addiction are mild indeed, with an annoying withdrawal characterized by severe craving for tobacco, loss of concentration, irritability, and a sense of extreme restlessness. There is usually increased anxiety, a fear of failure common to most drug withdrawals, and an increased appetite with weight gain. As a reminder, known prominent problems associated with cigarette smoking are listed in Table 30.

IV. CESSATION STRATEGIES

A. PREVENTION

Education in early life to reduce subsequent use of cigarettes and to delay the age of first use has been partially successful in America, with substantial reductions in adolescent

TABLE 30
Major Illnesses Resulting from Long-Term Use of Cigarettes

Respiratory tree
- Sinusitis, allergic rhinitis
- Asthma
- Emphysema
- Chronic bronchitis
- Carcinoma of lung

Cardiovascular
- Coronary artery disease
- Cerebral vascular disease
- Peripheral vascular disease

Head
- Carcinoma of lips, tongue, nasopharynx

Gastrointestinal tract
- Peptic erosions,
- Refractory to healing
- Cancer of esophagus, stomach, pancreas, colon

Genitourinary tract
- Carcinoma of breast, uterus, bladder

men from 1965 to 1985, when the process plateaued. Young women, in contrast, have continued to increase the use of cigarettes. Numerous reports indicate that early use of cigarettes occurs despite the known risk.[4] A substantially more effective strategy is to markedly increase the price of cigarettes. This has been shown to decrease use, particularly in adolescents and among the least affluent working men and women.[5]

The tobacco industry and its major advertising expenditures have made smoking attractive to many and counter education programs to avoid tobacco use. The reluctance of legislatures to ban smoking on airplanes and in public places is a clear reflection of these conflicting interests.

B. CESSATION PROGRAMS

The ingredients of successful smoking cessation programs have been well studied,[6] and the cessation rates in controlled trials have been from 6 to 40% better than controls. Since there is almost no stigma associated with cigarette use and subsequent cessation, usually under the imprimatur of a health problem, information and accurate follow-up is available.

Physicians may readily be trained in a 3-h seminar in how to aid their patients in a "Quit for Life" smoking-cessation program. The purpose of such training is to demonstrate and practice counseling about smoking cessation. In the initial hour physicians are shown a videotape illustrating this approach and then rehearse it.

The program involves five steps: (1) Ask all patients if they smoke, and ask smokers if they wish to quit. (2) Reinforce smokers' motivation to quit. (3) Help smokers who wish to quit make a plan for quitting that includes a specific quit date. (4) Give a signed Quit Date Prescription form with the quit date written on it and make at least one follow-up appointment. (5) Offer a self-help booklet about quitting.

In the second seminar, conducted one week later, participant physicians discuss their experiences with this program. As each obstacle is raised, the instructor offers specific ways to overcome it. Nicotine gum is recommended as an adjunct to counseling for those who have persistent withdrawal or who must smoke within one half hour of awakening. A videotape showing questions frequently raised by patients in follow-up and their possible solutions is presented.

The third session is held 4 to 12 weeks later. At that time additional tapes are shown to assist doctors with specific problems encountered in their patients.

A recent evaluation of this program indicated that physicians encountering smoking patients increased their advice and improved their success rate, with some 8% of all smokers verified as having stopped smoking by alveolar carbon monoxide measurement 6 months after this program.[7,8]

"Smokeless tobacco" is associated with far fewer health problems, and includes snuff that is inhaled, tobacco that is chewed, and forms of tobacco that are merely kept in the mouth. A recent evaluation of the health effects of smokeless tobacco indicated that the cardiovascular effects and the level of nicotine metabolic products in the blood were similar, but the mutagenicity of urine was lower than with cigarette smoking.[9]

Several papers have reported the use of clonidine for withdrawal symptoms in very heavy smokers during the early weeks of cessation with apparently good results.[10,11] Nicotine gum has certainly aided smoking withdrawal, and its use has been reviewed.[12]

V. LESSONS TO APPLY TO OTHER ABUSED SUBSTANCES

The toxicity of cigarettes is clearly separate from its addicting principle. The availability of nicotine medicinally and as a chewing gum to provide the drug in a manner free from the medical contraindications of smoking has helped us in understanding certain aspects of addiction. The legal nature of this abuse and the ease in quantitation of both use and cessation of use through measurement of CO in the breath or cotinine in the urine have allowed excellent short-term intervention strategies.

Clearly, the availability and use of nicotine chewing gum has assisted more people in successfully completing the transition from smoking to nonsmoking.[13] Equally clear, counseling, support, and reinforcement of some form at least each two weeks is useful in keeping a person from relapse. Using these principles, physicians and related programs have been able to get as many as 70% of private patients to cease smoking for at least 1 year.

The clear advantage in smoking literature is the absence of shame, illegality, and embarrassment in smoking, a marked difference from other addictions.

The smoking-cessation literature raises major doubts about some of the principles that will be enunciated for other drugs. These include the assumption that early education is the key to preventing use in adolescents. These efforts, though partially successful, have not worked for women, and are not now continuing to show progress. Regulation of supply through taxation may be more effective.

Use of an agent to assist withdrawal by reducing the dose has been effective in nicotine withdrawal. This goes against the grain of common wisdom in treatment of other addictions.

Health scare tactics are effective in decreasing use. This works only partially for cigarette smoking, and though used in all addictions, there may be misplaced confidence in its value.

REFERENCES

1. **Ashton, H. and Stepney, R.,** *Smoking: Psychology and Pharmacology,* Tavistock, New York, 1982.
2. **Cherek, D. R.,** Effects of smoking different doses of nicotine on human aggressive behavior, *Psychopharmacology,* 9, 1, 1981.
3. Smoking-attributable mortality, morbidity and economic costs, California, 1985, from *MMWR,* 38, 272, 1989, abstracted in *JAMA,* 262, 2942, 1989.
4. **Popham, W. J.,** Nationwide survey of eighth and tenth grade students on health risks, *JAMA,* 260, 1512, 1989.
5. Reducing the health consequences of smoking: 25 years of progress — a report of the Surgeon General, U.S. Department of Health and Human Services, Public Health Service, DHHS publication no. CDC 89-8411, Rockville, MD, 1989.

6. **Kottke, T. W., Battista, R. N., DeFriese, G. H., et al.,** Attributes of successful smoking cessation interventions in medical practice: meta-analysis of 39 controlled trials, *JAMA,* 259, 2882, 1988.
7. **Cohen S. J., Stookey, G. K., Katz, B. P., Drook, C. A., and Smith, D. M.,** Encouraging primary care physicians to help smokers quit: a randomized controlled trial, *Ann. Int. Med.,* 110, 648, 1989.
8. **Cummings, S. R., Coates, T. J., Richard, R. J., Hansen, B., Zahnd, E. G., VanderMartin, R., Duncan, C., Gerbert, B., Martin, A., and Stein, M. J.,** Training physicians in counseling about smoking cessation. A randomized trial of the ''quit for life'' program, *Ann. Int. Med.,* 110, 640, 1989.
9. **Benowitz, N. L., Jacob, P., III, and Yu, L.,** Daily use of smokeless tobacco: systemic effects, *Ann. Int. Med.,* 111, 112, 1989.
10. **Glassman, A. H., Stetner, F., Walsh, B. T., et al.,** Heavy smokers, smoking cessation and clonidine: results of a doubleblind, randomized trial, *JAMA,* 259, 2863, 1988.
11. **Green, J. J.,** Heavy smokers, smoking cessation and clonidine, *JAMA,* 260, 1552, 1988.
12. **Cummings, S. R., Hansen, B., Richard, R. J., Stein, M. H., and Coates, T. J.,** Internists and nicotine gum, *JAMA,* 260, 1565, 69, 1988.
13. **Tonnesen, P., Fryd, V., Hansen, M., et al.,** Effect of nicotine chewing gum in combination with group counseling on the cessation of smoking, *New Engl. J. Med.,* 318, 15, 1988.

Chapter 16

Alcohol and Sedatives

I. INTRODUCTION

Alcohol and a variety of street and prescription drugs in the categories of sedatives, hypnotics, and sleeping medications are the most commonly abused substances in North America if tobacco and caffeine-containing beverages are excluded. The group contains alcohol, barbiturates, benzodiazepines, and a few other agents. All of these substances show tolerance, cross-tolerance, and withdrawal syndromes. All act on the GABA benzodiazepine chloride ionophore, but they do not have the same specificity of reaction with this membrane receptor isolated from different parts of the brain. Bromide, largely unavailable in the United States for the last three decades, was a frequently abused, over-the-counter member of this group, delaying the entry of chloride by a slightly different interference.

Alcohol is widely and legally used in North America, with more than 80% of high school-aged young people having used the agent. More than 90% of metropolitan-dwelling adults use alcohol at least monthly, and an estimated 2 to 5% of any using group are judged abusers. Prescription drugs are legitimately provided by physicians for both clear indications and for patients who no longer have a clear indication. It is estimated that more than half the prescriptions issued for diazepam are inappropriate to the medical requirements of the patient. In addition, large numbers of prescription drugs are used outside of a physician's orders. An estimated 1.7 million Americans use sedatives nonmedically, or about 10% as many as abuse alcohol.[1]

II. ALCOHOL MANUFACTURE AND USE

Alcohol fermentation from simple sugars such as occur in ripe fruit (particularly grapes) is one of several forms of spontaneous spoilage when yeasts come into contact with monosaccharides. The technique of making wine was discovered in all fruit-growing regions of the world before recorded history when populations began to store agricultural products. Curiously, hunting civilizations usually did not make this discovery. Grains, in contrast to fruit, contain starches made up of complex polymers of simple sugars that alcohol-producing yeasts simply cannot ferment. It took humans 3000 to 4000 additional years to discover ways to break down grain so that yeasts could then convert it to alcohol. People in the Middle East allowed grain to sprout and thus develop its own enzymes to reduce starch to simple sugars (malting), and in South America, human saliva was mixed with grain for this purpose and thus beers were introduced. Beers and wines inhibit alcohol formation at 6 to 11% alcohol concentration, so this is the maximum concentration that can be obtained by fermentation. Alcoholic beverages can be made from any starch- or sugar-containing material by these processes. In early civilizations these beers provided essential nutrients, because the yeast was consumed with the beverage, and with it essential nutrients.

The ability to concentrate alcoholic beverages was first discovered in northern climates subject to freezing. A cider fermented to 10% alcohol content freezes by initially forming pure water crystals, raising the alcohol content of the unfrozen beverage by about twofold. This process is still employed in Canada and Northern Europe to produce "hard cider". Although distillation was introduced by the Arabs in the fourth century, it was not widely utilized to produce concentrated alcohol until the seventeenth century in Holland, when gin was invented and widely distributed. Distillation can readily concentrate ethanol to 95% pure. Distillation is carried out on naturally fermented material. The product is commonly named after the starting material. Thus bourbon is distilled from corn, rye from rye, scotch from barley, brandy from grapes, schnapps and gin from potatoes, and so on. Alcoholic beverages are always controlled as to alcohol content, and this is indicated as either the percentage ethanol based on volume or the proof value, which is twice the percentage. Some beverages, such as beers and table wines, are sold as fermented; some, such as dessert wines (port, muscatel), have extra pure alcohol added; and some, such as gin, vodka, and whisky, are distilled.

Alcohol is always taken orally, for no other route will provide the multigram quantities required. To produce even a mild glow, 10 to 30 g are required by a normal-sized person — the highest gram or molar dose of any addicting substance. Alcoholic beverages are used both ritualistically and socially. The usual portion of alcohol, regardless of the beverage, is about 10 to 20 g/portion, usually referred to as a "drink". An estimation of the daily consumption of alcohol is presented in the next chapter.

III. ABSORPTION AND METABOLISM OF ALCOHOL

A. ABSORPTION

Alcohol is absorbed slowly from the stomach, but extremely rapidly from the small intestine. Ingestion with food, particularly fatty or hypertonic foods, retards gastric emptying and slows absorption. After gastric surgery with gastroenterostomy, absorption is fast, comparable to direct duodenal instillation. Some 50% of a dose of intraduodenally administered alcohol is absorbed in 3 min. In contrast, 50% of an oral dose taken with a meal requires 30 to 60 min for absorption. There is a large first-pass effect of alcohol that is approximately 25% of the initial drink, but less as the liver enzymes become saturated. Alcohol is rapidly distributed in the total body water and also dissolves in bilipid membranes such that its volume of distribution is slightly greater than the body water content. Absorption is always complete.

B. EXCRETION AND METABOLISM

Alcohol is excreted in the breath in an exact relationship to the blood alcohol concentration and passes freely into the urine by glomerular filtration. Both routes together account for less than 8% of removal. The remainder is metabolized by the liver, with the first step, the conversion of ethanol to acetaldehyde, being the rate-limiting step. A liver cytosolic enzyme, alcohol dehydrogenase, an NAD-requiring enzyme, is the usual catalyst for this first step. When liver alcohol dehydrogenase is saturated, an additional microsomal enzyme (microsomal ethanol oxidizing system, MEOS) is induced which in alcoholics may metabolize as much as 50% of the ethanol.[2] Liver acetaldehyde dehydrogenase rapidly removes the acetaldehyde from the same liver cell in which it was formed, converting it to activated acetate, which enters the bloodstream and is used throughout the body as part of acetate metabolism. Acetaldehyde levels in the blood are undetectable in normal subjects, but increase in tolerant alcoholics, increase even more markedly in cirrhotics, and reach toxic levels in patients who drink while taking the enzyme inhibitor disulfiram.

Normal persons metabolize alcohol at a constant rate of about 20 g/h when the blood level is above 100 mg/dl. At lower levels the half disappearance time is 3 h. Most tolerant alcoholics increase the maximal rate of alcohol metabolism. The half disappearance time is under 2 h. Although very severe liver disease may retard the rate of alcohol removal from the body, nothing substantially accelerates its removal. Providing fructose increases the removal rate only about 5%, an effect that is not of value.

C. TOXICITY AND DRUNKENNESS

Ethanol is analogous to anesthetic agents in its suppression of various centers in the central nervous system. At low levels (0 to 200 mg/dl), progressive suppression of conscious centers occurs. At 200 to 400 mg/dl, unconsciousness occurs; and at 600 to 800 mg/dl, respiratory suppression and death intervene. Tolerance is both metabolic and neurological. Metabolic tolerance results from increased rate of liver metabolism of ethanol. Neurological tolerance indicates less impairment with the identical blood level of ethanol than would occur in an alcohol-naive or -intolerant person. Tolerant persons have a much higher fatal dose. As in anesthetized persons, if respiration and gas exchange are maintained, the person ingesting a fatal dose will recover. In such persons, alternative agents (such as methanol, and its accompanying acidosis) and head trauma must also be considered.

Drunkenness (synonymous with intoxication) is a clearly altered mental and physical state featuring muddled thinking and motor incoordination relating closely to the blood levels of ethanol. In a given person the pattern is stereotyped, but it varies widely in manifestations from person to person. Most states in America now accept a blood level of ethanol greater than 100 mg/dl as legal evidence of sufficient impairment to impair driving, but this level will not produce observable drunkenness. Twice this level is associated with an altered personality pattern, with garrulousness, talkativeness, or extreme taciturnity common. The subject seems warm relative to others in the area, and is awkward in fine movements of the hand such as writing a check, working a puzzle, or placing a key in a lock. There may be difficulty in "walking a straight line". At 300 mg/dl all persons have major alteration of behavior, many are sleeping, and many may be difficult to arouse though the vital signs are within normal limits. The degree of apparent intoxication is a function of both alcohol level and expectation. Submariners seeking release of intoxication after long underseas voyages were observed intoxicated after one or two portions of beer. Completely incoherent drunks have been sobered nearly instantly by a major fright. Ordinarily, blood levels of up to 100 mg/dl interfere with tensions and lead to a mild "high" to which many people drink. A 70-kg person requires four or five drinks to reach this level. Many perceptions of feeling good occur at much lower blood levels. At 100 to 150 mg/dl reaction time is appreciably impaired, and motor clumsiness ensues in many. The voice is inappropriately modulated,[3] and there is a clear perception of more warmth than others feel. At higher levels consciousness is progressively dulled, and then sleep occurs. Motor coordination is increasingly impaired; speech is slurred.

No drug increases the rate of metabolism of a given load of alcohol, but stimulants of pain (slapping face, ice to face), or caffeine assist in sobering up the person. The time-honored manner of attaining sobering is to allow the alcohol to burn off. In alcoholics the blood level may fall by 50% in 90 min, in others it may require 180 min to fall this much fall, but this will make a striking difference in the level of intoxication.

Alcohol poisoning is almost never seen in alcoholics because they know well the effects of a given quantity of ethanol. On the other hand, adolescents who think it smart to drink heavily may consume a 240-ml water glass filled with whisky, gin, or vodka. This amount can prove fatal by respiratory suppression. As in any depressant overdose, discussed in detail in Chapter 10, the history aids in recognition but the absent spontaneous respirations indicate the need for ventilation. With ventilatory support the effect will wear off in a few hours.

D. "HANGOVER" AND WITHDRAWAL AFTER HEAVY BUT NONADDICTED DRINKING

A person who is not tolerant will experience a most unpleasant syndrome during the interval 12 to 24 h after heavy drinking (5 to 15 portions of alcohol) ceases. At the peak blood levels there is a desire to sleep, but this is not restful for REM phase is suppressed in intoxication. When the person awakens he or she feels weak, fatigued, and is unable to concentrate on mental activities. There is invariably a diminished desire for food, an uneasiness, mild to marked headache, photophobia, an aversion to loud noise, and a slowness of thought and motion. This is self-limited and probably relates to mild brain edema and dilated central blood vessels. No single drug, including alcohol, completely reverses the unpleasant feelings, but nonsteroidal anti-inflammatory drugs (NSAIDs) are usually employed. The problem disappears in a day.

Tolerant individuals usually do not experience severe hangover but develop withdrawal symptoms and signs. As the blood level of alcohol falls under half the usual level, an internal uneasiness and consciousness of abdominal and heart sensations is present. A mild anxiety and limited ability to concentrate or complete a physical task develops. Tremor may be observed. There is a marked internal uneasiness, and the physical actions of the person become purposeless. Most chronic users recognize these signals as the need for an additional drink and remove the symptoms promptly by this means. Withdrawal is discussed more fully in Chapter 27.

IV. SEDATIVES

A. BARBITURATES

Barbiturates are widely abused as street drugs. Members of this group appear in FDA Schedules II, III, and IV, indicating their differing potential for abuse. Short-acting agents are used mostly as sedatives or hypnotics, and it is these agents that are commonly abused on the street. The major effect of barbiturates is depression of the sensory cortex, acting predominantly at the level of the thalamus. A separate effect is in anticonvulsant activity. All barbiturates are respiratory depressants in a dose-dependent fashion, and all alter the REM phase of sleep. Table 31 provides names and some data on commmonly used barbiturates. In this table we have divided them into long- and short-acting agents.

Secobarbital has the most rapid rate of onset of action either orally or intravenous, and phenobarbital one of the slowest, reflecting the high solubility of secobarbital in lipid membranes versus the low solubility of phenobarbital. The correlation of clinical findings with blood levels after toxic or stable dosing is useful. Table 32 provides the therapeutic range and the toxic range that often produces death by overdose.

TABLE 31
Some Properties of Barbiturates

Name/Brand	Half-life (h)	Duration (h)	Protein (percent bound)	First-pass (percent removed)	Excretion route[b]
			Short-Acting Agents		
Secobarbital Seconal (II)	15—40	3—4	50—70	25—50	L, K
Pentobarbital Nembutal (II)	15—50	3—4	70	15—25	L
			Intermediate-Acting Agents		
Amobarbital Amytal (II)	16—40	6—8	60	15—20	L
Aprobarbital Alurate (III)	15—40	6—8	40	15	L, K
Butabarbital Butisol (III)	50—140	6—8	25	25	L
			Long-Acting Agents		
Phenobarbital Luminal (IV)	53—118	10—20	20—45	15—20	L, K
Metharbital Gemonil (III)	50—70	10—12	60	20	L, K

[a] Controlled substances Schedule.
[b] L, liver excretion predominantly; K, kidney excretion prominent.

TABLE 32
Therapeutic and Sometimes Fatal Blood Concentrations of Barbiturates

Drug	Therapeutic range (μg/ml)	Fatal range (μg/ml)
Secobarbital	0.5—5	15—25
Pentobarbital	0.5—3	12—25
Amobarbital	2—10	30—60
Butabarbital	3—25	50—80
Phenobarbital	5—40	20—120

1. Toxic Reaction

Central nervous system depression and respiratory suppression are marked. There may be Cheyne-Stokes respiration, areflexia, pupillary constriction, lowered body temperature, and even a flat EEG. Treatment is respiratory support and, if necessary, cardiovascular support. In known-agent suicide attempts, removal of unabsorbed material by gavage or retarding absorption with charcoal is performed, but the results are of limited benefit. Usually, awaiting the metabolic removal of the agent while supporting the respirations is adequate treatment. A chronic toxicity is observed in abusers in which the predominant manifestations are irritability, trouble sleeping, and confusion.

2. Use by Addicts

A rapid high is desirable. Intravenous use of phentobarbital or secobarbital produces a high of short duration within 2 to 30 min. The sodium salts of the drugs are best absorbed

TABLE 33
Properties of Benzodiazopine Drugs

Name and trade name	Use[a]	Half life (h)
Agents with Sedative Metabolic Products		
Diazepam (Valium®)	Convulsions	20—70
Flurazepam (Dalmane®)		2.3
Chlordiazepoxide (Librium®)		5—30
Chlorazepate (Tranxene®)	Convulsions	50—100
Agents with Inactive Products		
Alprazolam (Xanax®)		12—15
Clonazepam (Clonopin®)	Convulsions	20—44
Lorazepam (Ativan®)	Convulsions	10—20
Oxazepam (Serax®)		5—15
Temazepam (Restoril®)		9—12
Triazolam (Halcion®)		1—3

All are sedative, hypnotic, and anti-anxiety agents.

on an empty stomach, but the first-pass effect for all is substantial. The degradation rate varies widely among normal humans as a genetically determined trait. There is a rapid onset of tolerance when high doses are used by any route, but the tolerance is more psychic and metabolic than some of the neurological effects. The chronic user, to obtain a high often becomes ataxic, dysarthric, and retarded in thought and movements. Withdrawal in chronic users occurs when the customary blood level falls to under half and is discussed in Chapter 27.

The short-acting agents are most desirable for abuse.

B. BENZODIAZEPINES

The benzodiazepines have a wide variety of differing properties and half lives, but share in common extraordinary safety and a marked sedative anxiolytic property. In ordinary therapeutic usage the addiction potential is low, and accordingly they are rated Schedule IV,[4] but in previously addicted patients this is a problem and there is some street drug trade in these agents.[5,6] The greatest abuse arises from doctors continuing prescriptions for patients initially requiring these drugs, but continuing them far beyond clear need.

These agents are not all interchangeable, differing from one another in their pathways of metabolism, their duration of action, and their ability to be absorbed by the intramuscular route. All of these agents are readily and completely absorbed orally, all are metabolized by the liver, many to an active agent, all are tightly bound to protein, and none is removed by dialysis. The longest-acting agent, diazepam (Valium®) has an age-dependent half life from 20 h at age 20 to approximately 70 h at age 70, with the more prolonged action coming from its active metabolic products. Other long-acting agents, with less effect of increased half life in older persons, include chlordiazepoxide (Librium®) and flurazepam (Dalmane®). Short-acting agents include lorazepam (Ativan®), triazolam (Halcion®), temazepam (Restoril®), oxazepam (Serax®), and alprazolam (Xanax®). Table 33 lists the most common drugs in this group and some of their frequent uses.

1. Use by Abusers

The relaxation and anxiolytic effects seem the predominant desirable effects. These agents are seldom abused alone as street drugs. They are not frequently chosen by street abusers because there is only a moderate high. Among physicians' patients these agents are abused in order to sleep, relax, escape, or diminish anxiety. It is common for them to be abused together with alcohol.

2. Toxic Reaction

Respiratory depression is very rare, and may not occur unless there is underlying disease. CNS suppression with confusion, drowsiness, dysarthria, and staggering gait are usual. There may be bradycardia and weakness to the point of being unable to walk. The agents are not dialyzable, so awaiting removal by metabolic action is the usual treatment.

3. Withdrawal

In consultative internal medicine work I have encountered more than a dozen patients who were addicted to doctor-prescribed benzodiazepines; usually diazepam was at least one of the agents. The patients were all middle-aged women with empty-nest syndrome, recent widowhood, or an unexpected divorce. They were consulting many capable physicians and had fine evaluations that found no organic disease, yet they had many complaints with insomnia, anxiety, inability to relax, extra worry, and somatization of complaints. Each of at least two and as many as four physicians prescribed benzodiazepine drugs, usually without a clear history that the patient was already taking them. In half the instances there was clear patient manipulation to increase the availability of the drugs, but in others there did not seem to be. The process developed over an average time of 22 months.

Withdrawal on an outpatient basis was possible in only one patient; the others were hospitalized and given decreasing doses of diazepam to complete withdrawal. Eight of the patients were judged to have depression with two of them bipolar, and all responded quite well to tricyclic antidepressants. Relapse was observed in one of the patients. The withdrawal may be prolonged over two weeks, when the addicting agent had active metabolic products, and patients may need to be treated for this period of time.

All doctors treating these patients were notified of the problem by mail with the patients' permission. The withdrawal period was more psychic than physiological trauma. When benzodiazepine addiction is encountered as part of multiple drug use, it is probably the least important. A review of 293 patients treated at the Mayo Clinic drug unit for benzodiazepine withdrawal indicated that only 39 of them had no other problem. It was correctly pointed out that in their patients and ones such as ours, withdrawal symptoms and anxiety are interpreted as a recurrence of the original symptoms and may pose special problems.[7]

C. OTHER SEDATIVE DRUGS

1. Methaqualone

No longer available as a prescription drug due to its demonstrated cardiovascular and respiratory depression effects, methaqualone is favored as a street drug because of its very rapid absorption from the GI tract and its very prompt high.

2. Glutethimide

Glutethimide is a Schedule III drug with cross-tolerance for this group of agents. It is erratic in absorption, with some people absorbing only half the drug, others hydrolyzing the biliary excreted conjugate once it reaches the gut and reabsorbing it. Its half life is 10 to 12 h with much variation. The lengthy duration leads to increased toxicity. The drug is highly dialyzable in overdose, which is an effective means for removal. For reasons unclear to this author, glutethimide is the most abused of the sedative drugs now that methaqualone is no longer readily available.[8]

3. Chloral Hydrate

Chloral hydrate is a Schedule IV substance that is well absorbed and mimics ethanol in its metabolism, except that it is 70% bound to protein. It has a prompt onset of action and a half life of 7 to 10 h. It is metabolized by the liver to trichloroethanol, which is further metabolized to inactive products excreted by the liver and kidney. Tolerance develops after daily use in 10 days. In overdose there is extreme obtundity, seizures, and suppression of brainstem function, with swallowing impairment, irregular heart beat, troubled breathing, and hypothermia common. In toxicity, peritoneal and hemodialysis have been carried out with good results. There is a withdrawal analogous to alcohol.

4. Ethchlorvynol

Ethchlorvynol (Placidyl®), is a Schedule IV controlled substance. It is rapidly absorbed, mildly bound to protein (30 to 50%), metabolized by the liver to a product excreted by the kidney, and has a half life of 10 to 20 h, but its duration of action is about 5 h. Overdose is similar to chloral hydrate. It is not very dialyzable.

5. Meprobamate

Meprobamate, a Schedule IV substance, has many trade names. It has a half life of about 10 h. It is an infrequently abused substance. Overdose is similar to other sedatives. Since portions are excreted unchanged in the urine, overdose is treated with mannitol diuresis.

D. SPECIAL PROBLEMS IN SUBSTANCE ABUSE WITH SEDATIVES

Nearly all sedatives used come from FDA-approved manufacturers, in which supplies for legitimate channels have been diverted to illicit use or prescriptions have been provided. The material is therefore free of adulterants, and the doses are known to the user. The two problems that one can encounter is the very long duration of action of these drugs, causing a withdrawal syndrome to occur over 2 weeks or more for the long-acting drugs such as phenobarbital, glutethimide, and diazepam. The other problem is management of deliberate overdose taken in a suicide attempt. Accidental overdose is nearly unheard of with these agents, but deliberate suicide is increased among addicts.

In suicide overdose, most common with the barbiturates but well known with glutethimide, the central nervous system obtundity is overwhelming. The brainstem is depressed, with irregular breathing and heart rate, and erratic temperature control. Hospitalization of such patients is essential. Barbiturates not tightly bound to protein are dialyzable, as is glutethimide, but the most important therapy is to maintain the vital functions until the dose is metabolized by the liver.

REFERENCES

1. Eliminating script scams, not drugs should be goal, *Medical World News*, American Medical Association, January 1989.
2. **Lieber, C. S.,** Biochemical and molecular basis of alcohol-induced injury to liver and other tissues, *New Engl. J. Med.*, 319, 1639, 1988.
3. **Pisoni, D. B. and Martin, C. S.,** Effects of alcohol on the acoustic-phonetic properties of speech: perceptual and acoustic analysis, *Alcoholism*, 13, 577, 1989.
4. **Woods, J. H., Katz, J. L., and Winger, G.,** Use and abuse of benzodiazepines, *JAMA*, 260, 376, 1988.
5. **Juergens, S. and Morse, R.,** Alprazolam dependence in seven patients, *Am. J. Psychiatr.*, 145, 625, 1988.
6. **Petursson, H. and Lader, M.,** Benzodiazepine dependence, *Br. J. Addict.*, 76, 133, 1981.
7. **Lin, S. C., Morse, R. M., Finlayson, R. E., and Palmen, M. A.,** Abuse of benzodiazepines, *J. Am. Med. Assoc.*, 261, 2956, 1989.
8. **Kales, A., Bixler, E. O., Tan, T. L., Sharf, M. B., and Kales, J. D.,** Chronic hypnotic-drug use: ineffectiveness, drug-withdrawal, insomnia and dependence, *JAMA*, 227, 513, 1974.

Chapter 17

Medical Problems in Alcoholics

I. INTRODUCTION

Medical problems in alcoholic subjects increase with quantity and duration of alcohol consumption and often increase with age of the user. Health problems do not appear when consumption is less than 50 g/day (four or five drinks) and are commonly seen only when alcohol consumption reaches more than 20% of total calorie consumption (about ten drinks daily). With a few exceptions there is no relationship to the specific beverage selected. Alcoholism-related diseases are caused by malnutrition (neuritis) and/or by alcohol toxicity (fatty liver). However, in most patients this differentiation loses meaning, for as alcohol intake surpasses 30 to 50% of caloric intake, both excess alcohol and malnutrition of protein, vitamins, and minerals are present.[1]

Every physician should learn to estimate the total alcohol intake of a patient undergoing evaluation. Alcohol is commonly consumed as beer (360-ml portions, 9 to 15 g alcohol), wines (120-ml portions, 10 g alcohol, fortified wines (60-ml portions, 10 g alcohol), or mixed drinks containing distilled spirits (60- to 400-ml portions containing 15 to 25 g/portion). It is reasonable to generalize that each portion of beverage alcohol (a bottle or can of beer, a glass of wine, or a cocktail) has about 15 g of alcohol and utilize this figure in estimating alcohol intake for a week or a month. Table 34 illustrates how this is done. For each patient weekly or monthly intake should be estimated and presented as grams consumed per day.

Normal drinking behavior rarely exceeds 50 g/day as an average alcohol intake; this is at least 350 kcal of energy and represents one sixth of the requirements of sedentary subjects.

TABLE 34
Estimation of Daily Alcohol Intake Based on 1 Week's Drinking

No. of beers consumed weekly	________	
No. of 4 oz. glasses of wine	________	
No. of cocktails	________	
No. of 1 oz. straight drinks	________	
Total	________	× 2
Equal grams alcohol used/day[a]	________	

[a] $\text{Total drinks} \times \frac{14\ \text{g/drink}}{7\ \text{days}}$

Above this level medical disease begins to appear. Alcoholism and its associated malnutrition produces a continuum of injuries from minimally recognized biochemical aberration of cells to clear cellular injury, cellular death, tissue injury and tissue death. Some injuries incite a striking inflammatory response (liver, stomach), whereas others are only cell loss (small intestine, central nervous system, muscle). The late stages, with cell death (and possibly inflammatory response), are clearly recognized as disease, but the earlier stages that produce only biochemical changes or mild malfunction are usually not recognized as disease because of their marked reversibility and minimal symptoms and signs. The medical challenge is to recognize the injury at a fully reversible stage and utilize the damage to motivate the patient to sobriety.

The cartoon in Figure 8 illustrates the major organs damaged in the alcoholic. Alcoholism is most frequently associated with damage to the central and peripheral nervous systems, the gastrointestinal tract including liver and pancreas, muscle, and the gonads.

In addition, recent alcohol use produces a variety of metabolic changes that are important for doctors to understand and occasionally are the basis for recognition of the drinking problem. Changes due to a metabolic or physiological adjustment to alcohol disappear within a week of abstinence; other reversible lesions require up to three months. To provide perspective, Figure 9 provides information on a large number of admissions to an alcohol detoxification unit. Abnormalities are listed as the fraction of the patients with that problem. Approximately half of all patients suffered withdrawal, some degree of liver disease, and some degree of CNS disease. Significant trauma, recent convulsions, use of other drugs, or severe malnutrition were present in about 10% of the patients.

II. NONSPECIFIC CONDITIONS MORE COMMON IN ALCOHOLICS[2]

A. TRAUMA

Trauma of all sorts is more common in alcoholics. Head injury occurs during intoxication and may not be recalled. Suicide is more common in alcoholics; occasionally a medical condition is the result of an unrevealed, unsuccessful suicide attempt. Trauma was found in 8% of the population in Figure 9.

B. ABUSE OF OTHER SUBSTANCES

Use of cigarettes, excessive dependence on caffeine, and a ready tendency to abuse over-the-counter, doctor-prescribed, or street drugs is characteristic of alcoholics. In the sample of male patients in Figure 9, 98% used cigarettes and 12% tested positive for a nonprescribed or illicit drug.

C. METABOLIC CHANGES

Metabolic changes are prominent in alcoholics.[3] Hypercholesterolemia, hyperlipidemia.

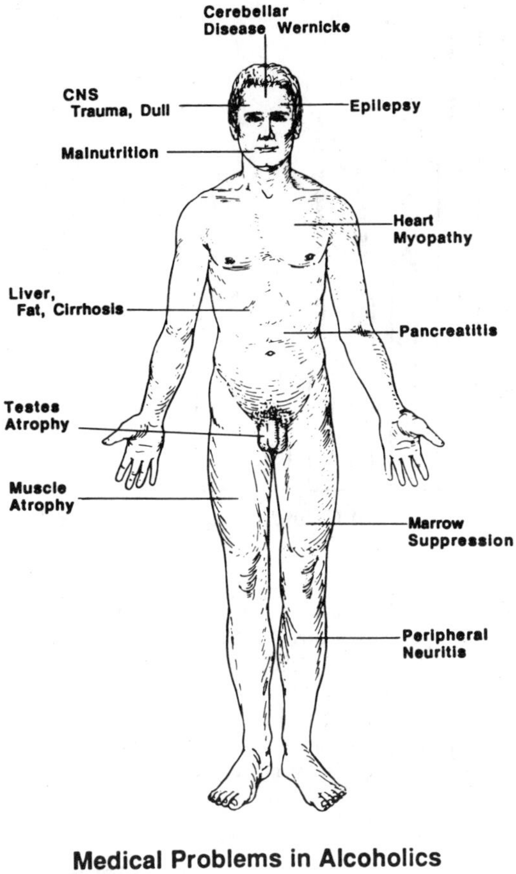

FIGURE 8. Cartoon of the many systems of the body injured in chronic alcoholism. This may be contrasted with Figure 11 (Chapter 20).

and hyperuricemia are frequent. There is a mild lactic acidosis more important in loss of potassium, magnesium, and calcium in the urine than in alteration of blood pH. Hypoglycemia may be a problem in prolonged fasting of at least 16 h duration, but in patients with access to food is extremely rare. Many drinkers when returned to normal diet have prominent hyperglycemia which will not persist after one week. Depletions of phosphorous, potassium, zinc, and magnesium may produce biochemical and clinical manifestations.[1,4]

D. FLUID AND ELECTROLYTE CHANGES

The chronic alcoholic may lose the diuretic response to alcohol due to inhibition of antidiuretic hormone. Dogs chronically exposed to alcohol become overloaded with salt and electrolyte,[5] but rats do not change in their ability to handle salt and water loads.[6] Human data is more like that of the dog, with overhydration during chronic drinking and diuresis during detoxification. Without gastrointestinal changes, chronic alcoholism is associated with an increased retention of sodium and potassium. However, diarrhea and vomitting are common, as are potassium, magnesium, and zinc depletions, and occasionally hypovolemia due to salt and water losses are observed. These factors combined with erratic food ingestion may be associated with depletions of selenium, phosphorus, or manganese. Chronic alcohol ingestion is usually wasteful of magnesium, zinc, and potassium in the urine. The wide range of observations in the literature is reviewed.[7]

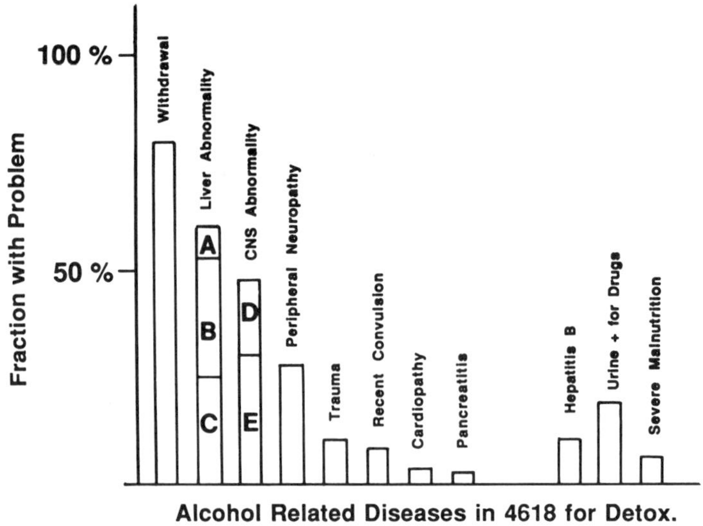

FIGURE 9. The prevalence of alcohol associated problems in 4618 patients treated in detoxification. The fractions of the patients manifesting the problem are displayed. Under liver abnormality, A is fatty liver, B is nonspecific hepatic abnormality, and C is cirrhosis. Under CNS, D is permanent impairment including CT scan atrophy, Wernicke, or cerebellar atrophy. E. is reversible memory loss. The fractions observed to have a positive serum test for Hepatitis B, a positive urine test for illicit drugs, or malnutrition sufficient to have one test $> 20\%$ below standards on anthropometric assessment are indicated.

E. INFECTIOUS DISEASES

Infectious diseases are more prevalent in alcoholics. Resistance to bacterial infection is lowered, with the appearance of many organisms thought to be of low virulence as infections, sometimes in unusual locations. In this way severe alcoholics are similar to other immune-suppressed patients. The detection of occult infection is one of the major challenges in screening these patients. A recent study found HIV-1 test positivity in 4.5% of inner-city alcoholics in Newark.[8]

F. IMMUNE SYSTEM CYRO CHANGES

The immune system is altered in major ways in alcoholics.[9] The deficiencies are mostly in cellular immunity but are even more marked when there is major organ damage such as cirrhosis or pancreatitis. They may mediate the slightly increased risk of cancer found in alcoholism.[10] This is believed to promote an increased occurrence of HIV-1 infection.[11]

III. CENTRAL NERVOUS SYSTEM CHANGES[12]

Mild but measurable, usually reversible, damage to the central nervous system (CNS) is quite common in alcoholics. It is common knowledge that heavy drinkers are a little "dull" for a few weeks after cessation of drinking, reflecting this global impairment. A great number of psychological tests have been used on this group of patients to demonstrate these abnormalities. Thus tests of spacial orientation, particularly those combining visual judgments, are markedly impaired in alcoholics, but other functions of the right hemisphere may be preserved.[13] A recent review indicates that brain damage is quite common in alcoholics; this is usually very mild, mostly reversible, and of no consequence at the time of evaluation or for prognosis, but of great value in motivating patients to treatment. There is also some epidemiological data that alcohol predisposes to subsequent cerebrovascular disease.[14,15]

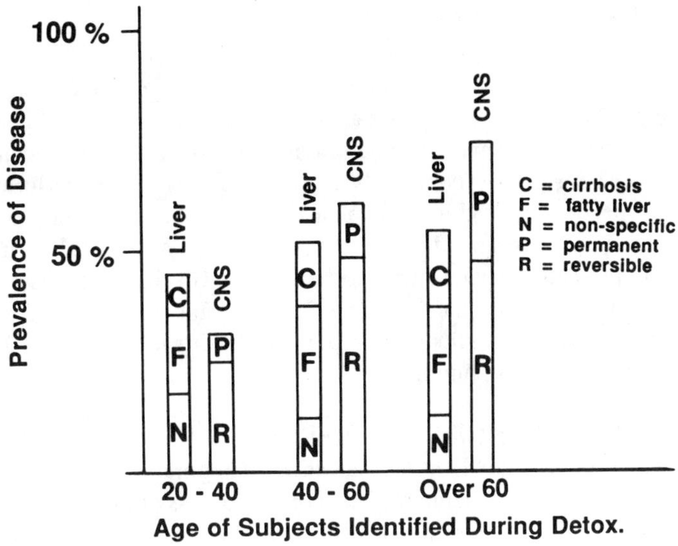

FIGURE 10. Change in prevalence of diseases of the liver and central nervous system (CNS) with aging in patients presenting for alcoholism detoxification. The sample is 194 patients aged 21 to 40 years, 668 patients aged 41 to 60 years, and 407 patients over 61 years of age. Note that liver disease increases with age, but the change is not significant. Both permanent and reversible CNS disease increase with the difference significant for each age group for permanent injury but significant only between the youngest group and each of the older groups for reversible disease.

Figure 10 illustrates data on the prevalence of central nervous system disease at various ages in comparison with liver disease to make the important point that older persons have more CNS disease. In this figure, permanent CNS disease included Wernicke-Korsakoff psychosis, cerebellar degeneration, and cerebral atrophy found on CT scanning. The most prevalent CNS lesion after withdrawal is complete is a defect in short-term memory, which disappears after 3 to 12 weeks of abstinence.

The increase in prevalence of CNS disease in this sample is significant in both reversible and permanent disease with increasing age. By comparable detection means, the prevalence of liver disease was higher than CNS diseases in younger persons but lower in the older group, though both increased.

A. EARLY CNS CHANGES

Loss of acute memory, deterioration in reasoning determined by psychological testing, and impairment in complex mental manipulations such as serial subtractions of 7's from 100, making change, or spelling common words in a reverse direction, is regularly demonstrated in alcoholics who drink 100 g/day for years. This "muddled mental state" is promptly recognized as not being normal, but quantitating its deviation is not readily done in most examinations. The orientation, verbal skills, and detailed cranial, motor, and sensory neurological examination are intact. The CT scan does not show loss of cortical matter. This assumes clinical importance in the elderly, who seem to be more susceptible to this change and may manifest severe forgetfulness that is clinically similar to multiple strokes or Alzheimer's disease. An occasional person under 50 years will be found to have deteriorated mentally to the level of inability to provide the level of leadership, thought, or decision-making activity of a few years previously. Depression, both clinically detected and present on overt psychological testing, is frequent in the early weeks after alcohol cessation.

B. MILDLY SEVERE CNS CHANGES

The most common condition is loss of cortical substance on CT scan, manifest by deterioration of mental function in specifically tested thought processes and memory (psychological testing) but rarely affecting verbal skills. The earliest losses of cortical tissue on CT scan require special measurements for detection. These patients may be evaluated because of inappropriate behavior in their home or business or very erratic job performance. Rarely, a withdrawal convulsion may lead to the evaluation. Cerebellar ataxia may be suspected by a complaint of new clumsiness and identified on examination. Most often the truncal muscles are involved and are readily demonstrated to be abnormal if the patient is asked to walk a tight circle of less than 2 ft in diameter. This is a frequent finding in patients whose job performance has deteriorated, particularly in physical labor such as construction, and evaluation is needed to plan for the future.

C. ADVANCED CNS CHANGES AND DISEASE

Wernicke-Korsakoff disease is a very advanced deterioration seen most commonly in alcoholics. There is usually a global loss of memory, with loss of most recent memory being prominent. There are often eye signs, with nystagmus and bilateral sixth-nerve palsies. Although cerebellar ataxia and peripheral neuritis are often present in the same person, they are not a necessary part of the syndrome. The sixth-nerve palsies respond promptly to thiamin injections, but the other manifestations may not respond or may respond only over one or two months. Although nearly all patients with Wernicke-Korsakoff syndrome have thiamin deficiency and this can be demonstrated by a decreased red cell transketolase level, in practice parenteral thiamin is administered to all who possibly have this problem to prevent progression.

Marked cortical atrophy on CT scanning with clinical impairment of memory is almost always irreversible, at least to the level of becoming normal.

D. EARLY RECOGNITION

The clinical suspicion of CNS disease arises during the taking of history and conduct of the physical examination. The history provided by family or work associates may be the first substantial suggestion of a problem. Cerebellar aberrations are recognized most sensitively from physical examination. Mental aberrations or depression may require psychological tests to establish the abnormality and to quantitate their level as the patient enters treatment. CT scans of the head are useful, particularly in early confirmation of the diagnosis of alcoholism injury to the cortex, but special techniques are needed to quantitate the size of the ventricles and the thickness of the sulci.

Patients with a clear problem should have a CT scan of the head, a neurological evaluation, and a careful functional assessment to determine improvement; this often requires psychological consultation. The prognosis for the mental function and depression changes is excellent; some amount of reversibility is always found, which rapidly improves for the first 60 days of abstinence. Mild degrees of cerebral atrophy may reverse on CT scan, but severe changes remain. Cerebellar injury is nearly always permanent in its clinical manifestations.

E. TREATMENT

All alcoholics with even the suspicion of CNS damage should receive parenteral thiamin of at least 100 mg and oral supplements of other B vitamins. Subsequent treatment is the restoration and maintenance of adequate nutrition, and the avoidance of alcohol. There are no other treatments. The rate of improvement of sixth-nerve ophthalmoplegia is rapid and typically complete in 2 days. The return of short-term memory is often complete in as little as 2 weeks. Other aspects of Wernicke-Korsakoff disease are less predictable in their re-

TABLE 35
Common Stages of Liver Disease in Alcoholics

Stage	Feature	Importance
Nonspecific liver damage	Liver tests normal in 10 days, AST < 3 × N, bil. < 3 mg/dl	Always disappears
Fatty liver	Hepatomegaly, liver tests as above	Precursor of severe stages, reversible
Alcoholic hepatitis	Systemic Sx, AST > ALT, PT & bil. predict survival	Cirrhosis precursor in 70+%, <30% heal
Cirrhosis	Portal hypertension, continuing hepatocyte failure, coma, ascites	Shortens life

covery. Evaluation after 3 months of abstinence indicates the degree of permanent damage. A recent evaluation of alcoholics 5 years after initial detection of brain injury by CT scan in 72% or by psychological testing in 49% showed continued improvement. All who ceased drinking for the 5 years showed improvement in the CT scan with partial reversal of the signs of cortical atrophy, and all showed improvement in one or more of the quantitative tests of central nervous system function.[16] A recent longitudinal evaluation on brain atrophy and performance found improvement over several years in both functions.

IV. PERIPHERAL NEUROPATHY

Symmetrical damage to the longer sensory tracts originating in the spinal cord is characteristic of the poorly nourished alcoholic and may be identified in as many as 40% of all alcoholics by nerve-conduction studies. Sensory loss such as light touch, two-point discrimination present symmetrically over the feet or hands or moving even higher is common. It is usually not recognized by the patient or may be associated with pain, particularly when walking. After vitamin repletion the pain will usually stop within 1 week, but the sensation may require a year or more to return to normal.

Motor damage, when asymmetrical, is usually traumatic and will improve depending upon the duration and site of the paralysis. Symmetrical motor damage has a remarkable tenacity and usually does not improve.

V. LIVER DAMAGE

Table 35 indicates four common stages of liver "disease" encountered in alcoholics.

A. NONSPECIFIC LIVER CELL INJURY

Nonspecific liver cell injury is the most common type of injury and is related to alcohol intake, not malnutrition. It is manifest clinically by mild hepatomegaly with or without tenderness and minimal abnormalities of the liver tests. The ALT and AST are rarely as high as three times normal, the bilirubin is < 3 mg/dl (50 μm/L), and the prothrombin time is usually normal. The GGPT is nearly always elevated, and the alkaline phosphatase may be any value. All of the chemical abnormalities will disappear by the eighth day of abstinence. This injury occurs in about 25% of all heavy drinkers (> 50 g/day) and may occur in a single weekend binge of drinking. It has no long-term prognostic significance and has no relationship to the subsequent development of cirrhosis. I envision this as patchy liver cell damage and death but only focal, never sufficient to produce submassive collapse essential to the formation of alcoholic hepatitis.

B. FATTY LIVER

Fatty liver is manifest by hepatomegaly, which is most often tender and may produce the largest livers clinically encountered. There may or may not be liver test abnormalities of the magnitude noted in Section V.A. The larger livers may be associated with splenomegaly and minimal-sized esophageal varices. This lesion also seems to be associated with alcohol consumption and does not require malnutrition for its production. If imaging is performed, the fatty liver has many internal echoes on sonography, irregular uptake on scintography, and may have nodularity on CT scan, but these methods are not required for diagnosis. The liver biopsy is diagnostic. In this diagnosis the liver tests are never severely abnormal, the bilirubin is less than 50 μm/L (3 mg/dl), the ALT and AST are only elevated up to three times normal, and the alkaline phosphatase may be elevated up to five times normal. With abstinence this disease resolves over several months and of itself is not permanent. This lesion occurs in 80 to 90% of drinkers in the 100-g/day range and is often present with other lesions. It is more likely to be present in diabetics or in the obese.

C. ALCOHOLIC HEPATITIS

Alcoholic hepatitis is an important precursor of cirrhosis and a useful concept in the spectrum of alcoholic liver disease. The injury is sufficiently severe to produce wide destruction of the liver (submassive collapse), and almost half the patients diagnosed already have findings of cirrhosis. Substantial malnutrition and alcoholism are both required to produce this lesion. There is a strong suggestion of a genetic factor, for once a person has alcoholic hepatitis there is a major likelihood that it will recur if the patient returns to drinking. There are several different histological lesions associated with alcoholic hepatitis, and their prevalence determines the predominant clinical course. The lesion leading to cirrhosis is a destruction of the central veins at the level of the lobule, or in the next two orders of larger veins. Surviving lobules show partial closure of the central veins, whereas complete blockage results in healing with a scar. Because of the focal nature of this lesion, it is seldom seen on liver biopsy.

The most common lesion on biopsy specimens is focal necrosis with polymorphonuclear cell infiltration. This is associated with ballooning and death of cells, and Mallory bodies, a peculiar eosinophilic clumping of intercellular cytoskeleton. Most active drinkers also have some degree of fat. These lesions disappear completely, leaving little or no evidence of their presence, whereas the lesions that interfere with venous drainage produce scars.

The majority of patients observed with this condition already have reached the stage of cirrhosis but have new reversible damage on top of established cirrhosis. As many as one third are completely reversible. There are prominent manifestations of liver injury, with hepatomegaly, liver tenderness, and signs of inflammation, with mild leukocytosis and anemia being common. Jaundice occurs in two thirds of the patients, and about half have manifestations of chronic liver disease including splenomegaly, collateral veins over the abdomen, ascites, and liver encephalopathy. Almost all show some signs of malnutrition, and it is severe in about one third.

In most cases the clinical findings worsen for a few days to several weeks. After 4 weeks the patient is clearly improving, and plateaus in improvement by the 12th week. Prognosis for survival is poor if the patient has prolonged prothrombin time, elevated bilirubin, or other organ damage. The index proposed by Maddrey et al.[16a] has proven useful. It is calculated by adding the bilirubin in milligrams per deciliter to the product of 4.6 times the prolongation of the prothrombin time in seconds. Patients with an index over 30 often die in the first month. The index relates closely to survival and subsequent complications.

The diagnosis is usually made on the clinical and blood biochemical findings. If there is fever or leukocytosis with no other cause, if the liver tests are abnormal in prothrombin time or show elevations of bilirubin $>$ 3 mg/dl (50 μm/L), if there is marked malnutrition or evidence of both acute and chronic liver disease with hepatitis negative immunological markers, the diagnosis is firm. A biopsy is made most of the time to overcome subsequent denial of a problem as the patient improves. Once the diagnosis is made, it is clear that the patient has liver disease which will recur with recurrent drinking. The treatment is largely nutritional support and control of the alcoholism. Androgens, propylthiouracil, and colchicine have been used with modest if any advantage. Corticosteroids are without advantage.

D. CIRRHOSIS

Cirrhosis differs from alcoholic hepatitis largely through the presence of portal hypertension. Cirrhosis shortens survival in all persons and has many typical complications. In the alcoholic, cirrhosis may be ''active'', meaning that new destruction of liver cells is currently present, or inactive. Active liver disease is most commonly due to continued drinking. Active liver disease has the manifestations of continued jaundice, continued elevation of the ALT and AST if they were elevated at all, continued presence of spider angiomata if they were present at all, and slow progression of the liver disease. With several months of sobriety, indices of activity will almost always arrest in alcoholic cirrhosis.

Cirrhosis is suspected from the clinical history and the physical examination. Marked jaundice, a typical complication of cirrhosis, firm hepatomegaly, splenomegaly, or abdominal collaterals of the portal vein often make this diagnosis highly likely. It is confirmed by biopsy, confirmation of portal hypertension on endoscopy or sonography, or by the course of the disease. Cirrhosis progresses because it is present, but may progress even faster if new liver disease occurs from further drinking. Thus abstinence is an essential form of therapy for alcoholic cirrhosis.

Portal hypertension and cirrhosis produce several highly treatable complications, including ascites, bleeding varices, and liver encephalopathy. Bleeding esophageal varices are controlled by sclerotherapy, ascites is controlled by diet and diuretics, and encephalopathy is controlled by diet, lactulose, and antibiotics. Severe or recurrent complications may require hospitalization. Hepatocellular carcinoma occurs in cirrhosis and may be recognized by serial imaging or the serum marker alpha-fetoprotein. Unfortunately, neither method allows recognition at a stage sufficiently early to effect surgical cure with any degree of reliability.

Mental changes as a complication of cirrhosis apart from hepatic encephalopathy are not usually thought about. A recent study by Van Thiel and Tarter[17] compared 18 neuropsychological tests assessing visuospacial, memory, language, and perceptual capacities in normals, cirrhotics, and alcoholics without cirrhosis. They found the most severe impairment in liver disease and found moderate improvement with treatment of the cirrhosis. The ultimate treatment of alcoholic liver disease and its complications is transplantation. The Pittsburgh group have had the most experience with this form of therapy and discuss the pros and cons of its use.[18]

VI. PANCREATIC DISORDERS

Pancreatitis occurs commonly in alcoholics, but is also frequent after abdominal trauma and passage of gallstones. The destructive process in alcoholism occurs in the very small ducts, and the process may be present without clinical manifestations in about half the cases.[19] Disease is most likely to become symptomatic when it simultaneously involves larger portions of the pancreas. Either the silent or symptomatic form can cause pancreatic calcification, pseudocyst, or pancreatic insufficiency.

Although symptomatic attacks decrease in patients who stop drinking, the disease may progress to pancreatic insufficiency.

Once an attack occurs, the process usually continues, at a much slower rate if drinking ceases, but it probably does not altogether stop. Although far fewer patients who drink alcohol ever get pancreatitis contrasted to the one in six who get cirrhosis, the disease seems to continue in those who go through the stages of acute pancreatitis to chronic pancreatitis and pancreatic insufficiency.[20]

A. ACUTE PANCREATITIS

The diagnosis is made upon identifying an elevation of the amylase (or lipase) and indications of inflammation in the area of the pancreas, usually associated with pain. There may be tenderness, ileus, or extensive peritonitis. On CT scan the gland may be normal, enlarged from inflammation and edema, or the inflammation may extend beyond the gland into surrounding organs or regions. A typical attack improves rapidly and is resolved in 10 days in half of all patients. In the more severe cases resolution is slower. Patients requiring hospitalization have severe pain, toxicity, fever, and both nausea and vomiting. Hemoconcentration, azotemia, postural hypotension, ileus, or low calcium upon presentation, and a requirement for more than 6 liters of fluid in the first 24 h, identify those patients with a poor prognosis for survival. Treatment is supportive, to provide adequate fluid and electrolyte support, sometimes orally, and to provide relief of pain. No medications appear beneficial.

B. COMPLICATIONS OF ACUTE PANCREATITIS

In pancreatitis, the activated pancreatic enzymes are highly destructive of tissue. At least 20% of patients have these enzymes outside the pancreas, producing the inflammation and pain. The extrapancreatic secretions and their associated inflammation frequently organize into an inflammatory cyst wall (called pseudocyst), and this may grow if the extravasation of secretion continues. A pseudocyst may produce symptoms and signs by its size (usually larger than 5 cm), or by its expansion (pain), or by the absorption of its contents (elevated enzymes). Most pseudocysts less than 5 cm resolve spontaneously. Those growing beyond this size produce complications increasingly as they grow and are usually controlled surgically if they have persisted for a month or so.

The same enzyme process may destroy pancreatic tissue and fill the area with inflammation (called a phlegmon), and this or a pseudocyst may become infected and form an abscess. The differentiation of a phlegmon from an abscess usually requires direct needling of the mass. Jaundice from pancreatitis may occur from blockage of the common duct due to the inflamed pancreas or pseudocyst. This harms the liver if chronic, and should be addressed, usually surgically. Hemorrhage from phlegmons or pseudocysts into the GI tract is an occasional complication of pancreatitis, usually recognized only at emergency surgery for GI bleeding.

C. CHRONIC PANCREATITIS

Chronic pancreatitis means many different syndromes. Recurrent acute pancreatitis, chronic pain believed to originate in the pancreas without recurrent attacks of pancreatitis, and pancreatic insufficiency are all included in this designation but require different management. Recurrent acute pancreatitis in the nondrinking alcoholic requires evaluation to identify and treat surgically correctable causes such as gallstones, stricture, and trauma to the pancreas. Pancreatic insufficiency requires identification (fat malabsorption, Bentiomide test) and treatment with pancreatic supplements and special diet. When chronic pancreatitis is manifest by fat malabsorption and weight loss, it is usually necessary to use pancreatic supplements with each intake of food (one to three capsules of Pancrease® is a typical dose), and treatment of diabetes mellitus may be required. Recurrent pain associated with chronic pancreatitis is frequent and a major problem in management.[21] Narcotic analgesics should not be employed for more than a month or so because of the high addiction potential. The pancreatic duct is usually evaluated by ERCP and based upon these findings some sort of surgical treatment undertaken.

VII. GASTROINTESTINAL TRACT CONDITIONS

A. PEPTIC INDIGESTION, ULCERS, GASTROESOPHAGEAL REFLUX DISEASE, AND GASTRITIS

Alcohol is highly injurious to the mucosa of the upper tract, particularly when ingested in concentrations as high as 20% ethanol. Contact with such a concentration of alcohol or higher (20% is nearly 4000 mOsmol/l) rapidly dehydrates cells of the esophagus and stomach with resultant cell death. Further ethanol produces a relaxation of the lower esophageal sphincter, a retardation of peristalsis, and a marked stimulation of the production of gastric acid. Although alcoholic beverages are highly secretory, very few of them have any acid neutralization effect. The net effect is that peptic indigestion is common, as are its associated conditions.

Ulcers occur at least twice as frequently in alcoholics as in the population at large. Death from unrecognized perforated ulcer is much more common in this group, and is possibly related to the suppression of pain from the perforation by the alcohol. Ulcers are often recurrent with relapse. Gastroesophageal reflux disease also has a higher prevalence in alcoholics. Both of these diseases are effectively managed with potent acid-inhibiting agents.

Gastritis is present in nearly all markedly malnourished alcoholics and in patients who use concentrated alcohol daily (usually 20% or higher). This lesion is aggravated by NSAID agents, which block prostaglandin synthesis. Although it accounts for mild indigestion, it heals very promptly once drinking ceases and proper eating is restored (usually in 7 days). It may produce occult or massive gastrointestinal bleeding. We have found that 25% of patients entering detoxification have positive tests for occult blood on the first or second day, and these disappear by the third day. Alcoholic gastritis accounts for 1.6% of gastrointestinal bleeding at the Hines VA Hospital. This is a service on which a third of all patients are actively drinking alcoholics. NSAIDs damage, ulcers, and Mallory-Weiss tears of the esophagus are far more common sources of GI bleeding. Treatment of the patient with fluid replacement, sucralfate each 2 h, and expectancy will result in stopped bleeding by the third to fifth day. Surgery is almost never required for either alcoholic gastritis or Mallory-Weiss bleeding in our experience.

After the first few days of abstinence we are reluctant to accept symptoms of pain, indigestion, nausea, or vomiting as being related to gastritis. This is characteristically an asymptomatic condition. Patients with persistent symptoms require endoscopy and specific appropriate treatment for the identified lesions.

Ulcers of the stomach may be refractory to healing in the drinking (and usually smoking) patient and have more complications of bleeding and perforation. If a patient is noncompliant with medications and cessation of drinking and smoking, surgical therapy may be required for control.

B. GALLSTONES

Gallstones are clearly more prevalent in alcoholic liver disease and may be more prevalent in alcoholics. The form is bilirubin pigment stones, which are usually multiple faceted. The small stones often produce transient obstruction of the cystic and common duct that is more difficult to recognize than the similar syndromes produced by the larger cholesterol stones.

There is no known method to prevent these stones, and treatment is surgical when symptoms occur.

C. MOTILITY DISTURBANCES

The motility of the entire GI tract is altered in alcoholism. There is a combination of adjustments to the chronic smooth muscle-relaxing effects of alcohol and injury to the autonomic nervous system. Practically, many nonspecific GI complaints may be encountered that will usually ameliorate in the first two weeks after drinking stops. Diarrhea may be the most annoying of these. This may start at the time of alcohol withdrawal and reach six to ten watery movements each day. Stool leukocytes are always absent, tests for specific agents are negative, and it is only poorly responsive to such drugs as loperamide or Lomotil®. The problem disappears spontaneously by the 14th day. Long-standing alcoholics have elevated pressure waves in the esophagus and hyperactive stomach motility during withdrawal, but this disappears along with the other symptoms.

D. SMALL BOWEL CHANGES

At least half of all alcoholics have malabsorption of fats while drinking and in the early weeks after withdrawal. In addition, there is a delay in the active transport of most trace nutrients such as thiamin and folate.

E. CANCER

The prevalence of cancer is increased in alcoholics, particularly in the esophagus, mouth, tongue and lips, and stomach. This fact encourages the physician to use careful examination of the lips and mouth during physical examination and a lower threshold for use of upper endoscopy for detailed inspection of the esophageal and gastric mucosa.

VIII. GONAD DAMAGE AND SEXUAL DYSFUNCTION

A. TESTICULAR ATROPHY

Testicular atrophy has been well characterized in alcoholics and results from direct alcohol toxicity. It correlates well with the total alcohol consumption in the patient's lifetime and seems to be largely irreversible. It is most readily confirmed by measurement of the testicular size on physical examination. Low sperm counts and low androgens in the serum are quantitative measures of the severity.

B. DIMINISHED MALE LIBIDO, POTENTIA, AND SEXUAL PERFORMANCE

Male libido, potentia, and sexual performance are all diminished in alcoholics as a group, but there is surprisingly little relationship between the magnitude of testicular atrophy as quantitated by androgen levels and these features of male sexual disfunction. There are many contributing causes to diminished sexual performance, and in most alcoholic patients there is a return toward normal function after 6 to 12 months of abstinence.

Testosterone therapy has been used with both prominent benefit and total lack of response.

C. FEMALE SEXUAL DYSFUNCTION

Ovarian damage is less prominent in women than is testicular damage in the male, possibly related to liver disease distorting androgen production to increased estrogen. Alcoholic women have irregular menses, anovulatory cycles, and problems in conceiving, implanting, and maintaining pregnancy while drinking. Fetal damage is discussed in Chapter 37.

IX. DAMAGE TO OTHER ORGANS

A. HEART

The heart is subject to muscular injury in long use of alcohol. The most important manifestation is probably arrythmia during withdrawal. A myocardiopathy is observed very frequently when searched for in heavy users, but it is reversible in nearly all cases. Permanent cardiomyopathy from alcoholism is an infrequent disease limited to very intensive drinkers.

Severe heart failure is associated with marked deficiency of nicotinic acid (beri beri heart), but this is no longer seen in the U.S. A review of heart injury in Philadelphia alcoholics found an increased ventricular mass, a reduced injection faction (less than 55% in one third of unselected heavy alcoholics), and abnormal biopsy in at least 6%. They concluded that cardiomyopathy was relatively frequent.[22]

B. SKELETAL MUSCLE

Severe drinkers often have muscular pains, elevation of the aldolase or CPK in the serum, and muscular atrophy. Occasionally this is associated with myoglobin in the serum and urine and may produce renal excretory problems. These problems are confined to very severe drinkers. With cessation of drinking the muscle returns to normal. Although this abnormality is frequent, it is not particularly important.[22]

C. SKELETON AND BONE

Aseptic necrosis of the hip occurs in alcoholics at a rate similar to that in patients on prednisone. It is manifest by pain and is recognized by vascular scanning of the femoral head or somewhat later at a much more advanced stage by hip X-rays. Replacement of the femoral head is effective in restoring ambulation. Osteoporosis has been described in a group of alcoholics, but the absence of liver disease was not sufficiently characterized.[23] Others are less clear on the frequency of this lesion.[24] Osteopenia, on the other hand, is common in all sorts of chronic liver disease, and is related to the duration and severity of the liver disease.

D. HEMATOLOGICAL SYSTEM

The most common abnormality in the hematological system is an elevation of the mean corpuscular volume, often employed as a marker of alcoholism. This is present in some 40% of all patients, but about 85% of derelict or public patients have this problem. It is not due directly to folate deficiency. Anemia is common in heavy alcoholics, and there are many contributing causes. A study from Harlem Hospital in New York found the mean hematocrit being 27% with multiple causes being identified in most alcoholic subjects.[25] Iron deficiency, however, is always a measure of blood loss; alcohol may play a role in increasing iron absorption, but it does not interfere with it. Low platelets, abnormal platelets, low leukocyte counts, and hemolysis are all observed.[26]

X. REASONABLE GOALS OF MANAGEMENT

Injuries that limit life, ability to work, or to enjoy pleasures are often reversible. Only cerebellar injury and symmetrical motor disturbances have failed to show substantial reversibility in 3 months. For all other conditions some form of alcoholism treatment combined with rehabilitation of the specific organ under question is of value for at least 3 months to learn about reversibility. At that time the degree of permanency can be assessed and a subsequent plan made.

There is no question that patients with organ damage who have had a life-long experience with the advantages of quality medical care respond better and comply with abstinence therapy. For this reason many of us use minimal to modest data on reversible organ damage to illlustrate to such patients the adversity of continued drinking and the objective advantages to be attained by abstinence. This therapy is ineffective in those who have had bad experiences with physicians.

REFERENCES

1. **Iber, F. L.,** Alcohol-associated diseases, in *Nutrition and Metabolism in Patient Care,* Kinney, J. M., Jeejeebhoy, K. N., Hill, G. L., and Owen, O. E., Eds., W. B. Saunders, Philadelphia, 1988, 429—44.
2. **Klatsky, A. L., Friedman, G. D., and Siegelaub, M. S.,** Alcohol and mortality: a ten-year Kaiser-Permanente experience, *Ann. Int. Med.,* 95, 139, 1981.
3. **Lieber, C. S.,** Interactions of alcohol and nutrition, introduction to a symposium, *Alcoholism: Clin. Exp. Res.,* 7, 2, 1983.
4. **Lieber, C. S.,** Biochemical and molecular basis of alcohol-induced injury to liver and other tissues, *New Engl. J. Med.,* 319, 1639, 1988.
5. **Beard, J. D. and Knott, D. H.,** The effect of alcohol on fluid and electrolyte metabolism, in *The Biology of Alcoholism,* Vol. 1, Kissin, B., Begleiter, H., Eds., Plenum Press, New York, 1971, 353—376.
6. **Tang, M. and Falk, J. L.,** Chronic alcohol dependence and water-electrolyte status, *Alcohol,* 3, 33, 1986.
7. **Pitts, T. O. and Van Thiel, D. H.,** Disorders of the serum electrolytes, acid-base balance, and renal function in alcoholism, in *Recent Developments in Alcoholism,* 4, Galanter, M., Ed., Plenum Press, New York, 1987, 311—339.
8. **Schleifer, S. J., Keller, S. E., Lombardo, J. M., et al.,** HIV-1 antibody reactivity in inner-city alcoholics, *JAMA,* 262, 2680, 1989.
9. **Dunne, F. J.,** Alcohol and the immune system, *Br. Med. J.,* 298, 543, 1989.
10. **Watson, R. R.,** Ethanol, immunomodulation and cancer, *Prog. Food Nutr. Sci.,* 12, 189, 1988.
11. **Plant, M. L., Plant, M. A., Peck, D. F., and Setters, J.,** The sex industry, alcohol and illicit drugs: implications for the spread of HIV infection, *Br. J. Addict.,* 84, 53, 1989.
12. **Charness, M. E., Simon, R. P., and Greenberg, D. A.,** Ethanol and the nervous system, *New Engl. J. Med.,* 321, 442, 1989.
13. **Cermak, S. S., Verfaellie, M., Letourneau, L., Blackford, S., Weiss, S., and Numan, B.,** Verbal and nonverbal right hemisphere processing by chronic alcoholics, *Alcoholism,* 13, 611, 1989.
14. **Klatsky, A. L., et al.,** Alcohol use and subsequent cerebrovascular disease hospitalizations, *Stroke,* 20, 741, 1989.
15. **Thomson, A. D., Pratt, O. E., Jeyasingham, M., and Shaw, G. K.,** Alcohol and brain damage, *Hum. Toxicol.,* 7, 455, 1988.
16. **Muuronen, A., Bergman, H., Hindmarsh, T., and Telakivi, T.,** Influence of improved drinking habits on brain atrophy and cognitive performance in alcoholic patients: a 5-year follow-up study, *Alcoholism: Clin. Exp. Res.,* 13, 137, 1989.

16a. **Maddrey, W. C., et al.,** Corticosteroid therapy of alcoholic hepatitis, *Gastroenterology,* 75, 193, 1978.

17. **Van Thiel, D. H. and Tarter, R. E.,** Mental changes in cirrhosis with or without alcoholism, *Alcoholism: Clin. Exp. Res.,* 12, 619, 1988.
18. **Van Thiel, D. H., Gavaler, J. S., Tarter, R. E., Dindzans, V. J., Gordon, R. D., Iwatsuki, S., Makowka, L., Todo, S., Tzakis, A., and Starzl, T. E.,** Liver transplantation for alcoholic liver disease: a consideration of reasons for and against, *Alcoholism: Clin. Exp. Res.,* 13, 181, 1989.
19. **Malagelada, J. R.,** The pathophysiology of alcoholic pancreatitis, *Pancreas,* 1, 270, 1986.
20. **Ammann, R. W., Buehier, H., Muench, R., et al.,** Differences in the natural history of idiopathic and alcoholic chronic pancreatitis, a comparative long-term study of 287 patients, *Pancreas,* 2, 368, 1987.
21. **Bockman, D. E., Buchier, M., Malfertheiner, P., and Beger, H. G.,** Analysis of nerves in chronic pancreatitis, *Gastroenterology,* 94, 1459, 1988.
22. **Urbano-Marquez, A., Rubin, E., et al.,** The effects of alcoholism on skeletal and cardiac muscle, *New Engl.J. Med.,* 320, 409, 1989.
23. **Spencer, H., Rubio, N., Rubio, E., Indrecka, I., and Seiten, A.,** Chronic alcoholism: a frequently overlooked cause of osteoporosis, *Am. J. Med.,* 80, 393, 1986.
24. **Bickle, D. D., Genant, H. K., Carin, C., Rechner, R. R., Halboran, B. P., and Strewler, G. L.,** Bone disease in alcoholics, *Ann. Int. Med.,* 103, 42, 1985.
25. **Savage, D. S. and Lindenbaum, J.,** Anemia in alcoholics, *Medicine,* 65, 322, 1986.
26. **Ballard, H. S.,** Hematological complications of alcoholism, *Alcoholism,* 13, 706, 1989.

Chapter 18

Psychiatric Problems in Addicts

I. INTRODUCTION

In considering psychiatric problems in addicts, we rapidly reach the unanswered enigma encompassed by "Which came first, the chicken or the egg?". It is clear, however, that in adhering to the rigid diagnostic criteria of the American Psychiatric Association (DSM III-R),[1] there are many aberrations from normal encountered in substance-abusing patients. The loss of brain mass as indicated by CT scan or MRI is widespread, but is discussed in Chapter 17.[2] A recent series of papers testing the regional glucose metabolism of the brain has found that chronic alcoholics without apparent central nervous system disease have striking regional differences in glucose metabolism. This is even more marked in those with forgetfulness and may be an important feature in the psychiatric as well as the neurological features of these patients.[3] Table 36 lists the several types of problems that will be discussed in this chapter.[4]

Psychiatric disorders that were clearly present before the addiction was discovered are discussed for purposes of differentiation in all of the subsequent sections. Manic and depressive states often self-medicate with addicting drugs or alcohol and seem extraordinarily prone to developing abuse. When observed, it is necessary to complete detoxification before a firm diagnosis and treatment plan can be made.

TABLE 36
Psychiatric Disorders Encountered in Addicts

1. Disorders clearly present before the addiction
2. Disorders with a very high association with addictions
3. Disorders clearly limited to the withdrawal period
4. Disorders appearing to be a toxic reaction to the substance abuse
5. Disorders identified during the addiction or during withdrawal that seem to be unrelated

II. DISORDERS WITH A VERY HIGH ASSOCIATION WITH ADDICTIONS

A. SUICIDE

Suicide is highly associated with addictions. In adolescents it is estimated that half of all suicides are promoted or closely related to substance abuse, and the figure is probably higher in adults. This poses a particular difficulty during withdrawal from alcohol, sedatives, or opiates, for the depression that is a normal consequence of the withdrawal period may have features that make a suicidal tendency difficult to distinguish. The important feature for the therapist is recognition of the propensity.

B. POSTTRAUMATIC STRESS DISORDER

Posttraumatic stress disorder (PTSD) is frequently identified in veterans who have been in combat areas, but is not limited to this group. It is now known to occur in anyone who is exposed to many weeks of prolonged, intense stress over which there is neither control nor an opportunity for relief. It is seen in bad marriages, certain occupations, adolescents unable to escape from home or school, or certain other situations in civilian life. Among combat survivors of the Vietnam War, 20% are variously estimated to have symptoms.[5] A recent survey of 89 such patients requiring treatment on an inpatient psychiatric ward found that 60% had problems with chronic alcohol abuse. No reason for the association was found, but the treatment of the PTSD with tricyclic antidepressants was equally effective in those with and without alcoholism, suggesting that the alcoholism may have been a self-help-seeking problem in this disorder rather than a primary illness.[6] Others who develop PTSD are exposed to prolonged periods of emotional stress, usually with responsibility for the welfare of other family members or employees. Their own sense of duty does not allow them to seek relief from this continued responsibility. We have been aware of this problem in self-made business executives who have not developed sufficient trust in other employees, in family members called upon to cope with severe and prolonged illness in a family member that produces extreme and prolonged financial and emotional drains, and in persons undergoing prolonged investigation and trials for wrongdoing whether the result is either exoneration or commitment to prison. One suspects that the addictions experienced by Betty Ford and Kitty Dukakis are representations of this syndrome.

C. DRY DRUNKS, FLASHBACKS, BLACKOUTS

The three phenomena of dry drunks, flashbacks, and blackouts are alarming aberrations of behavior that are common in abusing persons. Dry drunks, limited to alcoholism, and flashbacks, limited to nonalcohol substances of abuse, are similar phenomena that occur in a very heavy and prolonged abuser during extended abstinence weeks or months removed from the period of withdrawal. The subject experiences in psychic and physical behavior the identical experience encountered while using the agent. In the alcoholic, the behavior is drunkenness or an alcohol high, but completely dissociated from alcohol or other agent use, and is confirmed in its similarities by knowledgeable witnesses. It is alarming particularly to the patient. Fortunately, the event is infrequent among alcoholics and limited to very heavy and very prolonged users.

Flashbacks occur among users of concentrated forms of marijuana (hashish), LSD, other psychedelic drugs, and PCP. Reproduction of the psychic high with distorted time, space, color, and imagery without apparent cause or provocation is the experience, and it often produces fright in the person who experiences it and may by itself provoke panic. Both dry drunks and flashbacks diminish in frequency as the interval from drug use becomes longer and longer.

A blackout, most common in alcoholics but experienced in other sedative users and occasionally in other chronic abusers, is a period of amnesia, usually for a significant period of time. Witnesses to the event are not aware that the person is functioning abnormally, but the erased memory, often of a highly significant event, is very alarming to the person in whom it occurs. Such persons may awaken in a hotel room unaware of the city and how they got there, occasionally sleeping with a person whom they do not remember. Alcoholics Anonymous meetings frequently feature stories with blackouts being prominent. One such alcoholic told of awakening in a hotel room repeatedly with no remembrance of how or when he reached there; he developed the pattern of requesting a local newspaper to determine which city he was currently in. Another account was that of a sexually eager alcoholic in the careful and prolonged seduction of an associate. The stage was set for consummation, the blackout occurred, and the outcome at a later time was unknown to the raconteur, a frightening occurrence.

All of these manifestations are believed to be markers of brain injury of varying degrees of reversibility. All occur only in the most intense abusers.[7]

D. HOMELESS MEN AND WOMEN

Every American metropolitan area, and many cities of less than 50,000 in population, are experiencing increased numbers of homeless persons. These people frequent missions and shelters when they exist, may be sheltered in jails, but many are not identified from these records. There is a major amount of substantial mental illness in both men and women. A recently published survey from Baltimore found that 42% of homeless men and 49% of homeless women were classified as having major mental illness, with schizophrenia and major depression being most commonly identified, dementia being quite rare. Of the men, 75% were substance abusers with 68% alcoholics; and of the women, 38% were abusers and 31% alcoholics. In the cited study it was not clear as to which came first, the mental disorder or the substance abuse, for instances among the homeless of each were identified.[8]

III. DISORDERS LIMITED TO THE WITHDRAWAL PERIOD

A. PSYCHOSIS DURING WITHDRAWAL

Psychosis is infrequently seen during withdrawal from sedatives or opiates. In order to be secure in this diagnosis, a fully alert person must experience hallucinations or delusions without insight. This must occur within the range of expected time for withdrawal. Usually there has been a sequence of withdrawal symptoms and signs increasing in severity until the psychosis occurs. The psychosis typically occurs late in the withdrawal period and is accompanied by other clear signs and symptoms of withdrawal appropriate to the agent that was abused. With short-acting agents such as opiates and alcohol the onset of withdrawal is within 12 to 24 h of the last drug use; psychosis usually occurs at 36 to 72 h. With longer-acting drugs the withdrawal may not be apparent for several days, and psychosis may occur after 1 or even 2 weeks. Although such psychosis constitutes an emergency, the treatment is that of the withdrawal (see Chapter 27).

Differential diagnosis becomes a problem when it is not clearly identified that the person is a substance abuser. Trauma units and emergency rooms encounter a person with hyperactivity and hallucinations and who are unable to give a history, who are in withdrawal but may be temporarily thought to be psychotic. Since similar sedative treatment, often with haloperidol, will control both diseases, the correct diagnosis may be sorted out later without harm to the patient. When a history of drug use is clear, the timing of withdrawal is quite stereotyped for each drug. A toxicological screen will reveal an abused substance most of the time. Detoxification treatment is usually initiated and, with hallucinations or delusions that are bothersome, haloperidol treatment, 2 mg each hour until the patient is calm, is added. Infrequently, hospitalization is necessary.

Sedatives (including alcohol) are associated with a mentally clear person experiencing hallucinations on occasion. This is much more benign and easier to treat than a person experiencing hallucinations as a part of global mental disorientation and psychosis such as is typical of delirium tremens.

B. DEPRESSION DURING WITHDRAWAL

Depression is commonly seen immediately after withdrawal from sedatives, cocaine, amphetamines, and opiates.[9] This is depression in every sense of the disease, with the subject measuring moderately or more severely depressed on the Hamilton, Beck, or Zung psychological test. Even the measures of sluggish response of the pituitary-adrenal axis, characteristic of depression, are present in withdrawal. The majority of these patients progressively improve and no longer measure as depressed by psychological testing by the 21st day after withdrawal. There is no way to clearly distinguish preexisting depression from postwithdrawal depression except by the history and the subsequent improvement as the interval from agent abuse is prolonged. Preexisting depression is usually made worse at the time of withdrawal in an abusing person. An evaluation of alcoholics 12 to 13 days after detoxification by both basal cortisol levels and the ability to depress these with dexamethasone can be made in the hope of identifying those subjects with an underlying major depression disorder. A basal cortisol level below 7 μg/dl distinguished all alcoholics free of depression.[10]

C. DELAYED WITHDRAWAL

A variety of analgesic and sedative drugs partially treat withdrawal. Trauma patients after surgery are often treated with opiates, so withdrawal is completely suppressed and not recognized. On the 3rd or 4th day the need for analgesia is less, the drugs are diminished, and previously suppressed withdrawal appears. The inexperienced physician may treat this as "delayed withdrawal". In our experience treatment suppresses withdrawal, and very high doses of "treatment" drugs can prolong the state of tolerance and in this way delay the onset of withdrawal until they in turn are withdrawn. Thus for opiates and alcohol the withdrawal period should peak by the 48th hour and be entirely over by 7 days, for long-acting barbiturates the peak may be on the 6th day and the syndrome last 3 weeks.

Signs and symptoms of withdrawal extending substantially beyond these periods have essentially always proven to be due to another condition. Thus such patients should be evaluated for other treatable disorders. Although many authors prior to 1970 described delayed withdrawal or a severe form of withdrawal from alcohol (or opiates) occurring after 7 days, I have only found this described recently in a review by Naranjo and Sellers,[11] and I have simply not seen this in more than 20 years of observing all sorts of alcoholics. When hallucinations persist into the period more than 7 days, I have found that the patient has an underlying psychosis.

IV. DISORDERS APPEARING TO BE A TOXIC REACTION TO THE DRUG

An organic brain syndrome may be produced by a wide variety of drugs. Alcohol most commonly, depressants less commonly, and all other classes occasionally are represented. Solvent sniffing with toluene, when used aggressively to achieve a high, is associated with this problem, but the frequency is unknown. The history is usually chronic, aggressive, recurrent, high-dose use of one or more agents. The history often indicates use beyond an ordinary high, to the point where associates have concern of bodily harm. In the case of alcohol the use is intense and over many years, but the duration is often as little as 1 year for other agents.

The patient is usually found to be confused, disoriented, and to have decreased intellectual functioning. The syndrome may go unrecognized by those close to the patient, the dullness being attributed to use of their favorite agent. Often family or friends who have not seen the patient for a time are appalled at the state of mental deterioration and seek medical help. The addict with organic brain syndrome has no insight that a problem exists and often has other organ involvement, particularly in alcoholism. Many treatable conditions can mimic the findings of organic brain syndrome, requiring a laboratory and CT scan evaluation of all of these patients. Thiamin deficiency is usually corrected with parenteral thiamin 50 to 100 mg one time.

Psychological testing, with memory and intelligence test evaluation, is useful in both making the diagnosis and in identifying progression or incremental improvement. In very advanced cases the CT scan of the brain shows cortical atrophy as measured by an increased space between the tables of the skull and the surface of the brain, diminished thickness of the cortex from the ventricles to the surface, and larger grooves between sulci. After discontinuation of the abused drug, most patients slowly improve. Improvement has been observed over a period of as long as 5 years, though most occurs in the first 90 days. The subsequent management is determined by the degree of recovery. Such forgetful patients do not respond well to rehabilitation programs and frequently relapse to their original or new addictions. An excellent review of chronic alcohol use on memory has been written by the Toronto group, who have one of the most extensive experiences with this problem.[12] These chronic brain syndromes are one of the great tragedies of drug use, for patients are rendered functional at well below their potential, equal to that of a moron, but live long lives. The CT brain scans correlate poorly and in only a general way with the subsequent course of the patient.[13]

V. DISORDERS DETERMINED AFTER EVALUATION TO BE UNRELATED TO THE ADDICTION

All psychiatric disorders may develop addictions. Several factors probably increase this tendency. These include a familiarity with medications from their doctor-directed therapy, sometimes leading to self-treatment and addiction to drugs. The tendency to provide large quantities of medications to chronic psychiatric patients with prolonged intervals between visits makes this prone to happen. Depressed patients seem particularly prone to self-treatment with alcohol, depressants, and stimulants, common substances of abuse. Additionally, a psychosis sets a person apart and creates the setting for anger, resentment, and increased anxiety. Alcohol and other depressant drugs may initially be used for relaxation but later become an addiction.

One hundred ninety-five consecutive psychiatric outpatients were surveyed for covert illicit drug use by urine samples, screening for opiates, cocaine, barbiturates, and amphetamines. Thirteen percent were positive, and as a group these had a less favorable course with their therapy than did the controls. Demographic variables, patient reports, and personal psychiatrists' assessment were unreliable predictors of drug use.[14] The addicted psychiatric patient is often unmasked in the withdrawal period by atypical features of withdrawal. This may be manifest by withdrawal signs occurring far later than the highly limited withdrawal period or the occurrence of withdrawal-like psychotic symptoms, but at a substantially later time. This group of patients seems underdiagnosed in my experience.

Obsessive-compulsive disorders are widespread, according to a recent review.[15] When these take the form of bulimia, a substantial fraction are also abusers of alcohol. These disorders are remarkably refractory to treatment, but two agents affecting the serotoninergic systems have influenced the outcome favorably. These drugs, clomipramine and fluvoxamine, are sometimes called antiobsessional medications.[16,17] As yet there is no information on differences in response of those with and those without substance abuse in addition to their compulsive disorder.

A recent survey by the National Institute of Mental Health Epidemiologic Catchment Area[18] examined lifetime co-morbidity between mental disorder diagnoses and substance abuse. Patients with primarily mental disorder diagnosis had a 28% co-morbidity with substance abuse, mostly alcoholism. On the other hand, those with a diagnosis primarily of alcohol abuse had a 45% co-morbidity with a mental illness, and those with a drug abuse problem a whopping 71%. The important word here is abuse; when dependence is reviewed, the values are about one fifth of these.

Severe mental disorders, including schizophrenia, manic-depressive illness, and major depression, have the highest rates of co-morbidity with substance dependence. Of particular interest to primary-care physicians is the observation that 74% of those with depression are first seen by primary-care facilities.[19] If a depressive or anxiety disorder has its onset before age 30, it more than doubles the likelihood of substance dependency.[20]

Suicide is particularly important in these patients, for a clear history of depressive illness (48%) or alcoholism (23%) is present in completed suicides.[21] Again, primary-care physicians have the greatest likelihood of seeing these patients and play a substantial role in the prevention of suicide.

A study of homeless adults in Los Angeles investigated psychiatric diagnoses compared to an age-matched sample of households. All major mental illnesses were disproportionately high in the homeless, with substance abuse almost uniformly present in those over age 45 and increasing with age, and in Native Americans. Schizophrenia predominated as the reason for homelessness in the group aged 31 to 40, but substance abuse was extremely high in this group. The overall estimate of chronic major mental illness in the homeless group was 28% by DSM III R criteria and of substance abuse was 83%.[22]

VI. COMMENT ON TREATMENT

When psychiatric illness is clearly diagnosed and an addiction occurs, it may be essential to treat both concomitantly. When one has choices, usually control of the abused substance is essential if one is to attain usual treatment response to the basic psychiatric condition. This is particularly true when a less severe neurotic or behavioral pattern is to be treated in an addict.

A review of alcoholism occurring in depressed people has appeared and approaches both the diagnostic difficulty and the treatment. The authors favored treatment of the alcoholism initially to determine the severity of the depression and only after one or two months of persistent depression were antidepressive agents then recommended. Lithium was advised for the less ill person who had frequent relapses with alcoholism. A strong doctor-patient relationship was recommended as the most important aspect of therapy.[23]

REFERENCES

1. *Diagnostic and Statistical Manual of Mental Disorders,* 3rd ed., rev., American Psychiatric Association, Washington D.C., 1987.
2. **Zipursky, R. B., Lim, K. O., and Pfefferbaum, F.,** MRI study of brain changes with short-term abstinence from alcohol, *Alcoholism,* 13, 664, 1989.
3. **Sachs, H., Russell, J. A., Christman, D. R., and Cook, B.,** Alteration of regional cerebral glucose metabolic rate in non-Korsakoff chronic alcoholism, *Arch. Neurol.,* 44, 1242, 1987.
4. **Schuckit, M. A.,** Alcoholism and other psychiatric disorders, *Hospital and Comm., Psychiatr.,* 34, 1022, 1983.
5. **Egendorf, A., Kadushin, C., Laufer, R. S., et al.,** Legacies of Vietnam, Comparative Adjustment of Veterans and Their Peers, U.S. Government Printing Office, Washington D.C., 1981.
6. **Reaves, M. E., Hansen, T. E., and Whisenand, J. M.,** The psychopharmacology of the post-traumatic stress disorder, *VA Practitioner,* 6, 65, 1989.
7. **Goodwin, D. W., Crane, J., and Guze, S. B.,** Loss of short term memory as a predictor of the alcoholic blackout, *Nature,* 227, 201, 1970.
8. **Breakey, W. R., Fischer, P. J., Kramer, M., Nestadt, G., Romanoski, A. J., Ross, A., Royall, R. M., and Stine, O. C.,** Health and mental health problems of homeless men and women in Baltimore, *JAMA,* 262, 1352, 1989.
9. **Schuckit, M. A.,** A study of alcoholics with secondary depression, *Am. J. Psychiatr.,* 140, 711, 1983.
10. **Halbreich, U. and Castaneda, R.,** Depression during withdrawal; low basal levels of cortison distinguish detoxified alcoholics with major depressive disorder from non MDDS, *Alcoholism,* 13, 834, 1989.
11. **Naranjo, C. A. and Sellers, E. M.,** Clinical assessment and pharmacotherapy of the alcohol withdrawal syndrome, in *Recent Developments in Alcoholism,* Vol. 4, Galanter, M., Ed., Plenum Press, New York, 1986, 265.
12. **Wilkinson, D. A. and Poulos, C. X.,** The chronic effects of alcohol on memory, a contrast between unitary and dual system approach, *Recent Dev. Alcohol,* 5, 5, 1987.
13. **Wilkinson, D. A.,** Examinations of alcoholics by CT scans, *Alcoholism: Clin. Exp. Res.,* 6, 31, 1982.
14. **Hall, R. C., Popkin, M. K., Stickney, S. K., and Gardner, E. R.,** Covert outpatient drug abuse. Incidence and therapist recognition, *J. Nerv. Ment. Dis.,* 166, 343, 1978.
15. **Jenike, M. A.,** Obsessive-compulsive and related disorders, a hidden epidemic, *New Engl. J. Med.,* 321, 539, 1989.
16. **Jenike, M. A., Baer, L., and Minichiello, W. E., Eds.,** *Obsessive-Compulsive Disorders: Theory and Management,* PSG Publishing, Littleton, MA, 1986.
17. **Swedo, S. E., Leonard, H. L., Rapoport, J. L., Lenane, M. C., Goldberger, E. L., and Cheslow, D. L.,** A double-blind comparison of clomipramine and desipramine in the treatment of trichotillomania (hair pulling), *N. Engl. J. Med.,* 321, 497, 1989.
18. **Regier, D. A., Boyd, J. H., Burke, J. D., et al.,** One-month prevalence of mental disorders in United States, *Arch. Gen. Psychiatr.,* 45, 977, 1988.
19. **Shapiro, S., Skinner, E. A., Kessler, L. G., et al.,.** Utilization of health and mental health services: three epidemiologic catchment area sites, *Arch. Gen. Psychiatr.,* 41, 971, 1984.
20. **Brier, A., Kelsoe, J. R., Kirwin, A. C., et al.,** Early parental development of adult psychopathology, *Arch. Gen. Psychiatr.,* 45, 987, 1988.
21. **Goodwin, F. K.,** From the Alcohol, Drug Abuse and Mental Health Administration, *JAMA,* 261, 3517, 1989.
22. **Koegel, P., et al.,** The prevalence of specific psychiatric disorders among homeless individuals in the inner city of Los Angeles, *Arch. Gen. Psychiatr.,* 45, 1085, 1988.
23. **Pary, R., Lippmann, S., and Tobias, C. R.,** Depression and alcoholism: clinical considerations in management, *South. Med. J.,* 81, 1529, 1988.

Chapter 19

Opium Derivatives

I. INTRODUCTION

The medicinal value of the seed pod of the poppy *(Papaver somniferum)* was known by Hippocrates as a treatment for diarrhea and abdominal cramps. In the seventeenth century alcoholic extracts (paregoric, later laudanum) were used with improved efficacy. Smoking of opium was discovered in the Orient and Middle East and initiated recreational use and the recognition of addiction.

The use of opiates for gastrointestinal distress was known by the ancient Greeks, but the control of pain came about when purification occurred in the nineteenth century. Only in the twentieth century were the many chemical modifications of the basic principle morphine possible. Codeine, heroin, and hydromorphone were developed. In the 1930s synthetics followed. The concept of receptors and more detailed study of the pharmacology of pain relief led to agonist and antagonist hypothesis, a discovery of the 1970s. At present there are at least a dozen molecules that have morphine-like properties in various proportion and another group of substances with antagonist properties. Although some, such as codeine, morphine, and heroin, are derived from the poppy, most others are made synthetically. The opium poppy is grown extensively in the Middle East, Micronesia, and China for the illicit trade. The legitimate medical trade no longer requires this plant to produce essential medical products. The cultural and recreational use of opium in the Middle East is widespread, for Muslim culture does not interdict its use as it does alcohol. It is estimated in Iran that only a few percent of regular users, certainly less than 5%, become tolerant. This has a lot to do with the ritualistic and family use of the agent.

TABLE 37
Types and Significance of Morphine Receptors

(Animals — Not Known for Humans)

Name	Location	Function
Mu	CNS limbic, thalamus, midbrain, dorsal horns, spinal cord	Pain relief, addiction
Delta	All regions	Encephalin binding
Kappa	Cerebral cortex, spinal cord	Pain relief, specific for dynorphin
Omega	CNS	Subjective, psychoactive, PCP binds
Visceral	GI, GU, smooth muscle, and ganglia	Suppresses motility, secretion

II. MODE OF ACTION, AVAILABLE PRODUCTS, AND METABOLISM

A. MODE OF ACTION

A group of endogenous peptides, the encephalins, of which approximately 20 are known, react with the same CNS and peripheral receptors as does morphine. From animal studies it is known that there are at least four different receptors for morphine. These receptors bind differentially with morphine and encephalins and are responsible in animals for mediating several quite different effects of these drugs. These differing receptors and the effects that they are believed to mediate are outlined in Table 37.

All opioids of addiction potential have agonist properties for CNS receptors but differ from one another in the binding.

Although different opioids in animal models affect the receptors as noted in Table 36 in varying degrees, there is no clear data from humans that the effects are divorced except for the agonist and antagonist ones. Thus analgesia, a change in mood, overall relaxation, and a sense of well-being, as well as constipation, seem to go together with all of these agents. Individual variation from person to person produced differences in these effects as great as the use of different drugs in the same person.

B. AVAILABLE PRODUCTS

A wide variety of substances is available. These products are at least partially water soluble and are absorbed after oral ingestion, but many of the group are absorbed slowly. Heroin is the least well absorbed, with only about 70% of an ingested dose reaching the liver, whereas propoxyphene is rapidly and completely absorbed. All have a very high first-pass effect, which may remove as much as 80% of the absorbed drug. Products vary markedly in protein binding. Those with high protein binding move into the CNS slowly. All are rapidly inactivated by liver metabolism. Most of the available drugs have primarily agonist activity. Naloxone (Narcan®) has pure antagonist activity, and pentazocine is both an agonist and antagonist with the antagonist properties coming at a higher dose. Table 38 lists some properties of the available products.

Codeine and heroin are both converted to morphine but at highly different rates. All of the agents in Table 38 cross the placenta, and fetal addiction is a substantial problem.

C. PATTERNS OF STREET USE

Heroin is by far the preferred drug among addicts; others are used only when they are more readily available or among persons who obtain supplies from physicians. Although all routes — oral, s.c., i.m., and i.v. — are used, most addicts use the drugs i.v., or s.c. when the veins are blocked. The very high first-pass effect and relatively slow absorption of the major drugs largely eliminates the oral route in addicts. Tolerance develops rapidly in all

TABLE 38
Useful Pharmacology of Opioids

Potency is mg Equivalent of 10 mg i.m. Morphine

Drug, route	Potency	Protein binding	Duration (h)	Excretion	First pass
Butorphanol					
i.v., i.m.	2	>80%	3—4	72% renal	75%
Codeine					
Oral	200	None	4	Metabolism	30%
i.m., s.c.	120				
Hydromorphone					
Oral	7.5	50%	4	Metabolism	70%
i.v., i.m.,	1.5				
Levorphanol					
Oral	4	50%	4—5	Metabolism	50%
i.v., i.m.	2				
Meperidine					
Oral	300	>80%	2—3	Metabolism	80%
i.m., i.v.	75				
Methadone					
Oral	20	>80%	4—6	Metabolism	50%
i.m., i.v., s.c.	10				
Morphine					
Oral	60	<10%	4—5	85% renal	85%
i.v., i.m., s.c.	10				
Nalbuphine					
i.v., i.m., s.c.	10	50%	3—6	Metabolism	?
Naloxone (antagonist)					
i.v., i.m., s.c.	0.4	30%	2—3	Metabolism	? High
Oxycodone					
Oral	30	30%	3—4	Metabolism	40%
Oxymorphone					
i.m., i.v., s.c.	1	30%	3—6	Metabolism	?
Pentazocine					
Oral	180	50%	2—3	Metabolism	70%
i.m., s.c., i.v.	60				
Propoxyphene					
Oral	400	90%	4—6	Metabolism	70%

users of high doses, with metabolic tolerance related to increased enzyme in the liver and neurological tolerance related to increased numbers of receptors. When cancer patients are treated with self-administered doses of opiates by pump or through easy access to any necessary amount of drug, addiction is rare. This points up that most users do not become abusers, but once a person is identified as an abuser the tendency to do this with alternative substances is high.

III. PREDOMINANT EFFECTS AND TOXIC REACTIONS

A. EFFECTS

The preferred street drug is heroin; others are abused on the basis of availability. The effects of different drugs seem to be overall similar in producing at the same time analgesia, a high, overall relaxation, and constipation. At higher doses there is a clouding of mental function and a disturbance of motor and cardiac function with all types. Variation of these several effects from one person to another is about as great as it is with different drugs in the same person.

When these drugs are used for a high, snorting, i.v., s.c., or smoking is the usual route. All produce a surge of the drug, with a high following in 3 to 15 min. The duration of the high is less than 30 min unless continual administration is attained. The user moves into a state of arrested time and animation, floating in a cloud of ecstasy. The passage of time and physical or worldly problems are removed from awareness.

After the high there is most often a period of pleasurable slumber with complete relaxation and an awakening feeling refreshed and energized though to the surrounding nonusers the user looks debilitated and worn out. Tolerance and dependency develop as rapidly as with cocaine. Throughout the world and certainly in America, there are continual recreational users who do not develop substantial tolerance and who continue to function fully while occasionally using the agent.

Other systemic effects include peripheral vasodilatation and hypotension. There is marked miosis, unaffected by atropine. Enteric secretions are decreased, there is diminished gastrointestinal peristalsis manifested by a chronic and annoying constipation, uterine contractions are suspended, and there is oliguria. Sexual function and interest is impaired. Intravenous heroin use is occasionally associated with pulmonary edema. This is not altered by naloxone injection.

B. TOXIC REACTION

Toxic reactions occur frequently because doses are poorly standardized and a wide variety of adulterants are used to dilute street drugs. Toxic reactions are much more common among new users. In seasoned users, they are associated with a new source of supply. The person becomes comatose or semicomatose and the vital signs may be compromised with slow respirations. The pulse is usually rapid and there may be arrhythmia, but the blood pressure is usually low. The pupils are invariably pinpoint (miotic), and there is respiratory depression with clear signs of anoxia, often with striking cyanosis because of the combination of vasodilatation and oxygen undersaturation. Blood gases, if obtained, show retention of CO_2 in addition to severe hypoxemia. There may be prominent nausea and vomiting, and there is almost always marked vasodilatation though the extremities may be cold. There is impressive hypotension. Pulmonary edema may be prominent, and there may be cardiac arrhythmia. Injection of intravenous naloxone (0.4 mg), repeated once if no response, will invariably change the pupils, lighten the level of consciousness, improve the breathing and reflexes, and be associated with a rise in blood pressure but does not effect pulmonary edema, convulsions, or arrhythmia, which need specific treatment.

Treatment must be prompt to prevent permanent neurological injury. All sites possibly involved with such patients must have a supply of naloxone (0.4-mg ampules). If the diagnosis is suspected, respiration should be preserved and naloxone 0.4 mg should be given i.v., at least twice at 2 to 3-min intervals. This may be given with impunity even when the diagnosis is incorrect, for it is a pure antagonist. If the state of consciousness does not lighten immediately (1 or 2 min), the dose should be repeated. If nothing then happens, it is likely the diagnosis is incorrect. The patient should be in an appropriate environment for i.v. fluids, close monitoring, and treatment of arrhythmias if they are present, usually a specialized treatment unit or a hospital.

IV. SOCIAL ASPECTS OF USE

Illicit users nearly always avoid the oral route because of the first-pass effect, except for drugs like propoxephene. The majority of street users utilize i.v. or s.c. injections, but snorting of pure heroin or other pure drugs is a reasonable method of intake. Smoking of pure preparations is also possible. Street use of opiates in America is predominantly as heroin and is of two types, those using the drug irregularly for a high and not developing tolerance and those progressively developing tolerance with a multiple dose/day habit. The route of use does not determine which of these patterns predominates. The onset of tolerance is rapid, often developing in 3 to 7 days. It is clear that the majority of opiate addicts hold jobs and function fairly well even after one year of their abuse.[1] The Vietnam experience of U.S. soldiers suggests that more than half of those given an opportunity tried opiates, some became addicted, but nearly all who were drug free before Vietnam returned to this abstinent status after discharge from the armed forces.[2]

The most frequent illicit user is from a metropolitan area, under age 25, and from a minority group.[3] Users usually have had difficulty with the law for larceny, selling drugs, or drug use, and have used other drugs. Almost all have had school difficulties, less than 20% finish high school, and many have evidence of antisocial behavior in schools and with the courts by the time use is identified. For such juvenile users with poor social connections the prognosis is poor until they get about 20 years older. However, in persons with better backgrounds who do not have records of poverty, broken homes, school dropout, and many arrests, the prognosis for recovery is substantially better, particularly for those who enter treatment in the first six months after starting daily drug use. Long-term outcomes are dependent upon the group being followed. The prognosis varies from very, very glum, with one quarter dead and one quarter still addicted even after 20 years,[4,5] to substantially better than this.[6,7] The most hopeful aspect of the natural history is that remission is relatively common in those who reach age 40. As in alcoholism, the likelihood of relapse is highest in the first few months, and those abstinent for more than 24 months usually do not relapse.

Opiate addicts are extremely prone to use other drugs, both simultaneously and sequentially. Amphetamines and opiates are sometimes used at about the same time, presumably because the combined high is greater than the sum of the parts. When opiates are unavailable, a wide variety of drugs are used, but alcohol is the most readily available and is the additional drug most commonly abused. It is estimated that as many as half of opiate addicts become alcoholics either at the same time or immediately after cessation of their opiate abuse.[8,9] This becomes a very important issue in follow-up treatment.

Medical provision of opiates for patients with cancer-related pain, even when offered self-regulation of the dose, infrequently results in tolerance and progressively increasing doses. This is estimated to not exceed 5 to 10% of users for more than 3 months. A similar finding is observed in patients undergoing multiple sequential operations following trauma or those requiring opiates for the control of diarrhea. In contrast, alcoholics who develop painful chronic pancreatitis are estimated to have a 20% prevalence of drug abuse, often as incapacitating as the pain.[10,11] It seems that previous substance abuse may place the person at great risk for subsequent abuse.

V. RECOGNITION OF OPIATE ABUSE

Recognition of opiate abuse is quite easy in about three fourths of abusers, and extremely difficult in a few. At least half of all users promptly admit use, including the most recent history, but they are vague and uncertain on details as to amount and frequency. For those who do not readily provide the history, a physician relies most heavily on the setting and the accompanying history, physical findings, and laboratory examination. Table 39 indicates some of the features that permit recognition, even when the history is not clear.

It is quite common for opiate addicts to continue to use the drug while under active treatment, even in the hospital. For this reason repeated urine testing may be needed for diagnosis and certainly for management. Diagnosis is discussed more completely in Chapters 9 and 20. The naloxone challenge test is used in the office when a possible user with some physical findings, such as constricted pupils, is encountered who denies use. An intravenous injection of 0.4 mg of the drug is given and if there are significant changes in the pupils

TABLE 39
Recognition of the Opiate Abuser Even When Not Acknowledged

Setting
1. A former opiate abuser
2. Visiting multiple doctors with pain
3. Disadvantaged male <30 years, alienated
4. Improbable story, lost prescription or medicine
5. Illness with severe pain with many atypical features
6. Doctor, dentist, nurse, or pharmacist with access

Physical findings
1. Pigmented, infected, thrombosed veins
2. Severe constriction of pupils

Laboratory
1. Urine test for opiates
2. Naloxone challenge test

and other signs, this establishes recent use (in the last 6 to 8 h at the most). The test provides clarification of drug use status immediately but may precipitate opiate withdrawal syndrome.

VI. ASPECTS OF TREATMENT, INCLUDING METHADONE

Withdrawal management is presented in Chapter 27, and treatment for all opiate addictions is essentially alike. Heroin withdrawal has many features that are different from alcohol or other sedative withdrawal. The time course is similar, in that it begins within a few hours of the last dose, peaks by 48 to 72 h, and may last as much as 5 or 6 days. Within hours of cessation of heroin, the patient has a strong drive to obtain more drug and often is successful. Starting 6 to 12 h after the last dose there is prominent tearing of the eyes, running of the nose, and yawning, and this may be accompanied by profuse sweating and progressively increasing tachycardia. By 24 h, the pupils are dilated and there is hypersensitivity to environmental irritants. There is a very restless sleep and a mildly agitated state. There is a limited appetite, though vomiting is unusual, and there is often piloerection. Within 12 additional hours peak withdrawal occurs, with agitation and insomnia, GI upset, chills, flushing, and muscular pains. There is often abdominal pain, and the bowels may be loose. Ejaculation occurs in about half the subjects during this time. The syndrome rapidly improves after the peak at 72 h. With treatment, nearly all of the adverse symptoms are controlled. If the patient is pregnant, the withdrawal treatment must avoid fetal withdrawal, discussed more fully in Chapters 27 and 37.

If methadone is to be used for maintenance, it is useful treatment in withdrawal. Single doses of 20 to 50 mg are given orally, and if the symptoms and signs of withdrawal are not alleviated, repeated each 2 to 3 h, still using oral ingestion. The total dose required in the first 24 h is reduced by 20% and given the second day, with this process of reducing the daily dose by 20% or 10 mg, whichever is the higher reduction. No drug is used after the 4th day except for those undergoing maintenance methadone treatment.

Maintenance methadone can be administered only under the authority of licensed clinics in order to provide proper monitoring and to diminish the entry of methadone into street supplies of drug. Methadone, as noted in Table 38, is a long-acting opiate that acts similar to other addicting agents except that mental functioning and ability to work is less incapacitated by this agent than by others. The basic philosophy of this treatment is that a person is given the drug at very low cost and with limited effort. Patients can avoid withdrawal and will choose this method over street agents. The defect in this reasoning is that the cyclical superlative "highs" that addicts seek are not possible with the doses provided. Features of retention through detoxification in a methadone program have been examined.[12]

TABLE 40
Common Requirements of Methadone Maintenance Programs

Entry
- Detoxified and drug free
- Free of psychiatric illness
- Informed consent

Ongoing
- Daily appearance for liquid dose
- Drug testing up to three times weekly
- Continued treatment at least weekly

Two forms of maintenance are undertaken, a relatively low dose (30 to 40 mg of oral drug) used most commonly, and a higher dose (100 to 200 mg orally) used occasionally. For acceptance into a program, the client must be detoxified and drug free as determined by urine testing. An evaluation must show freedom from substantial psychiatric illness and a clear understanding of the responsibilities being undertaken as a member of the treatment program. Table 40 indicates common requirements of treatment.

Patients selected for methadone maintenance are usually those with a prolonged habit, usually of several years duration. Those without family, economic, and employment support systems or who have failed in other treatments are usually directed to such programs when they are available. Some clinics only accept clients with families and jobs, but most have a substantial population of the unemployed.[13] The most common clinic procedure favors lower doses of methadone for maintenance. The side effects are less and the supervisory problems somewhat simplified,[14] but there is substantial evidence that retention in therapy is greater with high-dose programs.[15]

Short-term evaluations of clients selected for methadone maintenance (or the slightly longer-acting methadyl acetate) clearly demonstrate improved work records, less street crime, and diminished burden on the criminal law section of society.[16] There are some substantial long-term consequences. The two most important of these are a depression that seems to develop in increasing numbers of patients as the duration of treatment is prolonged,[17] and the occurrence of the addiction of the fetus *in utero* as the client becomes pregnant, discussed in detail in Chapter 37. Constipation is almost invariably encountered, but can be managed with diet, and lactulose.

The lack of a client-acceptable high and the inability to regulate their own doses leads more than half the subjects on methadone maintenance to use other drugs, including alcohol at times, in an abusive fashion. This is the basis of the frequent drug testing (daily or three times weekly is optimal, but budget restrictions often limit it to very infrequently) and to the administration of the dose under observation in liquid form to prevent it from being diverted into illicit channels and substituting other drugs with a better high. In recent years many methadone programs have experienced budgetary cuts while the pressure to offer treatment to as many as possible has remained great. The decrease in drug testing and in counseling have usually led to inferior programs. The use of other drugs, particularly alcohol,[18] must be specifically addressed in any treatment program seeking to perform in the best manner for its clients.

Evaluations of methadone treatment programs are limited and are much more frequent during the first 6 months than after long-term treatment. An ingenious comparison of a methadone program abruptly terminated for loss of funding with a program that was not so disrupted indicated that after 2 years about 20% fewer patients had returned to heroin, and about 20% fewer had alcoholism, arrests, or were selling drugs on the street, in the group remaining in treatment.[19] There is no agreement as to how long persons should remain on methadone maintenance. Most agree that 3 months accomplishes nothing; some believe treatment should continue indefinitely or until the client feels that he or she should give it up. Others feel that tapering should begin after a year of treatment, lowering the dose very slowly at about a rate of 3% weekly.[20]

The cost of supervision and related counseling is high in maintenance programs, and experimentation to lessen the frequency of contact with the clinics has been made, but there are no evaluations that show that this is effective. As methadone maintenance patients gain in societal integration and prolonged abstinence, clinics liberalize "trusting" of the client with doses for vacations and prolonged holidays. Under such circumstance the client is given 3 to 15 days' supply of methadone at one time.

Patients on heroin for less than 6 months respond to traditional substance abuse therapy as discussed in Chapters 29, 30, and 31. For those who have failed these treatments or those with a more severe habit, therapeutic communities have been used with substantial effectiveness.[21,22] Volunteer groups have been of great value when they are available (see Chapter 32). Therapeutic communities developed with Synanon and others use a long-term communal residential setting that helps many. A recent evaluation of opiate addicts in England indicate that 45% were drug free and living in the community after 6 months, a more optimistic figure than most U.S. data.[23]

REFERENCES

1. **Caplovitz, D.,** *The Working Addict,* The Graduate School and the University Center of the City University of New York, New York, 1976.
2. **Robins, L. N., Helzer, J. E., and Davis, D. H.,** Narcotic use in Southeast Asia and afterward, *Arch. Gen. Psychiatr.,* 32, 955, 1975.
3. **Halikas, J. A., Darvish, H. S., and Rimmer, J. D.,** The black addicts 1. Methodology, chronology of addiction, and overview of the population, *Am. J. Drug Alcohol Abuse,* 3, 529, 1976.
4. **Vaillant, G. E.,** A 20-year follow-up of New York narcotic addicts, *Arch. Gen. Psychiatr.,* 29, 237, 1973.
5. **O'Brien, C. P., Woody, G. E., and McLellan, A. T.,** Long-term consequences of opiate dependence, *New Engl. J. Med.,* 304, 1098, 1981.
6. **Winick, C.,** The life cycle of the narcotic addict and of addiction, *Bull. Narc.,* 26, 1, 1964.
7. **Kandel, D. B.,** *Longitudinal Research on Drug Use,* Halstead Press, New York, 1978.
8. **Simpson, D. D. and Loyd, M. R.,** Alcohol use following treatment for drug addiction, *J. Stud. Alcohol,* 42, 323, 1981.
9. **Croughan, J. L., Miller, J. P., Whitman, B. Y., and Schober, J. B.,** Alcoholism and alcohol dependence in narcotic addicts: a prospective study with a five-year follow-up, *Am. J. Drug Alcohol Abuse,* 8, 85, 1981.
10. **Lass, H.,** Most chronic pain patients misuse drugs, study shows, *Hospital Trib. World Serve,* 6, 2, 1976.
11. **Banks, P. A.,** *Pancreatitis,* Plenum Medical Book Co., New York, 1979.
12. **Milby, J. B.,** Methadone maintenance to abstinence. How many make it?, *J. Nerv. Ment. Dis.,* 176, 409, 1988.
13. **Kosten, T. R., Rounsaville, B. J., and Kleber, H. D.,** Predictors of 2 — 5 year outcome in opioid addicts: pretreatment source of income, *Am. J. Drug Alcohol Abuse,* 13, 19, 1987.
14. **McGlothlin, W. H. and Anglin, M. D.,** Long-term follow-up of clients of high and low dose methadone programs, *Arch. Gen. Psychiatr.,* 38, 1055, 1981.
15. **Ling, W., Charuvastra, V. C., Kaim, S. C., et al.,** Methadryl acetate and methadone as maintenance treatments for heroin addicts, *Arch. Gen. Psychiatr.,* 33, 709, 1976.
16. **Stimmel, B.,** *Heroin Dependency: Medical, Economic and Social Aspects,* Stratton Intercont. Medical Book Corp., New York, 1975.
17. **Croughan, J. L., Miller, J. P., Koepke, J., et al.,** Depression in narcotic addicts — a prospective study with a five-year follow-up, *Comp. Psychiatr.,* 22, 428, 1981.
18. **Green, J. and Jaffe, J. H.,** Alcohol and opiate dependence: a review, *J. Stud. Alcohol,* 38, 1274, 1977.
19. **McGlothlin, W. and Anglin, D.,** Shutting off methadone: costs and benefits, *Arch. Gen. Psychiatr.,* 38, 885, 1981.

20. **Senay, E. C., Dorus, W., Goldberg, F., et al.,** Withdrawal from methadone maintenance: rate of withdrawal and expectation, *Arch. Gen. Psychiatr.*, 34, 361, 1977.
21. **Bale, R. N., Van Stone, W. W., Kuldau, J. M., et al.,** Therapeutic communities vs. methadone maintenance, *Arch. Gen. Psychiatr.*, 37, 179, 1980.
22. **Coombs, R. H.,** Back on the streets: therapeutic communities impact upon drug users, *Am. J. Drug Alcohol Abuse,* 8, 185, 1981.
23. **Gossop, M., et al.,** Lapse, relapse and survival among opiate addicts after treatment: a prospective follow-up study, *Br. J. Psychiatr.*, 154, 348, 1989.

Chapter 20

Medical Problems Related to Illicit Drugs

I. INTRODUCTION

Street drugs vary from chemically pure substances to the complete substitution of a drug with similar effects containing none of the alleged substance. Concentrated pure drug from the manufacturer is usually diluted to street doses locally through use of any white powdery material as the diluent. Local addicts are test subjects to be certain that the dilution is appropriate. This process introduces foreign matter into the drug and is somewhat haphazard in getting the dose correct. Common substances used to "cut" concentrated drugs such as cocaine or heroin for i.v. use include dextrose, lactose, dried milk, quinine, and occasionally talc. These adulterants are often responsible for anaphylaxis associated with i.v. injection.

The complications of alcoholism and drugs have been presented in separate chapters in this book, even though there is considerable overlap of the nonspecific complications. Thus neglect of self, increased accidents, trauma, suicide, and malnutrition are common to all addictions, whereas other medical problems are substantially different. Figure 11 indicates the major problems encountered in drug addicts that are further discussed below.

II. TRAUMA AND ACCIDENTS

Drugs have many effects promoting increased trauma. At low levels of use, detectable by chemical testing of the urine but not usually identified by family or examining physicians, the reaction time is prolonged. This means that the time taken from observation to appropriate

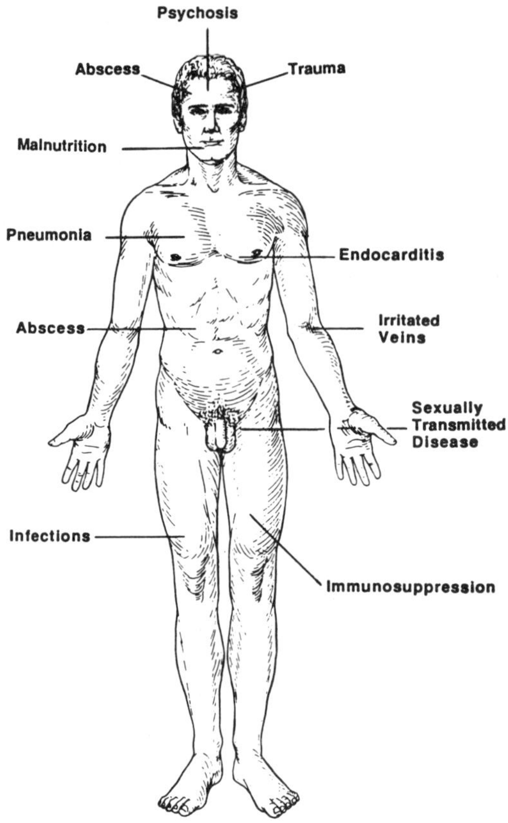

FIGURE 11. Illustration of common medical problems associated with addictions other than alcohol. Contrast with Figure 8 (Chapter 17).

reaction is longer than in normal circumstances. This delayed reaction contributes to increased motor vehicle, recreational, and work-related accidents where alertness for safety is important. At higher levels of use, some motor incoordination is present and further slows reaction time and coordination to prevent injury.

Chronic abuse impairs judgment; abusers are by the nature of their personality more willing to take risks than nonusers. This combination of increased risk taking and impaired judgment results in more chances being taken in all daily activities with an increased prevalence of injuries. Finally, abusers often are more irritable and sensitive and seem to become involved in more physical altercations than others.

The practical meaning of this is that addicts often have traumatic injury but are not always able to recall the history of its occurrence. I have encountered lacerations and stitches of recent origin in patients who cannot explain where or when they occurred. Any physician screening these patients must be aware that head, chest, and abdominal trauma with internal bleeding may in very short time convert a patient from one with minimal signs of injury into a one with life-threatening bleeding or infection. The screening for traumatic injury must be meticulous.

III. MALNUTRITION

Street drugs have no food value, so their abuse does not replace food in the diet. On the other hand, the craving for drug overwhelms all other emotional and body needs. Although

TABLE 41
Nutritional Assessment

Measurement	Malnourished level
I. Record for all Patients	
1. Weight, height	1. <80% of weight in table of normal weights
2. WBC and hemoglobin	2. <4000 & <120 gm/l
3. Appearance of nutrition	3. Look malnourished
II. Record in suspected malnutrition	
1. Triceps skin folds	1. <10 mm
2. Serum albumin	2. <28 g/l
3. Serum transferrin	3. <2 g/l
4. Upper arm circumference	4. <22 cm
5. WBC × % lymphocytes	5. <1200

amphetamines, opiates, nicotine, and caffeine specifically suppress appetite, this is minor, rarely accounting for substantive weight loss. Heavy addiction to any substance leads to neglected food intake. Malnutrition is limited to the more advanced users of any drug and is infrequent. When present, it renders the person much more susceptible to infectious diseases and to poor wound repair compared to normal subjects. For this reason it needs to be identified and treated, while treating the addiction.

Most hospital-trained physicians have experience in nutritional assessment. With training, the skills of observation during physical examination become as sensitive in identification of malnutrition as deliberate measurement. For those less certain, we include in this section some simple methods of quantitation of nutritional status. Table 41 lists these items and the standard that should lead to specific action for repletion.

Table 41 indicates those things that are required for all patients undergoing screening. Recording the height and weight offers the patient a basis to detect weight loss or gain from their usual, and the opportunity to compare the patient's current weight with charts for Americans of ideal body weight. Only those with one or more criteria of malnutrition or suspected poor eating habits from screening need further evaluation. With practice the physician becomes excellent at detecting malnutrition. Malnutrition can manifest itself in three rather different ways. (1) There can be deficient caloric intake for months, leading to loss of weight, triceps skinfold thickness, and upper arm circumference. (2) Protein alone may be deficient in addicts even though overall calories are maintained. This is more commonly seen in alcoholics than other addicts. This is manifest mostly by low WBC and hemoglobin, decreased albumin and transferrin, and possibly in loss of upper arm circumference. (3) Finally, specific vitamin or mineral nutrients may be lacking, and this is only detected by specific testing for each of them.

Recognition of malnutrition and its treatment will result in major symptomatic improvement even though the learned behavior to control the addiction has not yet occurred. Improvement gives confidence in the treatment team and encouragement to continue. Obesity may also be identified in addicts. In males, recording the waist and hip circumference, each at the maximum, is useful; if the waist exceeds the hips, more cardiovascular accidents occur. Again, attention to and counsel about future health and assistance in weight reduction indicates that you expect the patient to get better.

Patients who are depleted require repletion, and this is done by the provision of extra quantities of ordinary foods. Most addicts will readily eat and replete their body stores once they are through detoxification. Although supplements of vitamins and minerals are commonly administered in the early weeks of detoxification, there is no need for them for more than a week or two after normal eating has been resumed. Ordinarily, a person completely repairs the malnutrition within 2 or 3 months of cessation of drug use.

TABLE 42
Bacterial, Viral, and Other Infections and Infestations More Prevalent in Addicts

1. Bacterial endocarditis
2. Septic thrombophlebitis
3. Occult abscess, lung, brain, liver
4. Tuberculosis, including atypical
5. Pneumonia
6. All venereal disease
7. Urinary tract infection
8. Vaginal, pelvic infections
9. Hepatitis B & C
10. AIDS or HIV infection
11. Fungus infections
12. Amebiasis, giardiasis, other gut infections
13. Body lice, other ectoparasites

IV. INFECTIOUS COMPLICATIONS

The combination of illicit drug products contaminated with soil, bacteria, and fungi, i.v. and s.c. use, nonsterile injection technique, and shared needles largely accounts for the very high numbers and varieties of septic complications. If malnutrition is present, causing immunosuppression, then common infections may become unusually severe and uncommon ones may occur. Thus one encounters in addicts many of the same infections found in patients with AIDS or those undergoing extensive chemotherapy. The practice of sharing needles leads to the frequent occurrence of hepatitis B, hepatitis C, HIV infection, and other blood-transmitted diseases. Additionally, advanced drug users may share a derelict existence, participating in very marginal food and shelter, overcrowding, and communal living, which contribute to the higher incidence of communicable infection and infestations. Table 42 lists a number of bacterial and viral infections, and a few other communicable diseases, that are seen with increasing prevalence in drug addicts and street addicts that have little to do with the agent of abuse. These are more common following intravenous or subcutaneous use and are more severe in the malnourished person.

The identification of these problems requires suspicion, and a careful history and physical examination. Laboratory testing for specific diseases is undertaken if appropriate. The age and habits of the patient, and the complaints and findings upon examination, determine the degree to which these various problems are pursued. Most physicians identifying weight loss and would perform at least a tuberculin skin test for sensitivity and possibly undertake a chest X-ray. The ability to cure or correct almost all of the nonviral problems in Table 42 places a substantial responsibility on the physician. The unusual presentations challenge diagnosticians.

V. NEUROLOGICAL AND PSYCHIATRIC DISORDERS

A. NEUROLOGICAL DISORDERS

A great number of neurological complaints are encountered in addicts who reach a derelict existence but are infrequent in middle-class patients who continue in their jobs and with family. Peripheral neuritis is a common complaint, and asymmetrical paralysis of a foot, arm, or interference with hand movements is a basis for seeking help. These asymmetrical problems are almost always due to pressure on a peripheral nerve, and the patient responds over months. Splinting and physical therapy may be required for full return of function. Symmetrical sensory neuritis is usually associated with malnutrition and will also improve promptly with vitamin therapy in so far as pain is concerned, but return of sensation to normal is slow and often incomplete.

Cerebral vascular accidents are probably due to embolization with particulate material after intravenous injections are seen. Lesions in the eyegrounds, hematuria, and foreign bodies in liver or muscle biopsies usually accompany these. If the patient is young, the prognosis for complete recovery is excellent, but physical therapy may be needed. I encounter one or two patients each year with advanced contractures following a cerebral embolism who did not receive appropriate medical care. The good neurological outcome of this disease in this age group needs to be widely known to encourage earlier efforts to preserve and restore function.

Epilepsy is common. Convulsions may occur from toxic reactions, from emboli during intravenous injections, and from withdrawal. In addition, there is an increased occurrence of trauma producing injury and recurrent epilepsy. The issues of assessment and treatment are identical to that for the alcoholic as discussed in detail in Chapter 10.

B. PSYCHIATRIC DISORDERS

Psychiatric disorders were discussed in Chapter 18.

VI. COMPLICATIONS RELATED TO THE SITE OF ADMINISTRATION

Thrombosed veins, scars from frequent inflamed injections, absence of veins, skin abscesses, and pigmentation changes from hematomas over veins are all commonplace and well known to those working with intravenous addicts. Sometimes these findings on examination suggest that an addiction is present; Table 15, in Chapter 9, lists many of these findings. Occasionally a complication of septic veins is the compartment syndrome. The sheath in the arm or leg surrounding the vein, artery, or other structure becomes a phlegmon leading to ischemia. These problems require prompt extensive opening of the sheath and debridement. Gas gangrene has been reported.

Smoking of drugs, such as cocaine in the form of crack, opiates, or marijuana, leads to respiratory disorders. Allergic asthma, bronchitis, chronic cough, and increases in sinusitis have been observed. Taking drugs by nasal insufflation (snorting) produces prominent irritation of the mucous membranes with chronic rhinorrhea and even sinusitis in a few users. A recent report found orbital inflammation and optic neuropathy associated with sinusitis produced from habitual intranasal cocaine snorting.[2] It is rarely the basis for consulting a doctor and clears up promptly when snorting is discontinued.

VII. OTHER COMPLICATIONS

Cardiovascular toxicity relating to cocaine use is increasingly described. Coronary spasm, arrhythmia, and direct myocardial toxicity have been demonstrated. Although myocardial infarctions have been observed in young people, usually the injury is in subjects with a prolonged, intense habit.[3]

REFERENCES

1. **Miller, N. S., Nace, M. A., Brummitt, C. F., et al.,** Fungal infections associated with intravenous drug abuse: a case of localized cerebral phycomycosis, *J. Clin. Psychiatr.*, 49, 320, 1988.
2. **Goldberg, R. A., et al.,** Orbital inflammation and optic neuropathies associated with chronic sinusitis of intranasal cocaine abuse: possible role of contiguous inflammation, *Arch. Ophthalmol.*, 107, 831, 1989.
3. **Shi-Kaung, P., et al.,** Direct cocaine cardiotoxicity demonstrated by endomyocardial biopsy, *Arch. Pathol. Lab. Med.*, 113, 842, 1989.

Chapter 21

Cocaine and Amphetamines

I. INTRODUCTION

America currently is in an epidemic of cocaine use resulting partly from the ready availability of the "crack" form of cocaine. Popularization of use through wide publicity of celebrities using the agent has facilitated spread. Amphetamines have been used in similar epidemics and have remarkably similar effects to cocaine. Analysis of products sold on the street indicate that cocaine is often adulterated with the much less costly amphetamines and occasionally is only amphetamine. Both of these agents are popular drugs of abuse, with the majority of the amphetamines being diverted from legitimate medical supplies or synthesized in illicit American laboratories, whereas cocaine is all illicit in its supply channels, arising from the natural coca leaves grown on the slopes of the Andes in South America.

II. COCAINE

A. MATERIAL AVAILABLE

All cocaine arises from the coca leaf grown in South America and is refined in Central America and Mexico, with most being manufactured in Columbia. It has been used as a stimulant in the Andes areas of South America for centuries, but cocaine was first purified in 1860 and concentrates were used widely in tonics and soft drinks until the 1930s, when it was removed. It is available as a crude extract that is about 80% cocaine sulfate, and as the pure alkaloid (called the base) or as its hydrochloride. The pure base is the active volatile material sold as "crack" and is usually used by smoking. Only the pure base is sufficiently volatile to be taken by smoking, but other forms are used by nasal insufflation or intravenous injection. Most cocaine now arrives in the U.S. as a highly purified material and is usually diluted with any convenient white water-soluble material for street suppliers. Mannitol, glucose, or lactose are frequent diluents. Adulterated drug in which amphetamines replace the cocaine or large parts of it are common; a form of methylamphetamine called "crank" is quite volatile and can be smoked.[1] Mixtures of caffeine, benzocaine, procaine, and an amphetamine have been sold on the streets as pure cocaine.[2] Street names for cocaine include coke, snowflake, and crack.

B. MODES OF ADMINISTRATION AND EFFECTS

1. Administration

Cocaine is most commonly taken intranasally or smoked. For "snuffing" the powder is arranged on a clear glass surface in lines 2 to 3 mm wide and 3 to 4 cm long and inhaled through a straw or rolled paper inserted into a nostril. Each "snort" contains about 25 mg of active drug. Any of the street products may be taken in this manner. Smoking is a popular route, particularly with crack, which is much more efficiently vaporized at lower temperatures than other cocaine forms. Figure 3 (Chapter 5) illustrates the blood levels attained after taking cocaine via various methods. Smoking and snorting both produce a high within minutes, but both routes transfer less of the purchased dose into the blood than the intravenous route, with snorting providing greater efficiency. Both routes also avoid the many disease complications of intravenous injection. This drug is used intravenously for the most extreme high. With all of these methods of administration, the peak blood levels and the psychological high developed in 1 to 15 min. Nasal, intravenous, and pulmonary absorption occur very rapidly, with a euphoria probably surpassing that of all other drugs, followed in 10 to 15 min by a dysphoria and loss of euphoria leading to the further consumption of all available drug.

2. Effects

Cocaine is hydrolyzed in the blood by cholinesterase and metabolized by the liver leading to a half life of about 45 min. The extreme euphoria is over in 30 min after a single inhalation into the lung or i.v. dose, but is more prolonged after intranasal insufflation probably due to continued absorption. The high is always associated with increased adrenergic activity. Tachycardia, vasoconstriction, hypertension, and mydriasis are nearly always observed. Higher doses produce marked agitation and tachyrhythmias. Convulsions and death may occur. Toxic reactions with death are much more common after intravenous use.

The high is frequently followed by depression, and this becomes more and more marked with chronic use. At this time a mild withdrawal syndrome with fatigue, depression, and anhedonia is prominent. A biphasic response with lower doses improving motor function without tremor, and higher doses producing deterioration with severe tremulousness, has been observed.[3]

C. TOXIC REACTIONS

Fatal toxic reactions, usually from an overdose, have been well publicized in athletes and other entertainers. Drug-induced psychiatric disturbances are far more common. Toxic reactions may be manifest by convulsions, unarousibility, a clear acute stroke in a young person, hyperthermia, or unexplained cardiac arrhythmia. There are always some features of increased adrenergic function, and most of these are present: tachycardia, sweating, markedly elevated systolic and diastolic blood pressure, dilated pupils, and elevated temperature. Occasionally a prominent schizophrenia-like psychosis is present.

Evaluation and treatment to support vital signs should be concurrent. Other medical conditions whose toxicity may mimic cocaine overdose, such as septicemia, pulmonary embolism, and thyroid storm, should be considered. Blood and urine samples should be taken for drug analysis and, if possible, blood gasses obtained. If the overdose followed ingestion, prompt gastric lavage and or use of ipecac is recommended, leaving 10 to 15 g of activated charcoal in the stomach. Seizures are controlled with i.v. diazepam (10-mg increments over 2 min) or i.v. lorazepam (4-mg increments). An elevated diastolic pressure over 120 mm Hg is treated with i.v. phentolamine, 2 to 5 mg each 5 to 10 min, or propranolol, 40 to 80 mg i.v. each hour. Hyperthermia is usually treated with haloperidol (5 mg, i.m.), if not readily controlled with cold sponging or a hypothermic blanket.

Psychosis resembling acute schizophrenia, depression, or dysphoria meeting all criteria for chronic depression may occur in persons during a cycle of intense use of cocaine. In other instances, there may be a panic reaction with extreme fear of loss of sanity; an arrhythmia or even myocardial infarction may result because of the panic attack. Panic reactions are not recurrent, but may occur after any sequential use. Evaluation includes history and physical examination for trauma and other treatable diseases. Blood and urine are sent for drug screening. Blood gases are particularly useful in assessing the severity of the reaction and determining the need for hospitalization. Adrenergic hyperactivity will be observed with tachycardia, dilated pupils, severe sweating with warm skin, hypertension, and tachyrhythmias.

Reassurance and observation over 4 to 6 h will usually lead to marked improvement. Diazepam, 5 mg i.v., once or up to three doses may be necessary. Panic reactions mimicking heart attacks are often treated with propranolol orally, 40 to 80 mg, twice daily. If the problem does not clear up promptly, concerns about underlying psychosis, a more chronic drug-induced psychiatric condition, or another diagnosis are raised. Even with adequate sedation and a good home situation, thorough evaluation should be undertaken for reactions persisting beyond 2 days, usually in hospital.

D. MEDICAL AND NEUROLOGICAL COMPLICATIONS

A wide variety of medical and neurological complications have been described. Common ones include seizures, focal deficits, frank stroke, and vertigo.[4] An interesting series of case reports of cocaine initiating migraine-like headache has appeared.[5] The link between cocaine effects on serotonin uptake and the production of migraine is interesting.[6] Acute myoglobinuria with renal insufficiency has been described a number of times.

Increasingly acute myocardial infarction due to coronary spasm,[7,8] and myocardiopathy of a permanent or reversible form, are being described.[9] A new monograph on cocaine[10] and a very readable review of the toxicity and health complications of cocaine use has appeared,[11] as well as an encyclopedic review of unusual occurrences seen in hospital emergency rooms.[12]

E. TREATMENT

Treatment is not unique and is discussed in Chapters 26, 27, and 28. There is a trend in the recent literature to use many medications for both control of symptoms and relapse prevention, but the effectiveness of these medications has not been tested in controlled trials.[13] The available controlled trial literature indicates little basis for pharmacological intervention.[14] A possible exception may be that approximately one fourth of the patients who have clear depression are effectively treated with antidepressants, usually desipramine.[15]

III. AMPHETAMINES

A. GENERAL DATA

Amphetamines came into medical use in the 1930s to produce more energy in asthenic or depressed persons. After the ability to keep fatigued persons awake and appetite suppression were observed, these drugs were widely used medically and became a popular drug of

TABLE 43
Frequently Abused Amphetamines

Generic name	Trade name	Street names
Amphetamine	Benzedrine®	Bennies, uppers, ups
Dextroamphetamine	Dexedrine®	Dexies, uppers, truck drivers
Methamphetamine	Desoxyn®, Fetamin®	Speed, blue angels, crank
Methylenedioxy-methamphetamine (MDMA)		Ecstasy
Phenmetrazine	Preludin®	Uppers
Methylphenidate	Ritalin®	Uppers

abuse. Currently there are few medical uses; these include the treatment of narcolepsy, hyperactivity in children, and appetite suppression. Other drugs are available that produce comparable shrinkage of the nasal and respiratory mucous membranes associated with allergy or viral infections. Several epidemics of abuse of amphetamines in the U.S., Australia, and Japan[16] have led to limited medical use and some increased control. Amphetamines appear mostly in Schedule II of the FDA due to their high addiction potential with little medical value. It should be noted that euphoric and toxic effects of i.v. amphetamines are identical to those of cocaine. It is widely believed that users cannot distinguish i.v. cocaine from i.v. amphetamines. This leads to major adulteration of the more costly cocaine with amphetamines. Recently a volatile form of methamphetamine called ''crank'' has appeared. Table 43 lists the chemical, trade, and street names of the commonly abused amphetamines. These drugs are easily made in illicit laboratories from precursors readily available from the chemical industry. A recent paper detailed the large diversion of chemical to this industry.[17] Currently chemists in garage laboratories synthesize similar molecules that may not be controlled substances, yet have the same euphoric and addiction effects; these are called ''designer drugs''.

Three groups of abusers of amphetamines are identified. One group uses them to keep alert while moonlighting at several jobs with inadequate rest (including physicians, musicians, truck drivers, and air traffic controllers). Another is a group using them initially to control weight or narcolepsy who lapse into an abuse pattern. The third is a young population obtaining the drugs from friends or street sources and using them for a high.

B. METABOLISM AND PHARMACOLOGY

The amphetamines are effective orally and intravenously, and crank may be smoked. They have peak effects about 60 min after oral ingestion and last many hours. The half life of amphetamine is 10 to 30 h (shorter with acidic urine, longer with alkaline), of dextroamphetamine is 5 h, and of methamphetamine is 5 h. All are metabolized by the liver but predominantly excreted in an acid urine, thus accounting for the variation in half life with urine pH. Tolerance develops rapidly, but overdose toxic reactions are rare. They do commonly occur in group use when the same dose satisfying a highly tolerant user is employed by an intolerant one. It is estimated that about half of street amphetamines are diverted from legitimate medical sources and the other half are made in uncontrolled laboratories. The amphetamines have more peripheral adrenergic effects, so that sweating, muscle hyperactivity, and perception of excitement are more pronounced than with cocaine. The percentage of users who become addicts with amphetamines is less than with cocaine, as the euphoria is different and presumably less desirable.

C. TOXIC PROBLEMS AND EMERGENCIES

Drug supplies are usually pure but may not be supplied in precisely measured doses. Tolerance is rapid in onset, and as much as 10 times the dose used by a naive person may

TABLE 44
Signs and Symptoms That Suggest Amphetamine or Cocaine Abuse

Adrenergic signs and symptoms
1. A restless, hyperalert, and hyperactive state
2. Nervousness, increased heart rate and blood pressure
3. Widely dilated pupils in bright light, sunglasses worn even inside
4. Emotional irritability or outbursts
5. Cardiac arrhythmias unusual for age

Panic and psychosis
1. Fear of dying accompanied by tachycardia, dilated pupils, elevated blood pressure
2. Paranoia
3. Confusion with hallucinations
4. New-onset lethargy or depression

Findings
1. Needle marks from i.v. use
2. Bruises, or unexplained traumatic injury

Blood and urine taken for drug testing will provide definitive information

be needed for a high. Depending upon client needs, street doses may be selected to please tolerant persons. Overdose seems to occur only in a group situation when a nontolerant individual takes a dose that tolerant persons readily handle. The most common toxic reaction is psychosis, similar to that encountered with cocaine *(vide supra)* but much more common, particularly in persons undertaking "runs" of amphetamine use lasting over several days. In the naive user, particularly when strong preparations are used i.v. or intranasally, panic reactions may occur. Again, these are in every way identical to those for cocaine but probably a little more common due to the increased peripheral adrenergic effects of the amphetamines.

D. SUSPECTING AN ABUSER OF COCAINE OR AMPHETAMINES

Physicians are believed to identify less than half the regular users of these drugs in their patients because the majority have no medical problems and no desire to discuss the use. The user can be anyone, but workers in occupations that require sustained alertness or sudden and irregular shift changes, long-distance truck drivers, and hard-working employed students are at extra risk. Chronically obese people using diet tablets from time to time are at risk. Adolescents are also at risk. Certain social and cultural groups are frequent users, and use attracts new recruits. Professional athletes, entertainers, and those in the "jet set" have frequently been users. The use of these substances is suspected from the adrenergic overstimulation or from the occurrence of a typical psychosis. Some noted by Ellinwood are listed in Table 44.[18]

REFERENCES

1. **Sly L.,** New generation of drugs on way, US is warned, *Chicago Tribune,* September 1, 1989, 1.
2. **Siegel, R. K.,** Cocaine substitutes, *New Engl. J. Med.,* 302, 817, 1980.
3. **Cohen, S.,** *Cocaine Today,* American Council on Drug Abuse, Rockville, MD, 1981.
4. **Lowenstein, D. H., Massa, S. M., Rowbotham, M. C., Collins, S. D., McKinney, H. E., and Simon, R. P.,** Acute neurologic and psychiatric complications associated with cocaine abuse, *Am. J. Med.,* 83, 841, 1987.
5. **Satel, S. L. and Gawin, F. H.,** Migraine-like headache and cocaine use, *JAMA,* 261, 2995, 1989.
6. **Cunningham, K. A. and Lakoski, J. M.,** Electrophysiological effects of cocaine and procaine on dorsal raphe serotonin neurons, *Eur. J. Pharmacol.,* 148, 457, 1988.
7. **Lange, R. A., Cigarroa, R. G., Yancy, C. W., Jr., et al.,** Cocaine-induced coronary-artery vasoconstriction, *New Engl. J. Med.,* 321, 1557, 1989.

8. **Isner, J. M. and Chokshi, S. K.,** Cocaine and vasospasm, *New Engl. J. Med.,* 321, 1604, 1989.
9. **Chokshi, S. K., Moore, R., Pandian, N. G., and Isner, J. M.,** Reversible cardiomyopathy associated with cocaine intoxication, *Ann. Int. Med.,* 111, 1039, 1989.
10. **Spitz, H. I. and Rosecan, J. S.,** *Cocaine Abuse: New Directions in Treatment and Research,* Brunner/ Mazel Publishers, New York, 1987, Reviewed in *JAMA,* 262, 2308, 1989.
11. **VanDette, J. M. and Cornish, L. A.,** Medical complications of illicit cocaine use, *Clin. Pharm.,* 8, 401, 1989.
12. **Loper, K. A.,** Clinical toxicology of cocaine, *Med. Toxicol. Adverse Drug Exp.,* 4, 174, 1989.
13. **Kosten, T. R.,** Pharmacotherapeutic interventions for cocaine abuse, matching patients to treatments, *J. Nerv. Ment. Dis.,* 177, 379, 1989.
14. **Kleber, H. and Gawin, F.,** Psychopharmacological trials in cocaine abuse treatment, *Am. J. Drug Alcohol Abuse,* 12, 235, 1986.
15. **Gawin, F. and Kleber, H.,** Pharmacologic treatments of cocaine abuse, *Psychiatr. Clin. North Am.,* 9, 573, 1986.
16. **Ellinwood, E. H.,** Amphetamine psychosis: individuals, settings and sequences, in *Current Concepts in Amphetamine Abuse,* Ellinwood, E. H. and Cohen, S., Eds., National Institute on Mental Health, Rockville, MD, 1970.
17. **Sherrod, P.,** Chemical makers under fire in drug war, *Chicago Tribune,* May 7, 1989, Section 7, 3.
18. **Ellinwood, E. H.,** Emergency treatment of adverse reactions to CNS stimulants, in *A Treatment Manual for Acute Drug Abuse Emergencies,* Bourne, P. G., Ed., U.S. Government Printing Office, Washington, D.C., 1974.

Chapter 22

Marijuana

I. INTRODUCTION

Marijuana is an ancient drug, recorded as long ago as 2700 B.C., and remains even at the present time a widely used recreational drug in the Middle East and the Orient. It comes from the plant *Cannabis sativa,* which is an annual growing wild or readily cultivated under conditions that will grow tomatoes. The amount of active resin, found mostly in the flowering tops and upper leaves, increases with maturation and good growing conditions and diminishes with length of storage. It is believed to be second to alcohol in the numbers of North American users. Its active principle is delta-9-tetrahydrocannabinol (THC), but this is very difficult to manufacture. It is supplied illicitly as "grass", "pot", or "Mary Jo" for smoking or ingestion, or as hashish for smoking. Pure THC is probably never available on the street, but when sold illicitly is in fact other substances such as PCP or LSD. It is used mostly by young people, with peak age of use in the late teens. Data obtained in 1988 from a survey of high school seniors indicated that 65% are regular users of alcohol, 14% are regular users of marijuana, with cigarette smoking at 30%.

II. METHOD OF USE AND METABOLISM

THC is readily absorbed from respiratory mucosa, with about half the available drug reaching the smoker. Oral preparations are readily and completely absorbed, with a high first-pass effect. Onset of action is 5 to 15 min after the start of smoking, with the peak effect at 15 to 30 min and diminution in effect after 3 h. Onset after oral ingestion is after 30 to 60 min and persistence is 5 to 7 h. Good material contains about 5.0 mg of THC per cigarette. Although there has been continued investigation of the drug as an antiemetic for control of nausea, particularly in cancer chemotherapy, and for reduction of intraocular pressure in glaucoma, there is no FDA-approved indication for the drug in medicine. The drug is metabolized by the liver, and the inactive products are excreted in the bile and the urine. In the 1980s, street marijuana became 10- to 50-fold more potent than the material of earlier decades.

III. GENERAL EFFECTS IN THE USER

THC primarily produces euphoria, with relaxation and a sense of ultimate well-being sought and commented upon as the ''high'' that makes the agent popular. Short-term memory is impaired so consistently that conversation is interfered with and planned expressions are not completed. Coordination and balance are regularly impaired when critically tested, but ordinary muscular activities can be carried out.

Mood changes which may be prominent are highly dependent upon what the user expects to happen, the setting and companionship of drug use, and the potency of the dose or doses. Loss of time perception, heightened sleepiness, or sexual arousal may be seen. If intoxication is associated with intense stress, heightened aggressiveness is seen. At very high doses, hallucinations, usually visual, confusion, disorientation, and even panic may ensue.

At intermediate to high doses, or after repeated doses, there is tachycardia, elevation of the blood pressure, and reddening of the conjunctiva. There is no change in the pupillary size. Fine tremor, dry mouth, and nystagmus are observed with high doses, always after there is noticeable discoordination. There is no fever, but the respiratory rate is elevated.

In chronic use by smoking, bronchitis is frequent. In a well-followed group of patients, Weller and Halikas[2] found physical addiction, inability to control use, and social problems related to age of initial use, level of initial intake, and frequency of use. They also found future drug problems in their users. The drug may produce a withdrawal syndrome that is quite mild and may promote seizures in those who have had them previously. Probably the greatest health hazard is accidents occurring during use, due to both impaired judgment and impaired coordination.

IV. TOXIC AND CHRONIC RESIDUAL PROBLEMS

A. WITHDRAWAL

The reaction is mild and requires no specific treatment.[3,4]

B. TOXIC REACTIONS

Heavy use for a prolonged period of time, most often associated with use of concentrated resin such as hashish or ganja, may lead to visual hallucinations with paranoia. The mental processes are dulled, with prominent impairment of memory, learning, and problem-solving capacities. This may require up to 3 weeks to clear, and the patient may be hospitalized for safety. Lesser degrees of persistent mental alterations, particularly when mild, are probably common and unrecognized.

C. PRECIPITATION OF UNDERLYING PSYCHOSIS

There is a full literature of precipitation of overt psychosis through marijuana use, which in retrospective analysis had been present previously. Epilepsy, schizophrenia, and depression have all been rendered overt.[5,6] A wide spectrum of acute psychiatric reactions arise particularly in a university health service, where as many as 50% of the student body may be occasional users.[7,8] These include panic reactions, flashbacks, fear of losing one's mind, and occasionally injuries related to accidents during use evoking fear.

D. PERMANENT INJURIES

Fatal overdose is not known, though death has occurred from accidents. Animal work and detailed studies of chronic users indicate that the developing brain is more injured than the fully developed one, highly pertinent to use in adolescents. EEG tracings have been abnormal for up to 3 months in chronic users. Although chronic organic brain syndrome has been reported, this is not usually accepted as a permanent injury.[9]

V. TREATMENT

There is often a great deal of emotion connected with drug use, particularly when an adolescent or college-age person is determined to be a user in conjunction with some other social, behavioral, or legal problem. Weller and Halikas provided guidelines to differentiate recreational use, which needs no treatment, from abuse, which can benefit from treatment. They felt that someone addicted to marijuana required at least three of the following four: (1) adverse psychological reactions to the drug, including health problems; (2) problems with use (such as binges, use in the morning); (3) clear social or interpersonal problems, such as arrests or fights; (4) the expressed opinion of the patient or significant others with close contact that use has been too high. The withdrawal, if any, is mild and needs little or no treatment. If there are chronic residua, a protected environment may be required for a few days, seldom for as long as 2 weeks.

It is generally agreed that effective treatment of marijuana addiction is reasonably easy in the patient who is motivated by a frightening complication of its use. Such a patient is identified by a clear admission of excessive and regular use of marijuana with an event sufficiently alarming to make the patient consider treatment. In such a circumstance gaining the patient's confidence as a helper is the most important part of the treatment. Often as few as ten visits with a counselor is sufficient. Since such use indicates peer, school, or parental pressure, some examination of these to produce amelioration is of value. If the patient has no interest in treatment and does not accept that the addiction exists, then there is little value in forcing treatment unless the behavior pattern is sufficient to be health or life threatening, an infrequent problem with this drug. Hospitalization in treatment programs, preferably with subjects of a similar age, is then recommended.

The frequent use of other substances, and abuse of sedatives, requires the therapist to test for these at an early time in the evaluation and management of the patient and to avoid the ongoing use of sedatives. Since phenothiazines and haloperidol have the lowest potential for abuse, they may be used when such a drug seems necessary.

Recreational use of marijuana poses a very limited health habit and is of low risk for future health.[10,11] An excellent monograph has just appeared.[12]

REFERENCES

1. **Goodwin, F. K.,** Annual Survey of Drug Use by High School Seniors, University of Michigan Institute for Social Research, Reported in *U.S. Med.,* April 1989, 50.
2. **Weller, R. A. and Halikas, J. A.,** Objective criteria for the diagnosis of marijuana abuse, *J. Nerv. Ment. Dis.,* 168, 98, 1980.
3. **Jones, R. T.,** Clinical relevance of cannabis tolerance and dependence, *J. Clin. Pharmacol.,* 211, 1435, 1981.
4. **Kaymakcalan, S.,** Potential dangers of cannabis, *Int. J. Addictions,* 721, 1975.
5. **Halikas, J. A., Goodwin, D. W., and Guze, S. B.,** Marihuana use and psychiatric illness, *Arch. General Psychiatr.,* 27, 162, 1972.
6. **Ablon, S. L. and Goodwin, F. K.,** High frequency of dysphoric reactions of tetrahydrocannabinol among depressed patients, *Am. J. Psychiatr.,* 131, 448, 1974.

7. **Smart, R. G. and Adlaf, E. M.,** Adverse reactions and seeking medical treatment among student cannabis users, *Drug and Alcohol Dependence,* 9, 201, 1982.
8. **Pillard, R. C.,** Marihuana, *New Engl. J. Med.,* 283, 292, 1970.
9. Report of an ARF/WHO Scientific Meeting on Adverse Health and behavioral Consequences of Cannabis Use, Toronto, Ontario, Addiction Research Foundation, 1981.
10. **Rose, M.,** Cannabis. A medical question?, *Lancet,* 1, 703, 1980.
11. **Relman, A. S.,** Marijuana ''Justifies serious concern,'' in *Marijuana and Health,* National Academy Press, Washington, D.C., 1982.
12. **Gold, M. S.,** *Marijuana,* Plenum Press, New York, 1989.

Chapter 23

Hallucinogens and Phencyclidine

I. INTRODUCTION

This chapter discusses several classes of drugs. Lysergic acid diethylamide (LSD) shows cross tolerance for most of the other hallucinogens, but not for phencyclidine (PCP) or the atropine-like drugs. Only LSD and PCP are important agents of abuse, because they are readily synthesized in the U.S. and therefore widely available. Street drugs in these categories are often adulterated.

A. HALLUCINOGENS

Hallucinogens have been known to Native American culture for more than 1000 years, yet these agents were not substantially abused until the easily synthesized and widely available agent lysergic acid diethylamide (LSD) became available. Since its introduction into the drug culture in the 1940s, it has become a common street drug. There are currently no approved medical indications. A variety of plant-derived compounds with variable structures are included in this group. All of these agents induce false sensory experiences made up of complex stimuli that either do not exist or represent marked distortions of real sensory experiences. Perceived sensory experiences that do not exist are called *hallucinations* and, though commonly visual or auditory, may be tactile, gustatory, or kinesthetic. Actual sensory experiences that are highly distorted are termed *illusions*. The drugs in the group have variable actions, sharing in common only the production of illusions and hallucinations and these in various degrees. Studies of LSD have shown multiple actions at multiple sites in

TABLE 45
Hallucinogenic Drugs and Related Compounds

Hallucinogens
1. Indolealkylamines
    Lysergic acid diethylamide (LSD): "acid," "blue dots"
    Psilocybin, psilocin
    Dimethyltryptamine (DMT): "business man's lunch"
    Diethyltryptamine (DET)
2. Phenylethylamines
    Mescaline (peyote): "cactus," "mescal"
3. Phenylisopropylamines
    2,5-dimethoxy-4-methylamphetamine (DOM,STP)

Phencyclidine (PCP): "angel dust," "superacid"

Minor substances
1. Nutmeg, mace
2. Morning glory seeds

the CNS, with no single binding site predominating. Because these drugs are usually effective in microgram quantities, it is likely that binding sites accounting for this CNS sensitivity exist but have not yet been discovered.[1]

B. PHENCYCLIDINE

Phencyclidine (PCP) was introduced as an anesthetic in veterinary medicine and is readily synthesized. It is not a part of the hallucinogen group but is generally put in a separate classification. Its predominant addictive effect is a euphoria that requires meticulous dose titration to achieve. It is almost entirely available from illicit synthesis.

II. AGENTS AVAILABLE, SITES OF ACTION, AND METABOLISM

The agents available that will be discussed in this chapter are listed in Table 45. It should be noted that with the exception of LSD and PCP (which are always 80 to 99% pure), these are very impure substances. Often amphetamines are added as an adulterant to provide the prominent side effects that convince clients that they are getting active material. Only very rarely is a hallucinogen provided in pure form in street practice. Dilution with amphetamines is commonplace, and often the more exotic drugs are in truth combinations of LSD and PCP, both of which can be obtained synthetically much more cheaply than the naturally occurring substances.

A. SITES OF ACTION

Remarkably little is known about the sites of action in this group. LSD is the most potent of these agents, with as little as 25 μg producing its effect. At this dose it is presumed to have specific binding sites, but they are unknown, though labeled material is widely distributed in the brainstem. Onset of action after oral ingestion occurs within 15 min and may last up to 12 h. PCP binds to two known receptors, a binding site in the benzodiazepine-GABA chloride ionophore and one of the binding sites for morphine. Other binding sites are postulated.[2] It is used by ingestion, insufflation, and smoking. It is a weak base ionized at pH 5 or less, is concentrated in an acid urine and in gastric juice, and can be more rapidly removed from the body by acidifying the urine and aspirating gastric juice. Its hepatic metabolites are psychoactive. Although its half life is about 90 min, the effects due to the active metabolic products persists for about 6 h. Of the minor substances, morning glory seeds, nutmeg, and mace seem effective due to their atropine-like effect. These substances have prominent binding to cholinergic-sensitive neurons in the CNS.

B. METABOLISM

1. Methods of Administration

LSD is most commonly taken orally, with the 50- to 100-μg dose placed on a sugar cube. These drugs can also be taken nasally, but i.v. use and smoking are not common routes of administration. PCP, on the other hand, may be taken by any route, and injection, smoking, and nasal insufflation are known as well as ingestion.

Patterns of hallucinogen use tend to be sporadic and quite irregular, unlike most other abused drugs. These drugs are rapidly absorbed orally, and though there is a substantial first-pass effect, the rapid development of tolerance requires dose adjustment by chronic users to obtain the desired effect. These drugs are absorbed by nasal insufflation and faster but erratically by smoking. There is rapid development of tolerance and cross tolerance for other drugs of the group. There are several reasons that use is usually limited to fairly short periods of time. Only the chemically synthesized LSD and PCP are readily available in pure form; other agents are hard to come by and are irregular in potency. There is a limited margin of safety between a good trip and a bad trip with serious psychosis; few patients can continue use without experiencing bad trips. Tolerance is rapid in onset, requiring dose adjustment to get a good trip. Nearly all users also abuse other substances both simultaneously and sequentially.

2. Appearance

Drugs taken by insufflation, injection, or smoking produce the "high" within minutes, but after oral ingestion 30 to 45 min are required.

3. Metabolism

LSD and related hallucinogens are oxidized by the liver, and LSD is largely excreted in the bile, though other members of the group appear predominantly in the urine. Although the half persistence time in plasma is 3 h, the psychic effects of LSD last 8 to 12 h, in part due to active metabolic products. Other agents in this group require a great deal more drug, for they vary from 0.1 to 10% of the effectiveness of LSD. The psychic effect last only for 3 to 4 h. PCP is also metabolized by the liver to one or more active products that are eventually excreted in the urine. The native drug concentrates in acidic gastric juice and gastric suction have been employed to treat toxic reactions of the overdose type.

III. EFFECTS ON THE USER

A. HALLUCINOGENS

With hallucinogens the onset of action begins within 15 min after oral ingestion on an empty stomach and peaks after 45 to 60 min with the oral route. Other forms of ingestion peak more rapidly. The person has manifestations that are somatic, perceptual, and affective. Often euphoria is present, but interrupted with bursts of anxiety and lability of mood. Perceptual errors (illusions) are common, and there is almost always a deranged interpretation of sensory input analogous to the sensory-deprivation syndrome. Hallucinations occur in only a minority of uses, and these usually appear with higher doses. In nearly all users there are alterations in mood, distortion of time, and altered shapes and colors. This is not frightening and is usually depersonalized. An observer will witness rapid change in moods, hostility of expression, incoordination and ataxia, and may witness agitation, nystagmus, and inability to reach the person through ordinary conversation.

Hallucinogens variably effect mood. A majority report lability of mood or euphoria. Infrequently, loss of control, paranoia or panic may occur. Sympathomimetic effects are invariable, and there is usually defect in judgment. The effects on mood cognition, body image, and perception are dose related; at high doses a psychosis with prominent adrenergic findings occurs. Approximately one sixth of high school seniors in the U.S. have used hallucinogens at least once. When hallucinogens are used with a close and secure peer group, hallucinations and delusions can be experienced without loss of control. When used with an unknown group, loss of control and panic are much more common. The addicting property and unique feature of the hallucinogens is described as having a "capacity reliably to induce states of altered perception, thought and feeling that are not experienced otherwise except in dreams or at times of religious exaltation."[3]

B. PCP

Extreme euphoria results with the proper dose of PCP, but extensive dose adjustment is required because of rapid development of tolerance. There are distortions of body image and a rather constant distortion of the sensory input or illusions. Hallucinations are not frequent. There are rapid mood swings and irritability, and to an observer dysarthria, tremors, muscular rigidity, and nystagmus are common. If the dose is a bit too high, the patient is extremely depressed, with depression even of reflexes and paresthesia. Clarity of thought is invariably absent, and the subject is very difficult to communicate with. The user of just the correct dose may experience extreme relaxation and pleasure at the experience, but the user of an incorrect dose, either too large or too little, will count the experience very unpleasant. Severe somatic complaints of nausea, dizziness, and complete inability to concentrate may be experienced, or a panic attack may ensue through loss of control. The margin between a good trip and a bad one is slim, so that all degrees of alarming observations are made on ataxia, hypertonicity, myoclonic jerks, and even seizures that are not recalled by the subject. The effects are usually over by 6 h after dosing.

C. OTHER AGENTS

Mace, nutmeg, and morning glory seeds may produce confusion, illusions, and hallucinations after large amounts of ingestion, but the reactions are mild. Amyl nitrate produces a vasodilatation, a "rush" that is most widely employed to gain a penile erection.

IV. TOXIC REACTIONS

There are a great variety of toxic reactions to these agents, both acute and subacute; these have more in common than differences so they will be treated together. Very few users are fully knowledgeable of which drug they received, for LSD and PCP are inexpensive products on the street and mixed products as well as adulterated ones are common. Toxic reactions from too large a dose, panic states, and psychosis persisting substantially longer than the usual drug effects are frequent emergency problems. DSM III-R indicates hallucinogen abuse and organic mental disorders of hallucinogen affective and hallucinogen delusional disorders.

A. TOXIC REACTIONS

Toxic reactions are common and usually occur in an experienced user who has taken an unusually high or rapidly repeated doses of drug. Within 30 min a very exaggerated adrenergic response, with marked anxiety, prominent pounding of the heart, and anxiety, occurs. The pupils are widely dilated, the blood pressure and pulse are elevated, and there may be fever. In extreme circumstances vascular collapse and convulsions may occur. The psyche demonstrates hallucinations and loss of reality, and there is marked fear. Distortion and intensification of sensory perception is usually present, such as hearing color or feeling sounds. Depersonalization and confusion are often prominent. The symptoms disappear completely in 12 to 24 h. If hyperthermia is prominent, an ice bath or a cooling blanket may be needed. If the blood pressure is alarmingly elevated, phentolamine i.v. may be indicated. Convulsions are usually managed with phenytoin or diazepam. Anxiety is usually allayed by supporting the patient, and only rarely is a drug such as diazepam, 10 to 30 mg orally, repeated 10 to 15 mg each 2 h, required. With LSD the reaction is over in 24 h. If it persists, other drugs such as STP or PCP should be considered.

With these latter drugs, a toxic reaction may persist for up to 10 days. The patient may present with a catatonic picture and be unresponsive to any stimuli, even though the vital signs seem adequate. Most patients with PCP overdose have neurological findings that are more extreme than with other agents. Ataxia, muscular hypertonicity, hyperreflexia, myoclonus, and nystagmus are very common.

B. PSYCHOSIS

Hallucinations or delusions are almost always present, and strong support for the diagnosis is provided by the rapid clearing of the signs and symptoms, usually within 1 day, for all of the substances except STP, which may be associated with persistence for up to 10 days. Infrequently there may be violence. Preexisting schizophrenia and paranoia may be aggravated by hallucinogen use. Stable schizophrenics sometimes experiment with street drugs and present at emergency facilities that are unaware of their previous history.

Treatment is usually supportive. Control of the sympathetic overactivity may require diazepam; control of the hallucinations with haloperidol is usually undertaken when they persist for more than a day.

C. PANIC REACTIONS

Panic reactions almost invariably occur in a first-time user who believes he is losing his mind as he enters the visual hallucination effects. Reassurance is the only treatment that is needed.

D. FLASHBACKS

Flashbacks occur commonly in the frequent user but are very poorly understood. The subject experiences a partial repetition of the visual hallucination or the mental state of taking the drug at a time remote from actual usage. During a flashback the individual is able to function fully, and the interaction with physicians comes about most frequently from concern of an ominous meaning of the event, such as brain damage.

E. CHRONIC ORGANIC BRAIN SYNDROME

Multiple high-dose exposure or repeated use of hallucinogens over months may result in permanent loss of brain function. This may be observed by associates of the patient, who observe a loss of any form of motivation, a change in affect, or extraordinary forgetfulness. The condition may be recognized during recovery from a psychosis due to acute drug ingestion or evaluation of a flashback. Standard evaluation of mental function strongly suggests the problem through limitation in attention, poor digit recall and manipulations, and marked slowing of mentation. In extreme cases computed tomography may show loss of cortex. A psychological evaluation with testing may establish that impairment is present and allow one to quantitate its improvement. The prognosis for improvement is guarded until one has observed 3 months of abstinence; further improvement has not been observed after that time. This is in contrast to the comparable syndrome in alcoholics, which seems to improve over years.

V. SPECIFIC DRUGS

It is again to be noted that street drugs are often mixtures of LSD and PCP and may not be what the patients believe they are buying.

A. LYSERGIC ACID DIETHYLAMIDE

LSD is supplied by illicit manufacturers in the U.S. and is available in highly purified form. An effective dose in a nontolerant user is as little as 20 μg, and the street dose varies from 50 to 300 μg, usually dried on a sugar cube; the drug can be taken orally, snuffed, or injected. The onset of action by all routes is most rapid as regards adrenergic effects. Perception changes and visual imagery follow in 30 to 60 min for all routes of administration. A marked euphoria is a regular feature. The effects last from a few hours with low doses to a maximum of 20 to 24 h with higher ones.

B. MESCALINE

Mescaline (peyote) is available as ground dried buttons of the peyote cactus, with 300 to 1000 mg being the usual street dose. Synthetic material is also available. The onset is slower than with LSD, and the hallucinations are briefer in duration. Most purified drug sold on the street contains no mescaline, but is a combination of amphetamine with LSD and PCP.

C. PSILOCYBIN

Psilocybin is obtained from a wild native U.S. mushroom. Its street form is as dried mushroom containing up to 30 mg of active drug. It is in every way nearly identical to LSD. Although a synthetic form is available, it is far more common for PCP or LSD to be substituted for the chemical powder. Psilocin is a similar chemical substance.

D. PCP

PCP is synthetic material made both legitimately and in illegal labs and can be supplied in a pure form. It produces a dissociative state with essentially no depression of respiration. In humans the agitation and hallucinations following removal of the agent were annoying. This is the most readily synthesized drug in illicit laboratories and is widely available. Many street drugs are adulterated with PCP. It can be ingested orally, smoked, or injected into veins. It is very rapidly absorbed by all routes, with 2 to 15 mg being the average street dose. Its onset of action is within minutes by all routes, with prominent adrenergic and cholinergic effects. There is a rise in heart rate and blood pressure and a mild anxiety with pupillary constriction, prominent flushing, and increased salivation. As the dose increases there is dizziness, slurred speech, and clear intoxication of the alcohol type.

The mental state is one of suspension in time and space yet with considerable euphoria and mild pleasing anxiety. All experiences are heightened, usually pleasing, and pleasurable visual, sensual, or gustatory sensations are prolonged. As the dose increases, drunkenness becomes prominent. Confusion and psychosis are not features of the safe and desired doses, but are common as the dose absorbed exceeds 10 mg. Altered consciousness is usually present, with dullness, poor arousibility, or catalepsy stages identified before coma. The adrenergic signs of tachycardia and elevated blood pressure are always present. There may be severe salivation, drooling, nystagmus, wide open eyes with small pupils, and increased tendon reflexes. In severe cases there may be muscle spasms and convulsions. The mental and neurological state waxes and wains over the course of a day, but the toxic state may last as long as 4 weeks.

A drug testing laboratory is often necessary for diagnosis, for this is believed to be the most commonly abused illicit drug of this group and the one with the most serious toxic reactions. Blood and urine testing correlate poorly with the severity of the reaction but are invariably positive in toxic states.

The treatment of severe states is in hospital and follows a logical sequence to reduce life-threatening problems. Serious hypertension may require intravenous phentolamine. Good medical and nursing support will usually maintain the person until the drug disappears.

There is some basis for increasing drug removal by the urine by acidification of the urinary pH to less than pH 5.0 and by continuous suction on the stomach. Control of aberrant behavior usually requires drugs. Phenothiazines have been useful for sedation, for the blood pressure-lowering side effect is beneficial, but seizures may result. A variety of drugs, including propranolol and physostigmine, have been employed for specific disproportionately annoying symptoms.

The psychosis may be prolonged, lasting as long as 1 month, and is usually believed to be a part of a toxic reaction. An organic brain syndrome does not seem to occur with this agent.

E. OTHER AGENTS

Morning glory seeds, nutmeg, and mace do not have the toxic syndromes associated with more potent drugs. The many synthetic forms of hallucinogens mimic LSD in every respect.

REFERENCES

1. **Grinspoon, L. and Makalar, J. B.,** *Psychedelic Drugs Revisited,* Basic Books, New York, 1980.
2. **Zukin, S. R. and Zukin, R. S.,** Identification and characterization of (3H) phencyclidine binding to specific brain receptor sites, in *PCP (Phencyclidine): Historical and Current Perspectives,* Domino, E. F., Ed., MI NPP Books, Ann Arbor, MI, 1981.
3. **Jaffee, J. H.,** Drug addiction and drug abuse, in *The Pharmacological Basis of Theraputics,* 6th ed., A. G. Goodman and L. S. Gilman, Eds., Macmillan, New York, 1980.

Chapter 24

Miscellaneous Abused Drugs

I. SOLVENTS AND GLUES

Sniffing ether from a rag or bowl-like container and direct inhalation of nitrous oxide were recognized as problems shortly after these agents were introduced into medicine. Both anesthetic agents produce a diminution of worry and inhibitions, and a sense of relaxation as part of a high. Many substances containing volatile solvents have been used in this manner. The abuse of a given substance depends upon its wide availability and popularity in a specific group. Peer use largely influences what is currently being abused. Sniffing model airplane glue to produce mild euphoria from its ether content became widespread in the 1960s. It was soon discovered that a wide variety of plastic glues and cements, dry cleaning solutions, paint thinners, aerosols, and lighter fluids have these properties in common. The most popular active ingredients are toluene, hexane, xylene, trichloroethylene, acetone, volatile aromatic esters, naphtha, benzene, or petroleum ether, but freons, methyl chloride, amyl and butyl nitrate, methyl ethyl ketone, and methyl butyl ketone have been used. This list is by no means all-inclusive.

The solvent is usually used by teenagers by inhaling from either a paper cone or a plastic bag. Those in a spray can are sometimes inhaled directly. The active materials are rapidly absorbed and produce a mild euphoria and decrease inhibitions within minutes and the effect lasts for up to an hour; if used for a prolonged period, Stage I or II levels of anesthesia can be produced. Users develop a nearly instant ''high,'' with clouding of thoughts and suspension of sensation so that both time and animation seem arrested and a sensation of floating is achieved.[1,2]

A wide variety of side effects may be seen by a doctor that relate to intoxication and irritations. Deaths have been reported from suffocation related to a plastic bag occluding the airways. In prolonged or continual use, there is often nausea, vomiting, and diarrhea. Epilepsy, irregular heart rhythms of many sorts, and respiratory depression have also been noted.[3] Health problems commonly observed include eye and nose injection and irritation. Serious renal insufficiency,[4,5] liver failure,[2] and aplastic anemia have developed. Sudden death has occurred, but is rare.[6] The most common serious side effect is confusion and disorientation that persists for months. Tremor, staggering gait, nystagmus, but otherwise a normal neurological exam have been observed to persist for up to 6 months.[7]

The common findings are usually not severe and rapidly clear with cessation of the habit. The prognosis for the future is excellent, for few users continue with this habit. Although the same epidemiological characteristics are observed among smokers before age 10 and heroin users, a mildly different group engage in solvent use; they come from more stable homes, have fewer arrests, and do not go on to become hard drug users. Solvent sniffing is simply safer, less scrutinized by law enforcement agencies, and much less costly than other forms of abuse.

II. INFREQUENTLY ENCOUNTERED ABUSED SUBSTANCES

A. AMYL AND BUTYL NITRATE

Both amyl and butyl nitrate are sold over the counter in crushable glass ampules. They are readily absorbed on inhalation and are systemic vasodilators used for angina. They produce flushing, tachycardia, and hypotension, and a mild euphoria. They are widely used to enhance sexual pleasure and are used both to delay ejaculation and at the time of orgasm. Their street name is "rush," and they are widely believed to restore erections in those who have lost sexual interest, or to allow further sexual arousal when an orgasm is completed. There are probably no significant side effects.

B. ATROPINE-CONTAINING SUBSTANCES

A large variety of plant-derived substances provide extreme excitation when taken in large doses. Atropine-containing substances include atropine, hyoscine, and scopolamine from medical or over-the-counter drugstore purchases, and morning glory seeds, Jimson weed, datarum stramonium plants, nightshade, and belladonna plants from nature. Since impure preparations derived from plants are commonly used, toxic reactions occur. In a toxic dose, extreme confusion, hallucinations, and psychosis are accompanied by elevated body temperature, tachycardia, and striking dilatation of the pupils. Reversal with physostigmine is prompt. The history is the most reliable differentiation from cocaine toxic reaction.

C. BETEL NUT

Betel nut chewing is limited to those from South Asia and the Malaysia area, where some quarter of a billion persons are daily users. It is available in Oriental stores in America. Three ingredients (*Areca catechu* nut, calcium hydroxide, and betel fruit, *Piper betel*) are placed in the mouth and chewed. The taste is unpleasantly astringent and bitter, but alkaloids are absorbed that are stimulatory with effects not unlike coca leaves.

The chewing produces a bright red stain on the teeth and gums, a tell-tale mark of the chronic user. The user has a clouding of consciousness and a sluggishness of reason, but a heightened capacity for physical activity. There are usually contracted pupils, excessive tearing and salivation, and there may be looseness of the bowels.

D. COCA LEAF

Coca leaf chewing is limited to those from South and Central America, who must bring their own supply to this country. There are no tell-tale marks as in betel nut chewing, but the "cud" is almost always present. It produces an alertness and irritability not unlike caffeine and of itself is too weak to produce toxic reactions.

III. PRESCRIPTION AND OVER-THE-COUNTER DRUGS

A. OVER-THE-COUNTER DRUGS

Almost a quarter-million preparations are approved for over-the-counter sales by the FDA and can legally be shipped across state borders. Many more are sold only within a region and do not have to have FDA approval. There is a vague line between agents sold as health foods and those sold as drugs. Many of these contain weak agents that alter behavior to produce somnolence, alertness, and many other effects. Many over-the-counter preparations are mixtures of ingredients of which one or more modify behavior. Thus caffeine, alcohol, antihistamines, amphetamines, NSAID (nonsteroid anti-inflammatory drugs), atropine-like agents, and sympathetic mimetic agents are available. It is estimated that about one fourth of the population uses these regularly.[8,9] Probably half of the chronic users are taking them for a behavior-modifying effect. In practice, persons taking NSAID for fatigue, diet tablets for a pickup, or using a nasal inhaler to "clear their head" are common. Fortunately, except for caffeine, there seems to be too little active ingredient to produce tolerance.

Many over-the-counter sleeping medications contain the antihistamine pyrilamine maleate, sometimes with alcohol, acetaminophen, or other inactive ingredients. At ordinary doses these have very little direct effect and at high doses probably do not produce tolerance.

B. ABUSED PRESCRIPTION AGENTS

Prescription agents are better studied, and their side effects are better known than over-the-counter agents. There are also far better control systems in place to prevent their abuse. A thoughtful article recounts many of the ways that prescription drugs can be abused, and remedies for both potential patient and physician abusers are described.[10] When prescription drugs are abused, one or more doctors has to be involved for the patient to develop advanced tolerance.

All controlled substances are subject to abuse, but the common ones are benzodiazepines, sedatives, all sorts of hypnotics, amphetamines, and codeine. Prescription sedatives, in contrast to over-the-counter preparations, produce the most widely abused tolerances, that to benzodiazepines. Withdrawal symptoms are described, and dependent users may totally lose the desired effects.[11]

Initiation of treatment is almost always appropriate, but it is continued far too long, until there is either no indication, the indication is past, or the failure to respond indicates the need for more diagnostic evaluation. At least half the time the patient uses medication from several doctors to maintain the abuse, but careless office practice is sometimes the basis of continued abuse. Careful office records on the size of prescriptions and the anticipated duration as well as meticulous entry of refills and telephone approvals of refills will at least identify the problem in your own practice.

The identification of abuse in practice is difficult, and treatment once identification occurs is disappointing. Forty-six patients who sought outpatient treatment for abuse of prescription drugs were followed. Counseling, medical withdrawal, or medical maintenance with a chemically related drug were offered. Of these patients, 48% left treatment and relapsed within 30 days and another 17% relapsed within 3 months. Only 28% reported abstinence for 90 days, indicating that this is a serious problem to treat.[8]

The side effects of abused agents, whether over-the-counter or prescription medications, when they are not being taken for an appropriate cause is tragic. The renal damage, stomach ulceration, and hepatitis that occasionally arise with NSAID[12] are most frequent in patients for whom there is no indication for continuing the agent.

C. CAFFEINE

Caffeine is the most widely used and abused substance in North America, with more than 80% of all adults maintaining a continued detectable blood level obtained predominantly from coffee, tea, and cola-type soft drinks. Tolerance is widespread,[13] and a withdrawal syndrome is well described.[14] Headache is the most common symptom, noted 4 to 24 h after withdrawal. Severe fatigue, irritability, anxiety, and muscle tension are prominent in some patients. These are alleviated promptly with replacement of caffeine.

REFERENCES

1. **Glatt, M. M.,** Abuse of solvents, *Lancet,* 1, 485, 1977.
2. **Cohen, S.,** Glue sniffing, *JAMA,* 231, 653, 1975.
3. **Adriani, J.,** Drug dependence in hospitalized patients, in *A Treatment Manual for Acute Drug Abuse Emergencies,* P. G. Bourne, Ed., U.S. Government Printing Office, Washington, D. C., 1974.
4. **Stybel, L. J.,** Deliberate hydrocarbon inhalation among low socioeconomic adolescents not necessarily apprehended by the police, *Int. J. Addictions,* 11, 345, 1976.
5. Editorial, Solvent abuse, *Lancet,* 2, 1139, 1982.
6. **Fagan, D.G. and Forrest, J. B.,** "Sudden sniffing death" after inhalation of domestic lipid aerosol, *Lancet,* 2, 361, 1977.
7. **Lewis, J. D., Moritz, D., and Mellis, L. P.,** Long term toluene abuse, *Am. J. Psychiatr.,* 238, 368, 1981.
8. **Inciardi, J. A.,** Over-the-counter drugs: epidemiology, adverse reactions, overdose deaths and mass media promotion, *Addictive Dis., Ann. Int. J.,* 3, 253, 1977.
9. **Moss, A. J., Levy, A. S., Kim, I., and Park, Y. K.,** Use of vitamin and mineral supplements in the United States: current users, types of products and nutrients, *Advance Data,* 175, 1, 1989.
10. **Weiss, K. J. and Greenfield, D. P.,** Prescription drug abuse, *Psychiatr. Clin. North Am.,* 9, 475, 1986.
11. **Kales, A., Bixler, E. O., Tan, T. L., Sharf, M. B., and Kales, J. D.,** Chronic hypnotic-drug use: ineffectiveness, drug-withdrawal, insomnia and dependence, *JAMA,* 227, 513, 1974.
12. **Gilles, M. A. and Skyring, A. P.,** The pattern and prevalence of aspirin ingestion as determined by interview of 2,921 inhabitants of Sydney, *Med. J. Australia,* 1, 974, 1972.
13. **Procter, A. W. and Greden, J. F.,** Caffeine and benzodizepine use, *Am. J. Psychiatr.,* 139, 32, 1981.
14. **White, B. C., Lincoln, C. A., Pearce, N. W.,** Anxiety and muscle tension as consequences of caffeine withdrawal, *Science,* 209, 1547, 1980.

Chapter 25

Mixed Drug Abuse

I. INTRODUCTION

Substance abusers frequently use multiple agents during the same day or week. These agents are sometimes from the same group of agents for which they have already developed tolerance and therefore they experience cross tolerance; or they may be from a totally different group of drugs. Not infrequently tolerance to two or more groups of drugs is present in the same individual. The makeup of an individual that leads to the use of one drug also produces a tendency to use other agents. Thus the majority of abusing subjects are also heavy ingestors of caffeine and use tobacco. Table 46 suggests some of the commonly encountered circumstances under which this happens.

As tolerance develops in the use of sedatives, opiates, and cocaine/amphetamines, it is not identical in all of the minor effects of the abused drug. Often undesirable loss of alertness with sedatives, severe constipation and loss of appetite with opiates, and tremulousness with cocaine/amphetamine is present and is managed with other agents. This mixing of various classes of agents is sufficiently common that all therapists should be alert to the possibility. Alcoholics often use coffee heavily, opiate users often employ amphetamines, and cocaine/amphetamine users often use alcohol. Many are aware that the combination makes them feel and function better than a single drug.

Using any available drug to oblivion on a repeated basis is a manifestation of psychiatric illness. Such users should be evaluated in hospital. Because of its availability and cost, alcohol is most often the agent of choice for removal of consciousness. Most addicts experience periods of concern and guilt about drug use and make frequent abortive attempts to become drug free. Tolerance leads to bothersome withdrawal symptoms, and most ex-

TABLE 46
Frequently Encountered Circumstances of Mixed Drug Abuse

1. To counteract a side effect of the primary drug
2. Compulsion for mood alteration; any agent is better than no agent
3. To counteract symptoms during withdrawal
4. To counteract anxiety or depression during recovery
5. Supply of preferred drug interrupted

perienced users have personal experience with diminishing withdrawal symptoms. They are also well aware of drugs used by doctors that will counteract these symptoms. Benzodiazepine drugs are readily available on the street or from physicians and emergency rooms. Barbiturates are utilized for this purpose, and cocaine/amphetamine and opiate addicts often use alcohol.

After withdrawal is complete there is depression and anxiety arising from specific situations that the abstinent addict may choose to handle with another drug. Such a person may be well aware of the hazard of going back to his or her primary drug of abuse, but feels safe in using another agent. Most are aware that this is the approach used by physicians in such a circumstance.

Those using costly street drugs such as heroin or cocaine may employ a more available and less costly drug when their favorite is unavailable or unaffordable. I have often queried heroin users who have a "fix" as infrequently as weekly about this rare use. They have explained that it is the only drug they truly enjoy, but they use it only as a "reward" because they simply cannot afford it often. The net result is that about 20% of drug abusers or alcoholics use other agents, often to the point of abuse, at least some of the time.

A New York study suggested that one can predict future excessive alcohol consumption among patients on methadone maintenance by using a self-administered alcoholism screening test.[1]

II. IDENTIFICATION OF MIXED DRUG ABUSE

The history is often of very limited value in identifying mixed drug abuse because the abuser does not consider secondary drugs to be important. Persons using an occasional street or over-the-counter agent to control symptoms often deny the use, feeling simply that it is not pertinent to their diagnosis and treatment. Family members or household contacts are rarely knowledgeable about what is used unless there is sharing of all substances used. Admitted heroin or cocaine addicts are particularly at risk.[2,3]

Occasionally aberrant findings (dilated pupils in an opiate addict), or delusions when none are expected, may lead the health giver to suspect other agents. Urine screening tests are by far the most valuable when such a problem is suspected (see Chapter 11). Drugs that are commonly abused together are noted in Table 47.

Cross tolerance is the basis of some but not all of the use of drugs in sequence or combination. Thus cocaine and amphetamines produce marked cross tolerance; opiates abusers have cross tolerance for nearly all sedatives and alcohol. In other cases opposite effects are used to produce a prolonged "high". Amphetamine use with opiates is probably the most widely abused pair among the major drugs. More recently, intravenous cocaine has been used by opioid addicts.[4] Desipramine treatment has been proposed for such users.[5]

A recent letter addresses mixed drug abuse in those on methadone treatment. At two East Coast testing sites, 27% of the samples showed cannabis products and 4% a nonprescribed benzodiazepine at one site and 51% showed cannabis and 7% showed benzodiazepines at the other.[6] Others have noted the widespread abuse of benzodiazepines among street addicts.[7]

TABLE 47
Drugs Commonly Used in Combination

1. All addicts — cigarettes and excess caffeine
2. Opiate addicts — amphetamines, cocaine
3. Amphetamine addicts — prescription sedatives and alcohol
4. Alcoholics — sleeping medications and tranquilizers
5. Sedative addicts — amphetamines
6. Cocaine abusers — amphetamines, alcohol, and sedatives
7. Hallucinogen users — PCP
8. Self-conducted withdrawal — benzodiazepines, sedatives, and alcohol
9. Many former opiate addicts become alcoholics

III. EMERGENCIES

The most frequent emergencies result from a toxic dose of a drug experienced by a somewhat inexperienced user of a new drug or a new source. The appropriate dilution of drugs for street portions is generally well done because of the economic advantage to the seller, so overdosing because the supplier made a mistake is unusual. Toxic reactions are infrequently seen by doctors or emergency rooms when they are mild, but interference with vital signs, convulsions, or acute psychosis (see Chapter 18) are often the bases for an emergency visit.

Drugs have additive or even potentiating effects in many instances, and these are the basis of most problems, often unknown to the user.[8,9] Thus a blood alcohol level of 100 mg/dl combined with a barbiturate level of 10 wgm/ml, both subtoxic doses, has been fatal.[1] Combined alcohol-barbiturates, alcohol-marijuana, and alcohol-benzodiazepines have interfered with driving and airplane flying at levels that would be relatively innocuous for other activities.

IV. ASPECTS OF TREATMENT

Use of caffeine and nicotine is usually continued during treatment for more serious addictions, but should be interdicted during withdrawal because caffeine is a stimulant that increases undesirable hyperactivity and smoking is a fire hazard. After withdrawal, if the person has been off of smoking for a few days, continued abstinence from tobacco and all other drugs is used by more therapists than sequentially treating addictions including nicotine. Most opiate and sedative detoxification programs restrict caffeine-containing beverages for a week or so until the hyperactivity of the withdrawal period is over.

Drugs with sedative or antianxiety effects are widely used in the treatment of withdrawal without regard for whether or not there is cross tolerance. Agents with very long half lives are preferred because of the fewer doses needed. Thus diazepam and phenobarbital enjoy wide use (Chapter 27). Clearly the agent should not be continued beyond the first few days in opiate or alcohol withdrawal, but it may be needed for several weeks in phenobarbital or diazepam detoxification. Drugs with an addicting potential should *not* be utilized in treating addicts after withdrawal. Phenothiazine drugs, although they show cross tolerance, have a remarkably low addiction potential and therefore are the best group of agents if chronic sedation is required. A monkey addiction model dually addicted to cocaine and heroin has shown improvement when treated with buprenorphine, a mixed agonist-antagonist for opioids used for heroin addiction.[10]

Occasionally physicians provide large quantities of benzodiazepine drugs, usually diazepam, to chronic alcoholics. Most patients will willingly accept unlimited diazepam as an alternative to alcohol. Several excellent practicing physicians place alcoholic patients with liver disease on long-term, high-dose diazepam (approximately 60 mg/day) in order to permit the liver disease to heal on an outpatient basis. Though this retards rehabilitation from the alcohol addition, the liver will heal with this management.

Drugs taken in relatively small doses, or irregularly, probably interfere in no way with the rehabilitation process. Though volunteer treatment and self-help groups such as Alcoholics Anonymous (AA) and Cocaine Anonymous (CA) strongly support a totally drug-free person, there does not seem to be a clear scientific basis for this in all patients. The best we can suggest is to follow the rules of the program in which a person is entered and if AA or CA is prominently used, then the person must be substance free.

REFERENCES

1. **Stimmel, B., Sturiano, V., Cohen, M., et al.,** The ability of a self-administered alcohol screening test to detect future excessive alcohol consumption in persons on methadone maintenance, *Alcoholism,* 6, 362, 1982.
2. **Croughan, J. L., Miller, J. P., Whitman, B. Y., and Schober, J. G.,** Alcoholism and alcohol dependence in narcotic addicts: a prospective study with a five-year follow-up, *Am. J. Drug Alcohol Abuse,* 8, 85, 1981.
3. **Simpson, D. D. and Lloyd, M. R.,** Alcohol use following treatment for drug addiction, *J. Stud. Alcohol,* 42, 323, 1981.
4. **Kosten, T. R., Gawin, F. H., Rounsaville, B. J., and Kleber, H. D.,** Cocaine abuse among opioid addicts: demographic and diagnostic factors in treatment, *Am. J. Drug Alcohol Abuse,* 12, 1, 1986.
5. **Kosten, T., Gawin, F., and Schumann, B.,** Treating cocaine abusing methadone maintenance patients with desipramine, *Natl. Inst. Drug Abuse. Res. Monogr. Ser.,* 81, 237, 1988.
6. **DuPont, R. L. and Saylor, K. E.,** Marijuana and benzodiazepines in patients receiving methadone treatment, *JAMA,* 261, 3408, 1989.
7. **DuPont, R. L.,** Abuse of benzodiazepines: the problems and the solutions, *Am. J. Drug Alcohol Abuse,* 14, Suppl. 1, 1988.
8. **Cohen, S.,** Combined alcohol, drug abuse and human behavior, in *Perspectives in Alcohol and Drug Abuse,* Solomon, J. and Keeley, K. A., Eds., John Wright, Boston, 1982, 89.
9. **Kissen, B.,** Interactions of ethyl alcohol and other drugs, in *The Biology of Alcoholism, Clinical Pathology,* Vol. 3, Kissen, B. and Begleiter, H., Eds., Plenum Press, New York, 1974, 109—162.
10. **Goodwin, F. K.,** Potential pharmacotherapy for dual addiction to cocaine and heroin, *JAMA,* 262, 2654, 1989.

Chapter 26

Management of Substance Abuse — What is Treatment and What Does It Accomplish?

I. INTRODUCTION

This chapter discusses the goals we set out to meet in the treatment of substance abuse. There are some goals that treatment accomplishes about which almost everyone agrees, but there are many goals for which there is widely held disagreement as to whether treatment attains them or not. When an abusing client first presents to a therapist for evaluation, the consultation is nearly always sought as a consequence of a single crisis or an accumulation of problems. The addict, the therapist, and often the family and employer have differing goals that they wish to see attained from the treatment, and often these goals are unrealistic and sometimes incompatible. For example, a bank teller performing well at his job consults you 3 days after an automobile accident. At the time of the accident cocaine was found in his car and in his blood. He was arrested on charges of possession of cocaine, driving while intoxicated, and abusive behavior. A great deal of newspaper publicity was given to his arrest, because his car destroyed a popular fountain. He is also experiencing major marital and financial difficulties.

The expectations for treatment might be as follows. Addict: ''I hope I don't lose my job or go to jail''. Employer: ''The publicity is terrible, I hope I don't have to fire him for that reason for he is the best loan officer I have''. Wife:'' If only he could be like he used to be and we could pay some of our bills''. Therapist: ''I hope we can satisfy all these

TABLE 48
Goals of Treatment Reached by Nearly Every Substance Abuser

1. Relieve the stresses of the withdrawal period
2. Correct or arrest many progressive medical and psychiatric conditions
3. Prevent suicide
4. Provide a shield from hostile job, family, legal, and financial problems while improvement occurs
5. Learn about substance abuse, its remissions and relapses
6. Learn better and more durable interpersonal skills
7. Help family adjust to a member's addiction
8. Prolong survival
9. Achieve and encourage abstinence

TABLE 49
Opposing Veiws on What Treatment Accomplishes

Optimistic	Realistic
1. Patients regularly improve.	1. Patients enter treatment at a low point; the variation looks like improvement.
2. Complete abstinence is often attained for 6 months to 1 year.	2. About 3 to 5% conquer the addiction each year.
3. Treatment results in long-term abstinence.	3. Treatment only relieves some stresses and prevents some relapses.
4. Most treated patients improve.	4. Most improvement occurs despite treatment.
5. Without treatment, recovery is very unlikely.	5. Most recovered addicts do so without standard treatment.

people so he will stay in treatment long enough to make a difference''. Clearly, addressing the addiction is the most important problem, but it is not identified by any of the players in our drama.

Table 48 lists goals of treatment that may be reached by nearly all who undertake treatment. Table 49 lists in juxtaposition opposing views on what treatment accomplishes.

Tables 48 and 49 can be looked at in terms of our bank teller who uses cocaine. The addict clearly has identified treatment as a way to provide a shield from the hostile forces that may wrest his job and car from him, and he most wants to attain this realistic goal. His employer wants the bad publicity to go away (unrealistic) and for the bank teller to remain a productive employee (realistic). The wife wants her husband to be the way he used to be (unrealistic), and wants him cured of his addiction (unrealistic). The therapist believes that providing a shield from the current troubles and continuing treatment will lead to long-term sobriety, which may be unrealistic. The addict does not plan to give up cocaine permanently, the therapist considers this essential — a clear conflict. All believe that the addiction is somehow the basis of all the problems, which is unrealistic in that its absence will uncover many other problems.

A. SEMINAL IDEAS LEARNED FROM ALCOHOLISM

1. The ''addictive personality'' is a consequence of the abuse, not the cause.
2. Addiction over many years has ups and downs, with substantial improvement by any and all criteria from almost any circumstance.
3. Treatment prevents some relapses.
4. The pain and damage of addiction can be ameliorated.

The natural history of alcoholism was presented by Vaillant,[1] using data from two large and very long-term studies and by a review of the literature. From meticulous study of men long before and long after they became alcoholic, some important concepts emerged. Vaillant's study populations included longitudinal observations on large numbers of men who did not become addicted. He found that parental problems, broken homes, and childhood difficulties play only a modest role in the subsequent development of alcoholism. Although these factors appear frequently in the backgrounds of alcoholics, far more nonalcoholics also experienced them in similar degree, indicating that other forces can counter these adverse markers. Vaillant emphasizes that alcoholism has "a life of its own", producing a stereotyped set of behavioral characteristics that are a result of the addiction rather than the cause. Alcoholism (and other abuse) is different from other psychiatric illness in that it destroys the "very factors that facilitate recovery from illness — latent psychological (ego) strengths and social supports". Alcohol (and some other drugs) damage the central nervous system, rendering "kings and geniuses no different from paupers and imbeciles".

Vaillant demonstrates that recovery is a function of both definition and time; those who "recover" by any definition do so in almost all types of circumstances, only a few of which can be construed as treatment. Periods of prolonged abstinence, on the other hand, seem to be correlated with "treatment". Among those alcoholics most severely affected by destructive drinking habits, a new love relationship, frequent clinic contact, and Alcoholics Anonymous correlated with prolonged periods of abstinence, whereas willpower was the more valuable resource in those with a mild habit.

Vaillant's conclusions that the behavioral switch from alcohol "dependence to abstinence is mediated not by hitting some mysterious bottom but rather by forces that can be identified and understood by social scientists and harnessed by health professionals" have altered many treatment programs. In discussing treatment by professionals, he points to the dilemma encountered by all serious students of alcoholism (and, again, all substance abuse) that they are powerless over their addiction. On the other hand, to ignore a malady "as painful to the individual, as damaging to his health, as destructive to his family, and as refractory to willpower, motivation and to common sense" is unconscionable.

B. MODELS OF TREATMENT

Jerome Frank[2] presents a model of treatment that emphasizes both the relief of suffering and attitude change. He recognizes the ingrained habit in alcoholics of drinking in response to all sorts of stresses. Reasoning does not alter bad habits; the person's belief system must be altered. As paraphrased by Vaillant, "if you can win their hearts and minds, their habits will follow."[1] Frank advocates raising the patient's expectation of cure and reintegrating him with his societal group. To do this an interrogation accompanied by confession of sins is carried out by a person who assumes the rank of high-status healer in the eyes of the patient. The healer must be optimistic about future recovery and take substantial responsibility for the addiction from the patient following the confession, often by declaring alcoholism to be a disease. Peer support groups are effective to the degree that all of these elements are included. (1) The patient must assist others with a similar problem. (2) There is a firm and unequivocal conceptualization of the nature of the problem, which is accepted by all those involved with the group. (3) Major responsibility for the addiction and its accompanying pain is lifted from the individual. Alcoholics Anonymous provides all of these, and effective residential facilities also score highly on all counts. Many treatment programs, however, ignore one or even two of these.

The ingredients of treatment programs that hasten the onset of prolonged abstinence are well outlined in Vaillant's book and will be referred to in later sections of this book. It is important to emphasize at this juncture that treatments that destroy limited ego strengths or self-esteem may harm the spontaneous return to sobriety. Kissin and co-workers found that actively ignoring alcoholics[3] on a waiting list for treatment resulted in a spontaneous recovery rate far lower than other groups. Emrick, in a massive review of more than 300 papers addressing treatment outcome, failed to identify beneficial treatments but did notice harmful ones.[4] There is a large and useful literature on treatment methods and what they will accomplish. Bandura[5] and the Sobels[6] discuss behavioral treatment, with the latter attaining the best possible outcome; the very limited value of court-mandated programs is presented,[7,8] along with inpatient versus outpatient treatment,[9,10] and psychotherapy.[11] A book has appeared on evaluation of treatment and new research in this field.[12] A recent examination of the very long-term recovery process in alcoholics has been published, indicating that some valuable changes occur after many years.[13]

Compliance theory is an excellent model for examining the treatment of substance abuse. Usually the "health belief model" is employed to examine the patient's expected benefits of a certain behavior and is of great value in predicting outcome.[14] Several reviews of the health belief model emphasize the importance of self-management strategies to effect long-term change.[15] Aspects of patient-therapist communication, satisfaction with outcome, locus of control, social support systems, and treatment disruption to lifestyle important in addiction therapy have all been evaluated.[16,17]

II. WHAT TREATMENT IS ALL ABOUT — TENETS TO GUIDE THERAPISTS

We healers are helpless over substance abuse but can facilitate spontaneous remissions, prevent some relapses, and alleviate the suffering produced by active use. We must continually instill hope for the future in our patients and maintain the comfortable scientific confidence that things will be better when we are assisting a patient or a family at a time of crisis. To a large degree events are at their worst at such times, and conditions nearly always improve. We must be perfectly clear in the diagnosis and communicate this to the patient and others who are appropriately concerned and will participate in the recovery.

From this point on there are four issues to consider in treatment: (1) offering the patient a nonchemical alternative for his or her favorite substance; (2) reminding the patient repeatedly that a single use can lead to pain and relapse; (3) repairing the social and medical damage that can be identified; (4) restoring self-esteem. Treatment is not easy, and no single treatment addresses all of these needs. Entry into a hospital or treatment facility helps with the first three, but often damages self-esteem even further. Psychotherapy often does not aid self-esteem and is lax in reminding the person of the harmful nature of the habit. The best we can offer is that different modalities are needed at different times. A program the client will stick with is the best one for him or her.

III. OVERVIEW OF THE TREATMENT PROCESS AND THE ROLE OF THE IDENTIFYING PHYSICIAN

Figure 12 illustrates schematically what is happening in the early years of recovering from substance abuse. Eventual sustained and secure abstinence, a goal attained in about 25% of all abusers, comes about through a change in the person, his habits, his self-esteem, and his relationships with others. The input of formal treatment is most marked in the early months of recovery and diminishes rapidly during and after the first year. Self-help groups are the most widely employed early replacements for formal treatment services. They usually start in the first year and are urgent in the subsequent few years as the patient grows in strength of sobriety. Family, friends, and work-related companionship (networks) play an important but variable role. The early period of the recovery process from an addiction is outlined in Table 50. There is extensive variability in the amount of time required in each stage.

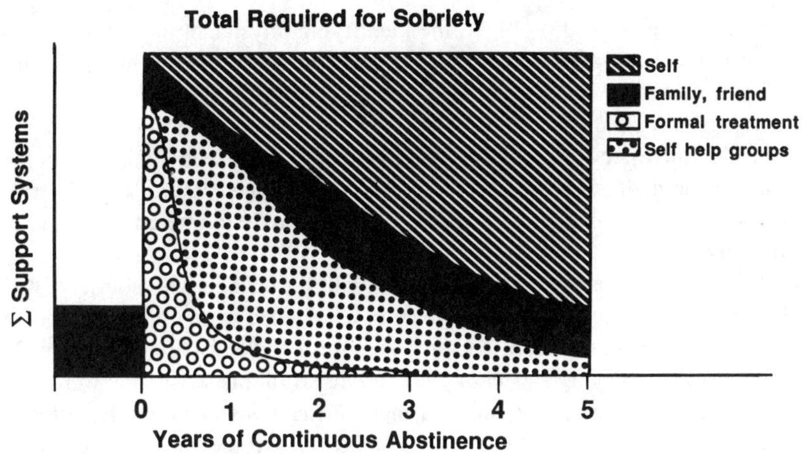

FIGURE 12. Schematic representation of the requirements for sobriety. The shaded areas on the ordinate represent all treatment and support systems in a summation fashion. Prior to the onset of sobriety, the influence of friends and family is simply inadequate to obtain substance-free existence. During the first year of treatment, formal programs, indicated by the open circles, are much more important than subsequently. Self-help groups are important in the early years. The most important factor in attaining lasting sobriety is the person.

TABLE 50
Recovery from an Addiction

Stage	Location	Duration
1. Withdrawal	1. Outpatient	1. 1—2 weeks
	Early Abstinence: First 3 Months	
2. Total support	2. Residential	2. 1—4 weeks
3. Subtotal support	3. Home, 3—5 h weekly	3. <3 months
	Late Abstinence: First Year	
4. At work	4. Home, 1—2 h weekly, family	
5. Growth	5. Group therapy	

The most intensive commitment of the identifying physician is in assisting the patient to enter therapy and in helping him or her to remain there during the early months. Detoxification can be readily carried out at home with the assistance of interested family in a determined patient. Often early treatment is carried out in a residential program to accomplish the first two periods of treatment away from the strains of home, family, and job. Nearly all prepaid health insurance plans will provide for residential treatment (including detoxification) for drug or alcoholism addiction at least once in any 2-year period, and such programs are to be preferred when they are available. Chapter 30 discusses the types of programs that are available and what can be accomplished.

In the early weeks a great deal of support is needed. Self-help groups are extremely beneficial and should be recommended by all therapists. Most private patients accept this slowly and a bit begrudgingly, possibly reflecting the attitudes of physicians. Group therapy is of greater value than individual counseling, for it is less threatening to the patient and often provides much practical advice that the counselor or physician is unable to provide. The range of opinions and personality types in a group add greatly to its value, for it is a microcosm of the real world.

If the patient has a medical problem, the identifying physician may choose to treat it or to refer. Even if there are no other problems, it is necessary for the physician to see the patient weekly or monthly. The physician should assess overall progress, discuss treatment, and test for relapse. All patients should attend self-help groups and be encouraged in this effort by their doctor. Specific problems, such as inability to sleep, fatigue, poor appetite, or edema, should be addressed by nonpharmacological means. Exercise, or warm milk to promote sleep, learning relaxation techniques to control anxiety, and conditioning exercises to overcome fatigue are useful and highly effective.

It is useful to remind treatment personnel that addicts change with sobriety. Kurtines et al.[18] demonstrated that addicts after many years of abstinence were much more normal upon extensive psychological testing than the same group immediately after recovery. Improvement was demonstrated in every aspect of their activities. In this sense they were remarkably analogous to prisoners of war, who showed marked maladjustment shortly after returning to free living in the U.S., with a high job instability, divorce rate, and alienation from family, all of which improved after a few years.[19,20]

The passage of time and with it changing values is a great force in therapy. Heroin abusers who start as inner-city youths with a background of poverty, broken homes, and criminality have very limited success in recovery until they reach age 40 years.[21,22] An interesting book has appeared describing addicts from many years ago who survived, usually with recovery.[23]

REFERENCES

1. **Vaillant, G.,** *The Natural History of Alcoholism,* Harvard University Press, Cambridge, MA, 1981.
2. **Frank, J. D.,** *Persuasion and Healing: A Comparative Study of Psychotherapy,* Johns Hopkins University Press, Baltimore, MD, 1981.
3. **Kissin, B., Rosenblatt, S. M., and Machover, S.,** Prognostic factors in alcoholism, *Psychiatr. Res. Rep.,* 24, 22, 1968.
4. **Emrick, C. D.,** A review of psychologically oriented treatment of alcoholism I, the use and interrelationships of outcome criteria and drinking behavior following treatment, *Q. J. Stud. Alcohol,* 35, 532, 1974, and II, the relative effectiveness of different treatment approaches and the effectiveness of treatment vs. no treatment, *Q. J. Stud. Alcohol,* 36, 88, 1975.
5. **Bandura, A.,** *Principles of Behavior Modification,* Holt, Rhinehart & Winston, New York, 1969.
6. **Sobell, M. B. and Sobell, L. C.,** *Behavioral Treatment of Alcohol Problems,* Plenum Press, New York, 1981.
7. **Ditman, K. S., Crawfor, G. G., Forgy, E. W., Moskowitz, H., and Macandrew, C. A.,** Controlled experiment on the use of court probation for drunk arrests, *Am. J. Psychiatr.,* 124, 160, 1967.
8. **Gallant, D. M., Faulkner, M. A., and Stoy, B.,** Enforced clinic treatment of paroled criminal alcoholics — one year followup, *Q. J. Stud. Alcohol,* 29, 77, 1968.
9. **Edwards, G. and Guthrie, S.,** A controlled trial of inpatient and outpatient treatment of alcohol dependence, *Lancet,* 1, 555, 1967.
10. **Willems, P. J. A., Letmendia, F. J. J., and Arroyave, F.,** A two-year follow-up study comparing short with long-stay in-patient treatment of alcoholics, *Br. J. Psychiatr.,* 122, 637, 1973.
11. **Hill, M. J. and Blan, H. T.,** Evaluation of psychotherapy with alcoholics: a critical review, *Q. J. Stud. Alcohol,* 28, 76, 1967.
12. **Lettieri, D. J.,** *Research Strategies in Alcoholism Treatment Assessment,* Haworth Press, New York, 1989.
13. **De Soto, C. B., O'Donnell, W. E., and De Soto, J. L.,** Long-term recovery in alcoholics, *Alcoholism,* 13, 693, 1989.
14. **Montano, D. E.,** Predicting and understanding influenza vaccination behavior. Alternatives to the health belief model, *Med. Care.,* 24, 438, 1986.
15. **Thoresen, C. E. and Kirmil-Gray, K.,** Self-management psychology and the treatment of childhood asthma, *J. Allergy Clin. Immunol.,* 72, 596, 1983.
16. **Stanton, A. L.,** Determinants of adherence to medical regimens by hypertensive patients, *J. Behav. Med.,* 10, 377, 1987.

17. **Janz, N. K. and Becker, M. H.,** The health belief model: a decade later, *Health Educ. Q.*, 11, 1, 1984.
18. **Kurtines, W. M., Ball, L. R., and Wood, G. H.,** Personality characteristics of long term recovered alcoholics: a comparative analysis, *J. Consulting Clin. Psychol.*, 46, 971, 1978.
19. **Hall, R. C. and Malone, W.,** Psychiatric effects of prolonged Asian captivity: a two year follow-up, *Am. J. Psychiatr.*, 133, 786, 1976.
20. **Sledge, W. H., Boydstun, J. A., and Rabe, A. J.,** Self concept changes related to war captivity, *Arch. Gen. Psychiatr.*, 37, 430, 1980.
21. **O'Brien, C. P., Woody, G. E., and McLellan, A. T.,** Long-term consequences of opiate dependence, *New Engl. J. Med.*, 304, 1098, 1981.
22. **Vaillant, G. E.,** A 20-year follow-up of New York narcotic addicts, *Arch. Gen. Psychiatr.*, 29, 237, 1973.
23. **Courtwright, D., Joseph, H., Des Jarlais, D.,** *Addicts Who Survive: An oral History of Narcotic Use in America, 1923—1925,* University of Tennessee Press, Knoxville, 1989, Reviewed in *JAMA*, 262, 3206, 1989.

Chapter 27

Drug Withdrawal: Recognition and Treatment

I. INTRODUCTION

Withdrawal from long use of alcohol or drugs is an essential first step in abstinence. Most withdrawal is undertaken by patients alone or with the assistance of friends and relatives, but quite frequently the physician is asked to participate at least in screening and sometimes in supervision of withdrawal. The majority of withdrawal occurs in the community. Although it is underutilized, the home should be the site of much medically directed withdrawal.

The early days of withdrawal are physiologically and psychologically unpleasant. For many the unpleasantness is known and avoided; for others the unknown is frightening. Symptomatic withdrawal is a major problem of chronic alcohol and opiate use and may be important in withdrawal from other sedatives. Withdrawal is differentiated from detoxification. Withdrawal is the transition from the tolerant to the intolerant. Medically speaking, withdrawal is a constellation of unpleasant and even life-threatening complications of marked tolerance when the ameliorating effect of drug is removed. Withdrawal lasts less than 1 week for alcohol and opiates, but may take longer for barbiturates. Detoxification refers to withdrawal and the correction of much nutritional and organ damage that accompanies abuse. Thus a construction worker using 1500 ml of vodka daily breaks his leg at work. Withdrawal is identified and treated over the next 4 days. At that time weight loss, muscular wasting, mild liver damage, and peripheral neuritis pose clear problems. Detoxification is accomplished over the next month as the patient's weight is restored, his vitamins repleted, and his muscle mass and liver tests returned to normal. There is an extensive literature on the

TABLE 51
Duration of Problems Encountered During Management of Withdrawal and Detoxification

1. Persistence of abused agent: $^1/_4$—10 days
2. Compensatory adjustments to membranes: 7 days
3. Fear of withdrawal symptoms or death: 7—14 days
4. Uncertainty of wisdom to withdraw: 3 days—?
5. Correcting the reversible damage: 30—90 days
6. Coping with problems revealed by abstinence (economic, social, interpersonal): 1—several years

causes of the withdrawal syndrome that in the last decade has relied on excellent data from animal models of withdrawal. This has led most reviewers to suggest that short-term withdrawal accounts for the acute aberrant behavior. The effects are most likely related to alterations in membrane receptor density and properties. There are also longer-term changes, such as localized differences in glucose consumption, which may be more refractory to reversal. Convulsions seem to be related to these longer-term changes.[1]

Withdrawal is most readily identified and managed with a knowledge of the setting in which it occurs, its precise time relationship to cessation of drug use, and its characteristic symptoms and signs. The setting of a withdrawal syndrome is use of alcohol, other depressants, or opiates to the point of tolerance. For alcohol the use must be daily and of at least 2 weeks in duration, but for opiates daily use for less than a week is probably sufficient. Table 51 reminds the reader of the timing after drug cessation when the events of detoxification occur.

The many processes occurring simultaneously during the withdrawal period offer the therapy team an opportunity to establish themselves as the subject's advocate and friend and assure commitment to ongoing therapy. All patients rapidly improve in both health and overall sense of well-being during withdrawal. A recent MRI study of the brain showed substantial increase in volume of the brain in alcoholics in as little as 2 months.[2] This improvement provides strong support for gaining their confidence. On the other hand, treating the withdrawal but failing to follow up with longer-term treatment is a tragic loss of opportunity.

II. FEATURES OF WITHDRAWAL

A. TIME OF WITHDRAWAL

The relation of withdrawal symptoms to time is quite stereotyped for alcohol and opiates. This precise relationship is useful in diagnosis of the syndrome and in making decisions about the intensity of withdrawal and accordingly the need for medications or even hospitalization. Figure 13 diagrams such a course with and without treatment. The timing of symptoms relative to the last dose of opiates or alcohol is strikingly constant, with symptoms beginning as early as 6 h after the last dose of drug, peaking no later than 48 h, and rapidly improving. Although the severity of symptoms varies widely, the course over time does not. Treatment diminishes the severity of symptoms but does not change the duration.

Figure 13 emphasizes the course of withdrawal after drug use ceases or in the case of alcohol is markedly curtailed. The time followed by alcohol and opiate withdrawal is sufficiently reproducible that after 36 to 48 h one is always on the improvement limb. In Figure 13 each D represents the administration of a dose of medication. The effect is to decrease the severity of the signs and symptoms of withdrawal.

B. SYMPTOMS AND SIGNS OF WITHDRAWAL

Figure 14 is a cartoon emphasizing the major features of alcohol and opiate withdrawal.

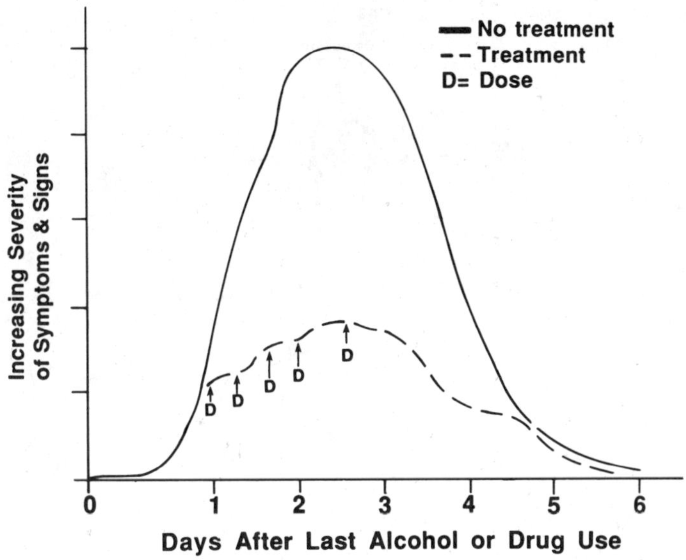

FIGURE 13. Time of withdrawal versus severity of symptoms and signs. The dashed line indicates the effect of treatment, with the Ds denoting a dose of medication. Although the severity varies from person to person, the time of withdrawal is quite constant with or without treatment in all patients following opiates or alcohol. Treatment diminishes the severity, but does not change the time course.

The earliest and mildest symptoms are those of anxiety and hyperactivity of the nerves, including the autonomic nervous system. The person feels an internal uneasiness, as though something is happening which may progress to nausea and even vomiting. Rest is disturbed, with many changes in position, sleep is disorganized, and the person does not awaken rested. There is mild tachycardia, slight elevation of the blood pressure, and a feeling of warmth when the room is cool to others. Tearing and salivation are more common in opiate withdrawal, and tremulousness may be apparent more in alcoholics. Initially the mind is clear and the patient is neurologically intact.

The more severe symptoms are discussed in the sections below on severity of withdrawal.

C. IDENTIFYING WITHDRAWAL

Identification of withdrawal from sedatives and opiates is quite direct when the history of use to tolerance is clear. However, if there is no history or the addiction is concealed, one must have a substantial index of suspicion and thorough knowledge of the sequential events of withdrawal. The sequence of increasing severity presented in Figure 12 during the initial 36 h is highly supportive of the diagnosis, and when a history is lacking may be the major basis of the diagnosis. Very long-acting benzodiazepines and phenobarbital will produce a withdrawal after 6 to 8 days. Trauma patients or those operated upon in an emergency and subsequently receiving analgesia may have their withdrawal suppressed until the 3rd or 4th day, but barring these infrequent occurrences withdrawal occurs in the 36 h following the last dose of drug.

The physical findings occurring in withdrawal progressively worsen until the peak is reached between 36 and 48 h and then improve.[2] The progressively more severe symptoms are listed in Table 52 and illustrated separately in Figure 14. The earliest manifestations are a consciousness of internal uneasiness, usually associated with a lack of desire for food and sometimes vomiting. The next, more severe stage permits diagnosis and is a hyperactivity of motion. The patient is unable to stay quiet, often moving unexpectedly, getting up, or

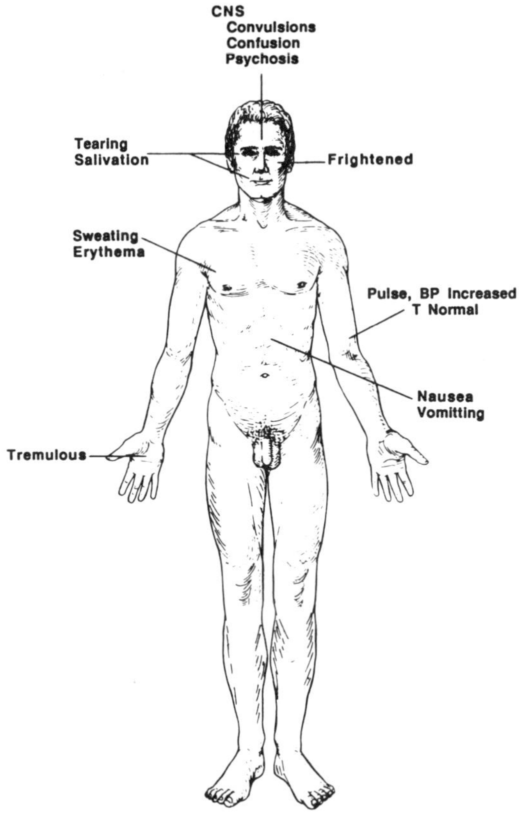

FIGURE 14. Major features of alcohol and opiate withdrawal.

TABLE 52
Observed Stages of Clinical Severity in Sedative and Opiate Withdrawal and the Times at Which They Occur

Stage	Description	Time from last dose (days) Alcohol	Phenobarbital
Minimal	Mild expressed anxiety, fidgets, mentally clear, pulse and temperature normal	1/2	3—5
Mild	Clear hyperactivity, appears anxious, sweaty, pulse rate up, mentally alert, restless	1/2—1	4—6
Moderate	Momentary mental lapses, marked agitation, sweaty, rapid pulse, fearful, severely restless, fairly cooperative	1—2	4—6
Severe	Hallucinations, mental lapses markedly interfering with communication, severe agitation, sweaty tachycardia, unable to cooperate, may have convulsion	1—2	4—7

taking a beverage in the middle of the interview and seeming not to be able to maintain contact. There is inadequate continuous eye contact, and the interviewer has an awareness of speaking a little louder to maintain contact. Although tremor may be prominent, it may also be absent.

The scales used to rate alcoholism withdrawal focus one's attention on detailed, non-

TABLE 53
Essential Ingredients of Screening an Abusing Person Who Is Entering Detoxification

1. To determine immediate hospitalization or detoxification needs:
   (a) Evaluate vital signs, including temperature, pulse, respiration, and blood pressure
   (b) Determine degree of orientation and contact with examiner
   (c) Evaluate for delusions, hallucination
   (d) History of previous withdrawals, trauma, convulsions, drug allergy
   (e) Determine degree of agitation
   (f) Search for occult infection, bleeding, and head trauma
2. To determine other medical needs:
   (a) Screening history if patient able
   (b) Screening physical examination
   (c) Screening lab appropriate to age and exposures of patient

specific findings that allow the examining physician to make the diagnosis even when the history of substance use is hidden. Binge users, or concealed users of drugs, may experience partial withdrawal during their short intervals of nonuse and not appreciate that this is withdrawal. A physician may be consulted for these symptoms.

Some change in energy level is usually prominent. The patient is usually agitated and hyperactive during the initial interview, shifting position of the arms and legs frequently and "fidgeting". There is often a complaint of sleep and eating difficulties, but somnolence and hyperphagia are rarely seen. There is inappropriate temperature regulation, with sweating and heat intolerance most common but inability to stay warm sometimes noticed. Pupillary dilatation, hippus, and tremor are common. There are no confirmatory laboratory tests for withdrawal. The electroencephalogram is fairly typical of withdrawal states, showing asymmetrical hyperactivity.

Table 52 indicates a series of recognizable but arbitrarily designated clinical stages in withdrawal, from least severe to most severe, with the time of usual onset. This series is in fact a continuum, with mild symptoms readily observed 12 to 36 h before severe ones occur in alcohol/opiate withdrawal and at least 2 full days before in phenobarbital withdrawal.

The majority of patients reach only the mild or moderate level of symptoms and require little or no specific treatment for withdrawal. This group can readily be treated for withdrawal at home. In alcoholism it has been determined that the patient who has not reached moderate severity by 24 h after drinking stops may be safely managed on an outpatient basis. The severe, alarming, and life-threatening symptoms simply will not occur.

III. SCREENING FOR PRESENCE OF, SEVERITY OF, AND TREATMENT REQUIREMENTS RELATING TO WITHDRAWAL

Screening an abusing patient is widely utilized to determine whether there are needs for immediate medical care or hospitalization. It is also possible to determine the appropriate medication and supervision needs for withdrawal management. Screening is usually performed by a physician or other trained person in an office or emergency room setting.

A. BASIC SCREENING

Basic screening is almost identical to the screening process outlined in Chapter 12, with a little extra emphasis on determining how severe the withdrawal will be, the urgency for treatment with medications, and whether or not bleeding, infection, or head trauma is present. Such screening can be accomplished by nearly all physicians and nurses, physician's assistants, and others, who can readily be trained to this task. Table 53 lists the essential ingredients of a screening process.

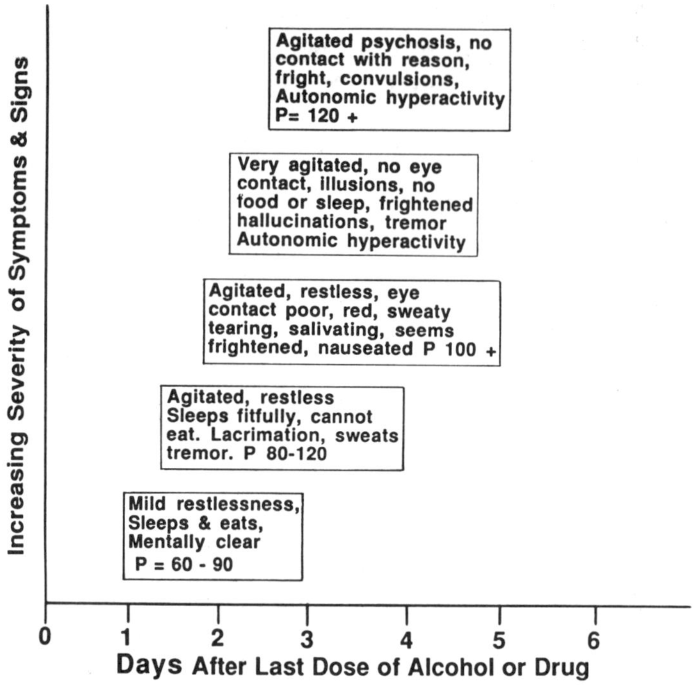

FIGURE 15. Time of symptoms and approximate duration of increasingly severe symptoms in alcohol or opiate withdrawal. Note that severity increases in a stepwise pattern, requiring 8 to 12 h to progress through each step.

Withdrawal may vary in severity from moderate to severe, with the latter requiring close supervision. Screening allows the observer to determine whether withdrawal has begun, to predict how severe it will be, and to determine if there are special factors in the patient that necessitate unusual treatment.

B. ANTICIPATING SEVERE WITHDRAWAL THROUGH SCREENING

Severe withdrawal is defined in Figure 15 and in the previous section. It includes all patients who reach the stage of frequent hallucinations and disorientation, who have a convulsion, or who otherwise cannot be managed in a home environment with an interested companion and some sedation.

The operative basis for predicting a severe withdrawal depends upon three points. First, withdrawals repeat themselves; severe withdrawals tend to recur in the same person. Second, there are historical and physical examination features which predict severe withdrawal. Third, once withdrawal begins, it runs a highly predictable course as shown in Figure 13. From the severity of the withdrawal at one point in time, one can readily estimate the maximum severity which will occur.[3,4]

Tolerance must be present for withdrawal to occur, and for sedatives and opiates at least 2 weeks of sustained use is required. Marked tolerance is associated with the most severe withdrawal; therefore, the more intensive the habit, the more likely is the withdrawal to be severe. Patients using alcohol, opiates, or sedatives for less than 2 weeks have no substantial symptoms of withdrawal. The compensatory cellular changes that account for tolerance required 3 to 7 days to disappear, which is the duration of the withdrawal period.

1. Predicting Severe Withdrawal Symptoms

The most severe withdrawals occur in patients who have the most tolerance (judged by the amounts of drug they are using). Thus an alcoholic using 1500 ml of vodka daily or a

TABLE 54
Predicting Severe Withdrawal, Need for Medication, and Need for Hospitalization

1. Accurate history of extremely high tolerance for abused drug
2. History of previous complicated withdrawals with acute psychosis, convulsions, violence
3. Fever above 101°F, from whatever cause, during withdrawal
4. Many marked manifestations of withdrawal, including confusion, anxiety, inability to rest, autonomic hyperactivity, tachycardia
5. More than one convulsion as part of withdrawal
6. Striking malnutrition
7. Confusion or acute psychosis
8. Severe, persistent abdominal or chest pain
9. Substantial instability of vital signs
10. Respiratory distress
11. Nausea and vomiting interfering with vital signs and renal function
12. Substantial bleeding
13. Documented requirement for massive sedation to control previous withdrawals

case of beer is much more tolerant than one satisfied with 500 ml of muscatel wine. A heroin addict taking six fixes daily is much more likely to experience severe withdrawal than one with a once-a-day habit. A further estimate of severity is the pattern of withdrawal experienced in the past, for there is striking reproduction of the features of convulsions, psychosis, approximate amount of sedation required, and even violence in subsequent withdrawals. Convulsions and violent behavior are particularly sought in the history or previous hospital records to anticipate these problems.

Severe malnutrition in an opiate or alcohol user often identifies heart injury and almost completely identifies the group who will die during withdrawal. Once a person has started the withdrawal process (invariably 6 to 12 h after stopping drug), the course follows the pattern outlined in Figures 13 and 15. For each 12 h without treatment, the withdrawal will increase at the most one severity unit. Thus, if a person is evaluated some 24 h after the last drug use and at that time the withdrawal is only mild, in the remaining time until the withdrawal reaches its maximum it can increase only one severity unit. Such a person can readily be managed on an outpatient basis.

Table 54 outlines issues of severity, need for drugs to treat the withdrawal, and hospitalization.

Fever at the time of withdrawal, like bleeding and severe abdominal or chest pain, is alarming and a basis for conducting the withdrawal where observations may be continued and hospitalization readily obtained if indicated. Fever is rarely above 100.5°F in withdrawal unless there is extreme muscular activity from psychosis. Higher temperatures usually indicate aspiration or infection. Hospitalization is usually indicated when vital signs are unstable, unless they can be stabilized with minimal therapy. Nausea and vomiting are common and are usually controlled with sedation. The assessment of malnutrition has been discussed in detail in Chapter 20.

2. Indices of Severity of Withdrawal

A number of indices of withdrawal severity have been developed and have been employed particularly in alcoholism. These assign a quantitative score to specific items observed in the patient. The pulse, blood pressure, temperature, and respiratory rate are always included. In addition, the ability of the patient to sleep and eat in the most recent 12 h, the quality of the eye contact, the presence of delusions or hallucinations, tremor, sweatiness, and clarity of memory are scored. These composite scores are a formalization of the process that the prudent physician undertakes but are a superior method for predicting withdrawal. Once a person has started withdrawal, if no treatment has been administered, a single evaluation is usually closely related to the most severe evaluation.[5-8]

TABLE 55
Minimal Care Requirements for Safe Withdrawal

1. A restful environment with other people who empathize with the problem and share some knowledge of the process
2. A bed or couch to lie on, some form of bland entertainment to avoid boredom, food and water
3. Impediments to the prompt availability of any abused substance
4. Continual and almost continuous availability of an interested, informed party to talk with; a counselor or recovered substance abuser is optimal, an interested relative is suboptimal
5. A backup medical plan should convulsions or other serious complications occur; transportation to an emergency room is adequate
6. Anxiolytic therapy in the form of conversation, compassionate companionship, or medicines

IV. TREATMENT OF WITHDRAWAL: REQUIREMENTS AND INPATIENT FACILITIES

Treatment of withdrawal as the first step in the treatment of an addiction is an excellent time to gain the support of the patient and his or her family for subsequent care. To accomplish this requires many skills and lots of time. Physicians must utilize other trained care givers, who provide compassion, attention to rest, relaxation, and food, and both listen to the patient and facilitate solutions when they exist and offer acceptance when solutions are unlikely. The specific training of nursing, social work, dietetics, and counseling are also required. The minimal essentials of withdrawal care are listed in Table 55.

It is apparent that much withdrawal treatment may be carried out at home or in the company of concerned persons. The ingredients provided by the physician often are not the most urgent ones required for the favorable outcome.

A. GENERAL

Trained staffs, whether in hospitals or special treatment facilities accustomed to treating substance abuse cases during withdrawal, undertake this with little fuss and minimal bother yet provide great comfort and reassurance to the patients. Hospitals without this experience have fears of the management of such patients and require a great deal of extra care and bother; the patients are dissatisfied and often feel rejected. If a detoxification unit is available, it is usually a better experience for the patient to undergo treatment there rather than in a general hospital. The staff is more knowledgeable and the treatment is better. The patients are far better satisfied and more likely to continue in therapy. The biggest difference between a standard hospital and a detoxification unit is in a clear plan anticipating most problems and reacting to them prophylactically or promptly. Most general hospitals await the full development of a problem before addressing it in this group of patients. Detoxification units recognize early signs of withdrawal and treat it appropriately and vigorously, delegating most treatment decisions to the staff at hand. Hospitals recognize withdrawal at a much later and more advanced stage and depend upon physicians to be called for treatment. Detoxification units recognize withdrawal at an earlier stage and authorize on-site staff, usually nurses, to administer appropriate treatment.

B. MAXIMS FOR DETOXIFICATION

Some Do's and Dont's are valuable for general medical wards to provide guidance in many of the common situations and help avoid frequent errors.

Do's

1. Do offer the patients food at each mealtime and calorie-containing fluids. This avoids fluid depletion and hypoglycemia.
2. Do use *one* drug for sedation. All staff become familiar with its profile of use and duration.
3. Do provide responsibility for sedation to the nursing staff.
4. Do encourage familiar clothes, persons, and objects to accompany the patient.

Dont's:
1. Don't use bed sides or restraints. They excite patients and produce injuries.
2. Don't use i.v. fluids unless clearly required. They retard the withdrawal and increase the amount of sedation required.
3. Don't use antiemetic and sleeping medications.
4. Don't use single rooms; encourage companionship.

Patients undergoing withdrawal are usually overhydrated but may be water and electrolyte depleted from vomiting or diarrhea. Giving calorie-containing foods will usually assist in recovery and avoid hypoglycemia. Intravenous fluids are seldom indicated; if they are required, give them in as little time as possible and discontinue the discomfort of the i.v. line.

Withdrawal is assisted by both sedative drugs and supportive, soothing conversation from an understanding, compassionate person; both can decrease the severity of withdrawal manifestations, as illustrated by the dashed line in Figure 12. To use a proper mix of "talk down" and drugs, all members of the team should be aware of the onset of action and persistence of the drug given and its expected actions. Units that use a variety of drugs of different potency and duration of action lose the close coordination of ancillary staff in assisting with the withdrawal. Units that place responsibility for dosing with the nursing staff more readily gain their assistance in all other aspects of patient management. The treatment area should be well lighted, have noise levels controlled, and utilize the company of other patients. Occasionally allowing a confused person to retain his or her own clothing and to remain in an armchair rather than a bed has led to peaceful withdrawal with a minimum of medication.

Bed sides, restraints, and i.v.s are highly stimulatory to the confused patient, and heavy sedation is usually required if they are employed. Simply not using them in most cases will result in the patient lying calmly in bed. If a patient has a tendency to get up, the bed should be temporarily removed and the mattress and bedclothes placed on the floor. This removes the hazard of falls, and the patient will usually remain there. Should this be objectionable, an easy chair with arms will usually work just as well. Confused patients are subject to cuts from broken glass and burns from smoking, and both should be anticipated by using only plastic and metal items around the patient and interdicting smoking and matches without companionship. Caffeine is stimulatory and is to be avoided during withdrawal. We use calorie-containing beverages rather than water, coffee, or tea. High-calorie caffeine-free soft drinks or Kool-Aid®, or instant soup mixtures made with hot water (Cup of Soup®), are less costly than fruit juices. Several calorie electrolyte solutions such as Orelsol®* have been developed specifically to replete alcoholics, but their value in repletion has not yet been demonstrated. They are pleasant to take and are clearly better than non-calorie-containing fluids.

C. RECOMMENDED DRUGS AND STANDING ORDERS FOR WITHDRAWAL

Short-acting agents such as alcohol and most opiates can be treated identically. Diazepam is the preferred drug in my experience, because there is already great familiarity with it and it is very inexpensive. It is very long acting, leading to fewer dosing decisions than with most other similar agents, but its single disadvantage is poor absorption when given i.m. Lorazepam is a similar drug that may be given i.m. The unit dose of diazepam is 10 mg. This is given orally as soon as the withdrawal is perceived to begin and repeated each hour until the progression of withdrawal ceases and sedation is attained. If a withdrawal score is used (see above), this should decrease within 1 h of ingestion of sufficient diazepam. If the physician gives the initial dose during the interview, he will be in a position to determine

* Orelsol®, made and marketed by Custom Laboratories, Inc., 930 W. Baltimore St., Baltimore, MD 21223, contains in each liter 15 mEq of Na, 10 mEq each of K and Cl, 4 mEq of Ca, 2 mEq of Mg, and 5 mEq of P, as well as 100 g of carbohydrate.

if a second or third dose is required as he completes his workup. The orders that I usually use for such patients are as follows:

1. Regular meals served in bed.
2. Diazepam 10 mg each 2 h p.o. for agitation. No dose to be given unless patient can sit and take medication plus glass of calorie-containing fluid.
3. Vital signs recorded t.i.d.
4. Restricted to room.
5. May smoke only sitting in chair with observation.
6. No restraints or bedrails.

On the second day I limit the diazepam to one half the total given the first day, and on the third day to one half of that on the second. No drug is used subsequently. Agents are not given to facilitate sleeping. Acetaminophen, up to four 300-mg tablets, antacids, up to 6 doses, and multivitamin tablets are available to all as they desire them. Each patient is given 1 mg of folate and 10 mg of thiamin i.m. or i.v. upon admission. Patients with a history of convulsions are given 300 mg of phenytoin p.o. daily for 5 days.

D. COMMENTS ON ALTERNATIVE MEDICATIONS FOR WITHDRAWAL TREATMENT

A variety of agents are advocated for the treatment of alcohol withdrawal, but several are superior in my experience. Use of a single agent in a unit leads to far superior withdrawal treatment than use of multiple agents. For 95% of sedative and opiate withdrawals, the very-long-acting agents diazepam and chlordiazepoxide are heavily preferred. The long action makes everyone's efforts easier, for when adequate sedation is attained (see treatment curve in Figure 12) so that withdrawal signs are decreasing, no further dosing is required. In a consecutive series of 100 patients adequately treated for withdrawal using chlordiazepoxide, the average patient required a total of 5.7 doses for the entire withdrawal. The mean dose in the first 24 h was 312 mg, and the mean in the second 24 h was 97 mg. In a subsequent study of 100 similar patients treated with diazepam, 6.3 doses were required (not significantly greater), with 43 mg used in the first 24 h and 28 mg used in the subsequent 24-h period. The very prolonged duration of action is desirable in uncomplicated withdrawal but may be less desirable when there is a question of serious head injury or impending surgery. The inability to give these two agents i.m. is their major disadvantage. Chlordiazepoxide has almost no anticonvulsant effect. An evaluation of withdrawal treated with a single 20-mg dose of diazepam has appeared.[9]

Oxazepam is very short acting relative to diazepam, has less anticonvulsant effect (comparable to chlordiazepoxide), and requires more doses. In 100 consecutive patients treated with this agent, 9.6 doses were required (significantly more than for diazepam and chlordiazepoxide). Lorazepam has potent anticonvulsive action and is well tolerated and absorbed i.m., but it is short acting. We have not studied this agent in consecutive patients.

Phenobarbital is an excellent choice for withdrawal, being highly effective, absorbed by all routes, inexpensive, and a potent anticonvulsive. An initial dose of 300 mg i.v. or i.m., followed if necessary 1 to 2 h later by 150 mg, is usually all that is required. Phenobarbital may be given i.v., i.m., or orally. It requires far more supervision than benzodiazepines, because it can suppress respiration enough to produce death. Many units employ only this agent with excellent results, but I do not recommend it because no one can safely advise a floor nurse by phone to administer an additional sedative dose of phenobarbital to a patient. To do this safely you must have personal knowledge that the nurse you are talking to can and has fully assessed the consciousness of the patient or you must personally review the patient's status. In contrast, you can safely request an orally administered benzodiazepine drug. Phenothiazine drugs such as chlorpromazine and haloperidol have side effects of hypotension that make them poor choices for use in withdrawal.

E. MANAGEMENT OF UNUSUAL PROBLEMS

1. The patient is disoriented and hallucinating upon admission. Such patients in full delirium tremens usually require i.v. administration of medications and are usually managed better with two agents in combination. If I can obtain an i.v. route, I administer 10 mg of diazepam immediately and repeat the dose each 10 to 30 min. I simultaneously administer 5 mg of haloperidol i.m. Usually the person is calmed by these two measures. Subsequent withdrawal is treated as in other, less severely ill patients. It is nearly impossible to keep an i.v. drip in such patients, and occasionally they are so combative that i.v. injections are impossible. Lorazepam in 2-mg increments can be given i.m. each 30 min until the desired sedation is obtained. Large inner-city detoxification centers frequently use phenobarbital for this purpose. They give an initial dose of 300 to 350 mg i.m. or i.v. and repeat half this dose in 90 min if needed.

2. A patient using 750 ml of Scotch whiskey daily has an automobile accident with head injury. CT scan shows a small subdural hemorrhage but no need for immediate evacuation. There is a right-sided ptosis but a large hematoma in that region. Close observation of the level of consciousness and the neurological examination is in order. Some 20 h after the accident the patient becomes increasingly agitated, with tachycardia to 130, marked tremulousness, and increasing difficulty in maintaining contact. Some treatment is essential.

Short-acting drugs are best for this purpose, the choice depending upon one's familiarity with particular agents. Intravenous alcohol or short-acting barbiturate (phenobarbital) would be the preferred treatments. A loading dose of 1.0 g/kg of absolute alcohol followed by a dose of 0.2 g/kg/h is usually sufficient for sedation, with a reduction of the infusion rate to 0.1 mg/kg/h when adequate reversal of withdrawal has been attained. Stopping the infusion of alcohol will lead to the person awakening for neurological evaluation in about 1 to 2 h; with the barbiturate it is much more rapid.

3. An alcoholic has been in a serious automobile accident and has a fractured pelvis and a ruptured liver and kidney necessitating several operative procedures. On the third day withdrawal is severe and there is concern of wound disruption. Immediate control is essential, and a long-acting drug is an advantage. Intravenous lorazepam would be my choice, for one needs effective treatment for only a day or two. Four milligrams initially would probably be all that would be needed. Alternatives would be a short-acting barbiturate i.v. maintained for a day or two.

A very delayed major withdrawal has been described occasionally in which hallucinations appear only after 5 to 8 days. In a vast experience with alcoholics I have not observed this syndrome except in mixed drug and alcohol abuse, usually including phenobarbital.[10]

V. DETOXIFICATION IN THE HOME OR IN THE COMMUNITY

Many metropolitan areas have detoxification facilities managed by volunteer groups that provide a restful environment with food and drink, knowledgeable and compassionate recovering users, and a good backup arrangement should emergencies develop. These facilities often operate without charge to the patient, provide excellent anonymity, and when acceptable to the client are a very satisfactory choice. There are a large number of residential substance-abuse treatment programs, nearly all covered by hospitalization insurance for at least one complete cycle each year, which provide minimal detoxification services. These facilities have a medical director who is available only a few hours each day and usually employ a single full-time nurse. Patients are usually screened in an emergency room for conditions that might require hospitalization and then cared for in the treatment facility. Finally, increasing numbers of addicts are withdrawn at home with the assistance of a nonaddicted companion. To utilize these facilities, screening must be effective and a system created to obtain additional medical care should the need arise. I have worked cooperatively with each of these types of detoxification and provided medications for most clients to assist with the withdrawal.

Screening usually reveals no problems that require immediate attention. If the signs of withdrawal are not severe, and there are no markers that predict a severe withdrawal, it is generally safe to direct the patient to a facility to complete withdrawal. In each case there should be written instructions for use of medications and for followup should that be necessary. In residential substance-abuse centers there is usually a written procedure governing the backup and control of medications. If there is any doubt, written instructions should be provided to the patient and the responsible person.

If screening reveals a health problem requiring hospitalization, the physician may undertake the detoxification and management of the health problem simultaneously or may refer the patient appropriately, but in most hospitals it is difficult to keep the substance abuse confidential.

When I send a patient home or to friends for withdrawal, I like to satisfy myself by interview that there is a nonabusing friend or relative who will reside with the patient for the next several days and who comprehends the problem and can control medication. I usually administer 10 mg of diazepam orally during screening, and if there is very limited effect, I may administer a second dose. I provide the nonabusing person with fifteen 5-mg diazepam caps with the following written instructions:

Instructions — (First and last name of patient, date of screening) was evaluated today for drug/alcohol withdrawal. No complications or health problems requiring immediate treatment were identified and treatment of withdrawal is being undertaken at home. It is important that food or liquids be taken at least 6 times a day. Fruit juice, ginger ale, or Seven-Up should be taken in a 12 oz. portion each few hours and he should have at least something to eat each meal. He may have anything he wants except alcohol. For the person or family who want more medications I have occasionally used the fluid prescribed to accommodate that psychic need. Gatorade®, or commercial and patented carbohydrate-electrolyte supplements[11] may be used for fluids but are certainly of no unique benefit. Coffee, tea, and cola beverages are to be avoided. He should not smoke without someone being present to prevent fire. He may be given one of the 5 mg diazepam tablets as frequently as each hour if he is wide awake, but should not be awakened to have one. After several tablets he will probably sleep. No tablets should be given after two days.

If you are concerned about pain, fever, bleeding or seeing things that are not there you may call me at 312-242-7200, or bring him to the Emergency Room at Grant Hospital. He has an appointment to be seen in my office on Nov. 19, 1990. All tablets left over after two days should be flushed down the toilet to prevent them from being used inappropriately. Encourage regular meal intake and exercise. After the 5th day he may have coffee, tea, and cokes again.

Comment on outpatient experience — The majority of withdrawal occurs at home utilizing the family or friends of the patient to provide food and shelter and continuous companionship and supervision. The physician can play a unique and invaluable role by providing screening (and, if appropriate, laboratory review), recommendations of nutritional supplements if appropriate, and specific anxiolytic therapy. The physician also is available to arrange backup. Chlordiazepoxide or diazepam are remarkably safe medications employed in these circumstances. After screening the patient to be sure that there is no contraindication to its use (severe chronic lung disease, liver encephalopathy stage 2), I often provide the nonaddicted companion or family with twenty-five 25-mg chlordiazepoxide capsules to be taken hourly as needed for anxiety. I instruct them neither to awaken the patient nor to give them more frequently. After 4 days the remaining capsules should be destroyed. In an experience with 100 consecutive outpatients so treated, 84 had successful withdrawals without the need for further consultation, 5 others were brought back for uncontrolled anxiety, and 11 returned to their substance (nearly all alcohol). I have also used 2.5-mg or 5-mg diazepam tablets in a similar fashion, providing 15 to 20 tablets depending upon whether I estimate a high or a low need.

On less frequent occasions I have carried out ambulatory detoxification of long-acting depressants and heroin. In this circumstance I have used combinations of chlordiazepoxide and phenobarbital. I have given the patient 120 mg of phenobarbital orally while still in my office (with an accompanying nonaddicted person) after initial health screening. I keep the patient there for an additional hour, and if the agitation has increased give either an additional 120 mg or 60 mg depending upon the increase. I then send the patient and companion home with sufficient phenobarbital to provide one dose daily such that on the second day the patient is given at one time the same dose as the first day (e.g., 180 mg given in the office, the same dose to be repeated the next day) and then the daily dose is reduced by 30 mg each subsequent day (150, 120, 90, 60, 30 mg taken over the next 5 days, respectively). In addition, the companion is given twenty-five 25-mg chlordiazepoxide capsules as noted above with the same instruction. This combination has been sufficient to provide detoxification in many patients. Many other drugs have been used. Clonidine[4] has not proven effective for all patients, and a recent trial of agonists to alpha 2 receptors has proven disappointing.[12] Horwitz and co-workers[13] describe their experience using atenolol as an adjunctive measure. All patients received benzodiazepine therapy but, based on the heart rate, one group was given either 50 mg (for heart rates under 80 beats/min) or 100 mg for heart rates over 80. Among patients with more active withdrawal the vital signs normalized, more patients remained in therapy, the patients were more alert, and craving for alcohol was significantly lower than in those receiving placebo. All patients were given oxazepam, either 15- or 30-mg tablets, up to four times daily.

A recent evaluation of inpatient versus outpatient detoxification has been published that randomized 164 low-socioeconomic-status veterans to a prospective trial and treated all with decreasing doses of oxazepam. The mean duration of treatment was significantly longer for inpatients (9.2 days) versus outpatients (6.5 days), but more inpatients completed detoxification. Neither group experienced serious medical complications of the treatment. Outcome evaluations at 1 and 6 months were similar, with significant improvement in both groups and no differences. Costs were quite different, with outpatient cost averaging $175 to $388 per patient depending upon the length and inpatient cost averaging $3319 to $3665. This study concluded that outpatient detoxification is effective and safe for patients with mild to moderate symptoms.[14] An editorial places alcohol withdrawal treatment in perspective.[15] Another review discusses recent improvements.[16]

REFERENCES

1. **Hemmingsen, R. and Kramp, P.,** Delirium tremens and related clinical states: psychopathology, cerebral pathophysiology and psychochemistry: a two-component hypothesis concerning etiology and pathogenesis, *Acta Psychiatr. Scand. Suppl.*, 345, 94, 1988.
2. **Zipursky, R. B., Lim, K. O., and Pfefferbaum, A.,** MRI study of brain changes with short-term abstinence from alcohol, *Alcoholism,* 13, 664, 1989.
3. **Pristach, C. A., Smith, C. M., and Whitney, R. B.,** Alcohol withdrawal syndromes — prediction from detailed medical and drinking histories, *Drug Alcohol Depend.*, 11, 177, 1983.
4. **Foy, A., March, S., and Drinkwater, V.,** Use of an objective clinical scale in the assessment and management of alcohol withdrawal in a large general hospital, *Alcoholism,* 12, 360, 1988.
5. **Naranjo, C. A. and Sellers, E. M.,** Clinical assessment and pharmacotherapy of the alcohol withdrawal syndrome, *Recent Dev. Alcohol,* 4, 265, 1986.
6. **Spehr, W., Andresen, B., and Stemmler, G.,** AMP-rated psychopathology in chronic alcoholics, *Eur. Arch. Psychiatr. Neurol. Sci.*, 235, 42, 1985.
7. **Foy, A., March, S., and Drinkwater, V.,** Use of an objective clinical scale in the assessment and management of alcohol withdrawal in a large general hospital, *Alcoholism,* 12, 360, 1988.

8. **Robinson, B. J., Robinson, G. M., Maling, T. J. B., and Johnson, R. H.,** Is clonidine useful in the treatment of alcohol withdrawal?, *Alcohol: Clin. Exp. Res.*, 13, 95, 1989.
9. **Sellers, E. M., Naranjo, C. A., Harrison, M., Devenyi, P., Roach, C., and Sykora, K.,** Diazepam loading: simplified treatment of alcohol withdrawal, *Clin. Pharmacol. Ther.*, 34, 822, 1983.
10. **Naranjo, C. A. and Sellers, E. M.,** Clinical assessment and pharmacotherapy of the alcohol withdrawal syndrome, in *Recent Developments in Alcoholism,* Vol. 4, Galanter, M., Ed., 1986, 265.
11. **Wright, C. and Talbott, G. D.,** The use of carbohydrate-electrolyte supplements in residential treatment of chemical dependence, *J. Psychoactive Drugs,* 20, 337, 1988.
12. **Cushman, P., Jr. and Sowers, J. R.,** Alcohol withdrawal syndrome: clinical and hormonal responses to alpha-2 adrenergic agonist treatment, *Alcoholism: Clin. Exp. Res.*, 13, 361, 1989.
13. **Horwitz, R. I., Gottlieb, L. D., and Kraus, M. L.,** The efficacy of atenolol in the outpatient management of the alcohol withdrawal syndrome: results of a randomized clinical trial, *Arch. Int. Med.*, 149, 1089, 1989.
14. **Hayashida, M., Alterman, A. I., McLellan, A. T., et al.,** Cost-effectiveness of inpatient vs. outpatient detoxification, *New Engl. J. Med.*, 320, 358, 1989.
15. **Lerner, W. D. and Fallon, H. J.,** The alcohol withdrawal syndrome, *New Engl. J. Med.*, 313, 951, 1985.
16. **Gallant, D. M.,** Improvements in treatment of alcohol withdrawal syndromes, *Alcoholism,* 13, 721, 1989.

Chapter 28

Entering Treatment

I. INTRODUCTION

The process of recovery from addictions is facilitated by treatment. The results of treatment were discussed in Chapter 26. A critical portion of the treatment process is its rejection by the addict at some time between identification and the first 3 months of therapy. It is the purpose of this chapter to discuss issues closely related to motivating and retaining addicts in therapy.

A. SEQUENTIAL REQUIREMENTS FOR ENTRY INTO AND RETENTION IN TREATMENT

The first things that must be accomplished are gaining the addict's and his family's confidence in the value of the therapist. This is intimately associated with presenting the diagnosis of addiction and overcoming some of the denial that will follow that disclosure.

The next three requirements are approached concurrently and are introduced as (1) keeping sobriety, (2) preventing relapse, and (3) building self-esteem. Initially, during intoxication, sobriety is usually enforced by physical removal of the addict from the agent and subsequently interposing major impediments to the further use of the agent. Subsequently, the patient's determination to keep sobriety is sufficient in most situations. Similarly, relapse prevention starts out as a physical separation of addict from agent, but at later times is reduced to counsel of avoidance, followed by the learning of alternative behaviors to avoid the need for the agent. Esteem is restored by successes in sobriety, reintegration into society, and reformation of substantial relationships.

The medical model of substance abuse employed by nearly all physicians is of great value in therapy. It gives the patient disease status rather than addiction status, which rates

TABLE 56
Prompt Benefits of Entry into Treatment

1. Sense of relief by patient, family, employer
2. Assumption of authority by an outside source
3. Improved overall health and sense of well-being
4. Improved mental faculties
5. Improved mental sanity
6. Removal of the unpleasantness of withdrawal

him much higher in the eyes of associates and thus builds self-esteem. Further, it removes some of the guilt for past actions and in this way assists self-esteem. Others have discussed whether or not addictions should be considered diseases,[1,2] and the issue is far from settled in the scientific sense; however, as a therapist with addicted patients you will perform better if you present no doubt.[3]

The longer-term goals of keeping sobriety and preventing relapse might be likened to an automobile journey after dark, into a completely new and very desolate area. Keeping sobriety represents features of the car (the patient), such as sufficient gas, appropriate brakes, good tires, and the like. Avoiding relapse represents the quality of the route, the types of roads, avoiding sharp curves, detours, and closed or hazardous bridges. The determination for sobriety is built into the patient and reinforced by therapy but as part of the addiction has a life of its own. Relapse prevention can be substantially enhanced by therapy. Alternative ways to provide the ''high'' of abuse, safe ways to control anxiety, and recognition of cues that precipitate addictive behavior are all part of the ongoing and progressive treatment process.

B. PROMPTLY ATTAINED RESULTS OF ENTRY INTO TREATMENT

There are a substantial number of positive results obtained almost immediately after entry into treatment, usually for withdrawal and detoxification. These benefits assist the addict in accepting the value of longer-term treatment as well as the value of the therapist, and partially overcome doubt about the decision to enter treatment. The physician treating substance abusers often feels insecure and uneasy at the moment of ''forcing'' a reluctant patient or family to initiate the treatment process. There are certain prompt rewards that follow, and these can be used to keep the patient's spirits high and to provide a factual support for the optimism you have presented to the family. Table 56 lists some of these that will be discussed.

Denial of the addiction usually involves the patient, the family, and often the employer. This has created anxieties, tension, and unrest on the part of many. The act of entering treatment of any form provides a sense of relief and saves the patient and the family from all the complex fabrications and coverups which have produced strained relationships and anxieties. There is comfort in the addiction family in having an outsider ''take over'' responsibility for an immediate phase of treatment. This allows the patient the luxury of simply getting better.

Mental clarity, better sleep, improved strength, and ability to eat return rapidly in the few days following withdrawal and continue to improve for 1 to 6 months. This is associated with an improved sense of well-being and of self. Appearances shift from unkempt to clean and neat. The well-developed system of excuses, fabrications, and coverups, which require so much of the patient's mental energies, is now no longer necessary. There is a sense of relief through understanding that many others have the same problem, that others understand its misery, and that this is sickness rather than personal inadequacy.

II. PRESENTING THE ADDICTION TO THE PATIENT; OVERCOMING DENIAL

A. PRESENTING THE ADDICTION

Presentation of the addiction is the basis of Chapter 14, and only a few points will be made here. Patients insist upon accurate diagnosis. The history, physical examination, and laboratory tests may each contribute to the recognition and diagnosis of an addiction. It is important that the physician who reaches a diagnosis of addiction resolve uncertainty or be prepared to communicate the uncertainty to the patient and his or her family. The diagnostic conclusions of addiction or abuse are presented by the physician just as any other serious chronic disease is discussed: ''You have multiple sclerosis.: The doctor then explains in appropriately simplified language what this means for current and future health and just what is involved in the appropriate treatment. Should there be treatment options, they must be presented. A few patients will accept the diagnosis and the recommendations for treatment outright, many will discuss the findings, and a few will debate the accuracy of your diagnosis. Although many will resist, only a few will vehemently deny the conclusions. Calmness, persistence, and repetition of the excellent prognosis for treatment usually will lead the patient to acceptance. In a rare case, the patient will leave the interview, but will return on his or her own volition for a subsequent appointment.

B. DEALING WITH DENIAL

When there is clear resistance to the acceptance of the denial, persistence and time to think about the initial presentation will often change this to acceptance. At the time of the presentation there are some common tactics on the part of the addict that recur sufficiently often to be discussed here.

1. Intimidation of the doctor to withdraw the diagnosis. This is usually avoided by being firm and not losing your equanimity. When initiated, it is appropriate to emphasize such action as a manifestation of the disease.
2. Threatened dismissal of the physician. Usually, if the patient threatens, it is mostly a bluff and can be overcome by calm understanding and optimism about the response to treatment. The suggestion that initial treatment be tried to determine whether it will be beneficial is sufficient. If the patient has walked out or failed to keep appointments, a call or note will sometimes bring him back, but most often he will be lost to your treatment.
3. Declaration that ''I can stop at any time,'' therefore there is no problem. Such a declaration is best confronted. Suggest a trial, providing the patient accepts blood or urine testing. Three negative tests will be the basis of accepting that the patient is correct.
4. ''You listen to my wife (or father) but you don't listen to me.'' Point out that the treatment will involve the whole family, who share in the misery, but persistently present the objective evidence of your diagnosis.
5. ''You don't understand my responsibilities, I can't undergo treatment at this time'' or ''I can't accept the shame, loss of job, etc.'' This is countered with reassurance that many others have the problem and many understand its treatment and will help. Address these anxieties appropriately in your plan of therapy.

C. LATE MANIFESTATIONS OF DENIAL

Denial, presenting as a major problem in the initial few months of treatment, keeps cropping up again and again throughout recovery. It should be openly discussed as a part of the addictive disease, but never in a form that indicates rejection of the patient. It starts

TABLE 57
Late Manifestations of Denial That Are Best Brought to the Patient's Attention

1. Enlarging minor medical complaints as basis of behavior (e.g., ''My sore back is why I use these drugs'')
2. Blaming use patterns on behavior of others (e.g., ''My boss doesn't like me so I get all the difficult jobs'')
3. Paranoia about others (e.g., ''The police just had to arrest so many that day'')
4. Comparing behavior favorably to others (e.g., ''I don't drink nearly as much as my wife'')
5. Minimizing (e.g., ''I only used coke two times in my life'')
6. Mass behavior (e.g., ''Everyone was shooting up so I had to do it'')
7. Fault finding with therapist or therapy, with a view to rejecting one or both
8. Generalization of failure of all therapy (e.g., ''I went to AA once but it didn't do me any good'')

TABLE 58
Stages in Recovery from Substance Abuse

Stage	Features	Treatment
1. Recognition of problem	1. Usually at a personal, social, or legal crisis	1. Some sort of detoxification support
2. Recovery of health (1—12 months)	2. Minor multiple organ damage	2. Nutrition, may require specific treatment
3. Restoration of job, family relationships (1—3 years)	3. Assistance for all	3. May require individual therapy
4. Stable new life	4. Infrequent relapses	4. None required
5. Relapses	5. Move to a lower number	5. As required

with assuring the patient that the choice for abstinence is largely the patient's. Therapists cannot prevent relapse; they can only assist the patient. Table 57 presents some of the ways in which denial is seen later in therapy.

Each of these behaviors must be calmly discussed in terms of its meaning. Discussion is needed to reverse the denial process, which will increase in the addict's mind until the problem of the addiction is totally overlooked. If there is disagreement, present yourself as knowledgeable about addiction and state that this is a part of that disease. Do not be manipulated into rejecting the patient. Under no circumstance should you lose your ''cool''. If a session becomes argumentative, emotional, and destructive, it should be terminated and rescheduled. Whenever possible, end the interview with an accurate but optimistic appraisal of events since treatment started.

III. STAGES IN THE TREATMENT AND RECOVERY PROCESS

In the movie *Sergeant York,* the hero is a farmer from Tennessee who becomes an alcoholic. One day during a drinking bout his rifle is struck by lightning and he is thrown to the ground. After that event he drinks no more. Such rapid attainment of prolonged sobriety is uncommon. Much more common is a prolonged course characterized by relapses and remissions. Table 58 presents some of the prominent stages of the recovery process and the customary treatments.

During these stages the autonomy of the patient changes in relation with the therapist. Initially, the ability to remain substance free is not placed at risk, so the patient is restricted to a treatment center, followed by return to a home that has been sanitized of alcohol and drugs to avoid temptations. Clear avoidance of sources of substances and situations for their use is prominent. As clear thinking, health, and coping skills improve, the patient assumes more and more control of his or her therapy and the selection of choices. At this time the therapist accepts and treats the patient as a more mature and autonomous individual. Then the therapist and the patient become co-conspirators in the search for better health, the physician serving primarily as an advisor of the pathways rather than a decision maker.

TABLE 59
Attainments Indicating Recovering

1. Continuous abstinence
2. Less frequent use of drug manifested by longer periods of abstinence, less destructive use, or self-initiated cessation
3. Correction of a substance-related physical or mental health problem
4. Repair of substance-related injury to family, job, and interpersonal relationships
5. Significant commitment of effort to a cause or relationship apart from self and substance abuse
6. Satisfactory performance in a job appropriate to skills and education
7. Development of significant relationship or acquiring a new friend

IV. GOALS AND MEASURES OF PROGRESS AFTER DETOXIFICATION

A. GOALS OF THERAPY AFTER DETOXIFICATION

During withdrawal you have made a strong case for the advantages of continued therapy and developed a relationship with the patient and his or her family. The diagnosis has been communicated and an optimistic outcome has been indicated. The four goals of subsequent treatment are (1) to offer the patient a nonchemical substitute for the dependency, (2) to remind the patient repeatedly of the addiction and its continued presence, (3) to repair the medical and social damage that has resulted, and (4) to build self-esteem.

The addiction is well ingrained into the fabric of the patient. Many common situations were formerly solved with drugs, and those situations will be solved in that fashion in the future unless alternatives are devised. As part of the treatment process, new methods to relax and reduce anxiety must be taught. Relaxation tapes used with a portable tape player are widely and effectively used. Tapes to encourage sleep are also effective. Exercise, reading, engrossing hobbies, gardening, and volunteer work are but a few of the nonchemical substitutes to which the patient can be trained to turn. Simultaneously, cues that precipitate reuse can often be identified and avoided. Examples of cues include barroom settings, the odor of stale beer, rock music, homosexual arousal, and unfair verbal abuse by a woman of a man.

The greatest builders of self-esteem are successes with sobriety, job, or intrapersonal relationships. Sincere belief in the medical model assists by placing the blame on the disease rather than the self. Learning that many others become addicted helps. Presenting "markers" of progress, as noted in the next section, can help the person understand that he is doing his part toward improving.

B. MARKERS OF IMPROVEMENT

Table 59 lists some readily evaluated features of recovering that may be identified and pointed out to the patient. They can also be used to encourage your staff and the family of the patient.

During recovery a drug use pattern that has been destructive to performance, health, and interpersonal relationships becomes less frequent and less destructive. This new status usually comes about through changes in both the victim and his or her family and friends. Thus, a marriage between an alcohol/benzodiazepine-abusing wife and a successful rising chief executive officer of a growing corporation may see these changes after a year of treatment during which a single 3-day relapse into drinking took place. The addict understands herself a great deal better, and recognizes her potential to relapse in stress-producing situations. She has developed alternative means to deal with stress, but to some degree has changed her life to avoid stressful situations. Her husband accepts her addiction, can talk comfortably about it with his associates, and no longer forces his wife into situations that she detests and that create great stress. He has learned to say that his wife does not like to be hostess at company affairs and invites other wives to share this responsibility. Her friends have changed, a few who have alcohol-centered lives have been dropped, others sharing her new interests have been identified.

The recovering process is lifelong, but the attainments set forth in Table 59 come about at various times. Stable abstinence is attained in many patients in 2 or 3 years. When stable abstinence is attained, the person can remain comfortably in a situation where drug or alcohol is available and avoid its use. Most former users identify stressful situations or cues that are likely to precipitate addictive behavior and as they improve seek assistance to support them through the anticipated crisis. The self-recognition of such threats to abstinence is an important step in recovery. Familiar cues that formerly precipitated drug use may now precipitate severe, uncontrolled, and somewhat illogical anxiety. The individual therapist can assist with cue identification, provide alternative means to deal with anxiety, and can offer pressure relief if the fear and anxiety become overwhelming through either temporary medication or hospitalization. The role of the physician who has recognized an addiction is twofold: to be a compassionate, understanding guide through the frightening initial treatment process, and to serve as an advisor in setting realistic goals with the client. Both these functions can be fulfilled as part of regular office visits and may be the glue that keeps a patient in treatment.

Group therapy, usually with a self-help group but also with a trained leader, is particularly helpful in meeting the goals of therapy in learning how to deal with the stresses of returning to work and to working again with people who have been harmed by the addiction. Issues of group identification enter into selection of treatment modalities even at an early stage. Treatment of women is discussed in Chapter 36,[4] ethnic group issues are discussed in Chapter 40, and adolescents are discussed in Chapter 35. It has been well documented that socially unstable patients treated with their peers subsequently perform much better than when they are treated in a program for middle-class patients.[5]

V. ASSISTING THE PATIENT IN SETTING REALISTIC GOALS FOR THERAPY

Realistic goals are an important part of the therapy process. Using these appropriately to facilitate therapy is discussed more fully in Chapter 31. These goals can be looked upon as ego-building attainments and therefore they must be readily achievable, clearly near at hand, and initially related to what is most in the patient's mind, relief from pain and guilt. The addicted person confronted with the necessity to acknowledge the addiction and commit to some course of action nearly always selects a goal that removes the immediate pressure and interferes minimally with the addiction. Thus "I'll cut back on my drinking", "I'll give up whiskey", "I'll quit taking those pills" are typical short-term goals to remove the pressure (of family, health, law). Often unrealistic statements such as "I'll never take another drop of alcohol as long as I live", "If I ever touch coke again I hope to drop dead instantly", "You can take my word for it, I'll never use any kind of medicine or drug again in my life" are made. It is useful to assist the patient in avoiding the unrealistic as well as setting goals that facilitate recovering.

The addicted person is impatient for success and relief of some of the pain brought about by the drug-induced behavior. Therefore, setting the initial goal as "Getting off the drug and getting health back", or "Getting through withdrawal" is highly praiseworthy, attainment can build self-esteem, and the goal can be achieved in at the most a week or two.

Addiction has a life of its own, and relapse is not a rejection of the therapist as a person or of his methods. As a therapist these things must be understood at all times, but expectation of a better future must be communicated as well as an unequivocal diagnosis of addiction. Successful outcome is almost always associated with occasional relapses, but they are short and not very destructive.

REFERENCES

1. **Szasz, T. S.,** Bad habits are not diseases: a refutation of the claim that alcoholism is a disease, *Lancet,* 2, 83, 1972.
2. **Keller, M.,** The disease concept of alcoholism revisited, *J. Stud. Alcohol,* 37, 1694, 1976.
3. **Jellinek, E. M.,** *The Disease Concept of Alcoholism,* Hillhouse Press, New Haven, CT, 1960.
4. **Chatham, L. R., Anderson, M. A., Person, P., and Keyes, J.,** Employed alcoholic women: the right to be the same or different, National Council on Alcoholism, Washington, D.C., 1979.
5. **Gerard, D. L. and Saenger, G.,** Out-patient treatment of alcoholism: a study of outcome and its determinants, *Brookside Monograph #4*, Toronto, 1966.

Chapter 29

Professionals and Others Providing Skilled Services to Substance Abusers

I. INTRODUCTION

Many different skills are required to bring addicts back to a normal life. The skills of a doctor, social worker, psychologist, and lawyer may be required in a single subject. In this chapter the unique contributions of other professions and training programs for helping addicts are examined. It is important for the physician who treats addicts to learn what other trained persons can accomplish and to reach some general conclusions as to what can be appropriately accomplished.

The training of dieticians, social workers, psychologists, and nurses provide skills that almost no other professionals regularly possess, and at times these unique skills are required. In addition, there are a large number of persons assisting addicts who have acquired their skills by practical, often extensive experience with addicts. Although this group varies widely and does not have a professional group controlling their competency, collectively they provide a lot of care, some of which is the best available for addicts.

Physicians who treat abusing patients rapidly develop a relationship with social workers, group counselors, and members of self-help groups in order to better assist their patients in recovering and to share some of the burdens of such care. In time each therapist encounters patients who relapse. When that happens they or their family telephone the therapist, often at awkward hours, needing prompt assistance. It is a comfort to the therapist to know that

TABLE 60
Factors Enhancing Relationship Between Abuser and Counselor

1. Similarity of culture, race, age, employment, and parents
2. Acceptance of authority
3. Conviction that "counselor can assist"
4. Reputation of hospital and individual
5. Comfort of early interactions

a relationship with a sponsor in a self-help group has been established. That sponsor will come promptly to the patient to provide comfort and assistance. The utilization of many different experts in substance abuse treatment is much greater in better programs than in many smaller practices.

Most professionals who treat abusers set limits on just what type of treatment will be provided and the circumstances under which it will be available. This is uniformly done by those with many addicts in their practice and is highly recommended, for it assists in keeping the therapist effective. Many therapists do not provide their home phone number but refer all patients to the hospital emergency room. Most therapists will not work extensively with a strikingly intoxicated person in the office or by phone. The involvement of several different disciplines in the treatment of a patient is often more effective and more economical.

Patients remain in treatment and are helped by treatment when they believe that the selected program will be beneficial. Such belief is usually established from events in the patient's life prior to entry into treatment. Patients with a long positive interaction with physicians are assisted by them. Patients who have never had a regular doctor and have derived their care from casual contacts with emergency rooms are often not assisted by physician therapy. Socially deprived patients are helped more by the self-help groups in attaining abstinence than they are by doctors.[1]

The cost of services charged to the patient, their family, or other resources is related closely to training. Physicians cost more per hour than social workers or psychologists, who in turn cost more than counselors. It is always worth asking if a less costly treatment can be substituted. On the other hand, no therapists should underestimate their value to recovery if they are bolstering sagging self-esteem and keeping people in treatment. It is not essential for the physician to provide a medicine or undertake a laboratory test to justify seeing the abusing patient. Table 60 lists issues that enter into determining the effectiveness of a therapist-client relationship.

Everything being equal, a person is more likely to be helped by someone with whom he identifies than by someone with appreciable differences. Sex, race, cultural background, and education all enter into effectiveness but are seldom spoken about. When highly credentialed and educated persons are utilized, the value of authority, reputation, and conviction that the person can assist override some of the differences. Abusers are sensitive to rejection, and any tension generated in the initial interaction is often misinterpreted as rejection which may permanently interfere with the relationship.

II. PROFESSIONALS AND WHAT THEY PROVIDE IN TREATMENT

A. PHYSICIANS

The American Society of Addiction Medicine has certified almost 1500 physicians as experts in such treatment. Of these, somewhat over half are from the primary-care specialties of internal medicine and family medicine, a little under a fifth are psychiatrists, and the remainder are from all other disciplines. A substantial fraction became interested in the field

TABLE 61
Treatments in Substance Abuse Undertaken by Physicians

1. Uniquely
   (a) Provide complex evaluations of changed alertness or vital signs
   (b) Provide emergency treatment
   (c) Diagnose and treat psychosis
   (d) Hospitalize
   (e) Prescribe drugs
   (f) Supervise disulfiram, methadone programs
2. Frequently
   (a) Administer and direct programs
   (b) Consultant to nonphysicians
   (c) Provide ongoing care and health maintenance to addicts
   (d) Assist with crises
3. Occasionally
   (a) Lead groups
   (b) Provide all care for abusers

through their own recovering process. Table 61 indicates the types of things done by physicians, uniquely, frequently, and occasionally.

Nearly all primary-care physicians (internists, family medicine practitioners), a majority of psychiatrists, and some others have specific training and skills in the care of addicted patients. Only a few physicians choose to care for addicted persons a majority of their professional time, and most of these have some special skill in attaining abstinence and recovery. Others who enter into the field should have special training. Although an experience of personal substance abuse and the many pains of recovering is valuable, that alone is not sufficient for someone to undertake modern treatment.

B. NURSES

Nurses undertake much of the ongoing care of substance abusers in professionally run detoxification facilities, in the triage of abusers in emergency rooms, and in the supervision of disulfiram and methadone programs. Although they do not possess under law the same authority as physicians, it is observed that when there are good relationships with their backup physicians, they can perform essentially all the duties that are outlined for physicians. Not infrequently they conduct initial screening, referring only patients with severe pain, bleeding, or disordered consciousness for evaluation by a physician. They are frequently the ones who recommend medication doses for the treatment of withdrawal and encourage their backup physicians to write discretionary orders that permit them to administer such medications. Many nurses have developed special training and facility for care of the psychotic abusing patient.

Nurses undertaking private counseling, group therapy, and other roles in substance abuse usually have special formal training or experience acquired from long and successful on-the-job training. As with other professionals, about half of those involved bring a background of personal or family substance abuse to the field. The majority of nurses are women, whereas the majority of abusers in programs are men. In many cases the gentler and less assertive nature of women is particularly beneficial to therapy.

C. PSYCHOLOGISTS

Clinical psychologists are licensed to counsel and treat behavior problems in most states after completing a supervised clinical internship of 1 year's duration. Most are not permitted to use drugs and work primarily by interview, counseling, and leading groups. They are skilled in using quantitative tests to measure functional deficits in the brain and behavior in order to accurately quantitate improvement or deterioration. These skills are sometimes

TABLE 62
Roles in Substance Abuse Undertaken by Psychologists

1. Unique
   (a) Quantitate functional impairment in mental function and behavior
   (b) Affirm the presence of psychosis
   (c) Initiate family therapy
   (d) Initiate group therapy
2. Frequent
   (a) Undertake group therapy
   (b) Offer individual sessions to improve ego, understand neurosis, remove destructive phobia or anxiety
   (c) Supervise residential programs
   (d) Direct programs
3. Occasional
   (a) Supervise methadone programs
   (b) Offer habit checkup — are you an alcoholic?
   (c) Provide inpatient services

TABLE 63
Roles in Substance Abuse Undertaken by Social Workers

1. Unique
   (a) Obtain emergency aid, shelter
   (b) Provide for battered child or wife
   (c) Identify treatment at little or no cost to client
   (d) Coordinate multiple public agencies
   (e) Offer compassion to families at times of crisis
2. Frequently
   (a) Advise on menu of services available
   (b) Plan programs of behavior modification and counseling
   (c) Offer family therapy
3. Occasional
   (a) Lead groups
   (b) Direct programs

needed to assess whether a person whose mental capacities were injured by substance use or related trauma has the capacity to return to former employment. As a group they have more training in conducting group therapy than any other professional discipline. Table 62 outlines some of the roles of psychologists.

D. SOCIAL WORKERS

Social workers as a group are uniquely equipped to coordinate programs involving many facets of society or many different public agencies. Problems of battered wives, children, or dependents who need temporary shelter, and emergency financial aid, are areas we are all familiar with. In many states, social workers can provide counseling on a fee-for-service basis and undertake individual therapy with abusers and their families. They often conduct group therapy. Table 63 lists some of the roles undertaken by social workers in substance abuse.

E. MINISTERS, PRIESTS, RABBIS

Religion is a powerful treatment in addiction, for recovery is associated with an inner conversion — giving up many bad values for a new (and hopefully better) set. In the acceptance of religion and its elements of forgiveness lies the ability to cleanse the ledger of previous bad activities and to start anew. This form of hope, understanding, and forgiveness is a potent force in recovering addicts. It is most effective in patients with some

TABLE 64
Roles in Substance Abuse of Ministers

1. Unique
   - (a) Assist with lifting guilt through forgiveness
   - (b) Invoke spiritual assistance for patient
   - (c) Explain the whys and wherefores of addiction
   - (d) Assist believing families
   - (e) Control access to many church-sponsored and -supported facilities
   - (f) Use of prayer to facilitate above
2. Frequent
   - (a) Provide client and family counseling
   - (b) Facilitate crisis management through church-related facilities, funds
   - (c) Encourage self-help volunteer groups by providing meeting sites, support
   - (d) Lend moral support to many treatment efforts
3. Occasional
   - (a) Provide group therapy
   - (b) Serve on community agency boards
   - (c) Home, hospital visitation

previous beliefs. In Vaillant's book, ''getting religion'' is often cited as the most significant event in attaining long-term sobriety.[2] Table 64 indicates some of the roles of clerics in treatment.

F. OTHER PROFESSIONALS

1. Dieticians

A dietician may be needed to work on special diets and can provide a lot of assistance with recovery. Selection of a nutritious diet and the socialization possible in the preparation and consuming of food can be used as excellent tools for rehabilitation.[3]

2. Lawyers and Judges

When the reasons that addicts alter their outlook and gain long-term sobriety are examined, it becomes clear that often some major external force created the continuing pressure for change. Loss of family, freedom, money, or a driver's license is sometimes such a force, and lawyers and the courts are frequently in the middle of the problem seeking a reasonable solution. Lawyers who have experience with substance abusers and the process of recovery can often use their capacity as counselor to assure entrance into treatment and sustained follow-up. It comes as no surprise that adults under a Driving While Intoxicated license suspension undertake treatment programs with great regularity.

III. NONPROFESSIONALS IN SUBSTANCE ABUSE

A. COUNSELORS

The term ''counselor'' designates a worker who has special training and attributes in providing treatment to individuals, but more often in groups. All counselors have had specific training covering one or several addictions, and have received on-the-job supervised preceptor training. Many have long experience as abusing persons in both the addiction and the recovery process. The formal training may cover as little as 6 weeks or as much as 2 years. Many counselors are among the most effective motivators in existence, and it is upon this group that the majority of institutional and public treatment depends. Certification of counselors is underway in some states, but these groups are underappreciated because any former addict can declare himself a counselor.

Counselors are usually avid members of volunteer groups if they have had the addiction and serve as excellent liaison persons to get patients interested and connected with such groups. They have a compassion about the addiction that is rarely found in others, and in the early period of recovery they are particularly valuable. They are uniquely effective in providing assistance to addicts who have not had a long good experience with the medical profession.

B. SUPERVISORS AT WORK

Though few work supervisors have formal training in substance abuse, they are important to therapy. Larger companies may have a special department, usually in personnel or the health facility, responsible for assisting the continued treatment of abusers. The assistance of an understanding person in the patient's workplace is most valuable in continuing therapy. Many large employers have Alcoholics Anonymous programs on site and permit attendance during company hours with full benefits and pay during the meetings.

Under new federal law, companies receiving funding from the U.S. government must undertake drug testing in the workplace. Upon identification they must offer rehabilitation treatment. These programs are required to be supervised by the employer, but they are permitted to contract such treatment to others, including physicians who are equipped to undertake this. Companies are increasingly learning that emphasis on healthy living habits, including early recognition of drug abuse, eliminating smoking, and control of alcohol intake, leads to a healthier workforce that costs less in health benefits, absenteeism, and retirement health benefits. Employment-based and -supervised treatment programs for alcoholism have the best outcome for recovery.

REFERENCES

1. **Gerard, D. L. and Saenger, G.,** Out-patient treatment of alcoholism: study of outcome and its determinants, *Brookside Monograph #4,* Toronto, 1966.
2. **Vaillant, G.,** *The Natural History of Alcoholism,* Harvard University Press, Cambridge, MA, 1981.
3. **Hauser, M. B. and Iber, F. L.,** Nutritional advice and diet instruction in alcoholism, *Alcoholism World,* 13, 261, 1989.

Chapter 30

The Range of Treatment and Rehabilitation Programs; Factors in the Selection of an Appropriate Program

I. INTRODUCTION

A wide range of treatment programs are available for addictive disorders: inpatient and outpatient; expensive and free; aimed at a single addiction, age group or even profession. For those of means there is a wide variety of choices, but for the indigent the choice is much more limited. Programs vary in location, emphasis, duration, and cost. In general, when assignment to treatment is completely random, outcome is more a function of the client's perception that the program is suited to his or her needs than to the content of the program. Poor Richard's adage, ''You can lead a horse to water, but you can't make him drink,'' is highly pertinent to substance abuse therapy — the views of the abuser must be considered in selecting a program.

Treatment is often selected and entered at a time of crisis, when the clear heads needed to make appropriate (and sometimes very costly) decisions are simply not available. The physician may provide a valuable service in guiding the patient and family to an appropriate choice. There is a major trend in North America to treat all substance abuse in the same facilities. Segregation by specific substance abused is decreasing in frequency. There is

TABLE 65
Issues to Consider When Selecting a Program

1. Does the evaluation show serious medical or psychiatric disease that requires hospitalization?
2. Does the evaluation indicate a severe withdrawal?
3. Is there a "track record" to consider?
4. What the client and family think will help?
5. How urgent is confidentiality?
6. Are there limits imposed by finances and insurance resources?
7. How does the choice relate to treatment at 3, 6, and 12 months?
8. What does an inventory of relatives and friends willing to assist reveal?

some basis in theory for this common pattern of treatment, as discussed in Chapter 4 and elsewhere.[1]

In this chapter we will introduce the types of programs available in the U.S. and discuss for whom they are suited and other issues that should be considered. Evaluation of treatment programs will be considered. Professionals involved with substance abuse treatment almost always have success with a limited variety of programs, and almost none have experienced the entire range of programs that are offered throughout the country.

The biggest division (and cost differential) is between residential programs that provide total care away from home and job, and outpatient, community-based programs that provide an hour or more of programing to patients who continue to live at home and to work. There are also intermediate programs, usually called day care. In these programs the person spends about 6 h each weekday at the treatment center but lives and has meals at home. In this chapter we will consider primarily programs that are available after detoxification has been completed.

II. WHAT TYPE OF PROGRAM IS NEEDED?

Table 65 presents issues that must be considered when planning a program for a person who has been identified as a substance abuser. It is well to review these factors each time this decision is to be made.

The majority of abusers attain abstinence at home with the assistance of family and friends, and sometimes the help of a physician. Most abusers can be managed without hospitalization, institutionalization, or specialized facilities relying on community resources, but the early phase of treatment is managed more readily and with less bother to doctor and family with a short stay in an institution.

A. POSSIBLE HOSPITALIZATION

A possible need for hospitalization will obviously influence your advice to the patient, for if there is a major medical or psychiatric condition that requires hospitalization, both withdrawal and evaluation and initial therapy can be accomplished at the same time. Fortunately, the vast majority of abusing patients do not have such conditions. Withdrawal from alcohol, opiates, or sedatives is physiologically and psychologically stressful, and often patients with heart arrhythmia or failure, or preexisting psychosis, are hospitalized to assure that there will be no complications. If a severe withdrawal is anticipated, a special site capable of treating such problems is necessary (see Chapter 27).

B. THE PATIENT'S "TRACK RECORD"

Subjects who have repeatedly failed to attain sobriety at home may need a short detoxification period in an institution to get them away from the viewpoint that "I'm hopeless". The anticipation of failure, on the other hand, is not the sole basis for hospitalization. The fact that a given program has failed to help the patient in the past may indicate the need to change the type of program. On the other hand, if there has been long-term benefit from a particular program, then there is every reason to try it again.

C. THE PATIENT'S VIEW AND THAT OF THE FAMILY

Outcome is clearly better in programs that patients think will help, and though less well evaluated a similar expectation is assigned to the family views. Patients are most likely to participate wholeheartedly in programs of their own election. We are all aware that celebrities go to certain institutions, and this knowledge alone may help. Abusing patients' biases more commonly reflect the kinds of people with whom they wish to associate, the need for anonymity, and whether services are administered by an M.D. or not than the type of rehabilitation program. Among employed persons, there is usually a bias toward private facilities rather than public ones.

D. NEED FOR CONFIDENTIALITY

Confidentiality is sometimes of great importance, particularly among those in the public eye, and may dictate the choice of treatment facility. It is nearly impossible to maintain confidentiality in a hospital; it is difficult if a local celebrity is in a local institution; and it may be sufficiently important to have a person hospitalized in another region of the country. Many clients raise this issue, but discussion often shows that it is of less importance than the family initially believed.

E. FINANCIAL RESOURCES

Financial resources are generally limited, and often the addiction has already strained family finances. Evaluations indicate that facilities costing in excess of $100/day offer essentially the same treatment and produce the same outcomes as programs that may cost $30/day or even public programs that are free to residents of a community or state. Prepaid insurance often carries a benefit for substance abuse hospitalization, and many clients are hospitalized solely because this benefit exists, even though hospitalization may not be appropriate. On the other hand, many people do not have such resources, and they and their families are sometimes made to feel derelict if they cannot borrow to provide costly institutionalization for loved ones. Detoxification and initiation of treatment are certainly easier in a residential program, and less trouble for the referring doctor than organizing everything from his office, but the outcome is not different.

F. LONG-TERM TREATMENT PLANS

There should be continuity of treatment and treatment plans. A better outcome is attained if the same persons involved with treatment in the first few days remain involved. A hospitalization at a distant city has the distinct disadvantage that continuity of care may not be possible.

G. HUMAN RESOURCES

Persons residing at home with a spouse or other family members are totally different in rehabilitation possibilities than persons who are living alone with no one available to provide assistance. In planning home detoxification and rehabilitation, the human resources available are of great importance.

III. TREATMENT FACILITIES

Table 66 presents the types of programs that are available, some of which are discussed below.

TABLE 66
Types of Programs Available for Addiction Treatment After Detoxification

- I. Inpatient programs, 21—90 days
  - A. Specialized residential programs
  - B. Programs evolving from self-help groups
  - C. Halfway houses
  - D. Veterans Administration programs
  - E. Subdivisions of psychiatric hospitals
  - F. Units within general hospitals
  - G. Public programs for indigents
    - 1. State psychiatric programs
    - 2. Specialized addiction programs
  - H. Public service programs for abusers
    - 1. Church sponsored
    - 2. Volunteer groups
    - 3. Salvation Army
  - I. Shelters
- II. Day-care programs
- III. Outpatient programs
  - A. Self-help groups.
    - 1. Alcoholics Anonymous
    - 2. Opiate groups.
    - 3. Cocaine groups
  - B. State or city programs
  - C. Veterans Administration programs
  - D. Follow-up after inpatient programs
  - E. Hospital clinics and programs
  - F. Private therapists' programs
  - G. Family programs
  - H. Group therapy

TABLE 67
Reasons for Selecting Inpatient Therapy Rather Than Outpatient Treatment

1. Destructive psychiatric, suicidal, or violent behavior pattern that cannot be managed on an outpatient basis
2. Inability to remain drug free in an outpatient environment
3. Severe withdrawal syndrome
4. Complex physical, psychosocial, or psychiatric condition requiring close observation and adjustment of medication
5. Lack of appropriate outpatient treatment in the community in which the patient resides
6. Lack of cooperation in the treatment program, as in some adolescents
7. Need for intensive treatment for a short, finite period of time

IV. INPATIENT TREATMENT PROGRAMS

A. GENERAL

The increased expense of inpatient therapy must be fully accepted and a clear indication for its use be present before it is recommended and undertaken. It is my bias that these programs are overused in the U.S. because insurance is frequently available to pay for them and many who recommend such programs have a financial interest in keeping the program utilized. Table 67 indicates some reasons for the clear choice of inpatient therapy over less costly, and for most patients equally effective, outpatient alternatives. It will be apparent that far more people are hospitalized than actually meet the above criteria.

B. ABUSE TREATMENT HOSPITALS

Several large chains of abuse treatment hospitals in the U.S. provide residential treatment from the time of cessation of use for either 21 or 28 days. All provide family therapy and aftercare. A typical program evaluates the patient as a condition of entry — sometimes in-house, sometimes through a local hospital, and sometimes through the patient's personal physician — to determine whether the facility can safely handle the patient; more than 98% of the time they can do so. Initial sedation is employed for detoxification. The subject is immediately introduced to the rules and the discipline, which usually includes responsibility for his or her own room, personal care, and laundry. The patient is provided a schedule of meals, activities, and appointments, and is expected to be on time for all. Participation in group, work and play therapy, self-help groups, and other activities is required. Communication with the outside is usually deferred until the second week to allow full concentration on the addiction. Each week there are at least three 2-h sessions of group therapy. Exercise, group games, and free time are all scheduled. There is individual therapy, and counselors and group leaders are usually experienced social workers, nurses, or psychologists. Such programs provide assured sobriety, a great deal of specific information about addictions, and a lot of practical training in social skills, authority acceptance, developing and maintaining relationships, and alternative ways to handle problems. A typical program costs $80 to $150 daily. These hospitals are a growth industry that return 15 to 20% profits to their shareholders.

Such programs have an excellent safety record and provide excellent programming for abstinence for those who undertake them in the correct frame of mind and continue in the aftercare. Family counseling in groups is usually available. Only if specialized medical care or psychiatric care is needed are additional charges made. These programs, if available in the community, are among the best available. They have evolved a daily program, staff training, and facilities that are optimum. Most are large enough to segregate subjects by age, permitting adolescents to be predominantly with others of their peer group. The infrequent person with major psychiatric or medical illness may not get the best care in such a facility, but my enthusiasm for their programs and outcome is high.

A large number of individual hospitals that specialize in the addictions have developed and justifiably maintain a high reputation for excellence in outcome. These usually emphasize a distinctive philosophy that is their trademark. Some, such as Father Martin's in Maryland, depend heavily on the charisma of a single person gently leading addicts into the ways of Alcoholics Anonymous. A number of Father Martin's presentations are available on video, and they are excellent.* Other hospitals use a rigid, proven program of discipline and self-help along group lines that has through many years of successful treatment become more and more professional. Hazelden offers an excellent inpatient program following AA principles but also provides one of the best lines of books and programs for group, physician, and self-education about the recovery process.** One group features aversion conditioning as a major portion of the therapy. These programs usually arrange follow-up in the community from which the patient comes and overall do an excellent job.

C. SPECIALIZED ADDICTION UNITS IN GENERAL OR PSYCHIATRIC HOSPITALS

Special inpatient units have been present for several decades in some general and psychiatric hospitals. In the last 10 years, with decreased hospital occupancy, many new units have been created to meet community needs and to counter low occupancy rates.

Such units are often an outgrowth of community need, but frequently do not have the range of services required for treatment. Hospital accreditation processes do not evaluate the program or its outcome but only the presence of a variety of professional inputs and

* Available from Kelly Productions, Inc., 8 Howard Street, Aberdeen, MD 21001, phone 1-800-638-5430.

** Hazeldon Educational Materials, Pleasant Valley Road, P.O. Box 176, Center City, MN 55012, phone 1-800-328-9000.

safety features. In general these units have less variety of staffing and less variability in programs available to the patient than do the specialized hospitals. However, they are community based, and aftercare is more readily arranged, although some hospitals may provide it only through private physicians. Further, they offer flexibility in duration of hospitalization that allows some goals to be met during inpatient status without the need to spend a stereotyped period of time in the unit. I would generally rate such programs in a general hospital as less effective on average than programs in specialized hospitals. Smaller programs offer fewer services and a more limited variety of rehabilitation experiences. All programs now mix alcoholics and other addictions, which is no substantial problem. Mixing adolescents and older adults and patients of substantially different socioeconomic conditions poses a greater problem in rehabilitation. The larger hospitals specializing in addiction recovery can usually devote groups to specific ages and specific backgrounds.

A special set of programs has been developed in most states and in a few cities that recognizes the responsibilities that these units have for the care and rehabilitation of indigent abusers. In some instances existing psychiatric facilities that are no longer needed have been converted for substance abuse programs; in other instances totally new programs have been created. These units vary widely in quality and in programming, from the extremes of being at the cutting edge of good programming to being little more than warehouses to remove undesirable addicts from main streams of society. For veterans, each Veterans Administration hospital has outpatient programs that are usually good. About half have specialized inpatient programs.

A limited number of occupation-specialized programs have been developed. Facilities exist for the recovery of health professionals and for clergy, and a few cater to celebrities.

D. HALFWAY HOUSES

All sorts of benevolent and self-help groups as well as communities have established halfway houses, to provide a transition from institutions (such as jails and mental hospital) to living and working at home. These are generally licensed as a boarding house for multiple occupancy, pass fire and sanitation inspections, but have only a director who enforces the rules and pays the bills. Subjects live and eat in the house according to its rules, and the inhabitants after a week or two usually have a voice in making these rules. All residents share in the work in the house and its kitchen and are expected to contribute work to the common good, pay within their means for room and board, and attend the rehabilitation programs. Assistance in returning to employment and regaining mental and physical health are provided. The duration of residence is indefinite. A typical home for addicts takes persons after they are through detoxification. Twenty to seventy persons, most often of a single sex, live together. Unemployed persons assist newcomers with conversation, discussion of the future, and ideas for abstinence. They are assigned progressively more work in the house and may be carried on credit or subsidized in the early weeks of residence. A daily meeting along the lines of Alcoholics Anonymous meetings is held.

Encouragement to seek work is offered, usually part time initially while continuing to live in the house. Only when he or she is fully integrated into the community does the person leave the facility.

There is little active treatment, periods of residence are long, and the cost is modest. The pressures of many programs to reach a specific degree of attainment in a specific time are absent. Some successful rehabilitation is accomplished, particularly for the person who does not wish to be pushed too fast. The halfway houses function as therapeutic communities and provide the key elements of (1) an understanding, supportive, and nourishing asylum that removes pressures to use drugs; (2) time away from family, job, and other social responsibilities; (3) building of self-esteem; (4) training in social coping skills; and (5) gradual reentry into the regular streams of employment and society, including family.

E. SHELTERS

Usually found in metropolitan areas, shelters offer food and shelter for addicts. There is no requirement for rehabilitation, but minimal medical, social, and rehabilitation services are available for those who both need and request them. Often these shelters allow a person to remain only 12 h, and provide only a bed, a shower, and a little food. Other shelters allow clients to remain in residence for long periods of time, and the resident directors turn their backs on continued substance abuse if it is not offensive to others living there. A small number of such inhabitants are directed to other programs, more aggressive in rehabilitation, as this becomes appropriate. Many of these long-term residential facilities exist to keep largely indigent men and women off the street and out of the public eye.

V. DAY-CARE TREATMENT

Many hospitals that treat substance abuse allow patients to remain at home with their families but to spend most of the day, from roughly 9 a.m. to 4 p.m. weekdays, with the treatment staff. The treatment program is identical but the cost is about one third that of hospitalization. The problem is that there are only a limited number of such programs. Day care is one of the most progressive approaches to public treatment programs and is widely used by the Veterans Administration. Such programs when available are a distinct advantage to the patient with a stable home situation. Although it is often maintained that such unpoliced abusers will take advantage of the limited supervision to continue their habit, this in fact proves to be a very infrequent problem.

VI. OUTPATIENT PROGRAMS

A. IN CONTINUITY WITH INPATIENT PROGRAMS

Nearly all programs recognize the need to provide weekly or twice-weekly support to alumni of their program, usually in the community at a time convenient for all, typically evenings or on weekends. These are almost always group discussions. They may involve families, a formal leader, or the leadership may arise spontaneously from the group. The important ingredients are that the leader continues to encourage abstinence, builds self-esteem in each individual, provides group coherence to recognize individual problems (return to drug use, unemployment), and provides group solutions (take the person back to the parent organization, assist with job procurement) and positive social outlets. The single biggest problem is that people lapse from the follow-up.

B. SELF-HELP GROUPS

Self-help groups are discussed in Chapter 33.

C. INDIVIDUAL COUNSELING

Psychiatrists, psychologists, social workers, ministers, and a few others provide counseling to assist abusing persons with specific problems. Identification of the overall problem and its correction, and assistance with individual problems such as job relations, marriage or family problems, or to tackle specific identified shortcomings in the person involved, such as a tendency to perfectionism, outbursts of anger, difficulties with parents or children, and sexual difficulties, are well addressed in such therapy. I recommend that everyone entering ongoing counseling set goals with their therapist so that both the client and the therapist can see clear attainment met each ten sessions or abandon the process. This leads to better satisfaction with the process, for specific, attainable goals can be agreed upon and usually reached. Although this form of therapy is often thought to be of great benefit, it is not nearly as helpful as treatment in groups if the client will accept group therapy.

D. GROUP THERAPY

Often group therapy is an outgrowth of individual therapy, conducted by the same or related therapist. The client enters into the group only after achieving some acceptance of the overall problem and understanding of the solution. Groups are a powerful means to learn and strengthen interpersonal skills, which are usually not well developed or practiced in the addict. The group can often do things with a person that individual therapy cannot, because (1) they represent many different perceptions and personality types; (2) they are an excellent microcosm of the larger world from which the person has been insulated by his or her addiction; (3) identification of problems in day-to-day living skills is quick; (4) the self-help attitude is present in all, so that when the client helps others it builds esteem; (5) the environment is protected to keep destructive forces at a minimum; and (6) there is a similarity of problems and solutions, so that as other group members discuss their problems and methods of handling them there is identity and information gained without the risk of personal exposure in that particular transaction.

E. FAMILY THERAPY

The majority of substance abusers still have intact families, and the last two decades have formally recognized the importance of structured family therapy. Sharon Wegscheider has produced a remarkably practical book on elements of family therapy for the counselor, which is highly recommended.[2] Though others have stated the ideas presented, they are articulated much more clearly in this book than elsewhere.

The family is caught up in the addiction process and becomes abnormal through the process of living with the addict. The common roles played by family members are clearly described, for they play similar roles in the recovery process. The addict in the family is called the ''dependent''. Although the consequences of the addictive behavior would be expected to threaten, or overwhelm, the dependent, the blow is softened and deflected by the ''enabler'', often a spouse or parent. The enabler saves the dependent from intense emotional pain but at great cost. The ''hero'' is usually the oldest child, who seems to have his or her life together but actually suffers greatly emotionally and contributes to the instability of the relationship between the dependent and the enabler. The ''scapegoat'' is usually the second or third child, but may be a less close household member, who because of dependency cannot vent frustration on its source and turns to very abnormal reactions.

Intervention usually starts with an overwhelming crisis that forces the enabler to take action; occasionally other principals take the action. Since diversity of views has characterized the nonactions of the family group in recent times, it is urgent for the family to take concerted action. Initial counseling is directed at getting them to realize that substance abuse is the primary problem and to consent to this action. This may take 4 to 6 weeks.

As part of this process the family needs to learn more about the dependent's addiction and how it behaves at various stages. They must collectively accept the dependent's addiction and stop covering up for him. They must see how the addiction has altered and substantially injured them all. Most family members are consumed by defensive behavior, denying their role in the process; this denial must be overcome. Once intervention starts, part of the therapy needs to be in a group setting with all of the family.

Once treatment is underway, the therapist and all participants must recognize that there will be no attempt to help them adjust to the substance-abusing family structure, but rather they must recognize that the former adjustment was sick and that *all* members of the family need to change. The overwhelming goal is removal of the chemical dependency; other problems (economic, employment) will take care of themselves in time. In the first 2 to 5 months of treatment, each person in the family group must have similar goals, approached in different ways and with different amounts of input, but all in the family must share in this therapy. The defensiveness of each must be overcome. This will cause extreme pain, but it must happen and with the therapist and the family providing support it will not be destructive but will provide relief. A list of common emotions such as love, embarrassment, fear, and need can be discussed openly. With the family's encouragement, positive feelings will emerge and each will understand his or her own role in the family's illness.

Treatment must continue for at least several years. The relief of the early treatment may allow the therapist and the family to let up, but relapses on the part of all are common.

The fact that wives of alcoholics often marry another alcoholic is a clear manifestation of failure to help these women. The use of volunteer groups such as Cocaine Anonymous or Alcoholics Anonymous is strongly recommended and is supportive of other therapies. A comprehensive review of the adaptive function of families to alcohol and drug abuse has appeared.[3]

VII. EVALUATION OF TREATMENT

When Betty Ford, Kitty Dukakis, and Elizabeth Taylor were hospitalized for the treatment of addictions, they and the hospitals they attended were given great publicity. Subsequently many persons chose the same centers for their treatment under the principle that if it was good enough for these celebrities, then it was good enough for them. Sometimes the public opinion of what is good determines vogues in addiction treatment. Other issues that prominently enter into a choice for treatment include the ability to guarantee anonymity or secrecy of the treatment.

Is the program good? Programs in hospitals are accredited and proudly display this credential. Unfortunately, the review process addresses only the numbers of different professions involved in the treatment and safety; it does not address the quality of the program or its outcome. Frequently, publicly funded programs (Veterans Administration, state, community, church groups) lack accreditation only because some costly aspect of the physical plant or a dietician is not funded, yet the programs are very good. It is essential to look a bit further. The director of any program should have credentials in addiction. Several groups supply special training and certification of expertise, and most effective programs are directed by certified persons. Further, what do professionals in that community think of the program? Do they refer patients there, and are they happy with the outcomes?

In a nonaccredited program the ingredients must be examined. At least 12 h weekly of structured, professionally directed groups should be available, and at least 2 h weekly of self-help programs. There should be review of health and psychiatric status for admission and facilities for evaluation of change. At least 1 h weekly should be devoted to an evaluation of progress. Facilities for follow-up should be clearly defined and arranged as part of the program. Methadone, disulfiram, and drug therapy as indicated should be available. If outcome is known, no less than 70% of the alumni should be abstinent for 3 months, and there should be no drug use at the facility. Some form of treatment should be available that involves the family in group sessions.

The facility should provide an ambience and amenities appropriate to the lifestyle enjoyed by the participant, and treatment facilities rise to meet this market. Usually the finest facilities are those in psychiatric hospitals catering to the highest economic strata.

Unfounded treatment bias is occasionally an overriding issue. Conditioned aversion therapy continues to thrive, though modified in recent decades to include more counseling and group therapy. Programs that feature almost all sessions conducted by physicians are thought by some superior. Other programs run by recovered alcoholics are even more widely perceived as being better than most. These biases are often well established in a potential client or a family member and must be given attention if the patient is to remain in the program.

Special group programs exist for clergy, physicians, lawyers, alcoholics, cocaine addicts, and many others. Some have a view that the more alike the treatment candidates are, the more effective the program will be. Again, this belief is without scientific foundation.

VIII. CONCLUSIONS ON RECOMMENDING PROGRAMS

Recovering from addictions is hard work for the family, the employer, the physician, and the addict. All are spared excess effort in the very difficult first few weeks if removal from the usual environment can be accomplished and treatment started in a residential facility, but such treatment is not essential — only conserving of all of the helpers for later use.

The choice of a long-term program that the person will use and stay with is the best choice. Volunteer self-help groups are highly valuable but often are not immediately accepted by many employed patients, who carry the bias that these are for the indigent. When choices exist, a program nearby that can readily be reached and involve the family is better than a distant one.

In the early months, involvement of at least an hour daily is needed. After many months this may diminish to an hour weekly or every other week. Overall programs that fall below this frequency are not as good as programs that meet it.

REFERENCES

1. **Schubert, D. S., Wolf, A. W., Patterson, M. B., Grande, T. P., and Pendleton, L.,** A statistical evaluation of the literature regarding the associations among alcoholism, drug abuse, and antisocial personality disorder, *Int. J. Addictions,* 23, 797, 1988.
2. **Wegscheider, S.,** *Another Chance, Hope and Health for the Alcoholic Family,* Science and Behavior Books, Palo Alto, CA, 1981.
3. **Smith, C. C.,** Alcoholism and family psychosocial interaction, *Recent Dev. Alcoholism,* 7, 147, 1989.

Chapter 31

Setting and Meeting Realistic Goals for Rehabilitation

I. DETERMINING THE GOAL OF TREATMENT

Much disappointment prevails in substance abuse rehabilitation because differing goals are present (but not expressed) among the principals. The addict may have the goal of getting out of current problems with wife, job, and debt, hopefully without losing the pleasures of the addiction; the wife may desire a single course of events that will forever free her and her husband of the bondage of drug use; the therapist may want to please both parties with prompt improvement so that they will remain in his care. Setting goals and reaching them is important to the process of recovering. The process of selecting goals is highly educational and plays a major role in acceptance of that which treatment can and cannot accomplish. Figure 16 is included here to illustrate that nearly all addicts relapse, so part of the goal setting must be directed toward relapse prevention.

For all addictions, some generalizations about treatment have evolved from long experience; these are an excellent basis for introducing possible goals and planning therapy. The goals eventually selected are those of the patient and the family, but the therapist plays a major role in the process. Table 68 sets forth some of the issues discussed in subsequent sections.

Most of the time the therapist becomes involved during a time of crisis, when emotion and desire for relief run high and rational thinking is limited. Under such circumstances, defusing the crisis by institutionalization may be the best action and the initial goal. The two issues that are addressed by the successful therapist in early contacts are hearing the

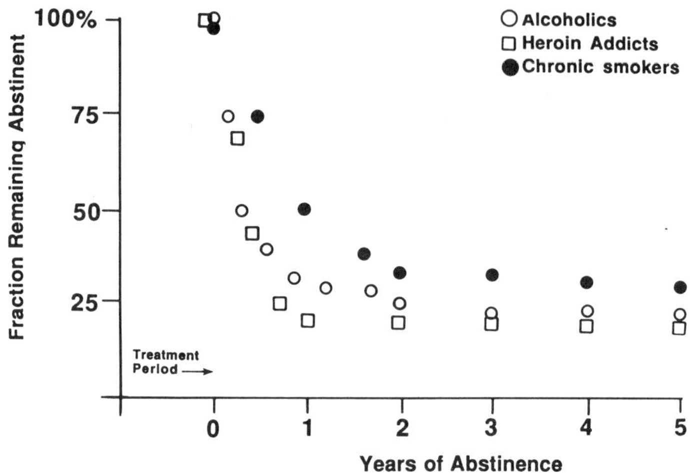

FIGURE 16. Follow-up data on all patients who enter treatment for various addictions. The relapse rate is rather uniform for each of these addictions and follows the same curve. Relapse is common and most frequent in the first 3 to 6 months. After 1 or 2 years without relapse, continued abstinence is more secure.

TABLE 68
Considerations in Planning Rehabilitation

1. Natural history
   (a) Relapses are common.
   (b) Without treatment there are remissions and relapses.
   (c) The overall situation will almost certainly improve from a time of crisis.
2. Retaining patient and family confidence
   (a) Be objective in diagnosis.
   (b) Explain decisions, provide choices increasingly with improvement.
   (c) Be honest with patient and family.
   (d) Recognize impatience for "quick fix".
   (e) Remain the patient's advocate despite adversity.
   (f) Commit openly to services that you can deliver over a long period of time.
   (g) Treat patient as an equal.
   (h) Don't commit to services you are not willing to deliver.
3. Treatment choices that you advocate
   (a) Tried and true is preferred to untested.
   (b) Abandon a treatment only reluctantly.
   (c) Safety and economy should always be considered.
   (d) Favor simplicity.
   (e) Those approaches favored by the patient work best.

goals of the principals involved, and overcoming the many faces of addiction denial in the patient. Often the patient, a family, an employer, and a party wronged in the crisis are involved in articulating goals. For example, an addict detected immediately following an automobile accident may have family, lawyer, police, and employer articulating as follows: family — "This has been going on for years and is wrecking us financially and emotionally"; lawyer — "Admit to nothing, create no records, but deny the problem"; police — "This is a serious misdemeanor in our state"; employer — "I hope this starts him getting straightened out. I don't want to dismiss him but I considered it before this happened."

Denial leads to concealment of facts about the addiction, usually related to frequency, intensity, and duration of use, and to an understatement and underrecognition of disruption in function. A variation on denial is hypercritical scrutiny of all aspects of therapy and the therapist in order to justify rejecting the therapy and dismissing the therapist. Denial is discussed more fully in Chapter 28. A special problem arises when the therapist speaks privately to the employer or the family. Holding such discussions in the presence of the patient avoids this additional area of concern to the patient, but doing so is not always practical. As a therapist, discuss openly the use of outside information in your presentations to the patient. Honor binding confidences, but encourage openness.

II. FEATURES OF EARLY RECOVERY AND APPROPRIATE GOALS

Once a patient has agreed to start treatment, there are many prompt improvements as discussed in detail in Chapter 28. These benefits operate in a positive manner to make the patient and the family feel better about the decision to enter treatment and serve to increase determination to continue.

Clearly, the earliest goal that all parties will readily accept is to complete the process of detoxification.

Detoxification, coupled with identification and treatment of medical and psychiatric disorders, starts the rehabilitation process in a highly positive fashion. In the initial weeks the havoc which the addictive behavior has wrought on interpersonal relationships within the family group and on the job, coupled with economic problems varying from extremely foolish to disastrous, are brought into clear focus. The patient's nerves are taut and coping skills somewhat limited, his patience runs thin, and during this time there are almost certain to be intolerance and blow-ups that without maturity and understanding may be destructive. In addition to providing understanding, the therapist may need to supply medications, relaxation techniques, or other means to defuse this anxiety. Goals set for this period need to address the coalescence of many problems in the addict's clearing mind.

An inventory of health, financial, family, and job-related problems is an appropriate goal, a judgment on each as to its probable alterability is useful. The addict must identify methods for relaxing and relieving anxiety. Although medications will be employed initially, nonchemical means must be explored. During this period, the environment must be tolerant of the patient's invalid status.

Goals are set and articulated with at least four clear purposes in mind. First, they permit all concerned to focus on one issue as preeminent and converge efforts toward this single end rather than in diverse directions. Second, attainment of the goal is a marker of improvement that patient, doctor, family, and others can see for themselves. Third, attainment of the goal builds the self-esteem of the patient. Finally, selecting the goal allows the therapist to discourage outlandish and preposterous expectations for treatment and focus on likely outcomes.

Early in recovery the therapist takes a much more heavy-handed role than later. In early recovery the patient is often muddled in thinking, and both he and family have been exhausted by the process that led to treatment. Later, as they learn more, their views will be more predominant.

Many different types of therapy and therapists are available to treat addictions, as discussed in Chapter 30. Often a social worker or a home-care nurse can better meet immediate needs than a physician. Orford and Edwards, in their classical study of treatment, pointed out that improved housing and better working conditions contributed in a major way to prolonged abstinence.[1] Vaillant discovered that the relationship of paroled heroin addicts to their parole officers played a substantial role in recovery.[2]

TABLE 69
Sequential Steps (Goals) to Be Climbed in Addiction Rehabilitation

1. Make a decision to totally stop use of addicting substance.
2. Complete detoxification.
3. Inventory mental and physical health; start needed treatment.
4. Identify nonmedicine aids to control worry, anxiety, insomnia, craving.
5. Identify clear cues to initiate addictive behavior and perfect coping mechanisms.
6. Inventory financial, family, and employment status and initiate solutions.
7. Enter group, family, individual, or other counseling to improve enjoyment of substance-free activities.
8. Reach 3 months of abstinence.
9. Test ability to cope with cues with support systems at hand.
10. Reach 6 months of abstinence.
11. Inventory and address personality, job, health, or avocations that interfere with contentment.
12. Reach 12 months of abstinence.
13. Cope with and terminate a relapse.
14. Have a relapse prevention plan in place.

III. CHANGING GOALS WITH RECOVERY — THE ANALOGY TO CLIMBING STAIRS

There are great advantages in setting goals that can be achieved fairly promptly. Early goals may require less active effort by the patient than later goals, and the concept of climbing stairs to sequential goals is often useful. Table 69 lists a continuum of goals that may be set. The attainment of the listed goals is a cause for positive celebration and reinforcement. The occurrence of a slip or failure to attain a goal is a proper basis for reassessment. It is important for all who have repeated contact with the patient to understand the stepwise setting and attaining of goals. These goals serve as clear markers of improvement and get others in the patient's life to focus on one goal at a time rather than many. Since an important therapeutic consequence of goal setting is the self-esteem boost from achievement of the goal, goals should be simple, particularly in the early period. It is of value to remember that addicts after a prolonged period of sobriety are much more nearly normal in their psychological makeup and their coping skills than they were early in abstinence.[3,4]

The goals in Table 69 can be used to define initial steps that upon attainment can be followed by another, more difficult step. Each attainment provides a basis for positive reinforcement. Failures allow the patient and the therapist to drop back to earlier goals, but usually some progress remains that forestalls complete reversion to the starting point. Throughout, the therapist is assisting the patient in seeing ever more clearly the growing advantages of abstinence over continuous addiction.

The substance-using addict develops behaviors that support the drug habit but that are almost always of no purpose and provide no positive meaning except in support of the substance use although they take a great deal of time. This time and these behaviors can be restructured, and goals may be selected that aim at this process. New social behaviors that will assist at work and in the family are commonly selected. A high priority must be given to those activities that build self-esteem, and such socialization or attainment activities should be emphasized. All abused substances produce for a time an exhilaration, a rush, a high, an energizing, an overcoming of depression that is seriously missed when the substance is not available. The resulting lethargy, depression, or feeling of fatigue is a major early impediment to remaining in treatment and poses a challenge to all therapeutic programs. It is most easily met by a network of understanding optimistic and enthusiastic people who understand the recovery process and provide encouragement through companionship and participation in work, play, or common chore activities. During this period the goal is to develop pleasure from small common activities such as eating together, shopping or preparing

TABLE 70
Sequentially Longer-Term Goals of a Type Useful for an Addicted Person

Early Months

1. Get off drug and through detoxification.
2. Stay abstinent a day at a time with all sorts of family and treatment help.
3. Regain pleasure from eating together, friends, family, and some recreation.

Later Months

1. Feel a sense of accomplishment in a single or few days' work being done well.
2. Enjoy yourself with companions, or associations from your addicted days.
3. Develop some behaviors that reliably provide a high when drugs are craved.
4. Add a friend each month who understands you and your problem.

food, working together, or planning the day's activities. Learning to make most interpersonal relations pleasurable rather than confrontational and how to avoid tension and anxiety are parts of this. Working with recovering addicts or alcoholics, or living together with others who are undergoing the recovery process, is very valuable in developing these new skills, but it is not essential. It is clear from a variety of studies that addicts become more normal in their psychological and interpersonal functioning as they are longer removed from their addiction.[5,6]

Slightly longer-term goals include understanding what the first fix of drug provided and considering other means to attain the same end in order not to need the drug. Maintaining esteem and accepting reality come about by avoiding such commitments as ''never'' or ''forever''. At about this time the concept of relapse as a very probably occurrence is introduced. Table 70 lists a series of ever longer-term goals that may be suggested as possible ones to adopt as earlier goals are attained.

REFERENCES

1. **Orford, J., Edwards, G.,** *Alcoholism,* Oxford University Press, New York, 1977.
2. **Vaillant, G. E.,** A 12-year follow-up of New York addicts IV: some characteristics and determinants of abstinence, *Am. J. Psychiatr.*, 123, 573, 1966.
3. **Gerard, D. L. and Saenger, G.,** Out-patient treatment of alcoholism: a study of outcome and its determinants, *Brookside Monograph #4,* Toronto, 1966.
4. **Costello, R. M.,** Alcoholism treatment and evaluation II: collation of two year follow-up studies, *Int. J. Addictions,* 10, 857, 1975.
5. **Finney, J. W., Moss, R. H., and Mewborn, C. R.,** Posttreatment experiences and treatment outcomes of alcoholic patients six months and two years after hospitalization, *J. Counseling Consulting Psychol.*, 48, 17, 1980.
6. **Gerard, D. L., Saenger, G., and Wile, R.,** The abstinent alcoholic, *Arch. Gen. Psychiatr.*, 6, 83, 1962.

Chapter 32

Volunteer Groups in the Treatment of Addictions; The Model of Alcoholics Anonymous

I. INTRODUCTION

The failure of traditional medicine to provide assistance to the large and growing numbers of substance abusers, mostly alcoholics, during the 1930s and 1940s led to the appearance of many self-help groups. A group of recovering alcoholics in Ohio, borrowing elements from other self-help programs, formulated a program that spread rapidly throughout North America and then the world. Although aimed initially at alcoholics, many mixed substance abusers and other substance users have received benefit from the Alcoholics Anonymous program.

For almost every type of abuse there are now specific self-help groups, such as Cocaine Anonymous, Heroin Anonymous, and many many others. All have incorporated the four elements of help needed by addicts and so clearly articulated by Vaillant.[1] First, the continuous peer support from former addicts, exposure to the most stable recoveries, and the presentation of hope provide a substitute for the experience of substance use. Second, the meetings are available every day, and even several times a day, and provide continual vigilance against the dangers of relapse. Third, membership in a group of concerned persons

TABLE 71
Important Elements in Self-Help Programs

1. Keep it simple
2. A day at a time
3. We are powerless over our addiction
4. Assistance for families
5. Networking
6. The power of a group
7. Recognition of a power greater than self
8. Assisting others with the same problem

who willingly share solutions to the common problems that greet recovering addicts assists with loneliness and with economic and emotional problems. Finally, the opportunity to help others stay abstinent assists in growth of self-esteem.

II. ELEMENTS OF SELF-HELP PROGRAMS

At the risk of oversimplification, I have listed in Table 71 some of the important ingredients in self-help programs. Many of the phrases have become standard in therapy, and are taken directly from Alcoholics Anonymous (AA), the oldest self-help program and the prototype for the rest.

A. KEEP IT SIMPLE

Detoxification or withdrawal from any abused substance is associated with muddled thinking, often reversible injury to the brain, and many pressing real problems and worries. It is not a time for complex and scientifically sound constructs but for simplicity. "You have a disease" communicates infinitely better than many sentences justifying this problem. The Twelve Steps of Alcoholics Anonymous, and the Alcoholic's Prayer epitomize the need for communication and are found in all such programs.

B. A DAY AT A TIME

The importance of not making goals about the years ahead, or the determination never again to utilize a needed and much cherished substance is recognized in this simple principle: one day at a time. Setting practical and attainable short-term goals builds self-esteem. The repetition of this motto even when abstinence is secure is a valuable reminder that relapse is possible.

C. WE ARE POWERLESS OVER OUR ADDICTION

Some groups present the addiction as genetically determined, others as a disease, but all remove the guilt and the concept of willful self-destruction. This has been found by all evaluators to be a useful portion of treatment in lifting some of the pain associated with addictions. However, it does emphasize that the first use of drug or alcohol is a place where the person has a choice.

D. ASSISTANCE FOR FAMILY

Alcoholics Anonymous, through its Al-Anon and Al-a-Teen programs for nonabusing concerned family and teenagers, respectively, recognizes and provides assistance for the disordered family structure of addicts (see Chapter 30 for more details). Separate guides and mottos have been produced for these groups to help them understand more about alcoholism and their role in helping the alcoholic recover. These no-cost programs are of great value to families even if the addict is not attending meetings.

Other addictions have incorporated AA ideas but have not formalized programs for family.

E. NETWORKING

The concept of networking is incorporated into most programs. The principle is to surround the recovering addict with assistance on all sides of his life, including employment, home, and social activities. Some programs, such as Alcoholics Anonymous, introduce the newly sober sufferer to persons in AA who may also be nearby in his life. Other programs encourage interested significant persons to come to meetings and to join in the group assisting recovery.

Many groups employ a "buddy system" or a sponsor in which the newcomer has a very special relationship to one more advanced in recovery. The sponsor has a special role in all phases of the newcomer's life to be certain that resources exist to provide assistance.

F. POWER OF THE GROUP

The group concept provides many useful tools to facilitate recovery. The addict can both hide his embarrassment and shame in the group, and can identify with the group or some of its elements. When there is a discussion, some things said are immediately identified as pertinent by another individual, others are not. When the person wishes to communicate, there are endless opportunities and types of people with whom to do so. The strength and support of the group become his, and his problems are taken up by the group and identified. No confession is shocking to a group with a similar problem, and judgments if made at all are usually quite charitable. At all times there are role models of successful coping with the addiction.

G. ACCEPTANCE OF POWER GREATER THAN SELF

"Religion is the opiate of the masses" identified a principle that is often overlooked by scientific therapists. Addicts feel defeated and helpless and at a very low point in their self-esteem. Religion gives back hope and improves morale. For an addict to remain stably abstinent, a dramatic personality change must occur, which is often thought of as a religious conversion. Finally, religion lifts sin and guilt and allows the pain and injury produced by addiction to be removed to permit a fresh start.[2,3] These elements appear frequently in the self-help groups in the constructs of God, a power beyond self, and take advantage of these issues. The Twelve Steps of AA illustrate this quite clearly.

H. ASSISTING OTHERS WITH THE SAME PROBLEM

The building of self-esteem and the providing of valuable assistance to less stable persons in the program through companionship, husbandry, understanding, and listening are valuable features of all self-help groups.

III. GUIDING A PATIENT TO A SELF-HELP GROUP

Although professional use of self-help groups is increasing, it is still not as widespread as it should be. Most large studies of sobriety indicate that short-term sobriety (1 to 2 years) comes largely from the program with which a person starts. Thus studies starting with the outcome of a clinic or a specific program find that this accounts for the majority of the patients who have recovered or remained abstinent after 1 or 2 years, but studies of long-term abstinence invariably show an increasing role for self-help groups. Figure 12, in Chapter 26, showed how this assumes greater and greater importance as one moves into longer-term sobriety. It is estimated that more individuals maintain sobriety through AA than through all other programs in the U.S. combined.[1]

Occasionally professionals in addiction have a financial relationship with a specific treatment facility and are influenced to favor its use for their referrals. Many persons working as counselors or in other roles are very much aware that their positions are dependent upon use of their skills and service. Although these considerations are usually suppressed when what is best for the patient is evaluated, they are not completely absent.

Analysis of who accepts Alcoholics Anonymous is revealing. In Vaillant's study, core-city men, mostly blue-collar workers or unemployed, accepted AA much more readily than the sample identified as college sophomores, even though the need and recommendation for AA occurred 15 to 25 years after the identifying study. He also found that an active effort to get patients to attend AA resulted in nearly twice as many persons becoming enrolled.[1]

It is not easy for a patient to enter a group. Although attendance at a meeting of a self-help group is readily accomplished, the fear of rejection, concern for the unknown, and an outlook of doom toward recovery leads most persons to reject such groups during and after their first session. The physician can assist greatly by enforcing three or more visits or by identifying and facilitating a meeting between patient and sponsor under the physician's guidance. Scientists have regularly shown the great value of AA[4,5] but have not identified a way in which to get more than two thirds of the patients into such programs.

IV. ILLUSTRATIONS FROM ALCOHOLICS ANONYMOUS

The story of Alcoholics Anonymous has been told by many of the early workers.[6] The program asks each of its members to take the following 12 steps:

Step 1. We admitted we were powerless over alcohol — that our lives had become unmanageable.
Step 2. We came to believe that a Power greater than ourselves could restore us to sanity.
Step 3. We made a decision to turn our will and our lives over to the care of God as we understood Him.
Step 4. We made a searching and fearless moral inventory of ourselves.
Step 5. We admitted to God, to ourselves, and to another human being the exact nature of our wrongs.
Step 6. We were entirely ready to have God remove all these defects of character.
Step 7. We humbly asked Him to remove our shortcomings.
Step 8. We made a list of all persons we had harmed, and became willing to make amends to them all.
Step 9. We made direct amends to such people whenever possible, except when to do so would injure them or others.
Step 10. We continued to take personal inventory and when we were wrong promptly admitted it.
Step 11. We sought through prayer and meditation to improve our conscious contact with God as we understood Him, praying only for knowledge of His will for us and the power to carry that out.
Step 12. Having had a spiritual awakening as the result of these steps, we tried to carry this message to alcoholics and to practice these principles in all our affairs.

V. HOW GOOD ARE SELF-HELP GROUPS?

AA was evaluated by following 393 members who had attended at least ten meetings of a single group in the years 1955 through 1960. Of the 244 who could be located, half were sober for all of the 4-year follow-up period and 19% more had 1 or more years of sobriety before relapse. Even if the patients lost are believed to be drinking, somewhat greater than 30% attained long-term self-reported sobriety.[7] The Rand study group evaluating short- and long-term usefulness of federally funded clinics for alcoholism found little benefit from AA in 2-year follow-ups starting with patients who had been enrolled in one of the targeted clinics. After 4 years, however, 14% of their total sample attended AA regularly, and of these 74 persons, 45% had been sober for a year. This was threefold better than other patients in the program.[8] Vaillant[1] found AA attendance associated with the best outcomes, and nearly half of those who attained stable sobriety after 6 to 8 years were active in AA. In the long-term follow-up, of 18 persons who had secure sobriety for more than 6 years using AA, the average number of meetings attended was 300.

Similar evaluations are not yet available for other self-help groups.

VI. REPRESENTATIVE SELF-HELP GROUPS FOR DRUG ABUSERS

A. HEROIN ABUSERS

A small study of heroin abusers compared halfway house treatment with a community self-help program. At 3 months following random assignment there were no differences in the number of reinstitutionalizations, the number of jailings, time spent in the program, and fraction of drug-free urines.[9] A descriptive self-help program for patients on methadone using Alcoholics Anonymous principles seemed to be of value.[10] A review of the history and nature of programs for Narcotics Anonymous has been published.[11] A presentation of how professionals may use self-help groups to the advantage of their client is provocative.[12] A very-long-term self-help group, used primarily by opiate addicts in New England, has provided treatment while in a working environment. The program goes on for years and is called recovery training and self-help.[13]

B. COCAINE ABUSERS

The differences between cocaine users and other addicts may be the greater tendency to relapse of cocaine users, and this is emphasized by one group using self-help.[14] One of the best ''hotlines'', in which clients and friends receive assistance from a free call-in number, is used for cocaine (Cocaine Helpline 1-800-Cocaine). Evaluation of callers reveals the profile of the users and overcomes some erroneous beliefs.[15] The unique value of professionals working with self-help groups even when using individual treatment is emphasized.[16]

C. OTHERS

A review of the Narcotics Anonymous program is available.[17] Groups are described for psychotropic drugs,[18] i.v. drug abusers with AIDS,[19] adolescents,[20] and noncompliant i.v. drug abusers.[21]

VII. SELF-HELP GROUPS FOR FAMILIES

Alcoholics Anonymous founded Al-Anon as a family self-help group, and this organization has assisted many families of addicts. Al-Anon aids the abuser toward recovery by helping nonabusing but enabling household members to get their acts in order. The important ingredients of such groups are very similar to those of the self-help abusing groups. These elements are listed in Table 72.

Shared attitudes, the cohesiveness of the members, and the feeling that they are not alone in their shame are among the most readily appreciated benefits of belonging to these self-help groups aimed primarily at families of abusers.

Most household sharers are intimidated by the abuser into a confused state in which they do not really know whether to support the person in certain behaviors or not. The group

TABLE 72
Common Features in Self-Help Groups for Families of Abusers

1. Powerlessness over the addiction
2. Family member is not to blame for cause or relapse
3. Understanding of the recovery process
4. Appropriateness of setting limits
5. Avoidance of abuse-supportive behavior
6. Emotional support
7. Practical assistance in day-to-day problems

can provide a great deal of practical advice in the appropriate limits to set, while assisting the person in handling the anger and guilt that are so very prominent.

A recent evaluation of self-help groups for the parents of young drug users indicated that they not only help the parents but assist in the recovery of their children.[22] Local self-help groups can be located through the National Institute on Drug Abuse (NIDA) Hotline at 1-800-662-HELP. A call while writing this chapter located three groups within 15 minutes of where I work in the Chicago area.

REFERENCES

1. **Vaillant, G.,** *The Natural History of Alcoholism,* Harvard University Press, Cambridge, MA, 1981.
2. **Robinson, D.,** *Talking Out of Alcoholism,* Croom Helm, London, 1979.
3. **Meyer, R. E. and Mirin, S. M.,** *The Heroin Stimulus,* Plenum Press, New York, 1979.
4. **Leach, B. and Norris, J. L.,** Factors in the development of Alcoholics Anonymous (AA), in *Treatment and Rehabilitation of the Chronic Alcoholic,* Kissin, B. and Begleiter, H., Eds., Plenum Press, New York, 1977.
5. **Kish, G. B. and Hermann, H. T.,** The Ft. Meade alcohol treatment program: a followup study, *Q. J. Stud. Alcohol,* 32, 628, 1971.
6. Alcoholics Anonymous: The Story of How Many Thousands of Men and Women Have Recovered from Alcoholism, 3rd ed., Works Publishing Company, New York, Alcoholics Anonymous World Services, 1976, 31st printing, 1988. Reviewed in *JAMA,* 261, 3315, 1989.
7. **Bill, C.,** The growth and effectiveness of Alcoholics Anonymous in a Southwestern city, 1945—1962, *Q. J. Stud. Alcohol,* 26, 279, 1965.
8. **Polich, J. M., Armor, D. J., and Braiker, H. B.,** *The Course of Alcoholism,* John Wiley & Sons, New York, 1981.
9. **Ives, W. R., Lounsbury, J. W., and Tornatzky, L. G.,** An experimental comparison of two community-based drug abuse treatment programs, *J. Community Psychol.,* 4, 253, 1976.
10. **Obuchowsky, M. and Sweben, J. E.,** Bridging the gap: the methadone client in 12-step programs, *J. Psychoactive Drugs,* 19, 301, 1987.
11. **Peyrot, M.,** Narcotics Anonymous: its history, structure, and approach, *Int. J. Addictions,* 20, 1509, 1985.
12. **Einstein, S.,** Self-help drug misuse intervention: a schema, *Int. J. Addictions,* 18, 559, 1983.
13. **McAuliffe, W. E. and Chien, J. M.,** Recovery training and self help: a relapse-prevention program for treated opiate addicts. *J. Substance Abuse Treatment,* 3, 9, 1986.
14. **Ehrlich, P. and McGeehan, M.,** Cocaine recovery support groups and the language of recovery, *J. Psychoactive Drugs,* 17, 11, 1985.
15. **Washton, A. M., Gold, M. S., and Pottash, A. C.,** The 800-COCAINE helpline: survey of 500 callers, *Nat. Inst. Drug Abuse Monogr. Serv.,* 55, 224, 1984.
16. **Millman, R. B.,** Evaluation and clinical management of cocaine abusers, *J. Clin. Psychiatr.,* 49, Suppl, 27, 1988.
17. **Wells, B.,** Narcotics Anonymous (NA): the phenomenal growth of an important resource, *Br. J. Addictions,* 82, 581, 1987.
18. **Shaw, C.,** A self-help group for patients on psychotropic drugs, *Practioner,* 227, 102, 1983.
19. **Friedman, S. R., Des JarLais, D. C., Sotheran, J. L., Garber, J., Cohen, H., and Smith, D.,** AIDS and self-organization among intravenous drug users, *Int. J. Addictions,* 22, 201, 1987.

20. **Ehrlich, P.,** 12-step principles and adolescent chemical dependence treatment, *J. Psychoactive Drugs,* 19, 311, 1987.
21. **Greif, G. L. and Price, C. A.,** Community-based support group for HIV positive I.V. drug abusers, the HERO program, *J. Substance Abuse Treatment,* 5, 263, 1988.
22. **Galanter, M., Gleaton, T., Marcus, C. E., and McMillen, J.,** Self-help groups for parents of young drug and alcohol abusers, *Am J. Psychiatr.,* 141, 889, 1984.

Chapter 33

Crises in Treatment

I. INTRODUCTION

The physician who provides chronic care for a substance-abusing patient has a very high probability of participating in a crisis with that patient. Doctors who work for a long time in substance abuse and avoid burnout have learned that these crises are part of the addiction, and if they have presented themselves appropriately as a helper, they will become involved.

Involvement means concern, doing what you can to contain the destruction of the crisis and relieve distress, but it falls well short of lending money, providing housing or transportation, or rescuing a person from jail. An older physician who provided care for many alcoholics kept on his desk and at his bedside a list of shelters, on-call lawyers, around-the-clock taxi services, and hospital emergency rooms to fulfill his role in being helpful.

In this chapter we will discuss relapse, unilateral termination of therapy, personal crises that may precipitate relapse, and the impact of deteriorating health.

II. RELAPSE

Almost any patient undertaking consultation for substance abuse who enters treatment will attain some period of sobriety. Our experience in 500 consecutive patients (11 women in the sample) who entered a Veterans Administration hospital alcoholism detoxification program is presented in Table 73.

It was observed that most patients who completed 5 days in the program managed to stay abstinent for 2 weeks. The relapse or loss rate (90% of those who were lost to follow-up were identified by a third party as having returned to drinking) was high during the first 3 months of follow-up but was substantially lower after that. Some three quarters of the

TABLE 73
Sobriety in 500 Persons Entering a Detox Program

Number	Issue	Method
500 (100%)	Entered Program	At least 6 h
461 (92%)	Completed 5 days	No. discharged
422 (85%)	Sober after 14 days	Self + family
371 (74%)	Sober after 1 month	Self + family
262 (52%)	Sober after 2 months	Self + family
189 (37%)	Sober after 3 months	Self + family
161 (32%)	Sober after 6 months	Self + family
152 (30%)	Sober after 1 year	Self + family

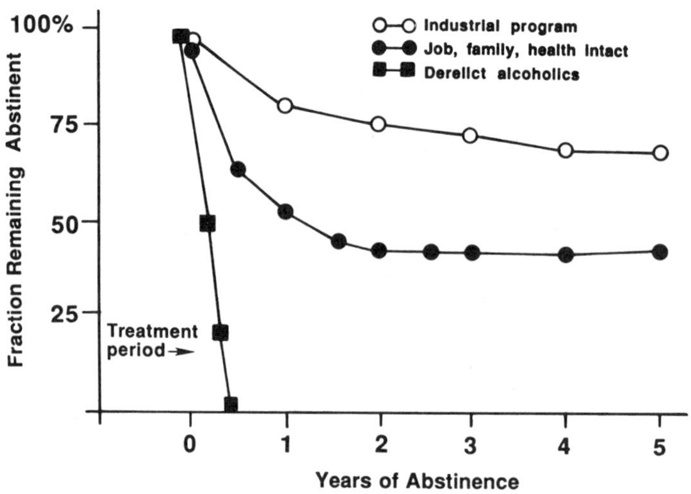

FIGURE 17. Long-term persistence of abstinence from alcohol in patients with different risk factors for relapse. The derelict alcohols relapse promptly, with all returning to drinking by the 6th month. Patients working in an industry with an on-the-job program as indicated by the open circles have the best record of prolonged sobriety, with 75% remaining abstinent for 5 years. Other patients employed and with intact families and health are intermediate in relapse rates. In all, relapse needs to be considered as a part of ongoing treatment.

patients who were sober at 3 months were still sober after 1 year. These data point up the major problems in relapse: the majority will relapse, most relapses occur in the early months after abstinence begins, but the relapse that occurs later is much more destructive to the rehabilitation process.

It should be noted, however, that the above data came from self-reporting by the patient and/or family, and self-reported outcomes are invariably better than actual testing of urines for substance will show. Two well-performed studies of this sort identified that the majority of alcoholics who were reported by self and others as sober had at least one positive urine when tested frequently. It is increasingly clear that diminution of the destructive aspects of the addiction rather than total abstinence (to chemical testing), is a realistic goal for treatment programs (Figure 17).

The causes of relapse are fully as elusive as the causes of alcoholism in the first place. The concept of "craving" is often evoked to explain relapse. In the laboratory setting, loss of control is nearly impossible to identify[1] and craving cannot be defined.[2,3] On the other hand, behavior psychologists have determined that craving results from environmental arousal of the need to drink by means specific cues associated with drinking. The music, the ambience, the company, the odors, and the time of day have all been shown to play a role, and when these things are linked together at one time the compulsion may be overwhelming.[4,5]

Marlatt, in an overview of relapse prevention,[6] places abusers who have entered abstinence in a state of perceived control that will maintain the desired behavior (usually abstinence) until the person encounters a high-risk situation. At this encounter, many show coping responses that are effective and increase self-efficacy and in the future diminish the probability of relapse. Others have ineffective coping responses, recall from experience the ''beneficial effects'' of their substance, and return to its use, at least for a single experience. This decreases self-efficacy, sets into motion a whole series of abstinence violation effects, and often is associated with increased probability of subsequent relapses. In analyzing a large series of relapses among alcoholics, smokers, heroin addicts, gamblers, and overeaters, negative emotional states accounted for more than a third of all relapses, with about 10% more caused by urges and temptations. Among external forces, social pressures accounted for about 20% of the relapses. In subsequent chapters of this book, plans to render these major forces less destructive are outlined, most of which are applicable in group or individual counseling.

From this and almost all experience it is clear that relapse is more likely to occur at times of extreme emotional duress, when anger, depression, boredom, or frustration are prominent emotions. To this end, groups and individuals that treat addicts will often provide play-acting to assist in dealing with these negative emotional states. A few physician therapists provide patients with a limited amount of a benzodiazepine to self-medicate as a coping mechanism during circumstances that precipitate such severe emotion, but I much prefer seeing the patient or conferring with him by phone or providing resources in addition to pharmacological ones. When drugs are recommended at such times of crisis it is invariably with the professional opinion that short-term use of these agents will be less destructive than returning to primary addiction.

In a patient with relapse, the self-esteem is diminished and remains particularly fragile, even more so when the period of abstinence was prolonged. Such a patient has a whole series of friends, professionals, and fellow sufferers who now have been let down. Any recriminations or rejection by well-accepted therapists or group members may be even more destructive. It is particularly important that the primary director of therapy recognize this vulnerability and combat its adverse effects by increased support.

The two major external forces leading to relapse are social pressures, accounting for about one fifth of relapses according to Marlett,[6] and interpersonal conflict, accounting for about one sixth. Counseling, particularly in groups, can be of great benefit in anticipating both of these problems and in providing practical skills to deal with them. Groups of similar age, employment, social habits, and addiction are particularly beneficial in providing day-by-day assistance on how to carry on with former associates when the opportunity and cues for substance use are present. An individual therapist usually cannot provide clear guidance for an alcoholic who must attend a business luncheon where cocktails will be served, yet those who have learned to cope with this common situation have developed many effective strategies. A common successful one to make prior arrangements with the waiter or bartender to be served a nonalcoholic drink in a manner that suggests it is similar to those being taken by others. Addicts, as a nearly stereotyped portion of their addicted behavior, seem to have lost the skill for resolving conflict and handling negotiation on an interpersonal basis. Because of past negative outcomes, close friends and family from the abusing days have learned to avoid conflict, and often continue avoidance patterns even after substantial periods of sobriety have intervened. Again, counselors and groups are far more helpful in discussion and instruction of methods to resolve conflict. Nearly all use the technique of simulated situations or review of actual experiences as a means for improvement.

Significant relationships, often with family, pose particular challenges to relapse prevention because there developed during the abusing days pathological patterns of denial that must be changed. Some aspects of family counseling have been discussed in Chapter 30, but usually a portion of therapy must be directed at both the client and significant others if the relationship is to survive.

III. COPING WITH AND TERMINATING A RELAPSE

The majority of patients will experience a relapse, with more than half occurring in the early months of abstinence. Successful living with an addiction involves the process of making the relapses shorter and less destructive. The patient and family in education about the natural history of addictive disorders need to know that the majority of people relapse. This should be the basis neither for rejection of the patient nor for termination of the therapeutic relationship but simply a short-term crisis in the recovery process.

When a relapse occurs, the initial goal must always be its termination, followed by a "circling of the resource wagons" to fend off the adverse effects of the "slip". Although termination has a better long-term prognosis for a good outcome when it is initiated spontaneously, the major losses in self-esteem and sometimes health and people resources associated with a prolonged relapse fully justify active and even occasionally coercive intervention. Often the physician is consulted by family or employer to confront and elicit cooperation, an undesirable but unavoidable task. Although a responsible request to stop and an offer of assistance with support and sedation is usually sufficient, sometimes denial of a relapse, outright lying about planned cooperation, or severe feelings of hopelessness and inability to cope are present. These latter are extremely difficult to deal with unless the patient is willing to accept confinement of one form or another. Under such strained circumstances, use of the close family is probably inappropriate; entry into hospital, halfway house, or another supervised living situation is better.

The fact of a relapse incurs a series of reactions that may be more destructive than the relapse. A job may be terminated, the return to the addiction may be considered a personal affront and a relationship disrupted, self-imposed guilt may surface, and a clearly communicated "you just can't be trusted" attitude at work and at home may be overwhelming. The wagons must be circled as far as possible to control these destructive effects but at the same time allow compassionate disapproval of the relapse to be comprehended. Preparing for relapses helps understanding and avoids the secondary destructive consequences of a relapse. Some of the consequences invariably occur and are appropriate. The relapsing addict needs support to rebuild that which was lost. As abstinence is again restored, a retrospective review of the relapse is of value in order to strengthen coping skills in that particular arena. Intensive therapy in the form of practical education, best arranged if acceptable to the client in groups, will most rapidly repair the damage. Sometimes this is the time to add additional forms of therapy that were rejected at an earlier time. Thus specific counseling to control anger or anxiety may be in order, or disulfiram (Antabuse®) treatment may be desired.

A few close relationships are probably more necessary to addicted persons than others. Sometimes misfits reach out to one another and the relationship continues only because of the addiction. Every professional has futilely attempted to reason or communicate with an intoxicated person, only to wind up losing his or her own self-control and even respect. This emphasizes the difficulty of continuing during sobriety relationships that developed during addiction. Some attention to improving lasting relationships is of value. One technique that often helps is for the addict to record a list of secret wishes of the significant other and now and then make some of them happen.

Marlatt and Gordon[6] note a technique that is most valuable. The addicted client, while abstinent and in treatment, is asked to list the major activities of the day and rate them in terms of pleasure and satisfaction. When possible, the activities should be changed if necessary to provide at least an hour each day of a highly pleasurable activity. I have adopted this to couple counseling with great advantage to the relationship.

Cues that may herald an impending relapse are often detected by the family and nearly always by the patient. The patients sense that they are losing ground to internal or external forces. If the client and the family can be induced to seek assistance at these times, there are less destructive ways of coping with the possible crisis rather than allowing a relapse to occur. Essentially any of the coping means effected by a physician are far less harmful to self-esteem. These include anxiety-relief techniques, a short hospitalization, or temporary use of sedative drugs.

IV. TERMINATION OF TREATMENT

Termination of treatment for whatever reason often is a time of crisis. If the patient terminates prematurely or against the advice of family and counsel, there is usually a substantial emotional anxiety created which brings the patient to this conflict and guilt-laden decision. If the physician terminates for reason of no further benefit, excellent response, or simply failure to influence the patient favorably, a similar state comes about.

A. CESSATION OF TREATMENT BY CLIENT

It is quite common that substance abuse patients lapse from treatment without this being clearly negotiated and agreed upon by all parties. The common mode is through cancellation or failure to keep appointments, with reluctance or total refusal to make subsequent ones, and with no explanation. When pursued, clients usually indicate that the treatment was not providing benefit that they could perceive, that it was no longer necessary, or that it interfered with other activities given a higher priority by the clients. Marlatt and Gordon note that feeling very positive about themselves, even cocky, or avoiding the realities of the recovery process are the basis of this cessation.

I have found no fully satisfactorily way to deal with unilateral cessation of treatment. Such clients do not make return appointments and usually do not respond to correspondence. An offer to arrange alternative treatment sent by letter is usually not acknowledged or responded to. Follow-up of such patients indicates that many have in fact found resources within themselves and their associates to continue without destructive return to abuse.

B. TERMINATION OF TREATMENT BY THE PHYSICIAN

Occasional patients are terminated from further therapy because the physician-patient interaction seems more destructive than helpful. Some personality pairs conflict, and alternative arrangements improve the therapy. Some patients simply do not fulfill their commitment to treatment with regard to attending meetings, groups, changing jobs (a bartending alcoholic has a substantial occupational hazard), or getting marital counseling. Under these circumstances, prolonging and accepting substantially subtherapeutic treatment may not be acceptable to therapist or patient.

On other occasions termination may be needed because the patient can no longer afford the physician, or the need for the physician's services in terms of either total program, other therapies, or overall progress simply indicates they are not needed. In all of these conditions a therapeutic relationship is breaking down, and some patients will interpret this as rejection because they are hopeless or in some way responsible. This is a particular problem when the patient is in fact responsible, but the best way to handle it is to blame it on physician or therapist shortcomings and speak to the positive aspects of the patient that can make the therapy better, with an even better outcome, with another therapist. The alternative treatment should be in place before the termination is completed. Substance abusers have a great tendency, even after years of abstinence, to anticipate rejection and difficulty. Planned therapy is often not effected because the client anticipated difficulty and avoided the difficulty by not seeking or keeping the appointment. The treating physician should negotiate alternative treatment and arrange the initial contact with the client and continue to see the client until this contact has occurred and the new arrangement seems satisfactory. Each person involved in therapy usually believes that he or she undertake some aspects better than other therapists, but all know that there are many therapies that accomplish the goals of improvement. This optimism should be transmitted to the patient and his family to diminish the feeling of rejection.

V. OTHER CRISES

Life is filled with highly stressful situations that may overcome the recovering abuser's stress-coping skills. Such issues as loss of a spouse, parent, or child, an arrest, a need for a major operation often are associated with relapse.

Therapists vary in their methods of intensifying support of the client under such circumstances. Some intensify interpersonal input, some work to diminish the stress (often impractical), and some use pharmacological support with sedatives or benzodiazepine drugs. A recent evaluation of the suitability of alcoholic cirrhosis patients for liver transplantation indicated that standard support by a therapist was sufficient to get the majority of patients through this complex and stressful situation.

VI. RECOVERING AFTER MORE THAN A YEAR OF ABSTINENCE

Relapse and remission are the rules of substance abuse during recovery. Although relapse prevention becomes more and more effective with treatment, the subject is at no time completely free from the possibility of relapse. Only a very few subjects obtain many years of relapse-free sobriety.

As recovering abusers move into the second and subsequent years of abstinence, several changes are common. Significant interpersonal relationships with spouses or live-in companions change frequently in a major way. Nearly one third of marriages or long-standing living-together arrangements, active during drinking years, are no longer viable when secure sobriety appears. Similar but less well-studied changes occur with other substance abuse. Living-together arrangements when both parties are abusers rarely survive prolonged sobriety. This is best understood through study of family dynamics. For a family to survive together during abusing years, each member must adopt abnormal and pathological patterns of denial that allow them to adapt to the condition of a major member being an abuser. When abstinence develops, these adaptations are no longer appropriate and create problems of themselves. Fortunately, many change and the family survives, but change is essential. A physician caring for a recovering abuser can inquire of changing relationships so that the medical record can reflect an up-to-date status should a slip or relapse occur and the "significant other" need to be contacted.

Many health conditions acquired during the years of addiction may produce incapacity at a later time. Other diseases increase in frequency and severity with aging or passing years. It is not uncommon to have a person during stable sobriety develop a new and incapacitating health problem at a time they had hoped everything was going better and this was behind them. Cirrhosis, clinically quiescent, may develop a hemorrhage from esophageal varices or a hepatocellular carcinoma. Chronic lung disease may reach the stage of beginning incapacitation during the years of sobriety, heart disease commonly comes on in the fifties, and is more common in drinking-smoking persons, and manifestations of Hepatitis B or C may become symptomatic. The loss of power over self indicated by a fatal or chronic disease requires many adjustments that may stress a recovering addict to the point of return to the addiction. Counseling is of great benefit at such times, recognizing that the recovering addict probably never becomes completely normal in coping with stress. It is to be emphasized, however, that the abnormal mental makeup of the actively drinking person returns nearer and nearer to normal with each passing year of sobriety.

VII. RETURN TO LIMITED AND NONABUSIVE SUBSTANCE USE

There is a substantial literature indicating that approximately 5% of former alcoholics are able to resume social drinking at a much later time and do not relapse into destructive drinking. This literature is somewhat analogous to Mr. Johnson's comment regarding a dog walking on its hind legs: "It is not how well he does it but that he does it at all." The literature is even more replete with instances of attempts to drink socially that precipitated a return to destructive drinking.

The vast majority of abusing persons "slip", returning to their earlier abused substance for at least one use if not full emersion in destructive addiction. A few are able to limit use to a nondestructive level. The most important point is that it allows each abuser the hope that with recovery all things will become possible, including the choice to use their substance again without destroying their life. The counsel provided by nearly all therapists is that such thinking is a major risk to continued abstinence, a risk that is seldom worth taking. The failures are vastly more common than the successes. Self-help groups adamantly counsel abstinence forever, and this is the best view.

One physician with whom I am acquainted, known by colleagues to be very successful with alcoholics, always starts his treatment by counseling patients to limit alcohol intake to three well-defined portions daily. Only when they fail in this counsel (which they usually do) does he undertake hospitalization and abstinence, but always with some regret that it did not work out *at this time* and that *it will probably work later*. He is at least as successful in keeping patients with medical illness abstinent as others, but he gain's the patients cooperation by their failing a trial of their own choosing.

Vallaint[7] addresses the issues of return to social drinking and the inadvisability of counseling this course. He notes in the alcoholism literature and in his own experience the inability to predict who will successfully accomplish this and those who will fail. Marlatt's work[8] is filled with practical strategies for substituting other activities during the early period of recovering such that these substitute for the desire and urgency to return to the formerly abused substance on a nondestructive basis. This monograph is highly recommended, and many of his ideas have been incorporated in other chapters of the present book.

REFERENCES

1. **Paredes, A., Hood, W. R.; Seymour, H., and Gollab, M.,** Loss of control in alcoholism: an investigation of the hypothesis with experimental findings, *Q. J. Stud. Alcohol,* 34, 1146, 1973.
2. **Mello, N. K.,** A semantic aspect of alcoholism, in *Biological and Behavioral Approaches to Drug Dependence,* Capell, H. D. and LeBlanc, A. E., Eds., Addiction Research Foundation, Toronto, 1975.
3. **Mello, N. K. and Mendelson, J. H.,** Experimentally induced intoxication in alcoholics: a comparison between programmed and spontaneous drinking, *J. Pharm. Exp. Ther.,* 173, 101, 1978.
4. **Keller, M.,** On the loss of control phenomenon in alcoholism, *Br. J. Addictions,* 67, 153, 1972.
5. **Allman, L. R., Taylor, H. A., and Nathan, P. E.,** Group drinking during stress: effects on drinking behavior, affect and psychopathology, *Am. J. Psychiatr.,* 129, 669, 1972.

6. **Marlatt, G. A.,** Relapse prevention: general overview, in *Relapse Prevention,* Marlatt, G. A. and Gordon, J. R. F., Eds., Guilford Press, New York, 1985.
7. **Vallaint, G.,** *The Natural History of Alcoholism,* Harvard University Press, Cambridge, MA, 1982.
8. **Marlatt, G. A.,** Cognitive assessment and intervention procedures for relapse prevention, in *Relapse Prevention,* Marlatt, G. A. and Gordon, J. R., Eds., Guilford Press, New York, 1985, 201—279.

Chapter 34

Prevention and Pertinent Public Health Issues

I. INTRODUCTION

Prevention is commonly divided into three phases, useful in planning, but in practice quite blurred in their distinctions. Primary prevention includes measures before a problem develops, secondary prevention is early recognition of a problem or a preproblem and the effecting of change. Tertiary prevention is late-stage intervention. The primary-care physician plays a large role in secondary prevention in advising all patients on unhealthy patterns in their lifestyle.

Prevention of abuse is the most cost-effective method of addressing the growing problems of substance abuse in the U.S. The incidence of cigarette and hard liquor use in American high schools has plateaued in the last decade and is declining for these two substances when all young people under age 30 are examined. In contrast, the use of other substances, particularly cocaine, is increasing. It is thus clear that prevention is a great deal more complex than a simplistic "just say no" and that much more study of the many forces that initiate drug used are needed if this problem is to be controlled. Table 74 indicates aspects of prevention that will be discussed in this chapter.

II. PREVENTION IN GROUPS AT HIGH RISK

A variety of genetic, socioeconomic, and early schoolroom factors identify individuals at very high risk of developing drug or alcohol dependence. Table 75 outlines some of these.

TABLE 74
Aspects of Prevention of Substance Abuse Pertinent to Physicians

I. Public health
   A. Limiting availability
      1. Control sales
      2. Tax use
      3. Interdict use
   B. Penalties for use
   C. Education for use, harm
   D. Diminishing adverse effect
      1. Driving while intoxicated
      2. Fetal problems in maternal abusers
   E. Elimination of critical occupations
      1. Pilots, engineers, drivers
      2. Physicians, intelligence operatives
II. Identification and treatment of early problems
   A. High-risk groups
   B. Physicians' practices
   C. Workplace
   D. Courts

TABLE 75
Factors Identifying Those at High Risk for Substance Abuse

1. Family history of drug, alcohol dependence
2. Broken home, single-parent home
3. Poverty
4. Lack of home or school discipline
5. Association with drug-dependent peers
6. Cigarette smoking before age 12 years
7. Poor work conditions or chronic unemployment
8. Occupations with high stress, or high exposure to abused substances

Children and particularly sons of alcoholic fathers are highly prone to develop subsequent alcoholism and other substance abuse. Childhood exposure to an abusing family member as well as specific genetic factors are measurably important.[1,2] The use of substances of abuse in the home is best covered in the alcoholism literature and is illustrated in the different patterns of use and abuse in various American ethnic groups (Chapter 40). The home environment is also important in many other ways. Broken homes or single-parent ones, those with low incomes, those with lack of discipline,[3] and those with clear neglect before age 8 are all associated with later life abuse to a higher degree than more normal populations. Early cigarette smoking,[4] and association with peers who are drug dependent,[5] are fairly obvious predictors. Occupational factors or working conditions,[2] and occupation are also important. Health workers, including physicians, nurses, and pharmacists as well as veterinarians, have both stressful lives and easy access to substances of abuse and are at increased risk. Bartenders and waiters have an obvious occupational exposure but, in addition, painters, high steel fabricators, and typesetters have increased alcoholism.

Physicians recognizing any of these increased risk factors, but particularly those of an abusing parent or household sibling, and occupational exposure should alert their client of the extra hazard of addiction and pay a little more attention to the mental health of the patient.

A number of longitudinal studies have attempted to intervene in the lives of sons of alcoholic fathers, to lessen the subsequent occurrence of alcoholism. These ongoing studies are so far inconclusive. Clear interdiction of the substance in the home is the most promising strategy to date.

III. EARLY RECOGNITION IN SELECTED SETTINGS

A. PHYSICIANS' PRACTICES

Recognition in physicians' practices has been discussed in detail in Chapter 8. It is estimated that some 50% of alcoholics and some 25% of other substance abusers seek aid from a physician or an emergency health facility each year. Recognition starts with the suspicion of abuse and requires chemical confirmation and meticulous probing for this possibility if higher fractions of these persons are to be recognized.

B. WORKPLACE

Some 80% of all industrial accidents, and more than half of absences, are believed to be related to substance abuse. Many industries have developed programs to train supervisors in the recognition of abusing employees, coupled with nonpunitive rehabilitation programs to prevent the vast loss of talent and absenteeism through this process. The National Council on Alcoholism in New York City has excellent programs for all sizes of companies and will assist in establishing programs. In many larger companies there has been clear documentation of the financial advantages of such programs in reducing absenteeism, increasing productivity, and preserving valuable employees.

C. LAWYERS, JUDGES

A common outcome of substance abuse may be an interaction with lawyers and the courts. The increased rate of accidents and marital difficulties, and a propensity for physical altercations, adequately account for this situation. Driving-while-intoxicated charges are common. Judges and lawyers increasingly recognize the role of substance abuse in divorce, battered-wife complaints, and public brawling or nuisance situations and are occasionally responsible for directing persons to effective treatment.

IV. PUBLIC POLICY

Many aspects of substance abuse and public policy interact. Public policy can control the availability and access to abused substances, and by fines and other punishments render abusive behavior in some domains (such as driving) unacceptable. In a permissive country, there is always a conflict between the rights of the individual and the needs of the larger population. Some of the issues currently in the news are presented here as examples of both problems and solutions.

A. IDENTIFICATION OF PROBLEMS

Substance abuse is widespread in North America; information comes from a variety of indirect sources and limited samples of population. There are surveys of high-school and grade-school children from all parts of the nation. Accident victims from traffic or in the home, hospitalized patients with a variety of illnesses, social agencies and courts have been studied for abused substances. Many studies in industry estimate the impact of substance abuse on productivity. Data exist on the amounts of alcohol used in America, the number of prescriptions filled, and the volume of raw materials available for the synthesis of amphetamines. All of these[6] have been utilized to indicate that Americans use substances liberally and that about 5% at any time have problems of abuse. From these data specific goals can be set, many of which have different solutions. Thus the goal to diminish automobile accidents resulting from driving under the influence of substances has a different approach than to diminish overall use of substances. Decreasing use during pregnancy to avoid fetal alcohol, fetal opiate, and cocaine syndromes in the newborn involves a different target group than raising the age of initial alcohol use.

B. EDUCATION

The reasons for avoiding illicit drugs and the responsible use of alcohol, tobacco, and medicines must be even more widely addressed in the school systems, starting with 6- to 9-year-olds. It has been established that programs now in existence have had a major impact in lessening drug and alcohol use in subsequent years.[7] Programs that feature at least videotapes of late health consequences of smoking, drinking, and use of street drugs, coupled with discussion to the extent of about an hour a week, are effective. Media presentations of the association of tobacco and alcohol with power, wealth, and sexual success encourage use, and the great power and wealth of illicit drug distribution personnel is treated far too favorably.[8,9]

Curricula have been developed that are highly effective both in grade-school children and in high-risk students as a means to diminish subsequent abuse. The following attributes seem to be critical: (1) Curricula reflect the norms of the community from which the children are drawn to assure community support. (2) Teachers are trained to teach objectively about drugs and alcohol and must be comfortable about such teaching. Examination of their own attitudes, values, and behaviors must usually be done to avoid teaching a specific bias. (3) Curricula cover multiple grades, some beginning as early as kindergarten. They clarify values including self-control, responsibility to others, and improvement of self-esteem. (4) Community education for parents and community leaders is almost always required for success.[10] This needs to be coupled with a control of advertisements to disassociate substance use from pleasure, smartness, sexuality, and sophistication. In addition, responsible use of alcohol, tobacco, and physician-prescribed medications must be taught in the later years of secondary education.

Special education aimed at target groups has been shown to be beneficial. Antidrug and anti-alcohol education as a part of prenatal clinic visits are effective. Similar education programs for those having motor vehicle or industrial accidents while associated with an abused substance have been effective.

C. LAWS TO CONTROL USE

From study it has been found that "happy hours", in which inexpensive liquor is available for a limited time, usually after work, has encouraged excessive drinking and many motor fatalities. Elimination of these has partially controlled the problem. Many studies have indicated aspects of bars that encourage drinking and those that discourage drinking. If full meals are served, drinking is far less; if there is live music and clients are offered dancing room, there is far less drinking than in bars with live music and no room for dancing. Other studies are needed on sites and amounts of substance used.

The price of alcoholic beverages markedly influences their consumption, and this is clearly a method of control of the use of alcohol and tobacco. Making users liable for their repeated use is an aspect of control for illicit substances that has been effective in some locations. It is just now being employed in the U.S.

D. LAWS TO COMPEL EARLY CASES TO ACCEPT TREATMENT

It is now possible to identify early and severe abusers at a time when treatment is much more likely to be effective, particularly in the workplace, in the military, and in many occupations. Yet many of these do not undertake any action to diminish the use. In contrast, we spend large amounts of money on the late-stage management of advanced addicts when the treatment offers little likelihood of substantial recovery. The workplace, doctors, courts, and screening identify many abusers. In Scandinavia, treatment programs are monitored throughout life. Although the incidence of abuse is high, the recovery rate is higher than in the U.S., probably because treatment follow-up is mandated.

REFERENCES

1. **Bewley, B. R., Bland, J. M., and Harris, R.,** Factors associated with the starting of cigarette smoking by primary school children, *Br. J. Prev. Soc. Med.,* 28, 37, 1974.
2. **Soueif, M. I.,** Some issues of major importance for prevention of drug dependence, *Natl. Rev. Social Sci.,* 11, 39, 1974.
3. **Tennant, F. S., Jr. and La Cour, J. L.,** Children at high risk for addiction and alcoholism: identification and intervention, *Pediatr. Nursing,* 6, 26, 1980.
4. **Tennant, F. S. and Detels, R.,** Relationship of alcohol, cigarette and drug abuse in adulthood with alcohol, cigarette and coffee consumption in childhood, *Prev. Med.* 5, 70, 1976.
5. **Murad, J. E.,** Drug abuse among students in the State of Minas Gerais, Brazil, *Bull. Narcotics,* 31, 49, 1979.
6. **Awni, A. and Westermeyer, J.,** *Manual of Drug and Alcohol Abuse, Guidelines for Teaching in Medical and Health Institutions,* Plenum Medical Book Co., New York, 1988.
7. **Beauchamp, D.,** *Beyond Alcoholism, Alcohol and Public Health Policy,* Temple University Press, Philadelphia, 1980.
8. **Tennant, F. S., Jr., Weaver, S. C., and Lewis, C. E.,** Outcomes of drug education, four case studies, *Pediatrics,* 52, 246, 1973.
9. **Tennant, F. S., Jr., Mohler, P. J., and Drachler, D. H.,** Effectiveness of drug education classes, *Am J. Public Health,* 64, 422, 1974.
10. **Finn, P. and O'Gorman, P.,** *Teaching About Alcohol,* Allyn & Bacon, Newton, MA, 1981.

Chapter 35

Special Problems of Substance Abuse in Adolescence

I. INTRODUCTION

Growing up in America produces many problems as one moves toward adulthood. Both parents working, broken or single-parent families, multiple moves, and too little money are substantial factors that are properly blamed as a cause of adolescent problems. However, among affluent two-parent families, too many advantages, too little to do, and boredom are blamed for some of the same problems. Many decades ago, adolescence was a low-pressure, slow changing process during which one moved from parental and home dependence to complete independence. In many ways we have prolonged the supervision and control of adolescence, with at least one third of Americans going on to college. For poor, inner-city kids and some others, the responsibilities of adulthood are foisted on them by a somewhat hostile society who have poorly prepared them for the responsibilities of American adulthood. This latter group have often been short-changed in education, more often than not come from a single-parent home, are raised with simply insufficient resources, and almost always have many peer-group exposures to substance use from early life. A recent conference on the characteristics of healthy adolescent development reported that 20% of ''normal'' adolescents have persistent psychological symptoms sufficient to impair their ability to function at least at times.[1] All would agree that adolescence is a most difficult time. Between the ages of 9 and 17 years the individual is expected to become an adult and assume a role in society, yet parents are so involved with the responsibilities of their own lives that appropriate attention to growing up is not given.

Peer pressure assumes dominance over parental influences during these years, and surveys throughout the country show that about half of all high school-aged young adults have sampled illicit drugs and about 80% have used alcohol. It is appalling to note that more than 20% of these use these substances at least weekly. Teenage addiction is well known, and its treatment has become a massive growth industry. In this chapter we discuss some features unique to this age.

II. CAUSES

Although the adolescents who become abusers come more frequently from broken homes, households that move around a great deal, single-parent homes, poverty, and had poor records of attainment earlier in school, the most remarkable thing is that of children who have these risk factors far more often emerge without addiction. This indicates that other influences are even more important. It will be seen that home tolerance, teaching in school and church, sibling and peer roles, and general satisfaction with life are important factors in overriding adverse home conditions.

Although genetic factors have clearly been identified as important in alcoholism and are likely important in other abuses, they account for a maximum of 15% of adolescent addiction. Addressing some of these other factors, a comprehensive self-reported questionnaire administered in the seventh, tenth, and eleventh grades in Australia indicated a high association between depression and families that were not close or loving. Depression correlated with prevalence of alcohol, cigarette, and marijuana use. The relationships were highly predictive of self-reported substance use in this study.[2]

Use of substances by parents or other family members has increasingly emerged as an important predictor of adolescent use. A recent review of 1380 youths from New Jersey interviewed at ages 12, 15, and 18 found at all ages that use of drugs and alcohol and minor problems from their use were significantly more prevalent in those with a positive family history of drinking or drug use than those with a negative one. On the other hand, there was no increase in escape drinking or drug use, or frequent intoxication.[3] The impact of substance use in parents and grandparents on childhood use seems little different than use in only one parent. In the same study this was simply one of many stressful life situations that were predictive of adolescent abuse in their sum but not individually.[4]

Permissiveness of substance use by parents or guardians, home examples of substance use and abuse, influence of older siblings, and peer pressure are highly important influences in adolescents who come from a setting suggesting that abuse is likely. Families and school counselors who recognize this problem have a substantial impact in prevention, and it is established that intensive school programs starting at ages 6 to 8 decrease the numbers of users in the high school years.

A recent evaluation of veterans using the findings of Cloninger divided alcoholics into those with age of onset before age 20 and who had fathers who also abused alcohol, and those without these risk factors. It was found that patients who started alcohol abuse at an early age (with or without the father also being alcoholic) had three times the likelihood of depression, four times the likelihood of suicide, and a significantly higher likelihood of being involved with crimes of physical violence than those who started alcoholic drinking after age 20.[5] A further study by the same author, looking at school-age children and following them into adulthood, found that the characteristics of novelty seeking, harm avoidance, and reward dependence were not correlated with one another but were predictors of later substance abuse. High novelty seeking and low harm avoidance were the most strongly predictive markers of early onset of alcohol abuse.[6]

TABLE 76
Special Problems in Adolescent Abusers

- I. Conditions related to physical and emotional age
  - A. Social responsibility poorly developed
  - B. Wide swings in mood and energy
  - C. Sex function and sexuality rushing forth
  - D. Intolerance of older viewpoints
  - E. Shaking off authority shackles
  - F. Rapid growth
  - G. Food and exercise needs
- II. Less clearly related
  - A. Increased suicide rate
  - B. Islands of remarkable naivete
  - C. Conformity to peer-group ideals

III. SPECIAL PROBLEMS OF ADOLESCENT ABUSERS

Table 76 lists some problems in adolescence that will be discussed in subsequent sections of this chapters.

A. PHYSICAL ASPECTS OF ADOLESCENCE

All children in the teen years experience a growth spurt, with increase in height, weight, and appetite. At such times of rapid growth the energy level may be a little sluggish, and between rapid growth phases it is endless. In most children the attention span is relatively short and a variety of sensory stimuli are needed, often to the annoyance of older persons. Sexual function becomes fully mature and sexuality is developing. All of these things happen during the teen years and may occur simultaneously or out of phase. Heavy alcohol or drug abuse may retard growth and appearance of sexual function; after withdrawal these may again accelerate. These many factors require that recognition and rehabilitation from substance abuse must provide for food and exercise in substantially increased amounts from standard programs and should recognize barely suppressed sexuality.

B. PSYCHOLOGICAL ASPECTS OF ADOLESCENCE

A moral and ethical sense, fully developed in adults in their forties, is far from developed in all adolescents and may be retarded further by abuse. Ordinary acts and pranks may be cruel and thoughtless, and those undertaken when existing restraints are paralyzed by substances may be heinous or repulsive. Crimes involving physical violence are most commonly committed by adolescents under the influence of intoxicants. Ordinary bounds of discipline may be tested and strained in a fashion much different from that involving older persons. The shorter attention spans, the need for multisensory stimulation, and the frequent wide mood swings are also different from older addicts. Depression is common, and suicide occurs more frequently in this group than in any other.[7] Successful programs to treat substance abuse in adolescents must take into account these unique psychological aspects of adolescents.

A group of adolescent cocaine users identified in an inpatient drug rehabilitation unit emphasized the frequent major problems in the lives before drug use began. In this study 86% of 28 patients had run away from home, 24% had dropped out of school, 96% had stolen, and 57% had destroyed property for no apparent reason. In this group of at least weekly users of cocaine, severe craving was present even after 1 month of abstinence.[8]

IV. OUTCOMES

A large group who used cocaine or marijuana as adolescents and who subsequently gave it up were examined for predictors of cessation. These predictors found in follow-up of 1222 addicts were conventionality in social role performance, social context unfavorable to the use of drugs, and good health. Prior involvement and cessation of use of licit or illicit drugs was also a significant factor, most strong for marijuana cessation. The most important predictor for cocaine cessation was cessation in one's friends.[9] The prediction of cessation of marijuana and cocaine use was examined in a large longitudinal cohort of young men and women. The same factors that predicted cessation of use in adulthood were those that predicted lack of initiation in adolescence: conventionality of performance of social role, social contexts unfavorable to the use of drugs, and good health. Those who had a prior involvement with substance abuse had a much higher failure rate in cessation than those without it for marijuana, whereas friends' use was most important for cocaine. Cessation is much more likely in those who use drugs for social purposes than those who use them for psychological reasons.[9]

V. INTERVENTIONS

A program addressing fourth-grade students called ''I'm special'', addressing in one hour a week improvement in self-esteem to avoid drugs was evaluated subsequently in the grades 5 to 7. Children completing the ''I'm special'' program (ISP) had significantly less use of substances in these later years than those from the same schools who did not have this program.[10] A program addressing family intervention within the home to attain drug-free behavior in adolescents has been described. Family unity in plan and action is essential, and use of drug testing, punishment, probation plans, and home detoxification are all practical solutions.[11]

A rapid growth industry is units for treatment of adolescent problems including addictions and other adjustment difficulties. These programs are useful in removing the young person from the stressful environment and in providing appropriate guidance for getting along with people, but evaluation indicating special value in assisting the addictions is not available.

VI. MISCELLANEOUS ASSOCIATIONS

Adolescents in a chemically dependent psychiatric population prefer unconventional music of the heavy metal type, compared to adolescents from the same community without similar chemical dependence.[12] A study of 63 adolescent rapists in California indicated drug abuse as a major factor that needed to be addressed as part of rehabilitation.[13]

A useful review of some of the behaviors found in alcoholism distinguished a group limited to adolescence with extra aggression, violent behavior, and increased personal and property injury as a consequence. These authors found this group to be more severe and less responsive to therapy.[14]

REFERENCES

1. Medical news: characterizing healthy adolescent development, distinguishing it from possible disturbances, *JAMA*, 262, 880, 1989.
2. **Reynolds, T. and Rob, M. I.,** The role of family difficulties in adolescent depression, drug taking and other problem behaviors, *Med. J. Aust.*, 149, 250, 1988.
3. **Pandina, R. J. and Johnson, V.,** Familial drinking history as a predictor of alcohol and drug consumption among adolescent children, *J. Stud. Alcohol,* 50, 145, 1989.
4. **Brown, S. A.,** Life events of adolescents in relation to personal and parental substance abuse, *Am. J. Psychiatr.*, 146, 484, 1989.
5. **Buydens-Branchey, L., et al.,** Age of alcoholism onset I, relationship to psychopathology, *Arch. Gen. Psychiatr.*, 46, 225, 1989.

6. **Cloninger, C. R., Sigvardsson, S., and Bohman, M.,** Childhood personality predicts alcohol abuse in young adults, *Alcoholism,* 12, 494, 1988.
7. **Brent, D. A.,** Suicide and suicidal behavior in children and adolescents, a review, *Pediatr. Rev.,* 10, 269, 1989.
8. **Smith, D. E., Schwartz, R. H., and Martin, D. M.,** Heavy cocaine use by adolescents, *Pediatrics,* 83, 539, 1989.
9. **Kandel, D. B., et al.,** Cessation of illicit drug use in young adulthood, *Arch. Gen. Psychiatr.,* 46, 109, 1989.
10. **Kim, S., McLead, J., and Palmgren, C. L.,** The impact of the ''I'm Special'' program on student substance abuse and other related student problem behavior, *J. Drug Educ.,* 19, 83, 1989.
11. **Quinn, W. H., Kuehl, B. P., Thomas, F. N., and Joanning, H.,** Families of adolescent drug abusers, systemic interventions to attain drug-free behavior, *Am. J. Drug Alcohol Abuse,* 14, 65, 1988.
12. **King, P.,** Heavy metal music and drug abuse in adolescents, *Postgrad. Med.,* 83, 295, 1988.
13. **Vinogradov, S., Dishotsky, N. I., Doty, A. K., and Tinklenberg, J. R.,** Patterns of behavior in adolescent rape, *Am. J. Orthopsychiatr.,* 58, 179, 1988.
14. **Yates, W. R., Meller, W., and Troughton, E. P.,** Behavioral complications of alcoholism, *Am. Fam. Phys.,* 35, 171, 1987.

Chapter 36

Special Problems in Women Abusers

I. INTRODUCTION

Drinking patterns and drug-associated diseases are different in men and women. Women are more likely to abuse alcohol, over-the-counter agents and prescription medications, whereas men are more into cigarettes, marijuana, and hard drugs.[1] More than 80% of all studies of substance abuse are confined to men, and these differences are often not appreciated and are usually overlooked in the establishment of treatment programs. The important problems produced by practicing addicts during pregnancy in terms of permanent injury to the unborn child, the production of withdrawal in the child at the time of delivery, and the transmission of diseases to the newborn, principally AIDS and hepatitis, are substantial economic burdens in our society and one of the costly, but less heralded side effects of addictions; these problems are discussed in the next chapter.

Women have undergone an extraordinary change in status in America in the last several decades. Liberation of women from childbearing, remaining at home, undereducation, and underpayment in the workplace have all occurred, with the result that women are the most rapidly growing group entering into the workforce, represent the most new college degrees awarded each year, and are rapidly increasing in the percentages of new Ph.D.s awarded. As a result of these advances the use of substances by females has also been liberalized, and problems of abuse have grown. Comparison of a 30-year-old working woman today with her aunts or mother of 25 years earlier indicates major differences in attitudes toward drug and medicine use, and evolution of these changes is continuing. In this chapter we explore some reasons for differences in addiction patterns in men and women, some differences in the complication profile, some issues of understanding and treating women abusers, and some issues on outcome.

II. DIFFERENCES IN WOMEN ACCOUNTING FOR SOME OF THEIR REACTIONS TO ABUSED SUBSTANCES

Women are smaller, contain a higher percentage of their body weight as fat, a lower fraction as water, and metabolize most substances 10 to 25% faster than men of equal size due to more intensive hepatic metabolism. Since most drugs are utilized in standard doses rather than on a weight-adjusted basis, women get higher blood and central nervous system levels of drugs and alcohol, yet they usually metabolize these faster and so experience wider swings in blood levels. If injury is from a liver product of the drug, as is possible in alcoholism, then the production of the toxic material is more rapid.

There is controversy about sex differences in blood levels of alcohol when corrected to the differences in body water. A study be Frezza et al.[2] found higher blood ethanol concentrations in women than in men. They examined the differences between blood levels after identical intravenous and oral doses of ethanol. This first-pass effect in women, which substantially related to gastric oxidation, was about 60% that of men considered and the first-pass effect was 23%. An accompanying editorial considered that this combined gastric and liver difference in women may account for the increased disease in women compared to men who drink excessively.[3] To add fuel to the controversy, a recent study found more rapid elimination of alcohol in women than in men.[4] A recent review concludes that women suffer more physiological deterioration from an equal amount of alcohol than men.[5] Although differences in drug and alcohol metabolism have been observed at different times in the menstrual and ovulatory cycle, these are inconstant and of only minor importance. Drugs such as opiates, sedatives including alcohol, amphetamines, and cocaine when used regularly interfere with the complex process of ovulation and subsequent implantation of the fertilized ovum, rendering pregnancy infrequent but far from impossible.

Women at all ages visit doctors more frequently than men, and in general are more compliant with medical recommendations and advice then men. Starting in adolescence and continuing throughout life, women use more medicines and more over-the-counter drugs and are given more prescriptions. In one study 67% of all prescriptions for mood-altering drugs were given to women.[6] Although most addictions to alcohol and illicit drugs find men in the majority, abuse of over-the-counter or prescription medications reverses this ratio, there being far more women users. The trends of the 1970s and 1980s show women rapidly gaining on men in their representation in alcoholism and drug abuse treatment centers.

The societal stigma of alcoholism or drug abuse, particularly for those over age 40, is much greater for women than for men, but is prominent for women of all ages, leading to more concealment of all forms of abuse. An unemployed woman can more readily conceal substance abuse than one who is employed. The increased availability of disposable funds and the ready availability of all forms of abused substances contribute to the increased use. A study addressing alcohol and drug use after treatment found that men used cannabis and tobacco significantly more than women, whereas women used more sedatives and minor tranquilizers than men.[7]

The increased use of illicit substances and the sustained high use of alcohol and abused prescription drugs affects both men and women, but in many circumstances the societal pressures on women are even greater than those on men, leading to the inappropriate use of substances to relieve tension and pressure. When we encounter an addicted female, particularly an executive or professional, most of us working with addictions have the impression that identification came late.

III. DIFFERENCES IN DISEASE SUSCEPTIBILITY BETWEEN ABUSING WOMEN AND MEN

The most striking identified difference is a fivefold increase in the rate of cirrhosis among women alcoholics contrasted to men manifest in the years 20 to 50, the peak prevalence years for this disease. This is partially related to the increased hepatic and blood levels of alcohol encountered in alcoholic women due to their smaller size, but is much more complex than this because, from epidemiological study, the damage occurs at much lower intakes of alcohol.[8] Data also seem to support an increased susceptibility to neuropsychiatric illness compared to men, but well-controlled studies do not yet exist.[9,10]

Although peripheral neuritis seems comparable in its distribution between men and women alcoholics, Wernicke-Korsakoff psychosis and cerebellar degeneration is increased at least threefold in male alcoholics. This probably reflects much higher and more prolonged levels of drinking in the alcoholics who acquire these disease. Pancreatitis seems to occur at much lower intakes of alcohol in women than in men.[11]

Accidents and trauma regularly have a male predilection, probably reflecting that more men than women drink and work or drive while under the influence of substances. The "macho" instinct in men almost certainly promotes risk taking, which is a factor in accidents and trauma. Men participate disproportionately in the risky hobbies of mountain climbing, technical rock climbing, hang gliding, motorcycle riding, and sky diving. Derelict drinking is less prevalent in women than men, possibly because they are less frequently represented among the homeless. The diseases of malnutrition and pancreatitis are seen less frequently in women.

Sexual habits of women account for substantial differences in diseases encountered in men and women abusers. Women have fewer sexual partners than men and therefore are less likely to acquire sexually transmitted disease. Homosexual women have far fewer partners than homosexual men. Chlamydia infections are far more prevalent in women than men, whereas gonorrhea is the other way around, independent of the issue of abuse.

A descriptive study found that depression occurred to a slightly higher degree and panic disorder much more often in alcoholic women than men.[12]

IV. ISSUES OF SEXUALITY AND SEX FUNCTION

Abusing women have many sexual problems. Women on heroin or cocaine often turn to prostitution to support their habit, but this is unusual among alcoholics and other drug addicts and is a function of social class and economic availability. Among abusing women there is often a poor image and self-esteem, leading to an increase in all forms of sexual subservience. Studies of recovery in abusing women reveal a great deal of sexual dysfunction, with less sexual activity, less orgasmic response, and less sexual satisfaction. Forrest even suggests that many women use drugs and alcohol initially to overcome problems of this sort, to become stimulated or to provide an excuse for failure to have orgasm. It is quite clear that advanced users of alcohol, heroin, or other sedatives are nearly totally unable to perform sexually.[13]

Women abusers are much more likely to live with male abusers, and to take up with them repeatedly in marriage or living arrangements, and in this manner are different from male abusers. Although these problems are present in extreme cases, the majority of female abusers have acceptable sexual performance. Fertility is diminished in substance abusers as a group, with changes occurring in both the neuroendocrine system[14] and reproductive function.[15] Injury to the unborn child and problems at birth are discussed in Chapter 37. Sexually transmitted disease is discussed initially in Chapters 17 and 20 but is particularly important one in women, with much recent emphasis on HIV infection. As a group, addicts and families of addicts get poor medical care, and manifestations of sexually transmitted diseases are acutely a little less prominent in women. Women addicts are frequently the sexual partners of male addicts. The most common group of new HIV infections transmitted heterosexually, in fact, are the consorts of male i.v. drug abusers who have acquired this disease from their partners.

After cessation of drug use, problems in fertility and sexual function continue for many years.

V. BACKGROUND FINDINGS IN WOMEN ABUSERS

Women alcoholics more often come from an alcoholic family than men alcoholics. Winokur and Clayton found that 28% of the fathers, 12% of the mothers, and 12% of the sisters of female alcoholics were alcoholic; the comparable figures for the male alcoholics were 21%, 3%, and 2%, respectively.[16] A frequent pattern noted by others is that the fathers of female alcoholics were long-standing alcoholics in as many as 50% of the cases.[17] In common with alcohol, it was found that more than half the families of heroin-abusing women used alcohol and drugs frequently in the presence of the children.[18] An emotionally brutal childhood with frequent family disruption such as loss of a parent or single-parent home was common in both alcoholic and drug-abusing women, again more so than for similar men.[19-21] The impact of loss of a parent before age 10 seems to be much more important to a female in producing later alcoholism or drug abuse than to a man.

VI. PERSONALITY FEATURES OF FEMALE ABUSERS

Most studies are based on observations after the addiction has developed; almost none are conducted before the addiction is present. A widely quoted study of use of licit and illicit drugs obtained from a large sample of households found that men tend to cope with alcohol, whereas women tend to cope with medications. Younger women, and men when they use agents, use stimulants, whereas older women use sedating and tranquilizing drugs.[22] A possibly related phenomenon is the observation on placebo effects in men and women compared to alcohol. Newlin observed in Pavlovian conditioning studies that men react to placebo in the opposite direction to their reaction to alcohol,[23] whereas women react in the same direction when expectancy of an alcohol effect is created.[24] Psychopathology is more frequent in women alcoholics and drug users than in males.[25,26] Depressive disease seems to be more common in women, with values as high as 27% observed. Rating scales identify more anxiety, guilt, tension, depression, hostility, and neuroticism in women than in men addicts.[27] It is possible that societal restriction of women and stigmatizing of addiction more for women than men may account for these differences. It also seems likely that only the more advanced cases come to attention to appear in statistical reports.

Women alcoholic behavior, from first becoming abnormal to becoming severe, is telescoped in time compared to that of men.[4] Women are more likely than men to become problem drinkers as a result of a single recallable traumatic event such as a divorce, loss of a child to college, or a health problem. The role of sex has received much attention by Wilsnack.[5] She found that employed married women had higher rates of problem drinking than unmarried women, and their sexual role behavior was often inconsistent with their own values. Among heroin and cocaine addicts the behavior of the male partner substantially determines the behavior.

Although, as a group, substance abusers are not good mothers, they are concerned about their children as much or more than other mothers. They handle separation from their children poorly, often placing the child with their own mothers. A great deal of concern arises and continues to arise about the problems in their own children and their role in the genesis of these problems.[28] Abuse of children is more common by active addicted parents.

VII. ISSUES OF TREATMENT OF WOMEN ABUSERS

The sex of the therapist enters into both treatment and choice of a therapist. Four reasons women prefer a female therapist have been outlined: (1) fear that men may have sexist values; (2) belief that a male therapist may be easily fooled into avoiding problem areas; (3) a wish to avoid erotic transference or involvement; and (4) the desire for a competent role model woman with whom to identify.[29] Education of the therapist and reassurance can overcome all but the last issue. Clearly, any therapist must have a firm grasp of issues that are important to women. A study of units devoted to treating alcoholic women indicated improved outcome, but the controls were treated identically.[30] Many public treatment programs are less available to women than to men, and finding a suitable program for women may require more effort. If there are young children, treatment in an institution nearly always involves interruption of the family, and this is of great importance to the woman. In most metropolitan regions there are more facilities and some of these are usually aimed exclusively at women, a factor that may lead to its acceptance.

In families in which both spouses misuse substances, there is a mutually supportive network which accelerates dependance. This is particularly prone to occur if the woman is the daughter of an abusing father,[31] and there is an excellent chance that during recovery the husband will abandon the wife. Such relationships rarely survive therapy, for there is no relationship without the drugs.[32] Families in which only the wife is an abuser are similar to other families in treatment. Female abusers select a male abuser as their live-in partner more than half the time; in contrast, male abusers live with female abusers infrequently.[33]

REFERENCES

1. **Blume, S. B.,** Women and alcohol: a review, *JAMA,* 256, 1467, 1986.
2. **Frezza, M., di Padova, C., Pozzato, G., Terpin, M., Baraona, E., and Lieber, C. S.,** High blood alcohol levels in women: the role of decreased gastric alcohol dehydrogenase activity and first-pass metabolism, *N. Engl. J. Med.,* 322, 95, 1990.
3. **Schenker, S. and Speeg, K. V.,** The risk of alcohol intake in men and women: all may not be equal, *N. Engl. J. Med.,* 322, 127, 1990.
4. **Mishra, L., Sharma, S., Potter, J. J., and Mezey E.,** More rapid elimination of alcohol in women as compared to their male siblings, *Alcohol,* 13, 752, 1989.
5. **Roman, P. M.,** Biological features of women alcohol use: a review, *Public Health Rep.,* 103, 628, 1988.
6. **Balter, M. and Levine, J.,** Nature and extent of psychotropic drug usage in the United States, *Psychopharmacol. Bull.,* 5, 3, 1969.
7. **Ross, H. E.,** Alcohol and drug abuse in treated alcoholics: a comparison of men and women, *Alcohol,* 13, 810, 1989.
8. **Norton R., Batey, R., Dwyer, T., and MacMahon, S.,** Alcohol consumption and the risk of alcohol related cirrhosis in women, *Br. Med. J.,* 295, 80, 1987.
9. **Ashley, M. J., Olin, J. S., le Riche, W. H., et al.,** Morbidity in alcoholics: evidence for accelerated development of physical disease in women, *Arch. Intern. Med.,* 137, 883, 1977.
10. **Saunders, J. B., Davis, M., and Williams, R.,** Do women develop alcoholic liver disease more readily than men? *Br. Med. J.,* 282, 1140, 1981.
11. **Mezey, E., Kolman, C. J., Diehl, A. M., et al.,** Alcohol and dietary intake in the development of chronic pancreatitis and liver disease in alcoholism, *Am. J. Clin. Nutr.,* 48, 148, 1988.
12. **Nunes, E., Quitkin, F., and Berman, C.,** Panic disorder and depression in female alcoholics, *J. Clin. Psychiatr.,* 49, 441, 1988.
13. **Forest, G. C.,** *Alcoholism and Human Sexuality,* Charles C. Thomas, Springfield, IL, 1982.
14. **Mello, N. K., Mendelson, J. H., and Teoh, S. K.,** Neuroendocrine consequences of alcohol abuse in women, *Ann. NY Acad. Sci.* 562, 211, 1989.
15. **Mello, N. K.,** Effects of alcohol abuse on reproductive function in women, *Recent Dev. Alcohol,* 6, 253, 1988.

16. **Winokur, G. and Clayton, P. J.,** Family history studies in comparison of male and female alcoholics, *Q. J. Stud. Alcohol,* 29, 885, 1968.
17. **Beckman, J. J.,** Women alcoholics: a review of social and psychological studies, *J. Stud. Alcohol,* 36, 797, 1975.
18. **Binion, V. J.,** A descriptive comparison of the families of origin of women heroin users and abusers, in *Addicted Women: Family Dynamics, Self-Perceptions and Support Systems,* NIDA Monograph, Department of Health, Education and Welfare, Washington, D.C., 1979, 77—113.
19. **Sandmaier, M.,** *The Invisible Alcoholics: Women and Alcohol Abuse in America,* McGraw-Hill, New York, 1980.
20. **Wilsnack, S. C.,** Alcohol abuse and alcoholism in women, in *Encyclopedia Handbook of Alcoholism,* Pattison, E. M. and Kaufman, E., Eds., Gardner Press, New York, 1982, 718.
21. **Corrigan, E. M.,** *Alcoholic Women in Treatment,* Oxford University Press, New York, 1980.
22. **Chambers, C. D. and Griffey, M. S.,** Use of legal substances within the general population, the sex and age variables, *Addictive Dis.,* 2, 7, 1975.
23. **Newlin, D. B.,** The antagonistic placebo response to alcohol cues, *Alcohol Clin. Exp. Res.,* 9, 411, 1985.
24. **Newlin, D. B.,** Placebo responding in the same direction as alcohol in women, *Alcohol Clin. Exp. Res.,* 13, 36, 1989.
25. **Winokur, G., Reich, T., Rimmer, J., and Pitts, F. N.,** Alcoholism III, Diagnosis and familial psychiatry illness in 259 alcoholic probands, *Arch. Gen. Psychiatr.,* 23, 104, 1970.
26. **Kaufman, E.,** Family structure of narcotics addicts, *Int. J. Addictions,* 16, 106, 1981.
27. **Bromet, E. and Moos, R.,** Sex and marital status in relation to the characteristics of alcoholics, *J. Stud. Alcohol,* 37, 1302, 1976.
28. **Corrigan, E. M.,** *Alcoholic Women in Treatment,* Oxford University Press, New York, 1980.
29. **Kaufman, E.,** *Substance Abuse and Family Therapy,* Grune & Stratton, Orlando, FL, 1985.
30. **Dahlgren, L. and Willander, A.,** Are special treatment facilities for female alcoholics needed? A controlled 2-year follow-up study from a specialized female unit vs. a mixed male/female treatment facility, *Alcohol,* 13, 499, 1989.
31. **Woodside, M.,** Children of alcoholics: a report to Hugh L. Carey, Governor, State of New York, Albany, New York State Division of Alcoholism and Alcohol Abuse, 1982.
32. **Rosenbaum, M.,** *Women on Heroin,* Rutgers University Press, New Brunswick, NJ, 1981.
33. **Ryan, V. S. and Moise, R. A.,** A comparison of women and men entering drug abuse treatment programs, Women Drug Research, Project Report, University of Michigan, Ann Arbor, MI, 1979.

Chapter 37

Problems of Addiction During Pregnancy And Problems in the Child

I. INTRODUCTION

Fertility is regularly reduced in women as addiction becomes more severe,[1] but there are still a great number of abusers who become pregnant. Pregnancy in drug and alcohol addicts is quite common in metropolitan areas throughout America, and the problems produced in the unborn child are myriad and are increasingly coming to the attention of doctors and legislatures.[2] The medical problems include permanent damage to the unborn child, lower birth weight of the child, withdrawal in the child, and all of the problems associated with lack of prenatal care. As a part of the continuing abuse, malnutrition, severe drug intoxication, and other diseases associated with addiction such as AIDS and hepatitis may also be present. Education about these problems is believed to have the greatest impact on the occasional user, but little or no influence on the habituated person. A recent review of Illinois data indicates that in 1988 at least 2160 children were reported as having a problem at birth or after, from addictions with opiates being most common, cocaine second most common, and alcohol and other drugs making up about 20% of the total.[3] The calculations of the cost to society of this problem for a single fetal alcohol child exceeds $1 million for life-long care. A recent urine screen of 1226 mothers receiving obstetrical care at Boston City Hospital revealed that 16% had urines positive for marijuana at delivery and 9% were positive for cocaine. An additional 11% who tested negative reported marijuana use, and

TABLE 77
Influence of Addictions During Pregnancy on Unborn Child and on the Newborn

1. Fetal alcohol syndrome
2. Nonspecific alcohol effects
3. Cocaine problems
4. Opiate problems
5. Other drugs affecting the child

an additional 8% reported cocaine use. Although cocaine or marijuana use were *not* associated with a shortened gestation period, mothers who used marijuana had a child on average 79 g smaller than average, and women who had used cocaine, 93 g smaller. The effect of the two drugs was additive, and both were made worse by concomitant smoking.[4] It is no surprise that, when specifically tested, marked underreporting of alcohol use during pregnancy was found.[5] Similar findings can be anticipated for illicit drug use. Table 77 indicates the problems that will be discussed in this chapter.

II. FETAL ALCOHOL SYNDROME

A. DESCRIPTION AND CAUSE

The adverse effects of drinking during pregnancy was recognized in the Old Testament (Judges 13:3—4) and by Aristotle[6] but were rediscovered in the modern era in the U.S. by Jones and Smith,[7] who described the brain and facial retardation produced by heavy alcohol intake throughout pregnancy. The process produces a permanent arrest in brain development (and with it facial development), and Jones and Smith described characteristic findings of prenatal and postnatal growth retardation, and poor head and facial development.

The estimated incidence ranges from 1.7 to 5.9 per 1000 live births[8] for the full syndrome and a much higher incidence for fetal alcohol effects. For pregnancies associated with an alcohol intake in excess of 50 g/day (five drinks minimum; most were drinking much more), the risk of fetal alcohol effects is 50%, and the full syndrome varies from a low of 3% to a high of 33%.[9] Further, there is clear evidence that reducing alcohol intake during pregnancy decreases the abnormalities.[10] It is not surprising that underestimation of alcohol use in pregnancy occurs.[11]

There are several prevailing views on the cause(s) of the syndrome, with the malnutrition hypothesis and the placental impairment hypothesis in my opinion having the most promise. The former holds that the alcoholic mother is not providing all trace nutrients to her unborn child and this is responsible for the abnormalities. Variations on this hold that acetaldehyde from the increased metabolism of alcohol produces a toxic effect.[11,12] The placental impairment notion is that injury to this organ prevents the appropriate transfer of macronutrients to the fetus.[13]

B. DIAGNOSIS

The history of alcohol intake throughout pregnancy is clear. The intake is in excess of five drinks daily and averages in various studies between 8 and 14; thus the person is typically taking 15 to 50% of their energy as ethanol. The child is undersized *in utero* for gestational age and is underweight at birth, with a greater than appropriate reduction in head circumference. There is always impairment of the central nervous system, including neurological abnormalities, developmental delays, or intellectual deficits. The cranial-facial appearance is typical, with at least two of the following present: microcephaly with the head circumference below the 3rd percentile, microphthalmia with short palpebral fissures, poorly developed philtrum, and hypoplastic upper lip.[14] A recent study reports fetal tachycardia in a mother taking alcohol during late pregnancy and during delivery.[15]

C. TREATMENT

There is no effective treatment, but withdrawal syndrome may occur with alcohol use up until the time of delivery. Major withdrawal has been reported at least 15 times. In alcohol withdrawal, abdominal distention and opisthotonos are common, but they are rare in narcotic withdrawal. In both withdrawals, increased muscle tonicity and tremors are common. Convulsions seem to be more common in ethanol withdrawal. This is treated with phenobarbital.

D. PROGNOSIS FOR FUTURE DEVELOPMENT

These children never catch up with their peers in mental function or in size. Unless they are identified as being of sufficient mental function to make it in society, they must be maintained in a dependent or institutionalized status life-long, somewhat like Downs syndrome or trisomy 23 children. A superb book by Michael Dorris[16] outlines the poignant saga of an author anthropologist who adopted a very young child who turned out to have fetal alcohol syndrome. It is an excellent guide to any family who live with this problem. The precise nomenclature to described the impact of prenatal alcohol use on the child has been discussed.[17]

III. NONSPECIFIC EFFECTS OF ALCOHOL USE

Mild retardation of intrauterine growth with underweight children is common among drinking mothers but probably requires three or more drinks throughout pregnancy. Such changes, though clearly identified and without permanent harm, are probably subclinical instances of the fetal alcohol syndrome. The difficulty is to precisely define a control group, and this has been most difficult, preventing a clear acceptance of alcohol-related injuries.[18] Suffice it to say that as little as two drinks per day during pregnancy results in increased spontaneous abortion. Full fetal alcohol syndrome developes in only 1 to 2% of those using five drinks per day throughout pregnancy and is much more likely to occur at higher levels. Between two drinks per day and higher levels there is less distinctive fetal injury, only some of which is reversible.

The ability to influence heavily drinking mothers by identification and education to decrease alcohol intake during pregnancy and to have a better outcome with healthy children[19] emphasizes the value of prenatal care, including review of alcohol and drug use habits and attempts to modify them. A prominent malpractice suit by a heavily drinking mother who gave birth to a child with the fetal alcohol syndrome as well as labeling of alcoholic beverages as to the hazard to the child's health have all facilitated the educational problem.

An interesting study addressed the issues of maternal alcohol use during breast feeding from the pioneering group studying fetal alcohol syndrome.[20] They found a significant effect at 1 year on motor development in all mothers who were regular drinkers during nursing, with more severe effects in those who were heavier drinkers. There was no adverse effect on the mental development of these infants.

IV. COCAINE

Women of childbearing age comprise a growing proportion of cocaine users in the U.S.[21] A recent review of 138 women who had used cocaine during pregnancy is of value.[22] These researchers found and compared 23 patients who used cocaine during only the first trimester with 52 who used cocaine continuously throughout pregnancy. Others used the drug in various patterns. Preterm delivery was prominent in both groups of cocaine users, with 31% of the patients using the drug throughout pregnancy delivering early. Cessation in the first trimester eliminated low birth weight and small gestational age, which were much more prominent (25 and 19%, respectively) in the patients using cocaine throughout pregnancy. Abruptio placenta was more common in all users. The weight, length, and head circumference was significantly larger in drug-free patients than in drug users, with use throughout pregnancy resulting in more severely affected infants.

The Neonatal Behavioral Assessment Scale indicated significant differences between the drug-free infants and the two groups of cocaine-exposed ones. The prominent intrauterine growth retardation in this study has been confirmed.[23] The amount or frequency of use was not as important as the number of trimesters used. Unfortunately, all the women using cocaine also used ethanol and tobacco. A later study by the same group found that users of cocaine during the first trimester who subsequently stopped produced no adverse effects on the child, but confirmed the adverse outcome in those who continued use in later trimesters with decreased birth weight, length, and head circumference. Both groups of exposed infants, however, had impairment of orientation, motor, and state regulation behavior.[21]

The authors believe that the action of cocaine in preventing dopamine and norepinephrine reuptake produces placental vasoconstriction, decreasing blood flow to the fetus, and may be the basis of the placental malformations. They also found seizures in six infants, and all of these had cocaine in their urine. Two infants in this study also had cerebral infarction, analogous to the coronaries and cerebral infarctions noted in young adult cocaine users.[24] A solid case for an infant withdrawal syndrome could not be made.

A further study noted cocaine-producing urogenital anomalies, suggesting they are five-fold increased in cocaine-using mothers.[25]

V. OPIATES

Opiates, most notably heroin, used up until delivery produces addiction in the child, which in turn produces a variety of problems in the newborn child. The child may be apneic, have a low Apgar score, and undergo withdrawal.[26] If the mother is seen during pregnancy, her withdrawal, if too rapid, may result in intrauterine death, leading many experienced obstetricians to maintain opioid-dependent women on a dose of methadone of about 20 mg daily throughout pregnancy.[27]

Fetal opiate syndromes are less clearly defined than fetal alcohol or fetal cocaine injury, in large part because multi-addictions, malnutrition, alcohol, and acquired disease are widely prevalent in pregnant opiate abusers, making specific identification of the cause of underdevelopment a major problem. Heavy users do not seek or receive prenatal care, are highly noncompliant with care, and have more underweight and underdeveloped infants, but no clear patterns have emerged.

A review of neonatal experience in children born of opiate-addicted mothers from a highly experienced unit is informative. Low birth weight and low 1- and 5-min Apgar scores are common.

Units that commonly deal with neonatal withdrawal handle it with almost no mortality, but the abstinence syndrome may be severe and persist as long as 3 months. Common findings include hyperirritability, gastrointestinal dysfunction, respiratory distress, decreased muscle tone, and uncoordinated sucking and swallowing reflexes. When the mothers have entered prenatal care, the infants have higher birth weights and less withdrawal. Methods to diminish the costs to the hospital have been outlined.[28]

A similar study of mothers on heroin versus mothers on methadone, using multiple regression analysis, concluded that infant birth weight and head size reduction were a function of maternal nutritional status. Although both groups of narcotic-exposed children caught up in head size, there was retarded intellectual performance in the drug-exposed infants.[29] A study one year after birth of 35 infants born of mothers abusing a mixture of drugs indicated no significant differences at 6 and 12 months, though the babies were smaller at birth than controls.[30]

A group of infants born to opiate-abusing mothers were found to have impaired ventilatory response to carbon dioxide and increased risk of sudden infant death syndrome, and this was observed to a lesser degree in children born to mixed drug abusers and PCP abusers but not in the control infants.[31]

Methadone treatment during pregnancy is not without its problems. Women of a certain age frequently become pregnant while in methadone programs; heroin addicts are often treated with methadone maintenance to keep them free of heroin during the remainder of the pregnancy. A recent study followed up 141 infants born of women maintained on methadone and compared them with 127 non-drug-exposed infants from similar mothers as regards age, race, and socioeconomic status. Methadone infants had smaller birth weights and head circumferences, but neither were thought to be of sufficient magnitude to be clinically significant. The initial Apgar scores were comparable, and evaluation of the majority of both groups at 6 months using the Bayley Scale of Mental Development indicated scores of 103 in the methadone-exposed infants and 105 in the comparison ones. This study concluded that there were no lasting developmental effects on infants exposed to methadone *in utero*.[32] There is a problem of narcotic withdrawal that can occur in methadone-treated mothers, affecting the infant at birth.

A longer follow-up of the development of children born to mothers on methadone maintenance extended to 4 years indicates no developmental disadvantage. This study discusses the above data[24] and concludes that socioeconomic and racial factors must be considered in selecting control patients.[33]

VI. OTHER DRUGS DURING PREGNANCY

Infant withdrawal syndromes have not been reported with stimulant drugs including cocaine and amphetamines, but have been noted with alcohol and other sedatives.[26] Other drugs used in treatment, including phenytoin and trimethadione, have been associated with adverse development.[34] Abnormalities have not been observed sufficiently often to assign a cause and effect to other substances of abuse.

Polydrug-abusing mothers had less impairment of birth weight and head circumference than well-controlled, low-dose methadone-maintenance mothers. Using the Brazelton Neonatal Behavioral Assessment Scale, the methadone-exposed infants showed more depression of interactive behaviors than those of polydrug abusers, and both were more depressed than in infants born of nonabusing mothers.[35] An interesting paper compared the infants born of mothers who abused alcohol only to those born of mothers who abused alcohol and opiates throughout pregnancy. The principal measure was malformations observed at birth, and these were much higher in alcohol abusers than in mixed abusers.[36]

Mothers identified during pregnancy to be abusing who accept treatment should be withdrawn gradually. Treatment of withdrawal in pregnant women is very similar to treatment of withdrawal in nonpregnant women, with the striking difference that it should be prolonged about threefold to assure adequate withdrawal of the fetus.

There are very limited reports of specific syndromes produced by other drugs. A recent report indicates that phencyclidine enters and persists for a long time in the brains of pups born of mother rats given PCP during pregnancy, but there was no clear statement on injury.[37] However, Olney and co-workers found that PCP produces a dose-related injury to neuron tissue, also studied in rats, but these were adult.[38]

VII. TREATMENT PROGRAMS

A comprehensive care program for pregnant addicts has been reported and evaluated. Early case finding and entry is important, for those entering the program early in pregnancy had a higher record of remaining in the program and more normal children were born of the pregnancy. The role of various elements in therapy has been discussed, but methadone maintenance for heroin addicts is recommended. Neonatal withdrawal severity and duration was related directly to prenatal dose and duration. Development by the Bayley Scales was usually normal, but if low, usually returned to normal by age 2.[39]

An interesting finding is that events associated with birth influence subsequent behavior in adults. These data from Stockholm reviewed the birth details in 412 forensic victims of suicide, alcoholism, and drug addiction and compared them with controls. Suicides involving asphyxiation were closely associated with asphyxia at birth, and suicides by violent mechanical means were associated with mechanical birth trauma. Drug addiction was associated with opiate or barbiturate administration to mothers during labor. The data on suicides confirmed an American study.[40]

REFERENCES

1. **Smith, C. G. and Asch, R. H.,** Drug abuse and reproduction, *Fertil. Steril.*, 48, 355, 1987.
2. **Lindo, M.,** Drug addiction, its effects on mother and baby, *Midwifery*, 3, 82, 1987.
3. **Reardon, P. and Pearson, R.,** Baby's drug death stirs mothers rights flap, *Chicago Tribune*, May 10, 1989, 1.
4. **Zuckerman, et al.,** Fetal growth in mothers using cocaine or marijuana during pregnancy, *JAMA*, 261, 2604, 1989.
5. **Morrow-Tlucak, M., Ernhart, D. B., Sokol, R. J., Martier, S., and Ager, J.,** Underreporting of alcohol use in pregnancy: relationship to alcohol problem history, *Alcohol*, 13, 399, 1989.
6. **Warner, R. H. and Rosett, H. L.,** The effects of drinking on offspring, *J. Stud. Alcohol*, 36, 1395, 1975.
7. **Jones, K. L. and Smith, D. W.,** Recognition of the fetal alcohol syndrome in early infancy, *Lancet*, 2, 999, 1973.
8. **Abel, E. L.,** Consumption of alcohol during pregnancy: a review of effects on growth and development of offspring, *Human Biol.*, 54, 421, 1982.
9. **Sokol, R. J., Miller, S. I., and Reed, G.,** Alcohol abuse during pregnancy: an epidemiologic study, *Alcoholism: Clin. Exp. Res.*, 4, 135, 1980.
10. **Rosett, H. L. A., Weiner, L., Zuckerman, B., McKinlay, S., and Edelin, K. C.,** Reduction of alcohol consumption during pregnancy with benefits to the newborn, *Alcoholism: Clin. Exp. Res.*, 4, 78, 1980.
11. **Fisher, S. E., Atkinson, M. S., Burnap, J. K., Jacobson, S., Sehgal, P., Scott, W., and Van Thiel, D. H.,** Ethanol associated selective fetal malnutrition: a contributing factor in the fetal alcohol syndrome, *Alcoholism: Clin. Exp. Res.*, 6, 197, 1982.
12. **O'Shea, K. S. and Kaufman, M. H.,** The teratogenic effect of acetaldehyde, implications for the study of the fetal alcohol syndrome, *J. Anat.*, 128, 65, 1979.
13. **Henderson, G. I., Patwardhan, R. V., McLeroy, S., and Schenker, S.,** Inhibtion of placental amino acid uptake in reats following acute and chronic ethanol exposure, *Alcoholism: Clin. Exp. Res.*, 6, 495, 1982.
14. **Rosett, H. L.,** A clinical perspective of the fetal alcohol syndrome (editorial), *Alcoholism: Clin. Exp. Res.*, 4, 119, 1980.
15. **Silva, P. D., Miller, K. D., Madden, J., and Keegan, K. A.,** Abnormal fetal heart rate pattern associated with severe intrapartum materal ethanol intoxication, a case report, *J. Reprod. Med.*, 32, 144, 1987.
16. **Dorris, M.,** *The Broken Cord: A family's ongoing struggle with fetal alcohol syndrome*, Harper & Row, New York, 1989, reviewed in, *J. Am. Med Assoc.*, 262, 3479, 1989.
17. **Sokol, R. J. and Clarren, S. K.,** Guidelines for use of terminology describing the impact of prenatal alcohol on the offspring, *Alcohol*, 13, 597, 1989.
18. **Rosett, H. L., Weiner, L., and Edelin, K. S.,** Strategies for prevention of fetal alcohol effects, *Obstet. Gynecol.*, 57, 1, 1981.

19. **Ouellette, E. M., Rosett, H. L., Rosman, N. P., and Weiner, L.,** Adverse effects of offspring of maternal alcohol abuse during pregnancy, *New Engl. J. Med.,* 297, 528, 1977.
20. **Little, R. E., Anderson, K. W., Ervin, C. H., Worthington-Roberts, B., and Clarren, S. K.,** Maternal alcohol use during breast-feeding and infant mental and motor development at one year, *New Engl. J. Med.,* 321, 425, 1989.
21. **Clayton, R. R.,** Cocaine use in the US: in a blizzard or just being snowed, in *Cocaine Use in America: Epidemiology and Clinical Perspectives,* Kozel, N. Y. and Adams, E. H., Eds., NIDA research monograph 61, U.S. Department of Health and Human Services, Washington, D.C., 1985, 8.
22. **Chasnoff, I. J., Griffith, D. R., MacGregor, S., Dirkes, K., and Burns, K. A.,** *JAMA,* 261, 1741, 1989.
23. **MacGregor, S. N., Keith, L. G., Chasnoff, I. J., et al.,** Cocaine use during pregnancy: adverse perinatal outcome, *Am J. Obstet. Gynecol.,* 157, 686, 1987.
24. **Cregler, L. and Mark, H.** Medical complications of cocaine abuse, *New Engl. J. Med.,* 315, 1495, 1986.
25. **Chavez, G. F., Mulinare, J., and Cordero, J. F.,** Maternal cocaine use during early pregnancy as a risk factor for congenital urogenital anomalies, *JAMA,* 262, 795, 1989.
26. **Zelson, C., Rubio, E., and Wasserman, E.,** Neonatal narcotic addiction: 10-year observation, *Pediatrics,* 48, 178, 1971.
27. **Finnegan, L. P., Ed.,** *Drug Dependence in Pregnancy: Clinical Management of Mother and Child,* Service Research Monograph Series, DHEW Publication No. ADM 69-678, Washington, D.C., 1979.
28. **Finnegan, L. P.,** Effects of maternal opiate abuse on the newborn, *Fed. Proc.,* 44, 2314, 1985.
29. **Lifschitz, M. H., Wilson, G. S., Smith, E. O., and Desmond, M. M.,** Factors affecting head growth and intellectual function in children of drug addicts, *Pediatrics,* 75, 269, 1985.
30. **Van Baar, A. L., et al.,** Behavior in first year after drug dependent pregnancy, *Arch. Dis. Child,* 64, 241, 1989.
31. **Ward, S. L., Schuetz, S., Kirshna, V., et al.,** Abnormal sleeping ventilatory pattern in infants of substance abusing mothers, *Am. J. Dis. Child.,* 140, 1015, 1986.
32. **Kaltenback, K. and Finnegan, L. P.,** Perinatal and developmental outcome of infants exposed to methadone in-utero, *Neurotoxicol. Teratol.,* 9, 311, 1987.
33. **Kaltenbach, K. and Finnegan, L. P.,** Developmental outcome of children born to methadone maintained women: a review of longitudinal studies, *Neurobehav. Toxicol. Teratol.,* 6, 271, 1984.
34. **Gal, P. and Sharpless, M. K.,** Fetal drug exposure, behavioral teratogenesis, *Drug Intell. Clin. Pharm.,* 18, 186, 1984.
35. **Chasnoff, I. J., Hatcher, R., and Burns, W. J.,** Polydrug and methadone addicted newborns: a continuum of impairment, *Pediatrics,* 70, 210, 1982.
36. **Iosub, S., Fuchs, M., Bingol, N., Stone, R. K., Gromisch, D. S., and Wasserman, E.,** Incidence of major congenital malformations in offspring of alcoholics and polydrug abusers, *Alcohol,* 2, 521, 1985.
37. **Pechnick, R. N., et al.,** Phencyclidine and pregnancy, a study in rats, *JAMA,* 262, 1439, 1989.
38. **Olney, J. W., et al.,** Neurotoxic effects of phencyclidine in rats, *JAMA,* 262, 1439, 1989.
39. **Suffet, F. and Brotman, R.,** A comprehensive care program for pregnant addicts: obstetrical, neonatal and child development outcomes, *Int. J. Addictions,* 19, 199, 1984.
40. **Jacobson, B., Eklund, G., Hamberger, L., Linnarsson, D., Sevall, G., and Valverius,** Perinatal origin of adult self destructive behavior, *Acta Psychol. Scand.,* 76, 364, 1987.

Chapter 38

Children of Alcoholics and Drug Abusers

I. INTRODUCTION

The association of multiple cases of alcoholism and drug abuse within the same family group has been known since the beginning of recorded history. Critical studies since the 1950s have dissected the relative contributions of environment, role models, and genetics, particularly in alcoholism. In this chapter we present some of the seminal information relating to the identification of children of addicts, particularly male children, as those at the highest risk for future addiction.

II. CHILDREN OF ALCOHOLICS

Margaret Cork, in her book, *The Forgotten Children,*[1] focused attention on the children of alcoholics. She and others[2,3] pointed out the high occurrence of subsequent alcoholism in these children (30 to 50% in various studies). She also brought to attention the major developmental, learning, and emotional problems present in these children. The long-term consequences on personality, inability to form intimate relationships, and attitudes toward alcohol have also been clarified.[4] Even now many behaviorists recognize a fairly specific syndrome associated with the abused and neglected childhood of a girl child and an alcoholic father. The features of these children of alcoholic fathers include inability to express emotion and to form intimate relations with either sex, and tendency to be self-sufficient and a loner in interpersonal relationships. There is an impaired social conscience often manifest by lying, petty thievery, and shoplifting.

Goodwin[5] was among the first to study twins born of at least one alcoholic parent who were separated for adoption and raised in homes separate from their biological parents or other relatives. The incidence of subsequent alcoholism was at least fourfold higher in such children than in twins from nonalcoholic parents, and the change was prominent in both men and women. Subsequent studies, particularly those of Cloninger et al.,[6] have shown the importance of genetic background and of environment. Further studies by these authors found personality factors in the child that predicted alcohol abuse in young adults. High novelty seeking and low harm avoidance were the most strongly predictive features of boys of early onset alcohol abuse.[7] In addition to alcoholism in the offspring of alcoholics, there is a substantial amount of other neurotic and psychiatric problems. A recent paper found cognitive and behavioral function to be impaired in school-aged sons of early-onset alcoholic fathers compared to matched controls and reviews this type of finding.[8] Others have found that the sons of alcoholic fathers are less affected by a dose of alcohol compared to controls.[9]

Most observers believe that similar features appear with drug addiction, but they have not been nearly as well studied in that case. Specific patterns of parenting may play a role. A survey in England that examined young addicts' perceptions of their parents compared to those of controls found that the addicts found their parents significantly more cold emotionally, indifferent, controlling, and intrusive in their development.[10] Although inheritance has been established as an important factor, it does not weigh nearly as heavily as parental substance abuse and tolerance of adolescent substance abuse by parents.[11] A longitudinal follow-up after 2 years of 518 children initially evaluated between 9 and 18 years of age found that family factors and school factors had an almost equal influence in promoting drug use; but school factors were important in ameliorating negative family factors.[12]

A variety of studies have observed minute details of the neurological, psychiatric, or psychophysiologic aspects of the offspring of alcoholic subjects. Knop[13] has identified many modest changes in the sons of alcoholics. Hesselbrock and co-workers[14] have found extensive minor differences in psychological tests showing impairment. Begleiter et al.[15] showed changes in visual and auditory evoked potentials indicating impairment in the offspring of alcoholics even before they have ingested their first drink.

In combination, these studies demonstrate that inheritance from alcoholic fathers (and mothers) produces many behavior, neuroanatomical, and neuropsychological changes and impairments that affect behavior in the future. Clearly, measures to prevent the emergence of alcoholism and drug abuse in this high-risk group are in order. Some of these are discussed below and in the chapter on adolescence, Chapter 35.

III. CHILDREN OF DRUG ADDICTS

A. CHILDREN BORN OF ABUSING MOTHERS

The multivariate social pathology entering into the early lives of children born of abusing mothers has not been fully sorted out, but these children have the highest identified prevalence of subsequent substance abuse and merit preventative measures. Major abnormalities by age 4 were documented in a study of amphetamine-abusing mothers. Almost half the children had measurable difficulties in adjustment.[16] The major problem of keeping such high-risk children in treatment was documented.[17] The instability of the subsequent home situation in children born of mothers taking heroin was documented; after 2 years only 6 of 23 followed infants were in homes with even temporary stability.[18] Battered children are common with abusing parents.

B. INFLUENCES THAT DETERMINE DRUG USE

The use and abuse of substances by high school-age persons is heavily influenced by patterns of use in the home by parents and siblings and after age 12 by use in peers. This can be countered by firm guidance from school or church. Most analyses find the influence of siblings and close friends to be quite similar. One recent study from New York neighborhoods found that school peer and family influences had a nearly equal impact on drug use. A positive force increasing the likelihood of use (family use, absent parents, no parent supervision, poor school performance or attendance, nonacceptance by predominant peer group) could be counterbalanced by strengths away from drugs in other areas.[19] Although abusing families are associated with a higher percentage of abusing youngsters, it is also apparent that the family can positively reduce the likelihood.

A recent review emphasized parent instruction that targeted behaviors appropriate for the adolescent's developmental status. The potential control that parents still have over much of the life of adolescents, when utilized, was effective in reducing drug experimentation and regular use.[20] Another study reviewed parenting patterns that promoted drug use and found that achievement pressure and conditional approval of drug use, particularly when in conjunction with unremoved irrational beliefs of the adolescent users, were important forces in promoting drug abuse.[21] A valuable study from Australia reviewed behavior problems including drug use patterns in children 12 to 15 years of age and found that the quality of the family relationship was by far the most important factor in avoiding drug use. A close and loving relationship was negatively associated with drug and cigarette use, whereas family depression, poor relationships, full-time working parents, or divorce were associated with increased drug use and other behavior problems in adolescents.[22]

Parental habits and attitudes clearly have a great deal to do with teenage use patterns. Homes in which drug or alcohol use is prominent have a much higher incidence of use in teenagers. Tolerance by parents is also an important factor in use by adolescents.[23] Older siblings often have a similar influence to parents, whereas younger siblings are more nearly akin to peers.[24] As use of illicit drugs increases, the peers assume greater and greater importance.

C. BROKEN HOMES, ABSENT FATHERS, OTHER

There is a modicum of research on the specific role of fathers on subsequent substance abuse. A fascinating study of fathers' impact on college-age daughters regarding marijuana use found that the fathers' greatest influence was mediated through peer groups, and through specific example behavior rather than through authoritative roles.[25] As in the alcohol literature, fathers' absence from the home assumes a great role, particularly in the preteen years[26] that is more marked for boys than girls.

IV. CONCLUSIONS

As yet there are no satisfactory twin studies of drug abuse to clearly separate out genetic effects, but these account for about 15% of alcohol use in the subsequent generation. Clearly a strong positive push toward substance abuse is provided by parental examples of substance use, whether of tobacco, alcohol, prescription medicines, or illicit substances, with the offspring most likely to abuse the same substance as the parents. A further strong influence is provided in the first 8 to 18 years of life by parental attitudes toward substance use. A strong negative influence and interdictive attitude may prevail over all other influences and is particularly strong through the early teenage years. In the teens, school and peer pressure becomes a more important source of attitudes than the home. There is no agreement on the role of advertisements, but the consensus is that the presenting of drugs, alcohol, and tobacco as being sophisticated, associated with sex, and success encourages use.

Children from broken homes, from a hostile, nonloving environment, children born of addicted mothers, and battered children have a far greater subsequent prevalence of all forms of behavior difficulties and acting-out including substance abuse. This group may be different than other users, but clearly are one of the highest using groups and need special targeted treatment.

V. TREATMENT

Evaluation of school programs aimed at decreasing drug use in *all* children indicates that the programs are effective. A program in the Philadelphia Public Schools using teacher training and then a program of 12 weekly sessions was quite valuable in increasing information levels, in decreasing the willingness to experiment with drugs, and in increasing strongly negative attitudes toward drug use.[27] A less objective evaluation in Wisconsin indicated a conception of great worth[28] by the administrators.

REFERENCES

1. **Cork, M. R.,** *The Forgotten Children,* Addict Research Foundation, Toronto, 1969.
2. **Cotton, N. S.,** The familial incidence of alcoholism: a review, *J. Stud. Alcohol.,* 40, 89, 1979.
3. **El-Guebaly, N. and Orford, D. R.,** The offspring of alcoholics: a critical review, *Am. J. Psychiatr.,* 134, 357, 1977.
4. **Pattison, E. M. and Kaufman, E.,** Family therapy in the treatment of alcoholism, in *Family Therapy and Margin Psychopathology,* Langley, M. R., Ed., Grune & Stratton, New York, 1981, 203.
5. **Goodwin, D. W.,** Alcoholism and heredity, *Arch. Gen. Psychiatr.,* 36, 57, 1979.
6. **Cloninger, C. R., Bohman, M., Sigvardsson, S., and von Knorring, A.-L.,** Pyschopathology in adopted out children of alcoholics: the Stockholm adoption study, in *Recent Developments in Alcoholism,* Vol. 3, Galanter, M., Ed., Plenum Press, New York, 1985, 37.
7. **Cloninger, C. R., Sigvardsson, S., and Bohman, M.,** Childhood personality predicts alcohol abuse in young adults, *Alcoholism,* 12, 494, 1988.
8. **Tarter, R. E., Jacob, T., and Bremer, D. L.,** Specific cognitive impairment in sons of early onset alcoholics, *Alcoholism,* 13, 786, 1989.
9. **Moss, H. B., Yao, J. K., and Maddock, J. M.,** Responses by sons of alcoholic fathers to alcoholic and placebo drinks: perceived mood, intoxication and plasma prolactin, *Alcoholism,* 13, 252, 1989.
10. **Schweitzer, R. D. and Lawton, P. A.,** Drug abusers' perceptions of their parents, *Br. J. Addictions,* 84, 309, 1989.
11. **Brown, S. A.,** Life events of adolescents in relation to personal and parental substance abuse, *Am. J. Psychiatr.,* 146, 484, 1989.
12. **Brook, J. S., Nomura, C., and Cohen, P.,** A network of influences on adolescent drug involvement: neighborhood, school, peer and family, *Genetic Soc. Gen. Psychol. Monogr.,* 115, 123, 1989.
13. **Knop, J.,** Premorbid assessment of young men at high risk for alcoholism, in *Recent Developments in Alcoholism,* Galanter, M., Ed., Plenum Press, New York, 1985, 53.
14. **Hesselbroch, V. M., Stabenau, J. R., and Hesselbroch, M. N.,** Minimal brain dysfunction and neuropsychological tests performed in offspring of alcoholics, in *Recent Developments in Alcoholism,* Vol. 3, Galanter, M., Ed., Plenum Press, New York, 1985, 65—78.
15. **Begleiter, H., Porjesz, B., and Kissin, B.,** Brain dysfunction in alcoholics with and without a family history of alcoholism, *Alcoholism: Clin. Exp. Res.,* 6, 136, 1982.
16. **Billing, L., Eriksson, M., Stneroth, G., and Zetterstrom, R.,** Predictive indicators for adjustment in 4-year-old children whose mothers used amphetamine during pregnancy, *Child Abuse Neglect,* 12, 503, 1988.
17. **Chan, L. S., Wingert, W. A., Wachsman, L., Schuetz, S., and Rogers, C.,** Differences between dropouts and active participants in a pediatric clinic for substance abuse mothers, *Am. J. Drug Alcohol Abuse,* 12, 89, 1986.
18. **Klenka, H. M.,** Babies born in a district general hospital to mothers taking heroin, *Br. Med. J. Clin. Res.,* 293, 745, 1986.
19. **Brook, J. S., Nomura, C., and Cohen, P.,** A network of influences on adolescent drug involvement: neighborhood, school, peer, and family, *Genetic Soc. Gen. Psychol. Monogr.,* 115, 123, 1989.
20. **Bry, B. H.,** Family-based approaches to reducing adolescent substance use: theories, techniques and findings, *NIDA Res. Monogr.,* 77, 39, 1988.
21. **Denoff, M. S.,** An integrated analysis of the contribution made by irrational beliefs and parenteral interaction to adolescent drug abuse, *Int. J. Addictions,* 23, 655, 1988.
22. **Reynolds, I. and Rob, M. I.,** The role of family difficulties in adolescent depression, drug-taking and other problem behaviors, *Med. J. Aust.,* 149, 250, 1988.
23. **Halebsky, M. A.,** Adolescent alcohol and substance abuse: parent and peer effects, *Adolescence,* 22, 661, 1987.

24. **Needle, R., McCubbin, H., Wilson, M., Reineck, R., Lazar, A., and Mederer, H.,** Interpersonal influences in adolescent drug use—the role of older siblings, parents and peers, *Int. J. Addictions,* 21, 739, 1986.
25. **Brook, J. S., Whiteman, M., Gordon, A. S., and Brook, D. W.,** Father's influence on his daughters marijuana use viewed in a mother and peer context, *Adv. Alcohol Subst. Abuse,* 4, 165, 1985.
26. **Stern, M., Northman, J. E., and Van Slyck, M. R.,** Father absence and adolescent ''behavior problems'': alcohol consumption, drug use and sexual activity, *Adolescence,* 19, 302, 1984.
27. **LoSciuto, L. and Ausetts, M. A.,** Evaluation of a drug abuse prevention program: a field experiment, *Addictive Behav.,* 13, 337, 1988.
28. **Fredisdorf, M.,** Alcohol and drug abuse prevention in Wisconsin public schools, *J. Sch. Health,* 59, 21, 1989.

Chapter 39

Problems of Alcohol and Drug Use in the Elderly

I. INTRODUCTION

The graying of America is resulting in more and more free-living Americans who are retired from the workforce. This group has the most resources to spend and the most leisure time. Although the majority of the elderly (over age 55) are healthy and living in private homes or apartments, increasing numbers are feeling financial strictures because inflation has outstripped many retirement plans. The presence of many chronic forms of illness along with diminished physical capacity is widespread, placing financial and emotional burdens that are often poorly met by local social and medical programs. The elderly use the most prescription medications and the most over-the-counter drugs. It is little wonder that there is an increasing recognition of problems of drug abuse and alcoholism in older subjects.

Age-related changes in drug metabolism have been extensively investigated with regard to therapeutic agents. Although examples of serious impairment are known, usually of agents requiring oxidative metabolism, the changes are on the whole modest. These investigations have been reviewed by Anderson,[1] and by Vestal and Dawson.[2] Drugs for which such changes may be important include benzodiazepines, barbiturates, and a few amphetamines. Alcohol metabolism has been systematically examined and shows very modest deterioration.[3]

Attitudes governing social and recreational use of drugs are established in earlier life, and there is little evidence of change after age 40. Thus the 80-year olds of the 1990s formed their habits in the 1950s. The elderly (usually defined as those over 55 or over 60 years), in keeping with their earlier life, consume prescription and over-the-counter drugs and

TABLE 78
Types of Patients Encountered with Problems of Substance Abuse at Ages over 55 Years

Problems with Onset Before Age 55

1. Chronic addict becoming older, use continues
2. Chronic disease developed from earlier addiction
3. Addiction in prolonged remission recurs over age 55

Problems with Onset After Age 55

1. Alcoholism with onset in elderly
   (a) Change in life situation
   (b) Change in health
2. Abuse of prescription or over-the-counter drugs
3. Symptomatic diseases caused by abuse
4. Hidden substance abusers
5. Falls and injuries resulting from abuse
6. Loss of mental faculties or incontinence resulting from abuse

alcohol, and use tobacco, but only infrequently use street drugs. It is anticipated that in 2010—2020 the patterns of abuse in the elderly will reflect the greater use of illicit substances in the population's formative years, i.e., the 1980s.

In addition, with retirement for many, along with retirement comes a steadily increasing loss of power over their lives, with declining purchasing power, declining health, and frequently deteriorating neighborhoods and household situations. Thus three intertwining patterns exist that may lead to a drug or alcohol abuse pattern. There are patterns of drug and alcohol from the first 40 years of their lives. A variety of drugs are prescribed by physicians, including sedatives, narcotics, tranquilizers, and soporifics, because they are temporarily indicated to control specific symptoms. Finally, there is too little to fill their hours and there is usually loneliness and loss of power over many features of their lives. These patterns together may lead to increased use of familiar agents, often alcohol. However, the problems in recognition of abuse contribute substantially to poor studies on prevalence, and response to treatment.[4]

II. PREVALENCE OF USE

A major household survey of the nutritional status of Americans found that some 85% of males aged 21 to 55 use alcohol at least occasionally, as do some 62% of women. Beyond this age there is a rapidly decreasing percentage of daily users, with 5% of men and 3.8% women aged 65 to 75 being daily users.[5] The frequency of use is much higher in institutionalized persons if access is permitted. A Boston study of free-living persons showed that drinking was increased in elderly with more income, those living with spouses, and, among men, those who smoked, with users averaging 11% of men and 8% of women.[6] A review of recent trends in Ontario failed to reveal any major changes in use of alcohol, sleeping pills, or tranquilizers in persons aged 60 or older in the past two decades.[7] In a Chicago study of veterans, a rapid decline in the number of those using alcohol daily was found after age 60. The group were those who presented at the outpatient area of a Veterans Administration hospital. Whereas more than 85% of those presenting up to age 60 were daily drinkers, in the next decade this dropped to 52%, and was 18% in the group aged 70 to 80 and 6% in those aged 80 or older.[8]

Table 78 lists some problems that may be encountered in patients over age 55 and indicates the way in which they will be discussed below.

Two valuable papers have appeared from the alcoholism and drug abuse unit at the Mayo Clinic. Patients over age 65 make up 10% of the total admissions to that unit. The prevalence of legally prescribed drugs as the substance of abuse made up 14% of their 216 admissions in the elderly group. Of these, 43% had cirrhosis, 25% had chronic organic brain syndrome, and 19% had some form of permanent CNS damage, indicating more disease as a group in these patients than in their younger counterparts. However, only 12% had an affective disorder. The response to treatment, despite increased illness, was about the same as for similar treatment of younger persons.[9,10] They found in their sample that about three fourths of the patients lived at home with a spouse and had many resources to call upon for support.

III. ALTERED SUSCEPTIBILITY TO ORGAN DAMAGE IN THE ELDERLY

A change in susceptibility to organ damage with age has been documented for alcoholism but can be expected to be true as well for other toxic materials that may be abused. Chapter 17 reviewed medical and neurological diseases encountered in alcoholics. As part of this review, Figure 11 illustrated an increased prevalence of central nervous system disorders among older patients. In these studies, 31% of alcoholics aged 20 to 40 entering detoxification treatment had CNS damage, well below the 44% with liver injury. In patients over age 60, 72% had CNS disorders and 57% had liver injury. This assumes even more significance when alcohol consumption at various ages is examined. A study of a subset of the above population indicated that alcohol consumption decreased on the average by 1% for each year over age 40 to 50 years, when the highest intakes occurred.[11]

It seemed a clear conclusion that the central nervous system is more susceptible at least to alcohol injury in older people. From animal studies of alcohol injury, it is clear that the effects of alcohol and aging are additive, but similar studies do not exist for humans. Changes in patterns of drug reactions are observed with aging, with a wider variety and a higher incidence in older persons.[12] The central nervous system disorders have recently been reviewed. The central nervous system disorders from substance abuse need particular efforts at recognition by general and geriatric physicians because of their reversibility.[13] A recent study used positron emission tomography to compare the regional glucose consumption in the brain in a group of newly abstinent chronic alcoholics free of Korsakoff's psychosis. The alcoholics showed a greater variation from region to region in glucose utilization, with many showing regions that were very low; this variability may help explain some of the CNS changes in alcoholics.[14] Increased sensitivity to drugs or alcohol in older persons may produce a great deal of confusion and mimic other conditions. One of the most reversible forms is that induced by low levels of drugs or alcohol, sometimes taken with a view of helping the patient. An excellent review has presented the problems of differential diagnosis.[15] Geriatric evaluation units find substance abuse or drugs to be the basis of these problems in 10 to 15% of all patients undergoing evaluation. Although the reversibility may be dramatic in a few patients, there has been no systematic study of either the exact frequency of this problem or the reversibility. It is simply one of those things that occasionally is of benefit.

In addition to CNS disease, liver disease and malnutrition were more prevalent in elderly alcoholics, even though they use on the average substantially less alcohol.[11] Malnutrition arises because of the displacement of more nutritious food by alcohol. This is usually manifest in very subtle ways with specific nutrients. Folate deficiency with anemia and elevated MCV is common, but vitamin A, pyridoxine, or thiamin deficiency may be predominant. A blood test for alcohol when the patient attends an outpatient visit is a useful way to confirm or rule out the diagnosis of there is patient denial about the problem. Liver disease seems to occur more readily in the elderly. There are no unusual features in this age group.

IV. THE CHRONIC ADDICT REACHING THE ELDERLY YEARS

The natural history of addictions is that they tend to diminish with increasing age. Thus, in a classical study of New York heroin addicts, the majority who survived 20 years had given up their addiction.[16] A further factor is that practicing addicts have a shortened survival time whenever studied, regardless of the age of onset. Traumatic deaths associated with increased risk taking, suicide, and the known complications of the particular substance chosen account for the majority of deaths. These two factors contribute to the infrequent occurrence of aged chronic addicts. In a study of ours,[5] we found that the majority of alcoholics identified over age 60 had their onset in the most recent 5 years, and this fraction was even higher with each additional decade of aging.

Occasional or even heavy users throughout adult life who never pass the threshold of abuse are common among the elderly who drink, particularly among the affluent. An alcohol "high" has been enjoyed for many years and is continued. Certainly drinking is enjoyed by the elderly, even though the group as a whole are more abstinent, consumption falls on the average, and regular drinkers drink less and less as they age. In this group, who continue to drink at about the same level as in their younger years, problems arise from the health effects of alcohol that were simply absent in the patients' earlier experience. It is impossible to delineate the prevalence, but I have identified falls, confusion, and new signs of alcoholic cirrhosis in this group without evidence that the drinking level has changed. By analogy I suppose that the increased susceptibility of the central nervous system to sedation would lead to prescription drugs producing similar problems. Certainly the epidemiology of falls in the elderly has identified sedative drugs as a problem.[17]

V. CHRONIC ADDICTION-CAUSED DISEASES IN OLDER PATIENTS WHO HAVE CONTINUED OR STOPPED ABUSE

Modest numbers of abusing patients acquire cirrhosis, organic mental disorders, cerebellar disease, or other conditions during abusing periods of their life and continue to live in their invalid state, most often by diminishing substance intake or becoming abstinent. As the ravages of age interact with a chronic disease there is often further incapacity, which brings such patients to medical attention. All of us deal with chronic emphysema initiated by cigarette smoking but getting worse with aging and are familiar with the problem.

The cirrhotic who reaches advanced years usually has good liver reserve, but bleeding esophageal varices or ascites may have had their onset decades after the diagnosis of cirrhosis was made either from alcohol use or acquired hepatitis. There are no unusual features in the management of such patients.

A more baffling problem is the organic mental disorders that may result from intense exposure to any agent. Organic brain syndromes resulting from LSD use or even vapor sniffing, Wernicke-Korsakoff syndrome from use of alcohol, or other forms of dementia caused by addictions may be well compensated for during the younger years but become a problem later. These syndromes are almost indistinguishable from Alzheimer's disease or multiple cerebral vascular accidents, and show little or no response to treatment. Only that infrequent person who continues substance abuse will respond to removal of the CNS-active drug.

VI. RECURRENT ADDICTION IN THE ELDERLY YEARS

Although addicts may relapse at any time in their lives, this problem is strikingly diminished after several years of abstinence. The elderly have many problems of loss of power over self and loneliness that require adjustment and produce stress. Retirement, with

TABLE 79
Factors that Increase Alcohol Use and Abuse in the Elderly

1. Situational
   - (a) Boredom
   - (b) Loneliness
   - (c) Loss of spouse or companion
   - (d) Anxiety over money, violence
2. Health related
   - (a) Loss of chewing ability
   - (b) Discomfort, inability to sleep
   - (c) Anxiety over cancer, loss of mobility
   - (d) Chronic pain

its loss of income and activity, loss of importance, failing health, and loss of companionship through death or relocation all contribute to stresses that may precipitate a return to substance abuse. However, addicted persons are much more apt to return to alcohol or abuse new agents supplied by physicians than to return to street drugs. This reflects that addicts readily abuse other agents. Even if street drugs were once abused, they are infrequently used in the twilight years, possibly because of increased costs and problems of supply. The abused substances are almost always alcohol, prescription drugs, or over-the-counter medications. A recent review addressed this problem in women. The reviewers felt that physicians were much more willing to give women prescriptions sedatives, psychotropics, and tranquilizers than they were men, and that this practice accounted for a substantial fraction of the abuse.[18] The management of recurrent addictions is little different than the management of new ones in the elderly.

VII. NEW ONSET OF ALCOHOLISM IN THE ELDERLY

The ready availability of alcohol makes it by far the most common substance of new abuse in the elderly. Table 79 lists some of the recognized problems associated with the increased use of alcohol in former drinkers.

As at other ages, no one knows why alcoholism begins, but the side effects of heavy drinking are much more marked in older persons. In most of the patients that we have studied with new onset alcoholism in the elderly years, major loss of family, independence, or health have been prominent. Alcohol abuse can occur at far lower levels of alcohol intake in the elderly, and can be readily concealed from the doctor and the family particularly when the patient lives apart from them.[19] Recognition may come from evaluation of a health problem, from apparent neglect of self leading to the consultation, or from a suspicious person evaluating minor nutritional markers, liver function test abnormalities, or an elevated MCV on the hematological profile.

As with other abusers, detoxification is necessary and can usually be readily accomplished on an outpatient basis if there is someone at home with the patient or they can move to the care of a friend or child for a week or two.

VIII. ABUSE OF PRESCRIPTION AND OVER-THE-COUNTER MEDICATIONS

A consciousness of side effects of drugs, particularly those with behavioral effects, and careful records on what has been prescribed and how often renewals have been given are essential to recognizing abuse of prescription and over-the-counter drugs in ones own patients. Since the elderly take many medications, often are under the care of several different physicians each of whom prescribes, the setting for abuse is obvious. Studies of drug abuse in nursing homes have addressed the unusual side effects. If we keep an index of suspicion of drugs when we evaluate patients with lethargy, clumsiness, forgetfulness, and erratic behavior, and carefully ask about what is being taken, it is usually possible to sort out these kinds of difficulties.[20] A workshop has recently made specific recommendations for all physicians in an effort to avoid this problem.[21] A particular problem of sedative use in the elderly is the increased likelihood of falls with resulting fractures.

IX. TREATMENT

Loneliness and loss of power over self due to loss of mobility, income, companionship, and sometimes health are problems that must be addressed in the elderly abuser. Since the abuse is nearly always alcohol or physician-given medications or over-the-counter ones, addressing the issue with family and friends and treating doctors will assist. A recent review addressed use of community resources such as Meals on Wheels, Golden Age clubs, and Eating Together programs.[4] In a comparison of treatment outcome in alcoholics, we found that older persons were more often sober after 3 and 6 months than younger persons (both groups encountered through entry into a detoxification unit). Many programs available to the elderly, such as Eating Together and Meals on Wheels, carry with them socialization that cannot be as readily attained by younger persons.

REFERENCES

1. **Anderson, K. E.,** Nutritional effects on hepatic drug metabolism in the elderly, in *Nutrition and Aging,* Prinsley, D. M. and Sandstead, H. H., Eds., Alan Liss, New York, 1989, 263.
2. **Vestal, R. E. and Dawson, G. W.,** Pharmacology and aging, in *Handbook of the Biology of Aging,* 2nd ed., Finch, C. E., Schneider E. L., et al, Eds., Van Nostrand Reinhold, New York, 1985, 744.
3. **Vestal, R. E., McQuire, E. A., Tobin, J. D., Andres, R., Norris, A. H., and Mezey, E.,** Aging and ethanol metabolism, *Clin. Pharm. Ther.,* 21, 343, 1977.
4. **Olsen-Noll, C. G. and Bosworth, M. F.,** Alcohol abuse in the elderly, *Am. Family Physician,* 39, 173, 1989.
5. **Finch, C. E. and Schneider, E. L., Eds.,** *Handbook of the Biology of Aging,* 2nd ed., Van Nostrand-Rheinold, New York, 1985.
6. **McGandy, R. B., Russell, R. M., Hartz, S. C., et al.,** Nutritional status survey of healthy noninstitutionalized elderly: energy and nutrient intakes from three-day diet records and nutrient supplements, *Nutr. Res.,* 6, 785, 1986.
7. **Smart, R. G., et al.,** Alcohol and drug use among the elderly, trends in use and characteristics of users, *Can. J. Public Health,* 79, 236, 1988.
8. **Iber, F. L.,** Alcoholism and associated malnutrition in the elderly, in *Nutrition and Aging,* Prinsley, D. M. and Sandstead, H. H., Eds., Alan R. Liss, New York, 157.
9. **Hurt, R. D., Finlayson, R. E., Morse, R. M., and Davies, J. L.,** Alcoholism in elderly persons, medical aspects and prognosis of 216 patients, *Mayo Clin. Proc.,* 63, 753, 1988.
10. **Finlayson, R. E., Hurt, R. D., Davies, J. L., and Morse, R. M.,** Alcoholism in elderly persons, a study of the psychiatric and psychosocial features of 216 inpatients, *Mayo Clin. Proc.,* 63, 761, 1988.
11. **Iber, F. L.,** The elderly alcoholic, in *Nutrition and Aging,* Hutchinson, M. I. and Munro, H., Eds., Bristol Myers Symposium, Academic Press, New York, 1986, 169.
12. **Roe, D. A.,** Drug effects on nutrient absorption, transport and metabolism, *Drug-Nutrient Interactions,* 4, 117, 1985.
13. **Willingbring, M. L.,** Organic mental disorders associated with heavy drinking and alcohol dependence, *Clin. Geriatr. Med.,* 4, 869, 1988.
14. **Sachs, H., Russell, J. A., Christman, D. R., and Cook, B.,** Alteration of regional cerebral glucose metabolic rate in non-Korsakoff chronic alcoholism, *Arch. Neurol.,* 44, 1242, 1987.
15. **Lipowski, Z. J.,** Delirium in the elderly patient, *New Engl. J. Med.* 320, 578, 1989.
16. **Vaillant, G. E.,** A 20-year follow-up of New York narcotic addicts, *Arch. Gen. Psychiatr.,* 29, 237, 1981.
17. **Ray, W. A. and Griffin, M. R.,** Benzodiazepines of long and short elimination half-life and the risk of hip fracture, *JAMA,* 262, 3303, 1989.

18. **Matteo, S.,** The risk of multiple addictions, guidelines for assessing a woman's alcohol and drug use, *West. J. Med.*, 149, 741, 1988.
19. **Atkinson, R. M.,** Alcohol problems of the elderly, *Alcohol and Alcoholism,* 22, 415, 1987.
20. **Abrams, R. C. and Alexopoulos, G. S.,** Substance abuse in the elderly, alcohol and prescription drugs, *Hospital and Community Psychiatr.*, 38, 1285, 1987.
21. Anonymous, Surgeon General's workshop on health promotion and aging, summary recommendations on the medication working group, *MMWR,* 38, 605, 1989; abstracted in *JAMA,* 262, 1755, 1989.

Chapter 40

Ethnic and Special Social Groups

I. INTRODUCTION

Different ethnic groups have major differences in their social makeup and values that to a major degree must be understood in evaluating and treating substance abuse. This is of substantial importance in evaluating patterns of substance abuse and tolerance of the abuse in the developmental stages. It is also important in using the family and the community to rally to the assistance of the abuser when rehabilitation is underway. This chapter is not meant to be complete but only to indicate something of the variation among groups and how this may influence outcome. Issues that arise in various cultures are listed in Table 80.

Examples of each of these issues will emerge below. Ethnic or cultural ties vary from total integration to total alienation, but this presentation will carry the assumption that some integration remains. Variation in regional use of drugs is well discussed by Arif and Westermeyer;[1] Cahalan[2] provides a wealth of data on national drinking practices in various regions, sizes of cities, and ethnic groups. We will present generalizations that are always at risk of being incorrect, but many references will be provided to allow further reading. There are now many studies on substance abuse comparing "old country" or "traditional" ethnic groups living in America with similar families still residing in the old country; and both groups often act in marked contrast to the new generation who are combining characteristics of the old along with their assimilation into America. Those groups which have been studied are listed in Table 81.

TABLE 80
Issues in Drug Use and Treatment That Vary Materially Among Groups

I. Role models and initial use
  A. Use in parents, older siblings
    1. Male versus female use
  B. Tolerance of certain drugs, complete avoidance of others
  C. Cultural view on self-control, drunkenness
  D. Size of "family" discussing personal problems
II. Issues altering early intoxication and abuse
  A. Authority of family matriarch or patriarch
  B. Importance of individualism versus conformity
  C. Traditional family control of money, recreation
  D. Cultural support systems for crisis intervention
III. Issues in treatment
  A. Networking in the greater family and ethnic community
  B. Acceptance of "strangers" as helpers
  C. Traditional acceptance of nonfamily assistance
  D. Openness in discussing problems outside family group
  E. Use of cultural traditions to enhance and reinforce recovery
  F. Use of unique cultural resources

TABLE 81
Ethnic Groups in America for Which Substantial Study of Response to Addictions Exists

1. Native Americans on reservations and in cities
2. Blacks
3. Latin Americans, east coast and west coast
4. Irish in America, Irish in Ireland
5. Orientals in America and in Hawaii
6. Italians in America and in Italy
7. Jews
8. Scandinavians in America and in Scandinavia
9. Slavic peoples
10. French in Canada, the U.S., and France

II. ISSUES COMMON TO MANY AMERICAN ETHNIC GROUPS

A. SITE OF RESIDENCE, SIZE OF ETHNIC CONCLAVE

Hispanics from the Caribbean and Central America residing in New York City may enter a group of like people so large that the requirement even to learn English may be modest and the cultural habits in their native land may be continued without much change. A Jamaican family living in Middletown, Ohio, on the other hand, may be required to live with Midwestern people, eat foods commonly available at that location, and adjust to Heartland habits and standards. The community in which a family lives and works and its provision and tolerance of the former culture, the availability of ethnic foods and supplies, and the types of co-workers are important issues in determining whether the abuse pattern is ethnic or American.

B. TYPE OF EMPLOYMENT

A Latin American or Asian physician, fully trained, possibly at least partly in America, who emigrates with family to a practice opportunity with predominantly native-born Americans is totally different from a refugee Vietnamese, or an illegal Mexican immigrant living with countrymen and performing an unskilled and poorly paid job in gardening. The latter are exposed to the frustrations of want in the land of plenty, are frequent victims of prejudice and violence, and are exposed to a sordid side of American housing, social and health services, and a heavy acquaintance with drug culture.

C. INNER-CITY POVERTY

In metropolitan areas the new immigrant, by reason of economic necessity, often lives, works, and interacts with people and places that are poor, run down, and heavily infested with drug abuse culture. These influences are visible and may be prominent, particularly in adolescents as they are exposed to two cultures.

III. NATIVE AMERICANS

Western Native American tribes have included peyote use in ritual for centuries. When alcohol was introduced to Native Americans by Europeans, the intensity of intoxication and the deep and recurrent inebriation was an early problem that made it illegal for a time to give an Indian alcohol. This problem continues in metropolitan areas where drinking to advanced drunkenness mimics that of Russians in the USSR. In a study of Minnesota Native Americans, high cultural affiliation diminished the severity of alcoholism and was associated with increased recovery, whereas lapse in close cultural relationship with tribe and relatives was associated with more severe drinking and less recovery.[3] This is reasonable because without a tribal relationship many American city dwellers develop anger and alienation.

A study of survival after the development of alcoholic liver disease found that Native Americans died more quickly than Caucasian or Black Americans, but at a rate similar to Puerto Rico Hispanics.[4] A group that looked at differences in alcohol-related mortality among tribes in Oklahoma found that 9% of Native American deaths were alcohol related, a much higher rate than among Blacks or Caucasians, and that there were substantial differences among tribes. Tolerance of drunkenness was offered as a possible explanation.[5] Surveillance of seventh graders found that American Indian adolescents living on reservations used far more drugs than similar-aged members of other ethnic groups. The reasons for this and intervention strategies have been discussed but not yet confirmed.[6] Similarly, in Washington state, the use of snuff and chewing tobacco was much higher among Native Americans than among others, based upon surveys of public schools. In this study 79% of Native Americans under age 12 used these products at least weekly.[7] A problem of inhalant use in very young reservation Indian youth was noted, with the predisposing factors clearly identified by the fourth grade.[8]

Consumption of illicit forms of alcohol by Native Americans was studied.[9] Use of features of tribal tradition in alcoholism treatment was evaluated by Hall.[10] The programs used by the Indian Health Service in treating alcoholism was presented in some detail and discussed, including not only traditional treatment programs but a very active program in prevention beginning in the early grades of school. This paper makes clear that treatment values established for other groups are quite effective with Native Americans and Native Alaskans.[11] This cursory review indicates that substance abuse begins at an earlier age in Native Americans than in most other populations. The prevalence and intensity of addictions, when studied in comparison with other ethnic groups, seems higher and much more intense. The disease profile may well be more severe, but treatment programs are quite similar. Use of unique features of the Indian culture assists in keeping people in treatment.

IV. BLACKS

The traditional Black American family has close family ties and is highly religious. This continues in smaller towns, but broken families and single-parent (almost always the mother) homes are very common in metropolitan areas. There is often a very strong mother figure in poorer families. Racism and discrimination are continuing important issues to all family members. Black fathers are more important in families than comparable white fathers. Talk-oriented therapy is not nearly as effective as highly structured therapy using examples, play-acting, or groups.[12]

Drinking patterns in Black youth followed the same predictors as in other populations, with great emphasis on what their friends and associates were doing and what was tolerated by their parents and teachers. In most parts of America the use of alcohol was lower than for other ethnic groups.[13] In a survey of high school drinking and drug use throughout New York State, Blacks and Orientals were less likely to be using either drugs or alcohol than Whites or Hispanics. This was most marked in cities of 150,000 or less in population but was present in all samples. Large-city exposure to heroin and cocaine led to more sampling in all groups, but in all the prevalance was highest among Whites and Hispanics.[14] In a study of different ethnic groups reaching treatment facilities, it was found that Blacks had the least network of helpers among family, employers, and friends, and that Blacks were the most likely to be referred to self-help agencies for therapy.[15] In a multicity evaluation of alcohol and drug abuse among Whites, Hispanics, and Blacks, all groups were similar at ages 21 to 30, with more Blacks being abstinent of both drugs and alcohol than the other two groups. Blacks and Hispanics were similar in greater use of heroin and heroin together with other drugs than were Whites. Blacks were found to be the most likely to need but not receive treatment.[16] Blacks with cirrhosis survived longer than Whites or Hispanics.[4] Different patterns of public and private alcohol consumption were observed when contrasting Blacks, Whites, and Hispanics. Blacks were the most likely to drink in parks, on the street, and in parking lots, and those drinking in those places were among the most heavy consumers. Whites were much more likely to drink in bars and restaurants. For all groups, young single men had the highest rate of drinking and drunkenness.[17]

Treatment seems similar in Blacks and other groups.[18] The use of Black therapists has been discussed.[19] My conclusions for Blacks indicate that close family ties are more likely to prevent early use and abuse than in other ethnic groups in America, but broken families, alienation, and poverty are the great producers of the Black addictions that are prominent in the public eye. Response to treatment seems greater when the program includes specific actions rather than being limited to groups or limited to discussion.

V. HISPANICS

Two somewhat separate cultural migrations in the U.S. are represented by the Hispanics of the Southwest, largely of Mexican origin, and those of the East Coast area from Florida to Boston, who are largely of Caribbean and Central American origin. In both groups the immigration waves are recent, with the entry of large numbers of people into low-paying jobs, and many are still at or below the poverty line. Thus Hispanics appear prominently in the inner-city drug culture and among derelict or street alcoholics. As a part of this large-city poverty existence, attitudes of rebellion as marked by surveys in grade school indicate increased substance use.

The epidemic use of cocaine, arising mostly in Columbia and passing through Mexico, has involved many Hispanics in the provision and street selling of this drug. There can be little question that this further encourages use in this ethnic group.

In America, the rosters of most severe problems produced by drugs and alcohol — cirrhosis, brain injury, injured children born of using mothers, and AIDS — contain a disproportionately high number of Hispanics.[20] One study reported more severe liver disease in Hispanics,[4] but this was not verified in another.[21] In a study conducted in New York, the most severe drinking patterns and the most brain damage was encountered in Hispanics of Puerto Rican extraction.[15] A study of Western Hispanics on methadone maintenance found that Chicano addicts did strikingly less well in the program than Anglos, despite better family support.[22]

Studies from California suggest that the Mexican-derived Hispanics are highly family oriented and committed to the larger family, and those reaching adulthood in Mexico before immigration have values that infrequently get them into street drugs. Alcoholism, however, is common among the men, but not among the older women. Younger Hispanics growing up in America reflect the peer values in the regions where they live. In San Diego and Los Angeles there are marked similarities to Hispanics in New York City. A persistent finding among Hispanics on both coasts was that alcohol use sufficient to produce health problems or arrests was not recognized as a problem as often as among Caucasians.[16]

The differences found in Hispanic youth in large cities are generally held to be more related to poverty and inner-city gang culture rather than being related directly to Hispanic culture.[23] To generalize, poverty and broken families, as among Blacks, play a major role in the development and severity of addictions. There is a tolerance of drug use even in American-based Hispanic families that is higher than in most other ethnic groups; there is also a belief that drug use and drunkenness is "macho" and therefore too often mimicked by male youth.

VI. RECENT-ORIGIN EUROPEAN CULTURES

A. IRISH

The Irish in both Ireland and in America have tolerated male drunkenness and almost considered it manly. It certainly has been an accepted escape from the harshness of life, leading many families to be highly matriarchal. This is clearly seen in the drinking patterns in the U.S. Curiously, female drunkenness is not tolerated in Irish culture. Vaillant, in his core-city men, did not find Irish-Americans drinking at an earlier age, but he did find them having far more (threefold) alcohol-related problems and eightfold more alcoholism than Boston residents born of immigrant Mediterranean parents. He felt that tolerance of drinking and drunkenness accounted for the difference.[24] In considering problems of American Irish in treatment[25,26] a high mistrust of strangers, and a tradition of hiding family secrets and treating frequent drinking as a family weakness not to be revealed, are common. Families are not assertive and rarely allow the therapist to know about discomfort or even improvement. They often comply with the therapist without changing. As a group, they rarely seek treatment, abused spouses seldom complain, and treatment is more often court or society mandated. The families often are matriarchal.[27,28]

B. GREEKS AND ITALIANS

Italian-American families,[29] in common with Greek-American families, give great importance to the extended family. They talk freely and reveal problems within the larger family but are reluctant to do so with outsiders. The therapist is a distrusted outsider and will undergo a series of tests of loyalty and skills before he or she can be helpful. Multiple family groups have been valuable in therapy.[30,31] These families provide careful instruction in responsibility about drinking, whether at home or in public, emphasizing personal responsibility. This has a great deal to do with the lack of street drug use among recently immigrated Mediterranean families, and abuse of alcohol or other substances is infrequent. Immigrant Italian familes have almost no alcohol problem until the second generation born in America, when family traditions have become weakened.[32]

C. OTHER EUROPEANS

Russians in Europe or in America are much heavier consumers of alcohol than most other groups, and all of the adverse problems of the alcoholic are more common in the

USSR. Drinking to the point of manifest intoxication is still a prominent feature of Russians in both Europe and America, and the net result is that the average alcoholic of Russian extraction consumes almost twice as much alcohol as his American drinking companion of non-Russian extraction.[33] French Canadians have been contrasted with European French in their drinking habits.[34]

D. JEWISH AMERICANS

Strong families with an excellent sense of family democracy and consensual decision making characterizes Jewish-American groups.[35] As families they value education credentials and careful, clear explanations to the entire family. They enter as a family into far more therapeutic decisions and prefer complex sophisticated interventions more than other groups. They are articulate and freely express their views.[36]

VII. ASIAN-AMERICANS

Family ties are quite close among recently immigrated Asians, and though recreational opiates are tolerated, alcohol and other street drugs are infrequently used when the original family ties are strong. In the next generation many of the same problems observed in other Americans are experienced, but a well-developed work ethic remains a distinguishing feature of nearly all Asians. There is a limited literature on these groups, mostly from the West Coast and Hawaii.[37,38] One study noted the dichotomy between the heavy drinking of young Asian-American men and the almost complete lack of drinking by their sisters.[39] The influence of Americans on cultural changes in Laos has been studied, indicating that the young of various Asian groups respond differently.[40] A study of drinking behavior among three different Asian groups in Los Angeles has recently appeared, with the Japanese-extracted Asians drinking much more heavily than the Koreans, and they in turn more than the Chinese.[41]

VIII. USEFULNESS OF ETHNIC INFORMATION

There is now a substantial literature on most of the major groups found in America and their handling of substance abuse. In the chapters on therapy it has been made clear that remaining in contact with some form of support system, one that the client will accept, is the single most important part of therapy, and this can be most important for people who believe they are different by reason of their ethnic background. Occasionally another person with the same background can reach them better than all others. Each person undertaking therapy needs to understand the more common differences of ethnicity present in their clientele in order to be a better therapist.

Differences in use patterns helps one understand whether the family and friends will be supportive or destructive to abstinence. Knowing something of the attitudes toward the addictions directs the therapist toward what can be problems that must be dealt with or resources that can assist in recovery.

There is a substantial literature supporting the view that therapists from the same cultural and ethnic group, when everything else is equal, are in fact better.

REFERENCES

1. **Arif, A. and Westermeyer, J.,** *Manual of Drug and Alcohol Abuse, Guidelines for Teaching in Medical and Health Institutions,* Plenum Medical Publishers, New York, 1988.
2. **Cahalan, D.,** *Problem Drinkers, A National Survey,* Jossey-Bass, San Francisco, 1970.

3. **Westermeyer, J. and Neider, J.,** Cultural affiliation among American Indian alcoholics, correlations and change over a ten-year period, *Ann. N.Y. Acad. Sci.*, 472, 179, 1986.
4. **Mendenhall, C. L., Gartside, P. S., Roselle, G. A., Grossman, C. J., Weesner, R. E., and Chedid, A.,** Longevity among ethnic groups in alcoholic liver disease, *Alcohol and Alcoholism,* 24, 11, 1989.
5. **Christian, C. M., Dufour, M., and Bertolucci, D.,** Differential alcohol-related mortality among American Indian tribes in Oklahoma 1968—1978, *Social Sci. and Med.*, 28, 275, 1989.
6. **Beauvais, F., Detting, E. R., Wolf, W., and Edwards, R. W.,** American Indian youth and drugs 1986—1987, a continuing problem, *Am. J. Public Health,* 79, 634, 1989.
7. **Schinke, S. P., Schilling, R. F., Gilchrist, L. D., Ashby, M. R., and Kitajima, E.,** Native youth and smokeless tobacco, prevalence rates, gender differences, and descriptive characteristics, *NCI Monogr.*, 8, 39, 1989.
8. **Beauvaise, F. and Oetting, E. R.,** Indian youth and inhalants, an update, *NIDA Res. Monogr.*, 85, 34, 1988.
9. **Burd, L., Shea, T. E., and Knull, H.,** "Montana gin", ingestion of commercial products containing denatured alcohol among native Americans, *J. Stud. Alcohol,* 48, 388, 1987.
10. **Hall, R. L.,** Alcohol treatment in American Indian populations, an indigenous treatment modality compared with traditional approaches, *Ann. N.Y. Acad. Sci.*, 472, 168, 1986.
11. **Rhoades, E. R., Mason, R. D., Eddy, P., Smith, E. M., and Burns, T. R.,** The Indian Health Service approach to alcoholism among American Indians and Alaska Natives, *Public Health Rep.*, 103, 621, 1988.
12. **Kaufman, E. and Pattison, E. M.,** Differential methods of family therapy in the treatment of alcoholism, *J. Stud. Alcohol,* 42, 951, 1981.
13. **Harford, T. C.,** Drinking patterns among Black and nonblack adolescents, results of a national survey, *Ann. N.Y. Acad. Sci.*, 472, 130, 1986.
14. **Welte, J. W. and Barnes, G. M.,** Alcohol use among adolescent minority groups, *J. Stud. Alcohol,* 48, 329, 1987.
15. **Babor, T. F. and Mendelson, J. H.,** Ethnic/religious differences in the manifestation and treatment of alcoholism, *Ann. N.Y. Acad. Sci.*, 472, 46, 1986.
16. **Hubbard, R. L., Schlenger, W. E., Rachal, J. V., Bray, R. M., Craddock, S. G., Cavanaugh, E. R., and Ginzburg, H. M.,** Patterns of alcohol and drug abuse in drug treatment clients from different ethnic backgrounds, *Ann. N.Y. Acad. Sci.*, 472, 60, 1986.
17. **Caetano, R., Herd, D.,** Drinking in different social contexts among white black and Hispanic men, *Yale J. Bio. Med.*, 61, 243, 1988.
18. **Iber, F. L.,** Treatment and recovery in alcoholism, contrast between results in white men and those in special populations, *Ann. N.Y. Acad. Sci.*, 472, 189, 1986.
19. **Thornton, C. I. and Carter, J. H.,** Treating the black female alcoholic, clinical observations of black therapists, *J. Natl. Med. Assoc.*, 80, 644, 1988.
20. **Schilling, R. F., Schinke, S. P., Nichols, S. E., Zayas, L. H., Miller, S. O., Orlandi, M. A., and Botvin, G. J.,** Developing strategies for AIDS prevention research with black and Hispanic drug users, *Public Health Rep.*, 104, 2, 1989.
21. **Smith, S. M. and Hoy, W. E.,** Frequent association of mesangial glomerulonephritis and alcohol abuse, a study of three ethnic groups, *Mod. Pathol.*, 2, 138, 1989.
22. **Anglin, M. D., Booth, M. W., Ryan, T. M., and Hser, Y. I.,** Ethnic differences in narcotic addiction II, Chicano and Anglo addiction career patterns, *Int. J. Addictions,* 23, 1011, 1988.
23. **Panitz, D. R., McConchie, S., Sauber, S. R., and Fonseca, J. A.,** The role of machismo and the Hispanic family in the etiology and treatment of alcoholism in Hispanic American males, *Am. J. Family Ther.*, 11, 31, 1983.
24. **Vaillant, G.,** *The Natural History of Alcoholism,* Harvard University Press, Cambridge, MA, 1982.
25. **McGoldrick, M.,** Normal families, an ethnic perspective, in *Normal Family Processes,* Walsh, F., Ed., Guilford Press, New York, 1982.
26. **McGoldrick, M.,** Irish families, in *Ethnicity and Family Therapy,* McGoldfick, M., Pearce, J. K., and Giordano, J., Eds., Guilford Press, New York, 1982.
27. **Bales, R. F.,** Attitudes toward drinking in the Irish culture, in *Society Culture, and Drinking Patterns,* Pittman, D. J. and Snyder, C. R., Eds., John Wiley & Sons, New York, 1962.
28. **Stivers, R.,** *A Hair of the Dog, Irish Drinking and American Stereotype,* Pennsylvania State University Press, University Park, PA, 1976.
29. **Lolli, G.,** The use of wine and other alcoholic beverages by a group of Italians and Americans of Italian extraction, *Q. J. Stud. Alcohol.*, 13, 27, 1952.
30. **Kaufman, E. and Kaufman, P.,** *Family Therapy of Drug and Alcohol Abuse,* Gardner Press, New York, 1979.
31. **Rotunno, M. and McGoldrick, M.,** Italian families, in *Ethnicity and Family Therapy,* McGoldrick, M., Pearce, J. K., and Giordano, J., Eds., Guilford Press, New York, 1982.

32. **Lolli, G., Serianni, E., Golder, G. M., and Luzzato-Fegiz, P.,** *Alcohol in Italian Culture: Food and Wine in Relation to Sobriety Among Italian and Italian Americans,* Rutgers Center for Alcohol Studies, New Brunswick, NJ, 1958.
33. **Segal, B. M.,** The Soviet heavy-drinking culture and the American heavy-drinking subculture, *Ann. N.Y. Acad. Sci.,* 472, 149, 1986.
34. **Babor, T. F., Hesselbrock, M., Radouco-Thomas, S., Feguer, L., Ferrant, J. P., and Choquette, K.,** Concepts of alcoholism among Americans, French-Canadian and French alcoholics, *Ann. N.Y. Acad. Sci.,* 472, 98, 1986.
35. **Herz, F. M. and Rosen, E. J.,** Jewish families, in *Ethnicity and Family Therapy,* McGoldrick, M., Pearce, J. K., and Giordano, J., Eds., Guilford Press, New York, 1982.
36. **Snyder, C. R.,** *Alcohol and the Jews, A Cultural Study of Drinking and Sobriety,* Rutgers Center of Alcohol Studies, New Brunswick, NJ, 1958.
37. **McLaughlin, D. S., Raymond, J. S., Murakami, S. R., and Goebert, D.,** Drug use among Asian Americans in Hawaii, *J. Psychoactive Drugs,* 19, 85, 1987.
38. **Sue, D.,** Use and abuse of alcohol by Asian Americans, *J. Psychoactive Drugs,* 19, 57, 1987.
39. **Welte, J. W. and Barnes, G. M.,** Alcohol use among adolescent minority groups, *J. Stud. Alcohol,* 48, 329, 1987.
40. **Westermeyer, J.,** Sex differences in drug and alcohol use among ethnic groups in Laos 1965—1975, *Am. J. Drug Alcohol Abuse,* 14, 443, 1988.
41. **Chi, I., Lubben, J. E., and Kitano, H. H.,** Differences in drinking behavior among three Asian-American groups, *J. Stud. Alcohol,* 50, 15, 1989.

Chapter 41

Substance Abuse Among Health Professionals

I. INTRODUCTION

Physicians, including medical students and residents, nurses, pharmacists, veterinarians, and dentists, have a higher prevalence of substance abuse than the population at large. This chapter is intended to assist in prevention, early recognition, and guidance to treatment of such problems.

A. RECOGNITION

The early recognition of substance abuse in health providers is an important goal, both to contain damage related to impaired judgment and to encourage therapy at an early stage. The key ingredients of any program are recognition through education of the possibility, confidential and nonpunitive evaluation to determine whether or not a problem exists, and supportive treatment under close supervision if a problem is found. People who deal with health workers, including colleagues, family, other professionals, and patients, need to be aware of systems once they are in place and of an orderly way in which the possibility of abuse can be reviewed without producing harm.

Model legislation has been developed in Georgia to allow professional groups (nurses, physicians, dentists, and others) to participate in the evaluation of possible abuse. In the best programs a well-publicized committee is available for evaluation of all complaints of possible substance abuse. The concern must arise from two different persons who identify themselves to the committee, but their identities remain anonymous in the committee's

TABLE 82
Indicators of Substance Abuse in Professionals

Behavior	Observers
1. Frequent use or intoxication	1. Colleagues, family
2. Uncharacteristic behavior	2. Staff, consultants
3. Missing substances, many times	3. Staff
4. Professional neglect	4. Consultants
5. Depression, suicide attempts	5. Family, personal M.D.
6. Pill or alcohol requirements for sleep or relaxation	6. Family, personal M.D.

private records. Two members of the committee then investigate the allegation, usually by a direct call upon the accused professional, and base their conclusions on this visit and possibly other inquiry following the visit. Their conclusions are first shared with the accused. If they find no evidence of abuse they tell the person this and enter the fact into their records to avoid further evaluation unless substantive new information appears. If they feel that abuse is present they outline with the abuser a program for recovery. This may include hospitalization for a time, attendance in a program for a time, taking a drug such as methadone or disulfiram, etc. Willingness to cooperate keeps the abuser from losing his or her license or the creation of open public records or an open hearing; failure to cooperate leads the reviewing committee to submit their findings to a disciplinary board for open hearings regarding licensure. Usually the lack of publicity is sufficiently attractive to assure cooperation. Some of the legal and administrative problems encountered in professional identification programs have been reviewed.[1,2]

The patterns of professional behavior that lead to recognition are noted in Table 82. The persons most likely to notice these behavior patterns are also indicated.

A 6-year study of residents' well-being was undertaken in Vancouver.[3] It was found that 14% of the house officers were impaired. Single women, chronically fatigued persons, and socially isolated persons were at the highest risk. Social deprivation and individual vulnerability, magnified by sleep deprivation, was the combination that produced the greatest risk for substance abuse. Another study of medical students found that abuse of drugs or alcohol correlated with history of previous drug use, use of tobacco, and missing classes.[4] A similar program at the Medical College of Wisconsin was a failure. Lack of careful planning in addressing legal, economic, and attitudinal problems was identified as the reason for failure.[5]

Recognition of abnormal patterns of substance use even in medical students is coming increasingly under study. One study of substance use in a population of medical students and physicians in training found that the medical group had slightly lower use rates than other age-matched populations. As in other populations, recreational drug use and drinking arose from sensation seeking, whereas therapeutic drug use was stress related and higher in the medical sample.[6] Another survey of drug and tobacco use in a Florida medical school found that lifetime and current use correlated, with higher use rates found in males, older students, and students who frequently missed classes. The use patterns had developed in high school and college and persisted. The study found that higher consumption of any recreational drug, including cigarettes and alcohol, predicted higher use of other recreational drugs.[4]

B. CAUSES

It is widely agreed that stress unrelieved by recreation is a setting that leads to use of drugs. The easily availability of drugs to professionals compared to others leads in part to this solution. A review of physicians in training suggested that as a group they used fewer drugs in high school and college as compared to the population at large, but that stress reduction contributed in a major way to increased use in medical school and during residency.[6] A review of hypothesized risk factors among physicians found an increase in access to drugs, family history of substance abuse, stress at work and home, emotional problems, and sensation seeking.[7]

C. PREVENTION

An educational program to foster early recognition is also of value in acquainting all of the helping professions with the potential high risk of their occupation with this problem. The increased numbers of group practices and sharing arrangements for solo practitioners, and the reduced hours-of-work requirements for residents, with more enforced recreation time, is of great benefit. Doctors, nurses, and others too frequently recognize the work-related stress that is common to health care but do not seek methods to alleviate it that they would readily recommend for their patients. Although nearly all training programs have access to free, excellent counseling and even prolonged treatment, these are underutilized. Two programs outlined the limitations of their prevention in young doctors due to budget and acceptance by their colleagues.[8,9] A primer for the substance abuse clinician has been published.[10]

II. TREATMENT AND RETURN TO PROFESSION

A. TREATMENT

Treatment results have been excellent, with at least 80% of the professionals recognized by substance abuse committees within the profession rehabilitated. A major portion of this success is the coercive aspects of treatment, which keep the person in both good programs and aftercare. The legal issues in coercing treatment have been discussed.[1] The importance of colleagues and the abuser's staff in treatment has been noted.[11,12]

B. SPECIAL PROBLEMS

A thoughtful paper points out the problems that formerly addicted physicians encounter upon reentry, particularly if they are applying for residency or hospital privileges.[13] The dilemma of such selections is between the desire to be fair and the statistical fact that former addicts are more prone to relapse than the population at large is to acquire the problem. Directors of hospitals and clinics are required for accreditation to obtain specific information on whether an applicant has been a substance abuser, and if the answer is positive require some documentation of treatment and cessation of the abuse. The application of these requirements and the protection of the rights of patients seem at times to be in conflict with the many antidiscrimination laws of the nation that protect the handicapped, but as yet there has not been a court case on this issue.

Recovering addicts are valuable adjuncts in therapy of abused substances. About half the successful candidates for Certification of Expert Training in Substance Abuse have had a background of personal abuse. These recovering persons bring a unique understanding to the treatment process. There are far more professional positions available in these fields than there are credentialed physicians to fill them. There is an excellent discussion of physicians in Alcoholics Anonymous which points out their role in helping one another.[14]

REFERENCES

1. **Angres, D. H. and Busch, K. A.,** The chemically dependent physician, clinical and legal considerations, *New Dir. Ment. Health Serv.,* 41, 21, 1989.
2. **Krizek, C. R.,** Addressing the problem of the impaired physician, *New Dir. Ment. Health Serv.,* 41, 11, 1989.
3. **Hurwitz, T. A., Beiser, M., Nichol, H., Patrick, L., and Kozak, J.,** Impaired interns and residents, *Can. J. Psychiatr,* 32, 165, 1987.
4. **Kory, W. P. and Crandall, L. A.,** Nonmedical drug use patterns among medical students, *Int. J. Addictions,* 19, 871, 1984.
5. **Lohr, K. M. and Engbring, N. H.,** Institution-wide program for impaired residents at a major teaching hospital, *J. Med. Educ.,* 63, 182, 1988.
6. **McAuliffe, W. E., Rohman, M., and Wechsler, H.,** Alcohol, substance use, and other risk-factors of impairment in a sample of physicians-in-training, *Adv. Alcohol Subst. Abuse,* 4, 67, 1984.
7. **McAuliffe, W. E., Santangelo, S., Magnuson, E., Sobol, A., Rohman, M., and Weissman, J.,** Risk factors of drug impairment in random samples of physicians and medical students, *Int. J. Addictions,* 22, 825, 1987.
8. **Lohr, K. M. and Engbring, N. H.,** Institution-wide program for impaired residents at a major teaching hospital, *J. Med. Educ.,* 63, 182, 1988.
9. **Kleber, H. D.,** The impaired physician, changes from the traditional view, *J. Substance Abuse Treatment,* 1, 137, 1984.
10. **Patrick, P. K.,** Self-preservation, A non-negotiable requirement for the substance abuse clinician, *J. Substance Abuse Treatment,* 1, 85, 1984.
11. **Clark, T. R.,** Hospital medical staff and the impaired or troubled physician, *N.C. Med. J.,* 44, 541, 1983.
12. **Twerski, A. J.,** You can help colleagues who have problems, *Legal Aspects Med. Pract.,* 8, 15, 1980.
13. **MacDonald, R. A., MacDonald, B. E.,** Alcoholism in residency program candidates, *J. Med. Educ.,* 57, 692, 1982.
14. **Anderson, C. T.,** Doctors in A.A., *American Medical News,* January 12, 1990, 33.

Glossary

Abstinent — Completely avoiding use of the formerly abused substance. The term does not apply to other substances unless specifically stated. Thus an alcohol abuser who no longer uses alcohol but who abuses diazepam is abstinent. The term sometimes refers to a person who by habit has never used a substance, but I prefer to call such a person, e.g., alcohol naive.

Abuse — Usually used, as drug or agent abuse. Regular use of an agent sufficient to produce a problem of health, relations with the law, or social functioning. A person using a drug in private is considered an abuser. Once the criterion of abuse is reached, the person is considered to be forever an abuser. Active abuse emphasizes current use of the abused substance. I do not limit the term abuse to use insufficient to develop tolerance or withdrawal. Use of an illicit substance does not constitute abuse. The thin line separating use from abuse is usually ill defined and varies with the beholder.

Addict — A regular user of a substance; tolerance may be present or unknown. Usually not used to refer to alcohol use or use of other legal substances.

Addiction — Heavy use of a drug sufficient to produce tolerance or withdrawal. This is synonymous with drug dependency.

Agent — The psychoactive substance being heavily used or abused. Approximately 20% of the time, there may be more than one agent.

Binge — A prolonged episode of intense use of a drug or alcohol. It may follow abstinence, or may simply be marked intensification of the pattern of use.

Blackout — A period of amnesia during or following drug use. It is most common in alcoholism and usually lasts for a few hours. The absence of memory is vividly recalled and is often quite frightening. It indicates brain damage.

Chronic brain syndrome — Loss of central nervous system function as determined by cortical atrophy on CT scanning or psychological testing lasting weeks. May be largely reversible.

Craving — An extreme longing for the effects of a drug or alcohol. Almost impossible to measure or quantitate objectively and distinct from withdrawal.
Cross tolerance — Tolerance for one drug resulting in tolerance for the second agent, even though the person may have had no previous exposure to the second agent.
Delirium — A mental disturbance characterized by illusions, hallucinations, delusions, excitement often progressing to the point of incoherence. The course is usually less than 3 days.
Delirium tremens — An acute mental disturbance with delirium. Agitation and visual or auditory hallucinations are nearly always present, followed by confusion. It almost never persists more than 8 days and is most frequent after alcohol or sedative abuse.
Delusion — A false belief that cannot be corrected by persuasion, reason, or even the patient's own senses.
Dependence — Use of an agent to the point of tolerance. The increased dose and the anticipation of withdrawal continues the habit. Used interchangeably with addiction.
Designer drug — Illicit drugs synthesized similar but not identical in structure to known opiates or amphetamines in order to avoid some of the legal entanglements of manufacturing and selling defined illegal drugs.
Detoxification — The process of treating a patient for drug removal, withdrawal, and repair of the clear nutritional and health deficits that respond in a few weeks. The term is much more inclusive than withdrawal.
Drink — A user's portion of alcohol, most often a customary portion usually containing 8 to 20 g of alcohol.
Drug — Any substance of abuse, usually excluding alcohol and inhalants but sometimes including these also. The term applies to both illicit and legally obtained agents.
Drug abuse — see abuse. To be distinguished from drug use.
Drug dependence — Chronic drug use sufficient to produce tolerance or withdrawal syndrome, usually associated with heavy use. To be distinguished from drug abuse. This term is synonymous with addiction.
Dry — Slang term referring to the absence of alcohol intake for a specified period of time. Occasionally used by analogy for other addictions. More often the word "clean" is used for a substance-free person when the abused substance is other than alcohol. Both terms are ambiguous about agents that are different from the primarily abused substance.
Dry drunk — Slang term used in alcoholism to describe behavior that is similar to that of drinking days with a similar behavioral pattern of drunkenness yet when no alcohol has been ingested. This is probably a form of anxiety attack. The term flashback refers to the same phenomenon experienced with other addictive substances when the person has been free of drug use for a prolonged period of time.
Fix — Slang for a single dose sufficient to produce a "high".
Hallucination — A vivid perception of the senses (visual or auditory) not based upon objective reality.
Hangover — The syndrome following a short binge of drug use. It is most commonly described after a bout of drinking alcohol and includes nausea, vomiting, irritability, conjunctival injection, headache, and inability to "clear the head" for serious thinking and decision making. It is more likely to occur in nonaddicted persons than addicted ones, but neither are completely free from its occurrence.
High — Slang for the euphoria developing after a psychoactive drug is administered. Usually refers specificially to the extremely satisfying plateau that may be only a portion of the drug experience.
Illusion — A misinterpretation of a real sensory image.
OD — Abbreviation for overdose.

Outpatient programs — Programs conducted in a center, often but not necessarily associated with an inpatient treatment facility. The patient lives at home and visits the treatment facility weekly or more frequently. A trained therapist must be in charge of the program. Usually means the same as ambulatory programs and is distinguished from residential programs and inpatient ones.

Outreach Programs — Programs with continuity from a residential or inpatient program that continue to provide services after the patient returns to home and community.

Overdose — A form of toxic reaction associated with an unexpectedly high dose of drug or a dose of a toxic drug that has features of a high dose. This could result from a suicide attempt or unknowingly because unusually potent illicit substance was purchased. Many toxic reactions are caused by adulterants and contaminants and are mistakenly called overdoses.

Polydrug abuse — Abuse of two or more drugs simultaneously or during same period of time. The practice is widespread. It may occur because the abuser cannot afford or obtain the most favored drug (common with cocaine, for which amphetamines are substituted) or is seeking relief from unpleasant side effects.

Program — Any organized and repetitive plan of treatment directed by a therapist. The provider undertakes some form of treatment for the client or patient, usually for a finite and stated period of time. The program may address all or only some of the client's needs. Thus there may be separate programs for the health problem, the addiction, and the underlying psychiatric problem, or they may all be handled in one program.

Provider — An organization, individual, or institution that provides a treatment program. This term usually carries the connotation of the administrative unit responsible for the program and is distinguished from therapist, who is the person directing the program. Thus an insurance company or an employer may be the provider of therapy, but deliver the program through a therapist.

Psychedelic drugs — Drugs that affect the mental processes, usually altering them sufficiently to distort reality of time, dimensions, and responsibilities. Delusions and hallucinations are common but not necessary.

Psychoactive agents — Drugs that primarily affect mental processes. Usually nicotine and caffeine are excluded, but the term includes inhalants, stimulants, depressants, tranquilizers, and hallucinogens.

Street drug — Street use. Illicit substance, use by purchasers of illicit drugs.

Talk down — A slang term for treating alcohol withdrawal, panic reaction, or a "dry drunk" or similar anxiety attack with protective, soothing, understanding, reassuring talk. It often takes the form of a unilateral conversation.

Therapy — Treatment of an abusing person by a person trained for such a purpose, usually with a degree or certificate; usually the therapist is paid. Although self-help groups and self-trained counselors are valuable in the recovery process and are major adjuncts to the treatment programs discussed in this book, they are called assistance, not therapy.

Tolerance — A physiological condition in which a dose of an agent that formerly produced a psychic or physiological effect no longer has that effect unless a higher dose is used. Usually the effect is marked, with doses 5 to 50 times the usual dose commonly observed. An abuser must use very high doses for several weeks to develop tolerance. Tolerance is not present in all users, because the dose is not always sufficient. Tolerance is usually associated with a withdrawal syndrome.

Toxic reaction — All unanticipated mental or physical findings occurring within an hour or two of drug use. They include overdose reactions, idiosyncratic reactions, psychosis, and reactions to adulterants which may be anaphylactic. A second group of findings often occurring after many uses of the drug are also included in this designation, such as skin rashes, confusion, myoglobinuria, and drug-caused hepatitis. Infections transmitted by the process of taking the drug are not included.

Treatment — Any form of program or emergency care provided to an abusing person by someone specifically trained for that which they are providing. It may be partial (such as treating fractures), short term (withdrawal only), or an effort at providing for all the patient's needs. Services provided by self-trained or untrained persons are designated assistance.
Trip — The entire experience following drug ingestion. A good trip produces euphoria without many toxic side effects, a bad trip produces many side effects.
Withdrawal — A condition following tolerance that occurs when the dose of alcohol, opiates, or other sedative drugs is reduced. It usually starts within 12 to 48 h and has run its course in 3 to 7 days. The more severe degrees are associated with extreme fright, hyperactivity, and cardiovascular stress, and occasionally result in death.

INDEX

A

B

C

D

E

I

J

K

L

N

O

P

R

S

T

X

Z